The aim of this volume is to establish that the period between the end of the Second World War and the beginning of the Cold War (1944–5 to 1947–8), hitherto neglected, represents an important conjuncture in the political and social history of Latin America in the twentieth century. The volume contains, besides an introduction and a conclusion by the editors, case studies of eleven of the twenty Latin American republics.

Despite differences of political regime, different levels of economic and social development, and different relations with the region's hegemonic power – the United States – there are striking similarities in the experiences of the majority of the Latin American republics in this period. For most of Latin America it can be divided into two phases. The first, coinciding with the Allied victory in the Second World War, was characterized by three distinct but interrelated phenomena: democratization, with a relatively high level of middle class and working class participation; a shift to the Left, both Communist and non-Communist; and unprecedented labor militancy. In the second phase, coinciding with the onset of the Cold War and completed almost everywhere by 1948, labor was disciplined by the state and in many cases excluded from politics; Communist parties almost everywhere suffered proscription and severe repression; reformist, "progressive" parties moved to the Right; the democratic advance was for the most part contained, and in some cases reversed. An opportunity, however limited, for significant political and social change, as well as for the first steps perhaps toward a Latin American version of social democracy, was lost. Instead, the institutional and ideological foundations were laid for Latin America's postwar "model" of economic growth without equity within a context of, at best, fragile and intermittent democracy.

# LATIN AMERICA BETWEEN THE SECOND WORLD WAR
## AND THE COLD WAR, 1944–1948

# LATIN AMERICA
# BETWEEN
# THE SECOND WORLD WAR
# AND THE COLD WAR,
# 1944–1948

*edited by*

LESLIE BETHELL

*and*

IAN ROXBOROUGH

CAMBRIDGE
UNIVERSITY PRESS

Published by the Press Syndicate of the University of Cambridge
The Pitt Building, Trumpington Street, Cambridge CB2 1RP
40 West 20th Street, New York, NY 10011–4211, USA
10 Stamford Road, Oakleigh, Victoria 3166, Australia

First published 1992

Printed in Canada

*Library of Congress Cataloging-in-Publication Data*
Latin America between the Second World War and the Cold War, 1944–1948
/ edited by Leslie Bethell and Ian Roxborough.
p. cm.
Includes index.
ISBN 0–521–43032–1
1. Latin America – Politics and government – 1830–1948.
2. Democracy – Latin America – History – 20th century. 3. Latin
America – Foreign relations. I. Bethell, Leslie. II. Roxborough,
Ian.
FI414.L278 1993
980.03'3–dc20
92–15357
CIP

A catalog record for this book is available from the British Library.

ISBN 0–521–43032–1 hardback

# Contents

# Contributors

ANDREW BARNARD is Honorary Research Fellow, Institute of Latin American Studies, University of London

LESLIE BETHELL is Professor of Latin American History, University of London

RODOLFO CERDAS CRUZ is Professor of Political Science, University of Costa Rica

JAMES DUNKERLEY is Professor of Politics, Queen Mary and Westfield College, University of London

STEVE ELLNER is Professor of History, Universidad de Oriente, Puerto La Cruz, Venezuela

JEFFREY GOULD is Assistant Professor of History, Indiana University

NIGEL HAWORTH is Senior Lecturer, Department of Management Studies and Labour Relations, University of Auckland, New Zealand

MARIO RAPOPORT is Professor of History, Universidad de Buenos Aires

IAN ROXBOROUGH is Professor of Sociology and Professor of History, State University of New York, Stony Brook

HAROLD SIMS is Professor of History, University of Pittsburgh

LAURENCE WHITEHEAD is Official Fellow in Politics, Nuffield College, Oxford

# Preface

This book has its origins in Leslie Bethell's interest in the historical fragility of democracy in Brazil, in particular his interest in the transition from the dictatorship of Getúlio Vargas to a limited form of democracy in 1945–6, and in Ian Roxborough's interest in the Mexican model of state-sponsored labor unions, which included an interest in the so-called *charrazo,* the intervention of the state to prop up a conservative union leadership in 1948. A historian and a sociologist, academic colleagues and friends, discovered almost a decade ago that they were both interested, initially for different reasons, in the history of Latin America during the period from the end of the Second World War to the beginning of the Cold War.

Comparing what we knew about Brazil and Mexico and drawing on our (limited) knowledge of other Latin American countries during the years 1944–8, we came to the conclusion that despite differences of political regime and different levels of economic and social development, there were striking similarities in the experience of a number, perhaps a majority, of Latin American republics, and that a period generally recognized as critical in the history of most other regions of the world in the twentieth century represented a more significant conjuncture in the political and social history of twentieth-century Latin America than had hitherto been recognized. Moreover, although Latin America's participation in the Second World War had been only marginal (in military terms at least), and although Latin America was not at first a focal point of conflict in the Cold War, the nature, and more importantly the outcome, of the postwar conjuncture was determined in Latin America as elsewhere not only by the changing balance of domestic political and social forces but also by the impact of the rapidly changing international context.

As a Fellow at the Woodrow Wilson International Center for Scholars in Washington, D.C., during the spring and summer of 1987, Leslie Bethell not only further pursued his research on Brazilian democratization at the end of the Second World War, but also initiated a new research project on Latin America's role in the post–Second World War political (and economic) international order. At the same time, Ian Roxborough continued his work on Mexican labor history during the 1940s, consulting material in the national archives in Mexico City, London, and Washington, D.C.

In an article published in the *Journal of Latin American Studies* in February 1988, we offered some preliminary reflections on the 1944–8 conjuncture in Latin America. For most of Latin America, we argued, the immediate postwar period could be divided into two phases: the first, coinciding with the Allied victory in the Second World War, was characterized by democratization, a shift to the left (both Communist and non-Communist), and unprecedented labor militancy; the second, coinciding with the onset of the Cold War and completed everywhere (except in Guatemala) by 1948, was characterized by the assertion or reassertion of state control over labor, the proscription and repression of Communist parties, and the containment – and in some cases reversal – of the advance to democracy. An opportunity, however limited, for significant political and social change in Latin America had been lost.

In the meantime, we had begun to invite other historians and social scientists to contribute case studies of the immediate postwar experience of particular Latin American countries (apart from Brazil and Mexico) to a volume we now planned to edit. Many of the chapters in this book were first presented as papers at a conference we organized, with financial support from the Nuffield Foundation, at the University of London Institute of Latin American Studies in October 1987. We also organized a panel on political change in Latin America between the Second World War and the Cold War at the Latin American Studies Association meeting in New Orleans in March 1988, and a conference comparing the impact on Latin America of the Second World War with that of the First World War at the London School of Economics in February 1989.

By this time we had come into contact with an even wider range of scholars working on related themes. For example, in December 1987 and December 1989 we both participated in conferences on Latin America in the 1940s that were organized by David Rock at the University of California at Santa Barbara. In March 1988 and April 1989, Leslie Bethell participated in meetings on the export of democracy as a theme in U.S.–Latin American relations in the twentieth century organized by Abraham F. Lowenthal at the University of Southern California in Los Angeles. Ian Roxborough presented papers at a conference on Communist parties in the 1940s organized by Geoff Eley of the University of Michigan, Ann Arbor, in November 1989 and at a conference on the Cold War organized by Alan Hunter at the University of Wisconsin, Madison, in October

1991. In one way or another at all these conferences we were able to test our ideas on the nature and significance of the postwar conjuncture in Latin America.

Many of the contributors to this volume commented on the chapters of their colleagues. We are especially grateful in this respect to James Dunkerley, Steve Ellner, and Laurence Whitehead. In addition, the following colleagues indirectly contributed to the volume at various stages with both their ideas and their encouragement: Alan Angell, David Collier, Ruth Berins Collier, Paul Drake, Valpy Fitzgerald, and Rosemary Thorp.

At the New York office of the Cambridge University Press, Katharita Lamoza was production editor and Kerime B. Toksu was copy editor. The index was prepared by Kathryn Torgeson. For her assistance throughout the preparation of this book, we should especially like to thank Hazel Aitken, Leslie Bethell's secretary at the Institute of Latin American Studies, University of London during his term as Director (1987–92).

# INTRODUCTION

## The postwar conjuncture in Latin America: democracy, labor, and the Left

*Leslie Bethell and Ian Roxborough*

The years between the end of the Second World War and the beginning of the Cold War, that is to say, 1944–5 to 1947–8, constituted a critical conjuncture in the twentieth-century history of Europe (both West and East), the Middle East, India, China, Southeast Asia, and Japan. In contrast, although important political changes occurred in several Latin American countries during these years – the rise of Juan Domingo Perón in Argentina, the election of Juan José Arévalo in Guatemala, the end of the Estado Novo in Brazil, the seizure of power by Acción Democrática in Venezuela, the Civil War in Costa Rica, for example – this period has not by and large been regarded as constituting a significant watershed in the history of the region as a whole, not least because of Latin America's relative international isolation. It is the aim of this volume to establish that although its participation in the Second World War had been only marginal (in military terms at least), and although it was not a focal point of conflict in the Cold War (in the early stages at least), the years 1944–8 nevertheless also represented an important conjuncture in the history of Latin America in the twentieth century.

Each of the twenty Latin American republics has its own history in the years immediately after the Second World War. Nevertheless, despite differences of political regime, different levels of economic and social development, differences in the strength and composition of both dominant groups and popular forces, and different relations with the United States – the region's "hegemonic power" – there are striking similarities in the experience of the majority of the republics.

This introduction is based in part on Leslie Bethell and Ian Roxborough, "Latin America between the Second World War and the Cold War: Some Reflections on the 1945–8 Conjuncture," *Journal of Latin American Studies* 20 (1988), pp. 167–89, and Leslie Bethell, "From the Second World War to the Cold War, 1944–54" in *Exporting Democracy: The United States and Latin America*, ed. Abraham F. Lowenthal (Baltimore, 1991), pp. 41–70, where a more detailed discussion of U.S.–Latin American relations can be found.

For most of Latin America the immediate postwar period can be divided into two phases. The first, beginning in 1944, 1945, or 1946 (depending on the country concerned), and often tantalizingly brief, was characterized by three distinct but interrelated phenomena: democratization, a shift to the Left, and labor militancy. Throughout the continent dictatorships fell, popular forces were mobilized, and elections with a relatively high level of participation were held. For the first time, a number of reformist, "progressive" political parties and movements came to power and successfully articulated the demands of the urban middle class and of the working class (though not yet those of the rural population) for political, social, and economic change. Even more notable perhaps were the gains, albeit more limited, made at this time by the orthodox Marxist Left, which for the most part meant the Latin American Communist parties. (Only Chile and to a lesser extent Argentina and Ecuador had Socialist parties of any significance.) The period at the end of the Second World War also witnessed strike waves, increased unionization, and a bid for greater union independence in those countries where the labor movement was closely controlled by the state. In a number of countries the incorporation of organized labor into democratic politics occurred for the first time.

In the second phase, beginning in some cases as early as 1945, and more generally in 1946 or 1947, and completed almost everywhere by 1948 (with the notable exception of Guatemala where the postwar "spring" lasted until 1954), organized labor was disciplined, brought under closer control by the state, and in many cases excluded from politics; Communist parties almost everywhere suffered proscription and severe repression, reformist parties moved to the Right, and the democratic advance was for the most part contained, and in some cases reversed. The popular forces, in particular the working class (but also in some cases the urban middle class), the Left, and democracy itself suffered a historic defeat in Latin America in the period immediately after the Second World War. An opportunity, however limited, for significant political and social change was lost.

The 1944–8 conjuncture in Latin America – and its eventual outcome, which had far-reaching consequences for Latin America's development in the second half of the twentieth century – can only be understood by examining the shifting balance of domestic political forces in each country. But it is also essential to explore the complex interaction between domestic and international politics as the Second World War came to an end, as a new political – and economic – international order was created in the aftermath of the war, and as, almost simultaneously, the Cold War began. And here the role played in Latin American affairs, both direct and indirect, by the United States is particularly important.

At the beginning of 1944 it could be argued that of the twenty Latin American republics only Uruguay, Chile, and, less convincingly, Costa Rica and Colombia, had some claim to call themselves representative democracies: their governments were civilian and had been elected (however limited the suffrage and however restricted the political participation); political competition of some kind was permitted (however weak the party system); and the rule of law obtained and basic civil liberties – freedom of speech, association, assembly, and so forth – were at least formally honored (however precariously at times). Of these four countries, Uruguay alone had (since before the First World War, though briefly interrupted in the 1930s) an executive freely and fairly elected by universal suffrage. Argentina had been democratic for a decade and a half before 1930, but during the "infamous decade" of the 1930s, Argentine democracy was distinctly flawed and in any event was overthrown in June 1943 in a nationalist military coup. Revolutionary Mexico was a special case: Presidents were elected (Lázaro Cárdenas in 1934, Manuel Avila Camacho in 1940) and were emphatically not eligible for reelection, but elections, though competitive, were firmly controlled by the official ruling revolutionary party, the Partido Revolucionario Mexicano (PRM). Mexican democracy was largely rhetorical, and the revolution itself remained the principal source of political legitimacy. Elsewhere in Latin America, narrowly oligarchical and often repressive regimes and military or military-backed dictatorships, some benevolent, some brutal, and most personalistic, predominated.

During the final twelve months of the Second World War and the first twelve months after the war, democracy was consolidated in those countries where in some limited sense it already existed. In Costa Rica in 1944, President Rafael Angel Calderón Guardía, elected in 1940, handed over power to Teodoro Picado, who had himself been elected (though not without accusations of fraud and intimidation). In Colombia, President Alfonso López, a Liberal, who had been elected in 1942 (though here, too, the elections had not been without violence and fraud), resigned in July 1945 and was replaced by his foreign minister, Dr. Alberto Lleras Camargo, as acting president. The presidential elections of 1946, in which one of the two Liberal candidates, Dr. Jorge Eliécer Gaitán, attempted for the first time to broaden the party's popular base, were won by the Conservative candidate Mariano Ospina Pérez running on a bipartisan National Union ticket, thus bringing to an end – democratically – sixteen years of continuous Liberal rule. In Chile, elections in 1946 brought to power Gabriel González Videla, the third Radical president elected in succession since the formation of the Popular Front in 1938.

These two years (mid-1944 to mid-1946) also witnessed significant moves in the direction of democracy in countries that were less obviously democratic, but not outright dictatorships. In Ecuador in May 1944, a popular rebellion, in which the Alianza Democrática Ecuatoriana (ADE) – a coalition of Socialists, Communists, Conservatives, and dissident Liberals – played a prominent role, led to the military coup that overthrew the fraudulently elected and repressive regime of Carlos Arroyo del Río and brought to power the leading opposition figure José María Velasco Ibarra (in exile at the time). The following year a Constituent Assembly was elected and confirmed Velasco in the presidency. Fulgencio Batista, who had dominated Cuban politics for more than a decade and served as president since 1940, permitted free elections in June 1944, which were won by Ramón Grau San Martín, the heir to the popular revolution of 1933–4 and the candidate of the opposition Auténticos. In Panama in May 1945, a Constituent Assembly was elected that appointed an interim president, Enrique A. Jiménez, who was supported by a coalition of opposition groups led by the Partido Renovador. In Peru, free elections were permitted for the first time in June 1945; they were won overwhelmingly by José Luis Bustamante y Rivero of the Frente Democrático Nacional (which had been formed the year before) with the support of Victor Raúl Haya de la Torre's Alianza Popular Revolucionaria Americana (APRA), Peru's most popular political movement. (APRA, which had been excluded from politics for more than a decade, had been legalized a month before the election and in January 1946 joined Bustamante's cabinet.) In Venezuela, still in the aftermath of the long dictatorship of Juan Vicente Gómez (1908–35), President Isaías Medina Angarita, toward the end of the war, pursued a policy of gradual liberalization in association with Unión Popular (the legal front of the Venezuelan Communist Party), but refused to allow direct presidential elections in 1946. On 18 October 1945, a military coup in the name of democracy backed by Rómulo Betancourt's Acción Democrática (AD) brought down the Medina administration and led to Venezuela's first experiment with democracy (1945–8). Even in Mexico the ruling party, in January 1946, introduced primary elections of candidates to posts other than that of president.[1] Miguel Alemán, the presidential candidate (albeit the first civilian and the first university-educated candidate) of the PRM was, however, chosen in the traditional manner and safely elected (also in the traditional manner) in July. The PRM was renamed the Partido Revolucionario Institucional (PRI) in December 1946.

More significantly, there were during the same period four successful transitions from military or military-backed dictatorships of various kinds to democracy broadly defined. In Guatemala, a popular uprising led to the downfall of the thirteen-year dictatorship of Jorge Ubico in July 1944

1  We owe this information to Blanca Torres.

and the election in December of Juan José Arévalo, the "spiritual Socialist" schoolteacher returned from exile in Argentina. In Brazil at the beginning of 1945, Getúlio Vargas, who had been in power since 1930, took the first steps toward the dismantling of the Estado Novo (1937–45). On 28 February, he announced that within three months a date would be set for presidential and congressional elections, and under the electoral law of 28 May national elections were indeed held on 2 December – the first relatively democratic elections in the country's history. In Argentina, May and June 1945 saw the reactivation of the liberal opposition to the nationalist military regime of Edelmiro Farrell and Juan Perón that culminated on 19 September in a massive demonstration by several hundred thousand people in Buenos Aires, "The March for Constitution and Liberty," and the first concrete steps toward democratic elections the following year (February 1946). Finally, the nationalist military government in Bolivia supported by the Movimiento Nacional Revolucionario (MNR) of Víctor Paz Estenssoro, which had come to power as the result of a coup in December 1943, was brought down in July 1946 by a violent popular revolt in which President Gualberto Villarroel was lynched. The driving force behind the revolt was a newly formed coalition of the Liberal Right and the Marxist Left, the Frente Democrático Antifascista (FDA), which immediately promised to hold democratic elections in January 1947.

Thus, there had been a sudden and dramatic advance of democracy throughout Latin America at the end of the Second World War. "The years 1944 and 1945," wrote a contributor to *Inter-American Affairs 1945*, an annual survey edited by Arthur P. Whitaker, "brought more democratic changes in more Latin American countries than perhaps in any single year since the Wars of Independence."[2] No single country moved in the opposite direction. Indeed, by the middle of 1946, the only Latin American states that could not claim to be in some sense popular and democratic in their origins, if not in their practice, were Paraguay and a handful of republics in Central America and the Caribbean: El Salvador, Honduras, Nicaragua, and the Dominican Republic. And most of these dictatorships that had survived the postwar wave of democratization had been shaken; some had been obliged to make at least token gestures toward political liberalization.

In El Salvador in May 1944 – a few weeks before the fall of Ubico in Guatemala – a popular uprising had actually overthrown the thirteen-year dictatorship of General Maximiliano Hernández Martínez, but in October an election campaign was aborted and a dictatorship restored. In Honduras there had also been disturbances in May 1944, but they were

---

2 William Ebenstein, "Political and Social Thought in Latin America" in *Inter-American Affairs 1945*, ed. Arthur P. Whitaker (New York, 1946), p. 137.

relatively minor and failed to dislodge Tiburcio Carías Andino. In Nicaragua demonstrations in June 1944, however, had forced Anastasio Somoza, dictator since 1937, to announce in September – and to reiterate during 1945 and 1946 – that he would not seek reelection at the end of his "term" in 1947. He permitted Leonardo Argüello, his opponent in 1936, to win the presidential elections in February 1947. (When, however, Argüello showed signs of independence and chose to work with the opposition, Somoza moved to overthrow him and reassert his personal control; Argüello was in office for only twenty-seven days in May.) Even Rafael Leónidas Trujillo in the Dominican Republic faced, for the first time since his seizure of power in 1930, opposition from both labor and the Left (including the Communist Left). This led to his engineering a carefully controlled opening at the end of the war and elections in May 1947 that were somewhat freer than earlier elections, but that he naturally won. In Paraguay in the summer of 1946, General Higinio Morínigo, "elected" unopposed in 1943, ended press censorship, relaxed prohibitions on political activities (and even included *colorados* and *febreristas* in a coalition cabinet), and promised to prepare Paraguay for a "return to democracy" (though no date was ever set for elections).

The principal factor behind the political changes in Latin America during the years 1944, 1945, and 1946 was the victory of the Allies (and thus of democracy over fascism) in the Second World War. Despite the strength of Axis, especially German, interests in Latin America and indeed widespread pro-Axis (and pro-fascist) sympathies throughout the region in the late 1930s and early 1940s, in the immediate aftermath of Pearl Harbor, all the Latin American states except Chile (temporarily) and Argentina (until March 1945) had lined up with the United States and severed relations with the Axis powers; eventually most, although until 1945 by no means all, had declared war. Formally at least, and in some cases with varying degrees of cynicism and *realpolitik,* they had chosen the side of freedom and democracy. The war itself had strengthened existing ties – military, economic, political, and ideological – between Latin America (except, of course, Argentina) and the United States. As it became certain that the Allies would win the war – the German defeat at Stalingrad in February 1943 marked the turning of the tide – and as the nature of the postwar international political and economic order and the hegemonic position of the United States within it became clear, the dominant groups in Latin America, including the military, recognized the need to make some necessary political and ideological adjustments and concessions,

There was also at the end of the Second World War considerable internal pressure for more open, democratic political systems, from the urban middle class, intellectuals, and students, and in the economically more developed countries, from the urban working class. War and postwar popular demands for democracy drew on a strong liberal tradition in Latin American politics and culture. But they were also the product of an extraordinary outpouring of wartime propaganda in favor of U.S. political institutions, the U.S. economic model, and the American way of (and standard of) life directed at Latin America. This was orchestrated above all by Nelson Rockefeller's Office of the Coordinator of Inter-American Affairs (OCIAA). By the end of the war, it should be remembered, press, radio, and the film industry throughout Latin America had been heavily penetrated by U.S. capital. Democracy, above all, emerged as a central symbol with almost universal resonance.

Thus, *indirectly*, the United States clearly played an important role in the democratization of Latin America at the end of the Second World War. *Direct* U.S. pressure in favor of democratization was not perhaps a decisive factor in most cases, but it undoubtedly played its part. The cornerstone of Franklin D. Roosevelt's Good Neighbor Policy had been a policy of nonintervention in the internal political affairs of the other American republics. Most (though by no means all) U.S. foreign policy makers preferred democracies to dictatorships, but they found it hard to reconcile a desire to promote democracy with respect for the principle of nonintervention. In any case, the strategic and economic interests of the United States – the defense of the Western Hemisphere against external attack or internal subversion, and the promotion of U.S. trade with, and investment in, Latin America – came first. At the outset of the Second World War the United States was primarily concerned that the Latin American states should be on the side of the Allies. Washington actively cooperated with all stable, friendly regimes in Latin America, dictatorships and democracies alike, that opposed the Axis powers. Indeed, indirectly through credits, purchases of commodities at prices favorable to producers, and military assistance (Lend–Lease), this meant maintaining many dictators – some of them like Trujillo in the Dominican Republic and Somoza in Nicaragua quite unsavory – in power. The United States' closest ally in Latin America – and the recipient of more than 70 percent of all Lend–Lease to Latin America – was Brazil's (relatively benevolent) dictator Getúlio Vargas.

Some U.S. officials both in Washington and Latin America were troubled by the inconsistencies and ambiguities of the U.S. policy toward Latin American dictatorships during the war, a war that was after all being fought for the Four Freedoms. There was a complex interaction between governments, oppositions, and U.S. embassies in Central America, for example, throughout 1944. But it appears that neither in El Salvador nor in Guatemala did the United States play a significant part in the downfall of Central America's two oldest dictatorships. Nor is there any evidence of U.S. involvement in Cuba's democratic elections of June 1944. In Mexico, Ambassador George S. Messersmith, the "diplomat of democracy," for a time favored and actively promoted the candidacy of Foreign Minister Ezequiel Padilla for the presidency in the interests of greater democratic choice, free enterprise, and good relations with the United States. But Padilla was quickly dropped when it became clear in 1945 that Miguel Alemán, who was strongly pro-United States, had the nomination sewn up. Washington preferred the maintenance of the status quo in Mexico, Central America, and the Caribbean for the duration of the war.

Nevertheless, with the growth of democratic opposition to dictatorships as the war came to an end, and with the overthrow and defeat of many dictators and semidictators, U.S. policy began subtly to shift. Washington positively welcomed the course of events in Guatemala at the end of 1944, for example, and quickly recognized the democratically elected Arévalo administration. In November 1944, Assistant Secretary of State Adolf A. Berle, Jr., in a circular to U.S. embassies in Latin America, underlined the fact that the United States would feel more favorably disposed toward "governments established on the periodically and freely expressed consent of the governed."[3] At the Inter-American Conference on the Problems of War and Peace (the Chapultepec conference) held in Mexico City in February–March 1945, the United States led the Latin American states in declaring a "fervent adherence to democratic principles." And during 1945 Washington began more openly to distance itself from, and demonstrate official disapproval of, Latin American dictatorships and "disreputable governments."[4] As the opening shots in the Cold War were fired (for example, in the conflict with the Soviet Union over democracy in Eastern Europe at the Conference of Foreign Ministers in London in September 1945), there was a new imperative behind the U.S. desire that its allies in Latin America be seen as democratic. Latin American dictators were now denied financial assistance and military aid. In December 1945, the State Department rejected a request from the Dominican Republic for export licenses for arms shipments on the grounds that it was "unable

---

3  Quoted in D. M. Dozer, *Are We Good Neighbors? Three Decades of Inter-American Relations, 1930–60* (Gainesville, FL, 1959), p. 213.

4  The phrase comes from a document, "Policy re Dictatorships and Disreputable Governments," by Spruille Braden, formerly U.S. ambassador in Bogotá and Havana and about to be appointed to the embassy in Buenos Aires, dated 5 April 1945. (It was a revision of a memorandum sent to the State Department from Havana in January.) Recommending "aloof formality" rather than friendly cooperation and, specifically, an end to financial assistance and military aid, it was circulated to all missions in Latin America by acting Secretary of State Joseph C. Grew on 28 May. See Bryce Wood, *The Dismantling of the Good Neighbor Policy* (Austin, TX, 1985), pp. 94–5.

to perceive that democratic principles have been observed there in theory or in practice."[5]

There is no firm evidence that the United States played any significant role in, for example, the decision to hold free elections in Peru in June 1945, or in the military coup that brought Acción Democrática to power in Venezuela in October – although both were warmly welcomed. The United States certainly did, however, intervene directly – and with some degree of success – in support of democracy in Argentina and Brazil in 1945, and in Paraguay and Bolivia in 1946. Persistent U.S. pressure in Asunción finally led to the democratization program of June–July 1946 as a result of which, in the words of *La Tribuna,* the Paraguayan dictator briefly became "the prisoner of a democratic cabinet" and the way was open for a new era of democratic politics in Paraguay.[6] In Bolivia, the U.S. embassy was equally active in forging an alliance between Right and Left against the nationalist military–MNR government that had come to power in December 1943. The FDA, which brought down Villarroel in July 1946 – and apparently opened the way for democracy in Bolivia – was strongly supported from Washington. The role of Ambassadors Spruille Braden in Argentina and Adolf Berle in Brazil is too well known to require detailed discussion here. Braden arrived in Buenos Aires at the end of May with the "fixed idea," according to Sir David Kelly, the British ambassador, that he had been elected by Providence to bring democracy to Argentina. He virtually became the leader of the opposition to the military regime, and especially to Perón, and before leaving in September to become Assistant Secretary of State, he had secured a time-table for free elections in February 1946 and a recognition that democracy was Argentina's "historic mandate." Throughout the first nine months of 1945, Berle had had no need to do more than quietly encourage Vargas's liberalization of the Estado Novo. His famous speech in Petrópolis in late September at a time when *queremismo* (mass mobilization in favor of Vargas's continuation in power) was threatening to derail the process of transition to democracy, and his discreet pressure after the military coup against Vargas at the end of October, guaranteed the elections of 2 December.[7]

5 See Jonathan Hartlyn, "The Dominican Republic: The Legacy of Intermittent Engagement," in Lowenthal, *Exporting Democracy,* p. 188.

6 See Michael Grow, *The Good Neighbor Policy and Authoritarianism in Paraguay* (Lawrence, KS, 1981), pp. 99–111.

7 Braden and Berle helped ensure that democratic elections were held in Argentina and Brazil. They had, however, no control over the results. In Brazil in December 1945, Brigadier Eduardo Gomes, the candidate of the União Democrática Nacional (UDN), a broad coalition of Right, Center, and Left forces opposed to the Vargas dictatorship, lost to General Eurico Dutra, Vargas's former

Significantly, the most sustained U.S. efforts in favor of democracy in Latin America had been directed at the countries to which for different reasons the label "fascist" could be most readily, though not necessarily convincingly, attached – Paraguay, Brazil, Bolivia, and, above all, Argentina. Fascism, not (yet) communism, remained the principal totalitarian enemy of democracy – and of U.S. interests – in Latin America at the end of the Second World War. It is interesting to note that throughout 1945 (and for that matter 1946 and even the first half of 1947), U.S. officials, in Washington and in Latin America, were not disturbed by the fact that Communists were playing a prominent part in the region's democratization. On the contrary, their participation was positively welcomed in, for example, Brazil, Bolivia, and Argentina. Nor was the United States concerned at this stage about the close relations between some Latin American governments and local Communist parties (in, for example, Chile, Costa Rica, and, to a much lesser extent, Peru).

An important feature of Latin American democratization at the end of the Second World War, as we have seen, was the number of "progressive" parties of the Center–Left – AD in Venezuela, APRA in Peru, the PRC–A (the Auténticos) in Cuba, for example – that came to power for the first time. Most of these parties were highly personalist and populist. They secured the support of the urban middle class (where it had not already been largely captured, as it had been, for example, by the Radicals in Argentina and Chile), sections of the working class, and in some cases peasants. While not always coming to power by democratic means, they offered an extension of democracy, social reform, and national economic development. Equally notable were the gains made by the Marxist Left, especially the Communist parties, at the end of the Second World War. After more than twenty years of weakness, isolation, and for the most part illegality, the Latin American Communist parties achieved for a brief period a degree of popularity, power, and influence – which would never be recaptured, except in Cuba after 1959 and (briefly) in Chile in the early seventies.

Communist parties were legalized or at least tolerated in virtually every country in Latin America. Total membership, less than 100,000 in 1939, had reached 500,000 by 1947.[8] United States intelligence reported that

minister of war, who was the candidate of the Partido Social Democrático (PSD) and the Partido Trabalhista Brasileiro (PTB), the two parties created by Vargas. In Argentina in February 1946, José P. Tamborini, the candidate of the Unión Democrática, a broad coalition of Conservatives, Radicals, Socialists, and Communists opposed to the military dictatorship, lost to Perón, despite an eleventh hour attempt by Braden, now assistant secretary of state, to discredit him by publishing a Blue Book linking him to the Nazis.

8  Fernando Claudin, *The Communist Movement: From Comintern to Cominform* (London, 1975), p. 309.

in February 1947 individual Communist parties claimed the following
membership: Brazil, 180,000; Argentina, 30,000; Chile, 50,000; Peru,
35,000; Venezuela, 20,000; Cuba, 55,000; Mexico, 11,000; Colombia,
10,000; and Uruguay, 15,000.[9] These figures are undoubtedly exaggerated, but they indicate an important presence of Communist parties in
all the major countries of the region. (In many of the smaller and less
industrialized countries, however, Communist parties failed to attract a
mass following.)

In competition with, at times cooperating with, their main rivals, the
reformist parties of the Center–Left and populists like Perón and Vargas,
Communists had considerable electoral success all over Latin America.
This was particularly the case in Costa Rica, Chile, Cuba, and Brazil. In
Costa Rica in 1944, Picado, like Calderón Guardía in 1940, was elected
president with Communist support. In Chile in September 1946, González Videla, a Radical but regarded as "the Communist candidate," was
elected president with Communist support and included three Communists in his cabinet. And in April 1947, 90,000 – 17 percent – voted
for the Partido Comunista de Chile (PCCh) in the municipal elections.
In Cuba, the Communist Partido Socialista Popular (PSP) garnered
130,000 votes in 1944 and 200,000 in 1946. And in Brazil, the Partido
Comunista do Brasil (PCB) secured 10 percent of the vote – 500,000
votes – in the presidential and congressional elections of December 1945
and again in the elections for governor and state assembly in January
1947. In contrast, however, Gustavo Machado, the Partido Comunista
de Venezuela (PCV) candidate in the presidential elections in Venezuela
in December 1947 secured only 3.2 percent of the vote. Even more
important perhaps, as we shall see, were the Communist advances within
labor unions throughout Latin America.

The explanation for the advance of communism in Latin America at
the end of the Second World War is, of course, to be found primarily in
the war itself and its outcome. Following the German invasion of Russia,
the breakup of the short-lived Nazi–Soviet pact, and the forging of the
anti-Axis alliance of Churchill, Roosevelt, and Stalin, Communist parties
in Latin America supported the governments in power, even though most
of these were authoritarian and reactionary, because they (with the notable
exception of Argentina) supported the Allied cause. As a consequence
many (though by no means all) Latin American governments softened
their attitude toward the Communist parties. At the same time, the Latin

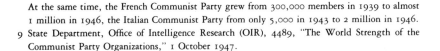

At the same time, the French Communist Party grew from 300,000 members in 1939 to almost
   1 million in 1946, the Italian Communist Party from only 5,000 in 1943 to 2 million in 1946.
9 State Department, Office of Intelligence Research (OIR), 4489, "The World Strength of the
   Communist Party Organizations," 1 October 1947.

American Communist parties, which had already abandoned their hard-line revolutionary strategy in favor of the strategy of the Popular Front in the aftermath of the Seventh World Congress (1935), now favored class harmony and class collaboration over class conflict in the interests of national unity.[10] This served to increase support for communism in various sections of the population and provided Communist parties with a degree of legitimacy. (It also led to increased tensions between Communist leaders and rank-and-file militants.) Furthermore, Communist parties were less obviously instruments of a foreign power. The Comintern (which had only "discovered" Latin America in 1928, and which had effectively ceased to function after the Seventh World Congress) was finally dissolved in 1943. During the Second World War, the Latin American Communist parties were largely neglected by Moscow and experienced a growing, though relative, independence of action. At the same time, they remained sufficiently identified with Moscow to benefit from the enormous, though temporary, prestige of the Soviet Union during and immediately after the war. Finally, since Communists had so evidently been on the side of democracy against fascism during the war, they were also among the beneficiaries of the victory of democracy and the democratization that occurred in Latin America at the end of the war.

The role of Communists in the process of democratization at the end of the Second World War was, however, complicated in some countries by the legacy of international alignments made during the war and the meaning attached to the terms "democratic" and "fascist." In Brazil, for example, the Communists supported or at least made an approximation with Getúlio Vargas in 1945, rather than with the democratic opposition, not only because Vargas had the support of labor, but also because he had supported the Allies against the Axis and was (therefore) in that sense "democratic." In Argentina, on the other hand, the Communists joined the essentially conservative Democratic opposition against Perón in 1945 even though he had the support of labor, not only because he was a leading member of the military dictatorship, but also because he had taken a neutral or pro-Axis stand and was therefore "fascist." Similarly, in Bolivia the Partido de la Izquierda Revolucionaria (PIR) joined the Right in an alliance against the military–MNR regime largely because, although it was reformist and had the support of labor, the MNR was authoritarian,

---

10 What became known as Browderism (the view, associated above all with Earl Browder, the general secretary of the Communist Party of the United States, that Communist parties should now favor class collaboration over class conflict even to the extent of voluntary dissolution) made headway in several Latin American countries (Cuba, Mexico, and Venezuela, for example). As the international Communist movement began to reassess its position in the postwar period, Browderism was denounced as a heresy (by Jacques Duclos as early as June 1945) and eventually abandoned.

nationalist, and above all, sympathetic to the Axis powers, and therefore "fascist," whereas the oligarchy, though deeply reactionary and notoriously antilabor, had favored the Allied cause and was therefore "democratic."

Another notable feature of the postwar years was the advance of organized labor as a major social and political actor in Latin America. By the late thirties, the export sectors had largely recovered from the World Depression and import substitution industrialization had accelerated in the more economically developed countries of the region. The Second World War gave a further impetus to industrial development, especially in Brazil and Mexico. At the same time, Latin America began to experience rapid population growth and rural–urban mass migration. As a result of all these factors, the working class grew in size and its character was transformed. In the early 1930s, the working class had been concentrated in the service and transportation sectors and, in those countries where mineral exports were important, in mining. Industry had been largely confined to textiles and food processing. By the end of the war, there was a significant expansion of industrial as well as state employment (including the formation of an important white-collar section of the working class). In Mexico, the number of workers in manufacturing had risen from 568,000 in 1940 to 922,000 in 1945, in Argentina from 633,000 in 1941 to 938,000 in 1946. In Brazil, over the decade between 1940 and 1950, the number of manufacturing workers rose from 995,000 to 1,608,000.[11] Although rises of this order of magnitude were not experienced by all countries, the rate of growth of the urban working class, and especially workers in industry, in Latin America as a whole during the war years was impressive. For the first time something approaching a recognizably modern proletariat was coming into existence.

This growth in the size of the working class was accompanied by a widespread expansion of union membership. In Argentina the number of workers enrolled in unions rose from 448,000 in 1941 to 532,000 in 1945 (and then shot up to almost 2 million in 1949, and 2.5 to 3 million by the end of Perón's first term in office). In Brazil, some 351,000 workers were unionized in 1940; by 1947 this had more than doubled to 798,000. Similarly, in Colombia union membership doubled between 1940 and 1947 (from 84,000 to 166,000). By 1946 between 3.5 and 4 million workers were unionized in Latin America as a whole.[12] The Confederación

---

11 J. Fuchs, *Argentina, su desarrollo capitalista* (Buenos Aires, 1966), pp. 260, 268; B. Torres Ramírez, *México en la Segunda Guerra Mundial* (Mexico City, 1979), p. 299; T. Merrick and D. Graham, *Population and Economic Development in Brazil* (Baltimore, 1979), p. 158.

12 L. Doyon, "Conflictos obreros durante el régimen peronista (1946–55)," *Desarrollo Económico* 17 (October–December 1977):440; L. Martins, "Sindicalismo e classe operária," vol. 10 of *História Geral da Civilização Brasileira*, ed. B. Fausto (São Paulo, 1981), p. 535; M. Urrutia Montoya, *The Development of the Colombian Labor Movement* (New Haven, 1969), p. 183; S. Baily, *Labor,*

de Trabajadores de América Latin (CTAL), founded in 1938 and still led by the Mexican Marxist labor leader Vicente Lombardo Toledano and to a large extent funded by the Confederación de Trabajadores de México (CTM), claimed to represent some 3.3 million members in sixteen countries. More importantly, the level of union membership in key sectors of industry and transportation was high, and this gave organized labor both industrial and political muscle.

Even more significant perhaps was the trend toward more centralized union organization, the search for greater autonomy from the state, and militancy over wages. During the war, real wages and therefore standards of living had generally declined: wages were held down by social pacts and no-strike pledges in the interests of the Allied war effort and the battle for production. At the same time, inflation rose as a result of shortages of imports and strong demand pressure, huge balance of payments surpluses from export earnings and accumulating reserves, and overvalued exchange rates. In some sectors, the labor market was increasingly tight, which improved union bargaining power. Although there was considerable migration to the cities and economic pressures of wartime inflation may have forced additional family members into the labor market, it does appear that employment opportunities expanded even more rapidly. Moreover, the war itself had increased expectations, and the new liberal political atmosphere at the end of the War provided the space in which pent-up demands could be released. The last year of the war (1944–5) and the first year after the war (1945–6) therefore witnessed not only political openings in a number of important Latin American countries, but a marked increase in the number of labor disputes and strikes throughout the region. Strike activity in Mexico, in fact, peaked early in 1943 and 1944 when there were 766 and 887 strikes, respectively, and then fell off in 1945 (220 strikes) and 1946 (207 strikes). And in the particular circumstances of the rise of Perón, labor in Argentina marched to a somewhat different rhythm from the rest of Latin America. But in Chile, for example, after only 19 in 1942, the number of strikes reached 127 in 1943, 91 in 1944, 148 in 1945, 196 in 1946, and 164 in 1947, and then fell to 26 in 1948 and 47 in 1949. In Venezuela there were 4 strikes in 1944, 32 in the period October 1945–December 1946, and 55 in 1947. Brazil witnessed two major strike waves at the end of the Second World War in March–May 1945 and in January–February 1946.[13] In

*Nationalism and Politics in Argentina* (New Brunswick, NJ, 1967), p. 101; V. Alba, *Politics and the Labor Movement in Latin America* (Stanford, 1968), pp. 211, 258.

13 For Mexico, see J. Wilkie, *The Mexican Revolution* (Berkeley, 1970), p. 184; for Chile, see B. Loveman, *Chile* (New York, 1979), p. 266, and the chapter by Andrew Barnard in this volume;

general, Latin America experienced in the years 1945–7 its most intense period of labor militancy since the end of the First World War (1917–19).

Since the early 1930s a variety of political forces had vied for control over labor movements in Latin America. And different governments had seriously begun to create a body of labor legislation that would incorporate labor into the political system as well as into the world of work. There was consequently intense political competition for influence over labor during the years between the Second World War and the Cold War. In this the Communist parties did not have things all their own way. They were often, in fact, in an ambiguous position. On the one hand, their reputation as advocates of broad reforms and their (at least verbal) defense of working-class interests attracted considerable support. On the other hand, their support for the no-strike pledges in support of the Allied war effort frequently led to rank-and-file movements bypassing the Communists. To a great extent the eventual outcome depended on the nature of the Communists' rivals in the labor movement. In those countries (such as Chile) where there was a well-established, non-Communist Marxist Left (the Socialist party), it was these forces that often prospered at the expense of the Communists. In other countries, older parties like APRA in Peru, relatively new parties like the Auténticos in Cuba and Acción Democrática in Venezuela, or personalistic movements of the kind led by Vargas in Brazil and Perón in Argentina emerged as serious (and often successful) rivals to the Communist parties.

Just as the Communist position on democracy was complicated by wartime international alignments, the attitude of organized labor toward democracy was complicated by class antagonisms. In general, unions supported the political openings of the postwar period. However, in Brazil and Argentina in 1944–5, for example, the labor movement supported Vargas and Perón on the grounds that, though dictators, they were positively prolabor, whereas the democratic oppositions were perceived as dominated by conservative oligarchies that were profoundly antilabor. In Mexico, where the official revolutionary party, although presiding over an essentially authoritarian system, had built a strong base of support among workers (and peasants), opposition forces, however "democratic," were even more clearly regarded as embodying reactionary positions. The relative weakness of the democratizing thrust in Mexico at the end of the war should come as no surprise.

Although democrats, leftists, and labor militants were not always and everywhere on the same side, the three features of Latin American politics

for Venezuela, see the chapter by Steve Ellner in this volume; and for Brazil, see the chapter by Leslie Bethell in this volume.

and society in the immediate aftermath of the Second World War that
we have examined in turn – the advance of democracy, the shift to the
Left, and labor militancy – were for the most part linked and mutually
reinforcing. They added up to a serious challenge to the established order,
at least in the perceptions of governments of the time. In every country
(except Guatemala and, to a lesser extent, Argentina) steps were quickly
and successfully taken to contain this challenge.

During 1947 and 1948 the postwar advance of labor, the Left, and
democracy throughout Latin America was brought to a halt and suffered
its first major setbacks. There was in the first place a general crackdown
on organized labor aimed at greater institutional and ideological control
by the state. Almost everywhere independent, militant, labor leaders
suffered repression, labor confederations were intervened, split, marginalized, or disbanded, antistrike legislation was reinforced, and a tough
stand was taken against strikes. This was particularly true in Brazil (where
the administration of Eurico Gaspar Dutra introduced new decree-laws
to bring labor under control as early as March 1946), Chile (where the
breaking of the coal strike of October 1947 was the central event), Cuba
(first under Grau in 1947 and more particularly under Carlos Prío Socarrás
after the elections of 1948), and Costa Rica (after the Civil War of 1948).
In Mexico, the so-called *charrazo* (September–October 1948) symbolized
the failure of the militant national unions of rail, mine, and oil workers
to prevent the governing Partido Revolucionario Institucional (PRI) from
strengthening its control over organized labor in the postwar period. Apart
from Guatemala and Venezuela (until November 1948), Argentina provided the only exception to this antilabor trend in Latin America in 1947
and 1948. Perón's regime was based on organized labor (and Perón owed
his election to the working-class vote). But he too established government
control over the major unions, purged Communist and independent leftists
from union leadership, and generally demobilized the working class. In
this sense Perón behaved like most other Latin American governments.

In general, Communist labor leaders found themselves purged from
major unions, even though they had been elected and in many cases were
notable for the relatively moderate positions they had adopted on strikes.
The Latin American Communist parties were virtually eliminated as a
viable political force in Latin America. In one country after another –
most notably in Brazil in May 1947, in Chile in April 1948, and in Costa
Rica in July 1948 following the victory of José Figueres and his supporters
in the Civil War of March–April 1948 – Communist parties were declared
illegal even though they had played by the rules of the democratic game
and, particularly in the case of Chile, had deep roots in politics and

society. (Many Latin American governments took the opportunity to break often recently established diplomatic relations with the Soviet Union.) Elected Communist members were removed from the cabinet and from Congress in Chile in August 1947, and from Congress (as well as state and municipal assemblies) in Brazil in January 1948. (In Peru, where the Communists were weak, it was APRA that was forced out of central and local government.) At the same time, reformist parties (with the notable exception of Acción Democrática, which remained in power in Venezuela until November 1948) generally shifted to the Right, reducing their commitment to socioeconomic change, even in some cases (APRA, for example) abandoning what democratic pretensions they once had. Only one entirely new reformist party, Lombardo Toledano's Partido Popular, which emerged belatedly, and as a result abortively, as a counterweight to the PRI in Mexico, was formed as late as 1948.

In those few countries where during the immediate postwar years dictatorships had survived – Nicaragua, El Salvador, Honduras, the Dominican Republic, and Paraguay – the (largely token) promises of liberalization that had been made were withdrawn or overturned. Trujillo was to survive in the Dominican Republic until 1961, the Somoza dynasty in Nicaragua until 1979. Morínigo in Paraguay, who under pressure from the United States had gone furthest in the direction of political reform, was replaced in February 1948 by Natalicio González after a five-month civil war, a *colorado* "terror," and a one-candidate tightly controlled "election." Six years later the thirty-five-year dictatorship of General Alfredo Stroessner began.

In at least four countries democratic expectations at the end of the war were not fully realized. Democracy in Argentina under Perón turned out to be highly restricted, and although the revolution that finally brought him down in 1955 called itself the Revolución Libertadora, it led to the first of a series of military governments that held power in Argentina for almost twenty of the following thirty years. In Ecuador Velasco Ibarra, who had himself suspended the Constitution as early as March 1946, was overthrown in a military coup in August 1947. In 1948, it is true, Galo Plaza Lasso, a progressive landowner, son of a former Liberal president, and candidate of the Movimiento Cívico Ecuatoriano, was elected to the presidency. But four years later the elections of 1952 were won by Velasco, who soon established an authoritarian, populist regime. In Panama elections were delayed until 1948, and were then fraudulent. José A. Remón, the chief of the National Police, emerged as the country's strongman in 1949. During the following three years, he made and unmade presidents and in 1952 was himself "elected" president. In Bolivia in 1947, the Frente Democrático Antifascista broke up and the country gradually evolved not toward democracy, but toward a reactionary and repressive military dictatorship. (This was, however, finally overthrown by the MNR-led Revolution of 1952.)

In those countries where democracy existed at the end of the Second World War and was consolidated – Uruguay, Chile, Costa Rica, Colombia – or where democracy of some kind was established and survived (at least for a while) – Cuba, Guatemala, Peru, Venezuela, Brazil – there was in 1947–8 (except in Guatemala under the reformist administration of Aré-valo) a marked tendency to restrict or curtail political competition and participation, to contain or repress popular mobilization, and to frustrate reformist aspirations. As early as September 1946, for example, Brazil's new "democratic" Constitution denied the vote to illiterates (more than half the population) and distributed seats in Congress in such a way as seriously to underrepresent the more densely populated, urban, and de-veloped regions of the country.

Toward the end of 1948, two democratic regimes were overthrown by military coups and replaced by military dictatorships. In Peru Bustamante, who had been struggling to stay in office for more than a year, was finally brought down in October 1948. General Manuel Odría, using draconian internal security legislation, immediately set about repressing APRA (Haya de la Torre spent the next five years in the Colombian embassy), the labor unions, and the Communists. One month later, on 24 November 1948, the democratic experiment of the *trienio* in Venezuela came to an end, and thus began the ten-year dictatorship of Marcos Pérez Jiménez during which AD, the unions, and (from May 1950) the Communists all suffered repression. The other democracies survived, but three more were overthrown in the early fifties. In March 1952, Batista brought eight years of Auténtico government in Cuba to an end and established himself in power in an outright military dictatorship. Colombian democracy sur-vived the *bogotazo,* the predominantly urban uprising that followed the assassination of Gaitán on 9 April 1948, but a state of seige in November 1949 led to the closure of Congress (for ten years). The elections in the same month were uncontested by the Liberals and produced a victory for the authoritarian Conservative Laureano Gómez. In June 1953, Gómez was himself overthrown in a military coup that brought General Gustavo Rojas Pinilla to power. Finally, in Guatemala, where a reactionary coup attempt by Colonel Francisco Arana had been thwarted in 1949, "ten years of spring" came to an end in June 1954 when Colonel Carlos Castillo Armas overthrew the government of Jacobo Arbenz (freely elected in November 1950 to succeed Arévalo) and began the process of dismantling the political, social, and economic reforms of the period since 1944.

At the end of 1954 there were no fewer than eleven dictatorships in Latin America (Guatemala, El Salvador, Honduras, Nicaragua, Panama,

Cuba, the Dominican Republic, Venezuela, Colombia, Peru, and Paraguay), thirteen if Ecuador and Argentina are included. Certainly there were more dictatorships in 1954 than in 1944. Not all, it should be noted, were military dictatorships born of military coups. Not all were hostile to labor, although all (except to some extent Cuba) were anti-Communist. Argentina and Ecuador were authoritarian, populist regimes that had their origins in reasonably democratic elections. Perón in Argentina controlled, but retained the support of, organized labor. There were now two revolutionary regimes in Latin America: Mexico and (since 1952) Bolivia. The former, however, was widely regarded as having become a single-party dictatorship. Only four democracies remained: Uruguay, Costa Rica, Chile, and Brazil. And not all these countries could be regarded as democratic without qualification. For example, Communist parties were proscribed in Costa Rica, Chile, and Brazil, and in Brazil more than half the adult population was disenfranchised by its illiteracy. Nor was it possible in 1954 to be confident about their futures as democracies. Chile in 1952 had elected as president a personalistic, authoritarian caudillo and former dictator (1927–31), Carlos Ibáñez del Campo. In fact, Chilean democracy was consolidated in the 1950s and 1960s and was only overthrown in 1973. Another former dictator, Getúlio Vargas, had been elected as president in Brazil in 1950. His suicide in August 1954, under pressure from the military to resign, produced a crisis that seriously threatened to end Brazil's first experiment with democracy after less than a decade. In the event, it survived until 1964. Uruguayan democracy survived until the military coup of 1973. Costa Rica alone has (since the 1948 Civil War) maintained democratic institutional continuity in the postwar period.

The outcome of the postwar conjuncture in Latin America can largely be explained in terms of the continuing strength of the dominant classes, rural and urban, and of the military. They had not been weakened, much less destroyed, by the Second World War as in so many other parts of the world. They had merely been temporarily forced onto the defensive at the end of the war, and after the war they were determined to restore the political and social control that was threatened by the political mobilization of the "dangerous classes," by labor militancy, by the advance of the Left, and perhaps even by democracy itself. The commitment of the Latin American elites (and the middle classes) to democracy, insofar as it existed in other than a purely rhetorical form, by no means implied an acceptance of broadly based popular participation in the democratic process, competition for power by parties of the Left as well as the Right and Center, or recognition of organized labor as a major political actor.

For their part, most progressive parties lacked deep roots in society, were often internally divided and in conflict with each other, and perhaps lacked a vocation for power. Labor unions, despite their impressive growth and the burst of militancy at the end of the war, were still relatively weak and inexperienced. And they still organized only a very small part of the total working population. Only the countries of the Southern Cone – Argentina, Uruguay, and, to a lesser extent, Chile – had developed essentially "modern" social structures characterized by urbanization, size-able middle and working classes, high levels of formal employment, small peasantries, and European standards of living for a substantial proportion of their populations. The societies of most Latin American countries, including the two giants Brazil and Mexico, were still predominantly rural. No Latin American economy, again not excluding Brazil and Mex-ico, had yet advanced far along the road to industrialization. Moreover, both parties and unions no doubt made strategic mistakes. The weakness of the commitment to democracy – most obviously on the Communist Left, but also on the non-Communist Center–Left (for example, APRA in Peru), and among those sectors of the working class susceptible to nationalism and populism – was also a factor in its defeat.

At the same time, domestic class conflicts – different in each country – were strongly influenced by the international environment in which they were played out, that is to say, by the beginning of the Cold War. Latin America was firmly situated in the United States' camp. Ambiguous and occasionally contradictory signals may have emanated from Wash-ington in 1945 and even in 1946, but the signals were clear in 1947 and 1948. At the very least, the Cold War and the international stance adopted by the United States reinforced domestic attitudes and tendencies, pro-viding an ideological justification for the shift to the Right, and for the counteroffensive against the Left and against those sectors of orga-nized labor under the influence of the Left that had in many cases already begun. Popular political mobilization and strike activity, whether or not Communist-led, suddenly became Communist-inspired, Moscow-dictated, and therefore "subversive" (not least of democracy itself).[14]

There was another, wider aspect of the interaction of domestic and international politics in the resolution of the postwar conjuncture in Latin America: the perception the Latin American ruling groups had of the new international economic order and Latin America's place in it. The end of the First World War had seen an international recession, and there was every reason to expect something similar at the end of the Second World

14 The Cold War did not, of course, introduce anticommunism into Latin America; it had been an element in the political culture of the Latin American elites since the Russian Revolution and the creation of the Comintern. The Catholic church, a powerful influence on Latin American politics and society, was a bastion of anticommunism.

War. There were considerable doubts about the likely performance of many of Latin America's principal traditional exports: their purchasing power at the end of the war was still more than 20 percent below their level before the World Depression and it was unclear what sort of demand there would be in the devastated postwar world. Many Latin American countries had accumulated substantial gold and foreign reserves during the war, but these were likely to be used to finance a postwar boom in imports. In any case, reserves held in sterling continued to be blocked, and the postwar rise in the value of the dollar was already eroding the real value of dollar reserves. The more economically advanced, semi-industrialized Latin American nations – above all, Mexico, Brazil, Argentina, and Chile – looked to promote economic development through an acceleration and deepening of the process of import substitution industrialization begun in the 1930s. To achieve this, considerable transfers of capital and technology – from the United States, in particular – would be required. It was by no means clear that U.S. capital would be provided for Latin American industrialization, or on what terms it could be attracted.

The Second World War, as we have seen, represented the inter-American system's finest hour. Against the Axis threat, both external and internal, the United States and Latin America (except Argentina) extended their economic as well as their military ties. The United States had provided financial and technical assistance to Latin America, mainly for the increased production of strategic raw materials, but also in some cases (in Brazil and Mexico, in particular) for the promotion of industrial development. And whereas the war had brought devastation and economic dislocation to Europe and Asia, it had generated an economic boom in the United States. Industrial output doubled, and the GNP rose by 80 percent – from $91 to $166 billion. At the end of the war many Latin American governments had expectations – or hopes – that the United States would continue and indeed expand its wartime role, providing them with long-term development capital.

The United States, however, which overwhelmingly dominated the international economy at the end of the Second World War, repeatedly headed off discussion concerning the economic problems of Latin American – at the Chapultepec conference in February–March 1945, for example, and at inter-American conferences in 1947 and 1948. Instead, the United States focused its attention on the security and economic rehabilitation of Western Europe, the link between the two being clearly recognized. The result was the Economic Recovery Program (the Marshall Plan) of June 1947. No single prominent American advocated large-scale economic support for Latin America. (At this stage the United States even refused to support the creation of an Inter-American Development Bank.) On the contrary, President Truman felt, as he said at the Rio conference in September 1947, that it was the "collective responsibility" of the people of the Americas to rebuild the "exhausted Old World." Latin America, it was argued, had suffered less in the war and had emerged at the end of the war in economically better shape than many other regions of the world. Moreover, Latin America would benefit indirectly from economic recovery in Western Europe. There was to be no Marshall Plan for Latin America.[15] As a result, in 1950 Latin America was the only area of the world without a U.S. aid program, apart from the meagerly funded Point Four technical assistance program established in 1949. Compared with $19 billion in U.S. foreign aid to Western Europe in the period 1945–50, only $400 million (less than 2 percent of total U.S. aid) went to Latin America. Belgium and Luxembourg alone received more than the whole of Latin America.[16]

Although there was some modest increase in lending by the Export–Import Bank after the war, Latin America, it was clear, would have to look to private foreign capital for its development. There was in fact very little new direct U.S. investment in Latin America in the immediate postwar period (and it mostly went into Venezuelan oil and Cuban sugar). If Latin America were, however, to put itself in a position to be able to attract more U.S. capital – and not only into the export agricultural and mining sectors but now, above all, into manufacturing industry – an appropriate climate for direct foreign investment had to be created, and various guarantees and assurances, both symbolic and real, given. There had to be a commitment to liberal, capitalist development and to an "ideology of production," and nationalism had to be curbed (no more "Mexican stunts" – Bernard Baruch's reference to the Mexican national-ization of oil in 1938). The Left, especially the Communist Left, had to be marginalized, and the working class brought firmly under control.

Both politically and economically there were good, domestic reasons for containing labor mobilization in Latin America in the period after the Second World War. In the more industrialized countries (Mexico, Chile, Argentina, and possibly Brazil and Colombia), the exigencies of macro-economic control in dependent economies with strong inflationary pres-sures required a certain level of labor market control by central government. (It was not possible simply to assume that in predominantly labor-surplus

15 At a press conference in Washington in August 1947 to celebrate VJ day, Truman specifically rejected the idea of a Latin American Marshall Plan. "There has been a Marshall Plan for the Western Hemisphere for a century and a half," he said. "[It is] known as the Monroe Doctrine." *New York Times*, 15 August 1947, p. 8.

16 Robert A. Pollard, *Economic Security and the Origins of the Cold War* (New York, 1985), p. 213; Stephen G. Rabe, "The Elusive Conference: US Economic Relations with Latin America, 1945–52," *Diplomatic History* (henceforth *DH*) (1978): 293.

economies, unemployment would prevent wages rising faster than productivity. In many countries, labor markets appear to have been highly segmented. Together with the oligopolistic nature of the modern industrial sector, labor market segmentation opened up the possibility of wage-push inflation.) However, the need to create and maintain an appropriate climate for direct foreign investment was an additional imperative. Strikes had to be kept at an acceptable level, institutionalized mechanisms for the efficient resolution of industrial conflict strengthened, and, in particular, wages in the modern manufacturing sector held at a relatively low level.

Above all, political stability was essential if foreign capital were to be invested in Latin American industry. This was not necessarily synonymous with the strengthening of democratic institutions. Here was a clear point of coincidence of different imperatives. Domestically, militant unions and an increasingly mobilized working class threatened dominant classes and elites, and indeed the middle classes, with moves in the direction of social reform and expanded democracy, which they found unacceptable. At the same time, quite apart from Cold War pressures and the revival of their latent anticommunism, they had urgent reasons in terms of the links between the domestic economies of Latin America and the U.S. economy, for taming labor and the Left and even, if necessary, for replacing democracy with dictatorship.

Thus, just as the United States *indirectly* promoted political and social change in Latin America at the end of the Second World War, it *indirectly* imposed limits on change in the postwar years. But did the United States also play a *direct* role in the overall defeat of democracy, labor, and the Left in Latin America? In approaching this question it is important to consider the place of Latin America in U.S. official thinking and policy making after the Second World War. The paramount importance of Latin America to the United States – both strategic and economic – was never seriously questioned. Although the external threat to the security of the Western Hemisphere from the Axis powers was largely eliminated relatively early in the war, the United States continued to plan for the preservation and strengthening of hemispheric solidarity after the war. This is clear, for example, from the Joint Army and Navy Advisory Board's Western Hemisphere Defense Program in December 1943.[17] Nelson Rockefeller, Assistant Secretary of State for the American Republics from December 1944 to August 1945, took the view at the United Nations conference in San Francisco in April 1945 that the United States could

17 See David Green, *The Containment of Latin America: A History of the Myths and Realities of the Good Neighbor Policy* (Chicago, 1971), p. 343; Chester Joseph Pach, Jr., "The Containment of US Military Aid to Latin America, 1944–1949," *DH* 6(1982):226.

not do what it wanted on the world front unless Western Hemispheric solidarity was guaranteed. Not insignificant was the fact that Latin America represented two-fifths of the votes – 20 out of 51 – at the United Nations, making it the most important single voting bloc. Moreover, Latin America remained the United States' most important export market and source of imports and, after Canada, the area in which most U.S. capital was invested.

However, the *primacy* of United States relations with Latin America was no longer unquestioned. Whereas, as Assistant Secretary of State Edward R. Miller wrote in December 1950, the Good Neighbor Policy had been "virtually our sole foreign policy" in the 1930s,[18] it was clear even before the end of the war that the United States had become for the first time in its history a world power in military, economic, and ideological terms, with global interests and concerns, and the ability to fashion a new postwar international order in its own interests. That the United States was now to play a world – not just a hemispheric – role was evident as early as February–March 1945 at the Chapultepec conference, and even more apparent at the UN conference in San Francisco in April where growing signs of the United States' distrust of the Soviet Union, its only rival at the end of the war, first emerged.

U.S. foreign policy at the end of the war and in the immediate postwar years was, it is important to stress, marked by hesitancy, confusion, and division. It took some time for a unified and coherent approach to develop. One thing, however, is certain: without exception the senior policy makers in Washington – Truman himself, Edward R. Stettinius, Joseph C. Grew, James F. Byrnes, George C. Marshall, Dean Acheson – showed little interest in, and for the most part were ignorant of, Latin America.[19] After the dismissal of Nelson Rockefeller as Assistant Secretary of State in August 1945, Adolf Berle commented, "Men [in high office] who know the hemisphere and love it are few, and those who are known by the hemisphere and loved by it are fewer still." In 1949, complaining bitterly about "sheer neglect and ignorance," Berle declared "we have simply forgotten about Latin America."[20]

18  *Foreign Relations of the United States (FRUS)* 1950, vol. 2, (Washington, D.C., 1976), pp. 625–6.

19  It is interesting to note that in a massive study of six men – Robert Lovell, John McCloy, Averell Harriman, Charles Bohlen, George Kennan, and Dean Acheson – who shaped U.S. foreign policy in the postwar period (Walter Isaacson and Evan Thomas, *The Wise Men: Six Friends and the World They Made* [New York, 1986]), there is no reference to Latin America until the Cuban Missile Crisis (1962). The most recent study of the Truman administration (Michael J. Lacey, ed., *The Truman Presidency* [Cambridge, 1989]), more than half of which is devoted to foreign policy, contains not a single reference to Latin America.

20  Quoted in Jordan A. Schwartz, *Liberal: Adolf A. Berle and the Vision of an American Era* (New York, 1987), pp. 268, 312.

A conference of American states in Rio de Janeiro to formulate a regional collective security pact against external attack under Article 51 of the UN Charter was planned for October 1945. But this was never given top priority and continuing problems between the United States and Perón's Argentina were permitted to delay it. The Inter-American Treaty of Reciprocal Assistance (the Rio treaty) was not signed until August 1947. In the meantime, no significant military assistance was offered to Latin America. An Inter-American Military Cooperation bill was drafted in May 1946, but it failed to make progress in Congress and was finally abandoned in June 1948. The Soviet Union had replaced Germany and Japan as the enemy, real and potential, of the United States. But there seemed to be no Soviet threat to Latin America. As the young John Foster Dulles wrote in *Life* magazine as early as June 1945, the Western Hemisphere represented the "outer zone" of Soviet penetration. The Russians had no atomic bomb, no long-range strategic air force, and an ineffective navy. From the point of view of the United States, Latin America was safe, whereas the Eurasian landmass – Western Europe and the Near East – was in great danger: the Truman Doctrine (March 1947) – the doctrine of containment – was a result of the perceived Soviet threat to Turkey and Greece. In addition, there were limits even to U.S. resources. Just as Latin America's economic needs were given less attention than Europe's, Latin America was given low strategic priority and remained firmly at the periphery of U.S. strategic concerns. The Mutual Defense Assistance Act (1949) allowed for the expenditure of $1.3 billion; not a cent went to Latin America.[21]

Latin America appeared secure from external aggression and to some extent it was safe for the United States to neglect it in global terms. This is not to say, however, that the United States was unconcerned about the possibility of internal subversion (from Communists rather than fascists now, of course). The Soviet Union had neither the military means nor the economic means to challenge seriously the hegemony of the United States in Latin America. But it did retain political and ideological influence through the region's Communist parties. And Communist-led or Communist-labeled insurgencies in Asia, however independent of control by Moscow, lent added credence to U.S. perceptions of a global threat of Communist subversion.

Whereas at the end of the war U.S. officials had been on the whole unconcerned about the growth of Communist parties, as the Cold War developed in the immediate postwar period Communist activities in Latin America were increasingly monitored by legal attachés (almost always FBI

21 Chester Joseph Pach, Jr., "The Containment of US Military Aid to Latin America, 1944–1949," *DH* 6(1982):242.

agents), military and naval attachés, and labor attachés in the U.S. embassies, and by CIA agents. The intelligence apparatus set up during the war for dealing with Nazi subversion was given a new lease on life. A CIA review of Soviet aims in Latin America in November 1947 contended there was no possibility of a Communist takeover anywhere in the region, but on the eve of the Ninth International Conference of American States meeting in Bogotá (March–April 1948), a conference that had been called for the express purpose of establishing a new institutional framework for the inter-American system in the postwar world, U.S. hostility to communism in Latin America was made explicit in State Department Policy Planning Staff document PPS 26 (22 March) and National Security Council document NSC 7 (30 March). Resolution 32 of the Final Act at the Bogotá conference asserted that even the existence of Communist parties as legal entities in Latin America was a direct threat to the security of the Western Hemisphere.

The United States was especially concerned about Communist penetration of the Latin American labor unions. As in Western Europe (especially France and Italy), and for that matter in the United States itself, organized labor was the major ideological battleground of the Cold War. There were important strategic issues at stake; in the late forties it was far from clear to the protagonists in the Cold War that a long period of mutual standoff and relatively peaceful coexistence was on the horizon. Were a Third World War to break out, Communist-controlled unions in Latin America would threaten the interests of the United States, especially in strategically important industries like petroleum (in Mexico, Venezuela, and Peru – virtually all U.S. petroleum imports at the end of the Second World War came from Latin America), copper (in Chile and Peru), sugar (in Cuba), and also transport (particularly railways, shipping, and docks), and in industry generally. Moreover, as in the United States itself, militant unions, whether Communist controlled or not, were a potentially destabilizing force hostile to postwar capitalist development – exerting direct economic and political pressure through strikes and demonstrations, and forming a base for both the parties of the democratic Left and the Communist parties.

In most Latin American countries – for example, Brazil and Cuba – it was not necessary for the United States to intervene directly, even behind the scenes, to secure the proscription of Communist parties and the purging of Communists and other militants from labor unions. Nevertheless, there was undoubtedly a general awareness of Washington's approval of such measures. In part this awareness stemmed from direct contact with U.S. officials, and in part from observing developments in the United States itself. The Truman administration took a tough stand against strikes by coal miners and railwaymen in 1946, and the passage of the Taft–

Hartley Act in June 1947 (albeit passed by Congress over Truman's veto), together with a series of moves to reduce Communist influence in the Congress of Industrial Organizations (CIO) and its constituent unions, especially the United Auto Workers (UAW), gave clear signals to Latin American policy makers that labor discipline and anticommunism were the order of the day.[22] The showdown in Europe between the more moderate sections of European labor movements and the Communists in 1947 and 1948 further reinforced the message. It might even be argued that U.S. pressure was anticipated. In Bolivia, however, the U.S. withdrawal of support in 1947 from the coalition that included the Marxist PIR was certainly a major factor in the decline in that party's fortunes and the marked shift to the Right in Bolivian politics in the late forties. And in Chile, which was particularly vulnerable to direct U.S. economic pressure, U.S. intervention in 1947 was perhaps decisive in persuading González Videla to take a firm stand against communism and the Communists.

In the meantime, on the international labor front, the American Federation of Labor (AFL) spearheaded the campaign to drive the Communists out of the ranks of the world trade union movement. Even during the war when the AFL had officially maintained good relations with the nationalist, pro-Communist Confederación de Trabajadores de América Latina (CTAL) in the interest of the war effort, the first steps had been taken in Latin America toward the creation of "free" trade unions based on the U.S. model. George Meany visited Latin America and two key figures in the postwar struggle for labor – Bernardo Ibáñez, the Chilean Socialist leader, and Juan Arévalo, the secretary of foreign affairs of the Confederación de Trabajadores de Cuba (CTC) – were invited to Washington in July 1943. The appointment of labor attachés in most of the U.S. embassies in Latin America during 1943–4 can be seen as part of the same process. But it was after the war that the major offensive was launched against the CTAL, which was now affiliated with the World Federation of Trade Unions (WFTU), a "Communist front" from a Cold War perspective. With State Department "informal assistance," AFL roving "ambassadors," like Irving Brown in Europe and Serafino Romualdi in Latin America, were sent out to organize support for pro-United States "free" trade unionism. By 1947–8 the anti-Communists had won the internal struggles in Latin American unionism. The major national union confederations disaffiliated from the CTAL, often after bitter internal conflicts and splits. In January 1948 at its meeting in Lima the CTAL split: the Confederación Interamericana de Trabajadores (CIT) – later to become the Organización Regional Interamericana de Trabajadores

---

22 The Taft–Hartley Act (1947) imposed considerable restrictions on strike activity and collective bargaining as well as making it illegal for Communists to hold union office.

(ORIT) was established. In December 1949 the non-Communist unions also left the WFTU and formed the International Confederation of Free Trade Unions (ICFTU).

It has been argued that from one perspective measures against Communist parties and Communist-led (and even independently militant) unions, albeit taken by democratic or semidemocratic governments – in Brazil, Chile, Cuba, Costa Rica, Peru, Venezuela, Mexico – represented a narrowing of the concept and practice of democracy in Latin America. However, from the perspective of Washington (and the dominant groups in Latin America) in 1947 and 1948, the removal of the Communists from the political and labor scenes *strengthened* democracy. Communism was no longer compatible with democracy; like fascism, it was an alien ideology that threatened it. Resolution 32 of the Final Act of the Bogotá conference (directed against the legal status of Communist parties) was entitled "The Preservation and Defense of Democracy in America." The Chilean Communist Party was outlawed by a "Law for the Permanent Defense of Democracy."

In its public rhetoric the United States continued to support democracy over dictatorship in Latin America. But after 1945–6, little was actually done to promote or even defend democratic principles and practices in Latin America (unless support for anticommunism is seen in this light). On the contrary, from 1947 – and perhaps the departure of Braden from the State Department in June 1947 was an early signal of this – there was a marked shift in U.S. attitudes. Dictators received fewer expressions of disapproval, although the government of Somoza's uncle Víctor Román y Reyes, who replaced Leonardo Argüello as president within a month of his election in May 1947, was denied U.S. recognition for almost a year. In the middle of 1947, licenses for the export of arms, aircraft, and vessels to Trujillo's Dominican Republic were granted again after a ban lasting three years. The United States not only refused to support, but at times positively opposed, the efforts of the so-called Caribbean Legion of exiled democrats, sponsored by José Figueres, Ramón Grau San Martín, Rómulo Betancourt, and Juan José Arévalo during 1947–9, to overthrow the dictatorships in Nicaragua and the Dominican Republic and the Communist-backed democratic government in Costa Rica (before the Civil War of 1948) – a form of collective intervention in support of democracy in the Caribbean and Central America. And at the end of 1948, despite statements deploring the use of force as an instrument of political change, the United States offered early recognition (and therefore, in the eyes of Latin American democrats, approval) to the military regimes of Manuel Odría and Marcos Pérez Jiménez after the overthrow of popularly elected, democratic governments in Peru and Venezuela. To have withheld recognition, it was argued, would have been to intervene in the internal affairs of Peru and Venezuela. Nevertheless, as the tide turned against democracy in Latin America, the overwhelming power of the United States was such that a U.S. policy of early (sometimes eager) recognition of dictatorships could in itself constitute a factor undermining democratic institutions.

In the new conditions of the Cold War, the struggle against communism worldwide, including Latin America, and the threat communism (and behind it the Soviet Union) was thought to pose to the strategic and economic interests of the United States inevitably had priority over efforts to promote democracy in Latin America. Democracies might still be preferable to dictatorships in the abstract, but if dictatorships proved more effective at dealing with communism (as well as more friendly to U.S. companies), they might be preferable to democracies.[23] It was only a short step to the view that circumstances might arise in which it was necessary for the United States to abandon the principle of nonintervention in Latin America in order to overthrow a democratic government that was "soft on communism" and install a dictatorship. A democratic government in Latin America now lived in the shadow of a vigilant and increasingly ideologically motivated United States. If it were to be "penetrated" by Communists – and in the atmosphere of the Cold War evidence for this could be merely the introduction of necessary, far-reaching social reforms, or even the toleration of strong independent trade unions and popular political movements of the Left – it could be seen to threaten the strategic and economic interests of the United States and could be undermined or even overthrown.

There is little evidence that the United States was actively involved in the overthrow of democracy in, for example, Peru in 1948, Cuba in 1952, or Colombia in 1953, although in view of the strength of U.S. economic interests in Peru and Cuba, in particular, further research would seem to be justified. In Venezuela, however, where the United States had crucial oil interests, where Communists had a good deal of influence over organized labor, and where the AD government, though anti-Communist, had refused to cede to Cold War pressures and outlaw the Communist Party (and had been lukewarm on the issue of communism at Bogotá), there is circumstantial evidence at least that the United States was no mere bystander when, on 24 November 1948, a military coup brought to an abrupt end the three-year experiment with democracy.[24] In contrast,

---

23 See, for example, George F. Kennan's memorandum to the secretary of state in March 1950, following his first and only trip to Latin America, quoted in Bethell, "From the Second World War to the Cold War," pp. 64–5. The full text of Kennan's memorandum can be found in *FRUS* 1950, vol. 2, pp. 598–624. See also George F. Kennan, *Memoirs 1925–50* (Boston, 1967), pp. 476–84.

24 See the chapter by Steve Ellner on Venezuela in this volume.

direct U.S. involvement in the overthrow of democracy in Guatemala in 1954 is unquestioned and has been extensively documented.[25]

Communist influence over the government of Arbenz – signaled in particular by the Agrarian Reform (June 1952) and the legalization of the Marxist Partido Guatemalteco de Trabajo (PGT) (December 1952), but undoubtedly exaggerated by Washington – was believed to pose a direct threat to U.S. corporate interests (specifically, the United Fruit Company). It was the most serious threat of this kind since the nationalization of the Mexican oil industry in 1938. Even more important, if in the judgment of the United States Arbenz had become a pawn of the Communists, Guatemala was a direct threat to the security of the United States. The Bolivian Revolution with its agrarian reform and nationalization of the tin industry could be tolerated: it was anticommunist; it did not threaten major U.S. economic interests; and, above all, it did not represent a threat to U.S. strategic interests. But the government of Guatemala stood accused of establishing a beachhead for Soviet imperialism in the Western Hemisphere and had to be removed. At the Tenth Inter-American Conference held in Caracas in March 1954, John Foster Dulles successfully secured the passage of a strongly worded anti-Communist resolution (the Declaration of Caracas), despite the reasonable apprehension of some delegates that it might be used to sanction U.S. intervention in Latin America, and specifically in Guatemala. In June 1954 the Eisenhower administration authorized CIA support for the invasion of Guatemala from Honduras. It proved decisive in the overthrow of the Arbenz government.

In this introductory chapter, we have described and tried to indicate the variety of factors, both domestic and international, that explain both the emergence and the eventual containment and defeat of democratic and reformist forces and aspirations in Latin America between the Second World War and the Cold War. The chapters that follow offer case studies of the immediate postwar experience of eleven of the twenty Latin American republics, including all the larger countries with the exception of Colombia. The picture that emerges is a complex one. There remains considerable scope for debate and disagreement about the details of the processes involved. We believe, however, that the evidence presented here substantiates our principal propositions.

---

25 See, in particular, Richard H. Immerman, *The CIA in Guatemala: The Foreign Policy of Intervention* (Austin, TX, 1982) and Stephen Schlesinger and Stephen Kinzer, *Bitter Fruit: The Untold Story of the American Coup in Guatemala* (London, 1982). See also Jim Handy, *Gift of the Devil: A History of Guatamala* (Toronto, 1984) and James Dunkerley, *Power in the Isthmus: A Political History of Modern Central America* (London, 1988). An important work published after the completion of this volume is Piero Gleijeses, *Shattered Hope: The Guatemalan Revolution and the United States, 1944–54* (Princeton, 1991).

It may well be that further research on the countries we have not been able to include in this book may lead to some modification of our general argument. We are particularly conscious of the need for consideration of Colombia, which in some respects had a rather different history from the rest of Latin America. We have been careful, however, to include two cases – Argentina and Guatemala – that seem to be at least partial exceptions to what has been presented as a general pattern of defeat for labor, the Left, and democracy in the immediate postwar period. In Guatemala, a democratic, reformist regime survived and the defeat of popular forces was delayed, though only until 1954. In Argentina, under Perón, the defeat was disguised by the fact that an authoritarian anti-Left but prolabor regime remained in power until 1955. Another possible exception is Uruguay where democracy survived (until 1973) and where, apparently, there was no move to contain either labor or the Left in the postwar period. It is not entirely clear why this should have been the case, though two hypotheses may be worth consideration. The first is that although the Left, and in particular the Communist Party, was influential in the labor movement, this was not translated into what was essentially a two-party political system dominated by the *blancos* and the *colorados*. Labor conflict was thereby restricted in its political impact and rendered manageable. The other hypothesis is that Uruguay successfully implemented, at an early stage, a form of social democracy whereby urban consumers were able to experience continually rising real incomes and had access to important welfare and social security programs. This precocious social democracy, basically subsidized by revenues from agrarian exports, held in check the incipient conflicts between accumulation and distribution.

There is certainly room for more research on all Latin American countries, and not only on labor and the Left, which we have argued are central to an understanding of the nature and outcome of the postwar conjuncture, but also on the Right, on the various elements that make up the Latin American elites, on the middle classes, on peasants (which played an important role in, for example, Bolivia and Venezuela), on the military, and perhaps on the church. Further study is needed of the precise operation of global forces and their impact on the ongoing processes of political and social change in each Latin American country. The relationship of the Second World War to the postwar "openings" is relatively well understood. The relationship of the Cold War to the subsequent "closures," however, calls for more research. We need to know more about the precise mechanisms by which the Cold War arrived in Latin America, how far anticommunism was sponsored by the United States, how it meshed with existing anticommunism and conservatism. Finally, we need more research on how not only the Cold War, but also the new international economic

# 1

# Brazil

*Leslie Bethell*

The outbreak of war in Europe in September 1939 forced Getúlio Vargas, who had been president of Brazil since the Revolution of 1930 (and dictator since the military coup and foundation of the Estado Novo in November 1937), to reassess the foreign policy he had successfully pursued throughout the 1930s. "Pragmatic equilibrium" between the three Great Powers with major strategic and economic interests in Brazil (the United States, Britain, and Germany) was no longer a viable policy. Brazil's options narrowed; choices had to be made. And despite pro-Axis, indeed profascist, sympathies in many sectors of Brazil's ruling elite, not least in the military high command, and some initial hesitation by Vargas, there was never much doubt that Brazil would eventually be driven by both political and economic considerations to join the United States in support of Britain against Germany. As early as January 1941 Vargas secretly authorized the construction of U.S. air base facilities in the strategically important Brazilian Northeast for a future war against Germany in North Africa in which the state of Natal was to be the "springboard to victory." In January 1942, after the Japanese attack on Pearl Harbor and the decision of the United States to enter the war and in accordance with agreements made at the Rio Conference of American Foreign Ministers, Brazil abandoned neutrality and broke off diplomatic relations with the Axis powers. In August, after Germany's persistent sinking of Brazilian vessels (with the loss of Brazilian lives), Brazil declared war.

During the Second World War Brazil was the closest ally of the United States in Latin America. Apart from providing bases in the Northeast (of diminishing importance after victory in North Africa), Brazil was a major supplier of strategic materials – above all, rubber and iron ore, but also chrome, industrial diamonds, manganese, nickel, bauxite, tungsten, and, not least, monazite sands (from which uranium and thorium, essential to the U.S. atomic energy project, could be extracted). Moreover, in July 1944 Brazil sent an expeditionary force of twenty-five thousand men to

33

the European theater – the only Latin American combat troops to see
action in the war (principally at Monte Castello in Italy in February–
March 1945). For its part the United States provided Brazil with military
equipment – including tanks and aircraft – under Lend–Lease. Brazil was
in fact the recipient of more than 70 percent of all Lend–Lease to Latin
America. Senior Brazilian officers – the largest contingent of Allied officers
– were trained at Fort Leavenworth and elsewhere. The United States
remained the main market for coffee, Brazil's principal export, and other
foodstuffs. And although unable to supply Brazil with all the manufactured and capital goods it required, not least because of restrictions on
shipping, the United States offered loans (notably the Export–Import
Bank loan for the Volta Redonda steel complex in the state of Rio de
Janeiro) and technical advice and assistance (by means, for example, of
the Cooke mission in 1942), which considerably accelerated Brazil's economic – and especially industrial – development.[1]

As the tide turned in favor of the Allies and victory over the Axis (and
therefore of democracy over fascism) was assured, it became increasingly
unlikely that the Estado Novo – a dictatorship that had not entirely
avoided the label "fascist" – would long survive the end of the war.
Barbosa Lima Sobrinho, the distinguished journalist and politician, once
offered the provocative proposition that the German defeat at Stalingrad
(February 1943) sealed the fate of the Estado Novo. The U.S. ambassador
to Brazil, Jefferson Caffery, forecast at the time that after the war Vargas
would feel "impelled to restore some sort of democratic process."[2] This
was a view shared by the British ambassador, Sir Noel Charles: "His
[Vargas's] position at the peace conference and in postwar Brazil alike
require him to conform in an increasing measure to the basic principles

1  On relations between Brazil and the United States during the Second World War, see Frank D.
   McCann, Jr., *The Brazilian–American Alliance 1937–1945* (Princeton, 1973); Stanley E. Hilton,
   "Brazilian Diplomacy and the Washington–Rio de Janeiro 'Axis' during the World War II Era,"
   *Hispanic American Historical Review* (henceforth *HAHR*) 59(1979):201–31; McCann, "Critique,"
   *HAHR* 59(1979):691–700; R.A. Humphreys, *Latin America and the Second World War*, Vol. 2,
   *1942–1945* (London, 1982), pp. 59–85; Gerson Moura, Brazilian foreign relations, 1939–1950:
   The changing nature of Brazil–U.S. relations during and after the Second World War (Ph.D.
   diss. University of London, 1982); Monica Hirst, O Processo de alinhamento nas relações Brasil–
   Estados Unidos, 1942–5, (Master's thesis, Instituto Universitário de Pesquisas do Rio de Janeiro,
   1982); Marcelo de Paiva Abreu, Brazil and the world economy, 1930–45: Aspects of foreign
   economic policies and international economic relations under Vargas (Ph.D. diss. University of
   Cambridge, 1971); Marcelo de Paiva Abreu, "Anglo–Brazilian Economic Relations and the Consolidation of American Pre-Eminence in Brazil, 1930–45" in *Latin America, Economic Imperialism
   and the State*, ed. C. Abel and C.M. Lewis (London, 1985), pp. 379–93.
2  Caffery, no. 10029, 6 February 1943, RG 59, Department of State, 832.00/2–643, National
   Archives, Washington, D.C.

for which the United Nations are fighting."[3] It would in the end, Caffery and Charles believed, prove impossible to resist the inevitable domestic pressure for liberalization. The Sociedade dos Amigos da América, founded in December 1942, and the Liga de Defesa Nacional, founded during the First World War and revived during the Second, used every Allied military success as an opportunity to express the hope that representative government would be restored in Brazil. "If we fight against fascism at the side of the United Nations so that liberty and democracy may be restored to all people," declared the signatories of the opposition Manifesto dos Mineiros in October 1943, "certainly we are not asking too much in demanding for ourselves such rights and guarantees."[4] At the same time external pressures would eventually oblige Brazil to adopt a more liberal political system. An editorial in the Rio de Janeiro newspaper *O Jornal* in February 1945 gave clear expression to the realities and imperatives for Brazil in the emerging new international order:

The moral and political atmosphere of the world has been decisively transformed with the defeat of the totalitarian states and the triumph of the democratic systems. . . . The peace conference is drawing near, a conference in which we should play a part that measures up to the responsibilities we have assumed and the sacrifices we have made during this war. We could not, however, take our place at the conference table with the full force of our prestige, if in our own country we had not put completely into practice the democratic principles for which we fight.[5]

The United States brought no *direct* pressure to bear on its ally Brazil in favor of political liberalization, at least not until the closing stages of the war. In Brazil, as elsewhere in Latin America, the United States was pleased to accept the support of – and indirectly to support – a dictatorship, provided it was committed internationally to the struggle against the Axis and for democracy. "From the American standpoint (when they are honest with themselves) Vargas is admittedly a tyrant," an official at the Foreign Office observed, "but (like another great Allied leader) he is a tyrant on the right side and therefore ceases to count as such."[6] The Good Neighbor Policy toward Latin America, the cornerstone of which was nonintervention, even for the promotion of democracy, was in any case by now well established. President Franklin D. Roosevelt was, more-

---

3 Charles, no. 95, 11 May 1943, Foreign Office (henceforth FO) 371/33678, Public Record Office, London.

4 Quoted in John W.F. Dulles, *The São Paulo Law School and the Anti-Vargas Resistance (1938–45)* (Austin, TX, 1986), p. 127. See also Hélio Silva, *1945: Por Que Depuseram Vargas* (Rio de Janeiro, 1976), pp. 62–77.

5 1–7 February 1945. Quoted in McCann, *Brazilian–American Alliance*, pp. 450–1.

6 Allen, Foreign Office Minute, 1 March 1945, FO 371/44806.

over, on particularly good personal terms with Vargas. And Vargas was, of course, no Trujillo or Somoza. However, toward the end of the war – in, for example, a circular written by Assistant Secretary of State Adolf A. Berle, Jr., to U.S. embassies in November 1944 – the United States became more open in its declarations that it felt greater affinity with, and was more favorably disposed toward, democracies than dictatorships in Latin America.[7] In February 1945 Secretary of State Edward R. Stettinius, Jr., visited Brazil on his way back from Yalta en route to the Inter-American Conference on the Problems of War and Peace (the Chapultepec Conference) in Mexico City. At Yalta it had been agreed that there would be "free elections of governments responsive to the will of the people" in liberated countries (and at Chapultepec there would be declarations in favor of democracy in Latin America). There is no evidence, however, that Stettinius specifically raised the issue of elections in Brazil during his brief stay in Rio de Janeiro, although the British embassy believed that he did. (The visit was "evidently one of more than courtesy.") The story circulated in Rio that Stettinius's gift to Vargas, a radio, was to enable the Brazilian dictator to discover what was going on in the rest of the world.[8]

Brazil's entry into the Second World War on the side of the Allies undoubtedly stimulated domestic opposition to the Vargas dictatorship. This opposition had its roots, however, in the nature and "illegitimacy" of the regime. The Estado Novo was the outcome of a military coup in November 1937 carried out to prevent presidential elections in January 1938 in which, under the Constitution of 1934, Vargas himself could not be a candidate. There was, however, a potential time bomb: under the "Constitution" of 1937 Vargas's presidential mandate was six years after which there would be a plebiscite. As November 1943 approached, therefore, the opposition to the regime from a variety of clandestine and semiclandestine groups intensified. The Manifesto dos Mineiros was merely the most public manifestation of a fierce debate on the legal foundations of the regime and of a rising tide of opinion throughout 1943 and 1944 in favor of political liberalization.

The opposition to Vargas can be divided into two main elements. The first, and much more important, consisted of those traditional, liberal-conservative, regionally based political families and parties, especially in São Paulo but also in Minas Gerais and even in Rio Grande do Sul, that had held power during the First or Old Republic (1889–1930), that had

---

7 On the United States and democracy in Latin America generally at the end of the Second World War, see Leslie Bethell, "From the Second World War to the Cold War, 1944–54," in *Exporting Democracy: The United States and Latin America,* ed. Abraham F. Lowenthal (Baltimore, 1991), pp. 41–70.

8 Gainer, no. 64, 19 February 1945, FO 371/44812; McCann, *Brazilian–American Alliance,* p. 451.

been defeated in the Revolution of 1930 (and in the Civil War of 1932), and whose resurgence by means of elections in January 1938 had been halted by the coup of November 1937. Many of their leading members were in exile in New York, Paris, and Buenos Aires. Their main political objective was not the establishment of democracy per se – their democratic credentials left a great deal to be desired – but a restoration of liberal constitutionalism. The *paulista* and *mineiro* representatives of the export-oriented landed oligarchy also sought a return to liberal economic policies, opposed as they were to state intervention in the economy – except in defense of export agriculture, especially coffee – and the "artificial" industrial growth that had occurred and had eventually been promoted by the Vargas regime during the Depression years of the 1930s and during the war. The second anti-Vargas element consisted of the bulk of the liberal, professional middle class – journalists and lawyers, for example – together with liberal intellectuals and, above all, students. The São Paulo Law School, especially its Frente de Resistência, was particularly active and combative, despite government repression.[9] This element was more genuinely democratic and formed the ideological backbone of the emerging *ampla frente democrático*. It attracted the non-Communist Left but not for the most part Brazil's Communists, who at the end of the Second World War were to play a significant role in Brazilian politics for the first time.

Founded in March 1922 the Partido Comunista do Brasil (PCB) had been allowed to operate legally only during March–July 1922 and January–August 1927. Like the liberal opposition, it had suffered persecution and repression at the hands of Vargas, especially following the attempted Communist putsch in Natal, Recife, and Rio de Janeiro in November 1935. Most of the party's national and regional leaders were in fact in prison during the Estado Novo, including the most famous, Luis Carlos Prestes, ex-*tenente*,[10] convert to communism in the early 1930s, and honorary president of the Aliança Nacional Libertadora (Brazil's Popular Front) in 1935. The PCB was, therefore, a clandestine party. Membership was small and consisted of intellectuals, the professional middle class, and lower middle class elements as much as industrial workers.

The Second World War deepened divisions that already existed within the PCB. Two broad groups can be identified. One consisted of the Rio de Janeiro Communists together with some, for the most part Bahians, living in São Paulo and favored *união nacional democrática contra nazi-*

---

9 See Dulles, *São Paulo Law School*, passim.
10 The *tenentes* (lieutenants) were young, reform-minded army officers who in the 1920s instigated a series of military uprisings against the oligarchical economic, social, and political system of the Old Republic.

*fascismo.* They put the need for national unity in support of the struggle of the Allies (including the Soviet Union) against the Axis – and ultimately for democracy – before immediate political change in Brazil. In this sense, then, they were pro-Vargas, at least for the duration of the war. The group's self-styled Comissão Nacional de Organização Provisória (CNOP) took the initiative in convoking in 1943 the Second National Conference of the PCB. Fourteen delegates met at Barra do Piraí near the Mantiqueira mountains in the state of Rio de Janeiro on 27–29 August. A provisional party organization was formally reestablished and Prestes was elected secretary general in absentia. A second group (predominantly from São Paulo), however, rejected both this position and the right of the CNOP to institutionalize it. By putting the emphasis on *união democrática nacional* and the struggle for democracy in Brazil, they were essentially part of the anti-Vargas opposition. Toward the end of 1943 they formed their own organization, the so-called Comitê de Ação. But many left the Comitê for the CNOP/PCB when, first in March and then in June 1944, Prestes, although demanding amnesty (he was himself still in prison), the legalization of the party, and the restoration of individual liberties, defended the Mantiqueira line that Communists should support Vargas unconditionally in the war against fascism. Prestes rejected both liquidationism (a reference to those who favored the dissolution of the party in view of the dissolution of Comintern – a variation of Browderism)[11] and the leftist sectarianism of those who attacked Vargas. Some Communists, however, especially *paulista* intellectuals and students, continued to play a role in the broad opposition front. The first Brazilian writers' congress held in São Paulo in January 1945 – a key event in the mobilization of the liberal opposition to Vargas – was attended not only by prominent figures on the non-Communist Left but by two of the nine founders of the PCB in 1922: Astrojildo Pereira and Cristiano Cordeiro.[12]

Getúlio Vargas had never shown any enthusiasm for democracy, at least not for *democracia liberal,* which he associated with the semi-representative but essentially oligarchical politics of the First Republic. Ideologues and propagandists of the Estado Novo referred to *democracia nova, democracia auténtica,* or even *democracia autoritária* [*sic*]. Individual freedoms, political parties, and elections for both executive office and legislative assemblies all may have been undermined and in most cases abolished in 1937, but

11  On Browderism, see Introduction, note 10.
12  On the Partido Comunista do Brasil during the Second World War, see Ronald H. Chilcote, *The Brazilian Communist Party: Conflict and Integration, 1922–72* (New York, 1974); Leôncio Martins Rodrigues, "O PCB: Os Dirigentes e a Organização" in *História Geral da Civilização Brasileira,* vol. 3, pt. 3, ed. Boris Fausto (São Paulo, 1981); Edgard Carone, *O PCB,* vols. 1–2 (São Paulo, 1982); John W.F. Dulles, *Brazilian Communism 1935–1945: Repression during World Upheaval* (Austin, TX, 1983).

the power of the central state, economic and especially industrial development, national identity and pride, and citizenship in a social if not a political sense (for the urban population at least) had all been advanced under the Estado Novo (or Estado Nacional, as Vargas began to call it).[13]

For Vargas, the Second World War was a reason (or excuse) for delaying discussion of Brazil's political future. Stability, continuity, and national unity became overriding considerations. Opposition demands for political change around the time of the sixth anniversary of the November 1937 coup were largely ignored. In April 1944 Vargas told the Brazilian Press Association that elections would have to wait until the end of the war (which gave the opposition *Diario Carioca* the opportunity to run the headline "President Vargas promises elections after war").[14] In July he appointed as the new police chief in Rio de Janeiro Cariolano de Góes, described by the British ambassador as "thoroughly brutal and repressive." The Sociedade dos Amigos da América was proscribed in August (prompting the resignation of Osvaldo Aranha, Vargas's distinguished foreign minister, who had recently been elected the society's vice-president). There were renewed waves of arrests during the following months. Opposition hopes of engendering political change before the end of the war were finally dashed.

Nevertheless Vargas had come to recognize that if Brazil wished to play a role in a postwar international political order dominated by the United States – and Brazil aspired to a permanent seat on the Security Council of the United Nations, the structure of which was under discussion at Dumbarton Oaks during the second half of 1944 – and if Brazil wished to secure much needed U.S. development aid and U.S. direct investment (especially in manufacturing industry) after the war, at least some "adjustment" of Brazil's political structure would have to be made. Ambassador Caffery reported as much as early as June 1944.[15] In his Independence Day speech in September, Vargas for the first time explicitly promised free elections after the war. Equally important, the military, the main pillar of the Estado Novo, had arrived at the same conclusion. Late in October 1944 General Eurico Gaspar Dutra, minister of war since 1936 and no democrat, returned from an inspection tour of the Brazilian forces

13 A key source for the study of the ideology of the Estado Novo is the official journal of the regime, *Cultura Política*, edited by Almir de Andrade and published by the Departamento de Imprensa e Propaganda (DIP) from March 1941 to October 1945. See Lúcia Lippi Oliveira, Mônica Pimenta Velloso, and Angela Maria Castro Gomes, *Estado Novo: Ideología e Poder* (Rio de Janeiro, 1982), and Silvana Goulart, *Sob a Verdade Oficial: Ideología, Propaganda e Censura no Estado Novo* (São Paulo, 1990).

14 On 13 July 1944 *The New York Times* carried on its front page the headline "Vargas promises Brazil democracy."

15 Caffery, no. 16668, 29 June 1944, RG 59, 832.00/6-2944.

in Europe convinced that the bulk of the officers, under the influence as they now were of the United States, and looking to U.S. military assistance after the war, supported the establishment of "democratic representative institutions" in Brazil. In November General Pedro de Góes Monteiro, former minister of war (1934–7) and former army chief of staff (1937–44), on leave from Montevideo, where he was serving with the Inter-American Defense Committee, joined Dutra in arguing for an end to the dictatorship sooner rather than later. Vargas finally instructed Alexandre Marcondes Filho, who was both minister of justice and minister of labor, to draw up, in consultation with Brazil's senior generals, a program of political liberalization, including elections, the speedy implementation of which he promised in a speech to the military on 31 December 1944.

Vargas and the military were confident they could control the process of *abertura* and could indeed win any elections that might be held. Thus democratization need not mean the overthrow of the Estado Novo, a return to the status quo of before 1937 or even 1930, or the restoration of a largely discredited *democracia liberal*. The opportunity was there for the transformation of the Estado Novo, an advance to *democracia social*. There had, after all, been no breakdown of political power. Vargas controlled the state apparatus (the military, the police, the state *interventores*, the municipal *prefeitos*, the bureaucracy, the judiciary, etc.). He could count on considerable political support from the non-export-oriented sectors of the rural oligarchy (in Rio Grande do Sul, Minas Gerais, and the Northeast), from the industrialists who backed and benefited from his development policies and the "social peace" he guaranteed, and from the middle class, especially in the enormously expanded public sector. Finally, and most importantly, if elections were to be won, Vargas believed with justifiable confidence that he and the regime had the support of organized labor.

Compared with that of Argentina, for example, the Brazilian working class was relatively small and heterogenous. It numbered some 2 million in 1945, approximately 15 percent of the 13–14 million *assalariados* in Brazil's population of 40 million. More than two-thirds of Brazilian workers were still employed in agriculture, cattle raising, and rural industries. The working class had expanded during the 1930s and especially during the Second World War. It had also become more Brazilian, due to urban population growth and the beginnings of a mass migration from countryside and small town to city rather than European (and Japanese) immigration, which had been restricted during the 1930s. Half of Brazil's workers (around 1 million) were employed in only two cities: Rio de Janeiro (the Federal District) and São Paulo, which had become to some extent "proletarian cities." Before 1920 urban workers were concentrated in public utilities, railways (and other means of transport), ports, banks, the construction industry, commerce, and, least important, manufacturing industry (mostly textiles and the processing of food and drink). By 1945 however, more than half of Brazil's urban workers (1.1 million) found employment in approximately seventy thousand small and medium-sized *fábricas* (few employing more than 1,000 workers) in the areas of textiles, food and drink, but also metallurgy, chemicals and pharmaceuticals, cement, tires, vehicle assembly, and so forth. There was also a significant force of white-collar state employees.[16]

In 1945 a quarter of the urban labor force – half a million workers (approximately twice as many as before the war) – was unionized. The "old" *sindicatos*, independent, with anarchist, socialist, and (after 1922) Communist leadership, had suffered severe repression following the great strikes of 1917–19. After 1930, under Decree 19.700 (March 1931) of the revolutionary government, they had been gradually supplanted by labor unions closely controlled by the state, that is to say, by the newly created Ministry of Labor, Industry, and Commerce. A more liberal Decree 24.694 (July 1934) in accordance with the Constitution of 1934 permitted some revival of independent unions and, at least until the state of seige in November 1935, some renewed influence of the Left. Finally, however, under Articles 138 and 139 of the corporatist Carta Constitucional of the Estado Novo (1937), inspired by the Carta del Lavoro of fascist Italy, and Decree 1.402 (August 1939) state control of unions was restored and reinforced. All decrees and regulations on unions were consolidated in the Labor Code (the Consolidação das Leis do Trabalho) of May 1943.

A central feature of the relationship between the state and organized labor in Brazil during the Estado Novo was the *sindicato único,* that is to say, one union per industry per locality. There were 800–900 recognized unions in Brazil. Each broad sector (for example, industrial workers, commercial workers) and each category (for example, textile workers, bank workers) could organize state federations and national confederations. But no "horizontal" inter-union organizations across sectors (for example, textile workers and metal workers in São Paulo) were permitted. Above all, the law did not allow for a single *national* organization of all workers like the Argentine Confederación General del Trabajo (CGT) or the Mexican Confederación de Trabajadores de México (CTM). Moreover, international affiliation with the Confederación de Trabajadores de América Latina

---

16 For the size and composition of the Brazilian working class at the end of the Second World War, I have drawn on the monthly reports of Edward J. Rowell, the U.S. labor attaché in Rio de Janeiro (U.S. embassy in Rio de Janeiro post files, labor affairs RG 84/850. 4, National Record Center, Suitland, Washington, D.C.), and a most interesting document prepared for the Bureau of Labor Statistics of the U.S. Department of Labor by Jules Henry, "Developments in Brazilian Labor Organization since VJ Day," which was later published in *Monthly Labor Review* (March 1947).

(CTAL), founded in 1938 by the Mexican Marxist leader Vicente Lombardo Toledano, was expressly forbidden. Another feature of the relationship between state and labor was the degree of control over unions exercised by the Ministry of Labor through legal registration, the "election" of officials who were in fact appointees (known as *pelegos*), and financial regulation. Unions were financed by means of the *impôsto sindical* (introduced in July 1940). This was the compulsory contribution by all workers (whether union members or not) of union dues at the rate of one day's pay per annum deducted at source by the federal government. In the absence of free collective bargaining, negotiations between capital and labor were conducted through labor courts. Finally, Brazilian workers lacked a legal right to strike.[17]

This close, corporatist relationship between state and *sindicatos* was reinforced by an ideology of class collaboration, class harmony, social peace, and government as arbiter between capital and labor. The ambiguities in the relationship have been the subject of much discussion. On the one hand, unions lacked autonomy and were subordinate to the state. Workers were not permitted to engage in political activity, nor to strike, even though wages failed to keep up with inflation. In addition, a long tradition of working class struggle to improve wages, hours, conditions of work, and conditions of urban daily life was crushed, or at least subdued, under the state of seige that followed the *intentona comunista* in 1935 and under the Estado Novo beginning in 1937, especially during Second World War. On the other hand, unions were legally recognized and union leaders had some (limited) political influence. There were regular wage increases, at least until 1943, and in 1941 a minimum wage had been introduced. In addition, limited social welfare benefits (pensions, healthcare, etc.) were extended to increasing numbers of employees and their dependents. As Clifford German, the British labor attaché, wrote in the review of Brazilian trade unionism with which he introduced his first report from Rio de Janeiro, the Brazilian workers had "a number of rights not enjoyed in any democratic country, such as guaranteed stability of employment after ten years' service; equal pay for equal work for both

---

17 On Brazilian *sindicatos* and the legislation relating to *sindicatos* in the period 1930–45, see Aziz Simão, *Sindicato e Estado* (São Paulo, 1966); José Albertino Rodrigues, *Sindicato e Desenvolvimento no Brasil* (São Paulo, 1968); Luis Werneck Vianna, *Liberalismo e Sindicato no Brasil* (Rio de Janeiro, 1976); Maria Hermínia Tavares de Almeida, Estado e classes trabalhadores no Brasil (1930–45) (Ph.D. diss. Universidade de São Paulo, 1978); Leôncio Martins Rodrigues, "Sindicalismo e Classe Operária (1930–1964)" in *História Geral da Civilização Brasileira*, vol. 3, pt. 3; Antonio Carlos Bernardo, *Tutela e Autonomia Sindical: Brasil 1930–45* (São Paulo, 1982); Maria Celia Pinheiro-Machado Paoli, Labour, law and the state in Brazil 1930–1950 (Ph.D. diss., University of London, 1988).

sexes; and every employee after a month's service is protected by provisions similar to those of the War-time Essential Order system in Britain."[18]

It is not clear whether Vargas, who had been president continuously since 1930 but never directly elected, intended or hoped to offer himself for election in 1945. Certainly he was impressed by Roosevelt's reelection (for the fourth time) in November 1944. The invention of *trabalhismo* and the intensification of state propaganda (especially the *Hora do Brasil* radio program begun in August 1944), aimed at reminding *os trabalhadores brasileiros* of their economic and social gains under the Estado Novo, have been seen as the beginnings of an electoral campaign in favor of Vargas.[19] The monthly meeting of union leaders in Rio de Janeiro on 21 February 1945 chaired by Dr. José Segadas Viana of the National Department of Labor was reported as having "degenerated into a Vargas campaign rally."[20] Posters appeared throughout Brazil proclaiming, "Ontem Getúlio Vargas estava com os trabalhadores. Hoje os trabalhadores estão com Getúlio" ("Yesterday Getúlio Vargas was with the workers. Today the workers are with Getúlio"). There was much speculation about Vargas's intentions by foreign observers at the time. The British embassy in Rio and the Foreign Office in London, for example, always assumed Vargas would run.[21] Roosevelt went so far as to express the hope that Vargas would run – and be elected.[22]

On 28 February 1945 under Constitutional Amendment no. 9, Vargas decreed that elections would be held later in the year on a date to be announced within ninety days. The Departamento de Imprensa e Propaganda (DIP) abolished press censorship. It had in any case collapsed with the publication in the *Correio da Manhã* on 22 February of Carlos Lacerda's famous interview with the novelist and former presidential candidate (in 1937) José Américo de Almeida ("the most comprehensive attack on the Vargas regime for many years," the British embassy reported).[23] The DIP was then itself abolished. Under a new Rio de Janeiro police chief, ex-*tenente* João Alberto Lins de Barros, repression of opposition political activity also ceased. On 18 April an amnesty was proclaimed and all political prisoners (including Luis Carlos Prestes) were released. Under

18 German, Monthly Labour Report no. 1, 17 June 1946, Ministry of Labour, LAB 13/498, Public Record Office, London.

19 See Angela de Castro Gomes, *A Invenção do Trabalhismo* (Rio de Janeiro, 1988), p. 299.

20 Daniels, 16 March 1945, RG 59, 832.00/3–1645.

21 E.g., Gainer, no. 24, 18 January 1945; Allen, Foreign Office Minute, 5 March 1945; McQuillen, Foreign Office Minute, 17 March 1945: FO 371/44806.

22 See U.S. Ambassador Adolf Berle's diary (14 March 1945) in B.B. Berle and T.B. Jacobs, eds., *Navigating the Rapids 1918–71: From the Papers of Adolf A. Berle* (New York, 1973), p. 476.

23 Gainer, no. 74, 23 February 1945, FO 371/44806.

the Lei Eleitoral of 28 May, presidential and congressional elections were scheduled for 2 December, with elections for state governors and state assemblies the following year. The ballot would be secret and supervised by independent tribunals; all men and women over eighteen years old (provided they were literate) would have the right to vote; and the vote would for the first time be obligatory. The electoral law contained one unusual feature: automatic voter registration for lists of employees (including many who were in fact illiterate) in both the public and the private sectors. This was designed to expand significantly the political participation of the urban working class while maintaining the severe restrictions on the participation of the (mostly illiterate) rural population. Finally, the law established regulations to ensure that the parties that would contest elections would be – for the first time since the foundation of the Republic in 1889 – *national* parties.

The three parties that would dominate Brazilian politics during the next twenty years (until their abolition by Brazil's military government in 1965) were all formally constituted between February and May 1945: the Partido Social Democrático (PSD) by the *situacionistas,* the *homens do poder,* and especially the state *interventores;* the União Democrática Nacional (UDN) by a broad coalition (Right, Center, and non-Communist Left) of Vargas's opponents; and the Partido Trabalhista Brasileiro (PTB) by Ministry of Labor officials and union bosses.[24] The PSD made Vargas its president but, under military pressure, chose not Vargas but Eurico Dutra, the minister of war, as its presidential candidate. There was, among other factors behind this move, an important tactical consideration: if Vargas became a candidate and resigned the presidency (as he would eventually be obliged to do), the regime might lose control of the transition from dictatorship to democracy. The UDN confirmed as its candidate Eduardo Gomes, ex-*tenente* and air force brigadier who had been in effect leader of the opposition to Vargas since the middle of 1944. The PTB, at this early stage much the weakest of the three new parties, also made Vargas its president but did not nominate a presidential candidate.

Thus in May 1945 the electoral contest in Brazil was essentially between

---

24 On the PSD, see Lucia Hippolito, *De Raposas e Reformistas: O PSD e a Experiência Democrática Brasileira (1945–64)* (Rio de Janeiro, 1985); on the UDN, see Maria Victoria de Mesquita Benevides, *A UDN e o Udenismo: Ambigüidades do Liberalismo Brasileiro (1945–1965)* (Rio de Janeiro, 1981); on the PTB, see Castro Gomes, *Invenção do Trabalhismo,* pp. 288–303, and Lucilia de Almeida Neves Delgado, *PTB: Do Getulismo ao Reformismo 1945–1964* (São Paulo, 1989), which came to my attention after this chapter was written. See also J.A. Pinto do Carmo, *Diretrizes Partidárias* (Rio de Janeiro, 1948); Phyllis Peterson, Brazilian political parties: Formation, organization and leadership, 1945–1959 (Ph.D. diss., University of Michigan, 1962); Helio Silva, *1945,* pp. 162–73; and Maria do Carmo Campello de Souza, *Estado e Partidos Políticos no Brasil (1930 à 1964)* (São Paulo, 1976).

a party for and a party against the Estado Novo and what it represented, but both parties were of the dominant class (supported by different sectors of the middle class). Their candidates for the presidency were both drawn from the high ranks of the military and neither had much popular appeal or support. *Democratização pelo alto* had come down to a choice between *democracia do general* and *democracia do brigadeiro*. At this point, however, the Brazilian people, or to be more precise the Brazilian working class, entered the political scene. The six months from May to October 1945 witnessed an unprecedented level of political mobilization in Brazil's major cities orchestrated in part by the PCB, but more particularly, as we shall see, by the so-called *queremistas* (from the slogan "Queremos Getúlio"). Brazilian politics were dominated not by the two presidential candidates, Dutra and Gomes, but by two politicians who were able to appeal more effectively to the working class – Prestes and, above all, Vargas.

During the first half of 1945, partly as a consequence of the political *abertura* initiated by Vargas but more as a reaction to wartime hardships and deprivations, there were for the first time in more than a decade significant manifestations of popular discontent in cities throughout Brazil. Popular protest was directed not so much against the dictatorship (much less the dictator) as against low wages, long hours, bad working conditions, poor housing, inadequate transportation, and, above all, the rising cost of living. Early in 1945 the American Chamber of Commerce in Rio de Janeiro calculated that prices in general had more than doubled during the war (up 250% between June 1939 and December 1944) and the price of food had tripled (up 317% between June 1939 and December 1944). At the same time, wages had increased by only 50% since 1941 and there had been no general wage adjustment since November 1943.[25]

In late March and in May in particular, the Brazilian labor movement, which (as we have seen) had doubled in size during the war, emerged from a decade of relative passivity to display a militancy unequalled since the end of the First World War. Several hundred strikes occurred – in the transport sector (especially railways), in public utilities (e.g., gas and electricity), in the banking sector, in the docks, and in industry (e.g., the Matarazzo cotton textile mills and the Goodyear tire plants). Rio de Janeiro, São Paulo, Santos, Campinas, Juiz de Fora, Belo Horizonte, and Porto Alegre were all affected. In São Paulo 300–400 strikes involving 150,000 workers were estimated to have taken place in less than one week in May. The climate there was described as that of a general strike. There developed, according to the U.S. consul general, "what amounts to little

---

25 Rowell, Monthly Labor Report no. 8 (February–March 1945), 9 May 1945, RG 59, 850.4.

short of panic among the propertied classes."[26] Many of these strikes were successful, at least to the extent of securing wage increases of around 40 percent.

Emerging from a decade of repression and isolation and permitted to organize openly beginning in mid-April, the Communists were quick to seize the opportunities offered, even though they had no previous experience in mass organization. They soon had *sedes* in every city in every state. They claimed a membership of over 50,000. They extended their influence over neighborhood Comités Democráticos Populares (or Progresistas), which sprang up all over Brazil. Above all, they penetrated the official corporate union structure, although how far to take control of it, how far to reform it, and how far to replace it with an independent parallel structure remains a matter of some dispute. The Communists were always ambivalent about "spontaneous" working-class action, especially strikes, committed as they still were to class collaboration and national unity, and concerned with ensuring an orderly transition to democracy that would guarantee the legal status and survival of the party.

On 30 April, 300 Communist labor leaders from thirteen states came together to form a central inter-union front, the Movimento Unificador dos Trabalhadores (MUT). The declared objectives of the MUT were: (1) reform and revitalization of the union structure; (2) union autonomy (and in particular less control of union finances and elections by the Ministry of Labor); (3) free collective bargaining (i.e., a reduction in the powers of the labor courts); (4) the right to strike over wages and conditions; (5) the improvement of the social security system; (6) the extension of labor and social security legislation to the countryside; (7) mass unionization; (8) the creation of "horizontal" union organizations (city, state, and, above all, national); and (9) affiliation to international labor organizations.[27] The MUT grew rapidly in Rio de Janeiro, São Paulo, and Minas Gerais in May and June, absorbing a number of other recently formed, independent labor organizations like the Liga dos Trabalhadores Democráticos.[28] Although never officially recognized by the Ministry of Labor, the MUT was allowed to function and grow. It was even given permission to send two delegates (claiming to represent 150,000 workers) to the second meeting in Paris in October of the World Federation of Trade Unions (WFTU) to which the CTAL was affiliated. From June on, however, the wider political struggle in Brazil tended to overshadow the struggle for control of the unions. At the same time, workers were invited by the

---

26 Cross, 3 July 1945, RG 59, 832.00/7–345.
27 On the foundation of the MUT, see Rowell, no. 358, Monthly Labor Report no. 9 (April 1945), 8 June 1945, RG 84/850.4; and German, Monthly Labour Report no. 1, 17 June 1946, LAB 13/498.
28 Dulles, *Brazilian Communism*, p. 213.

MUT to abjure "irresponsible" strikes and demonstrations and to tighten their belts (*apertar o cinto*) in the interest of ensuring a peaceful transition to democracy and a legal future for the PCB.

The secretary general of the PCB, Luis Carlos Prestes, was a former leader of the Prestes Column (1924–7), for almost a decade (1936–45) the most prominent political prisoner in Latin America, and the subject of a best selling biography, *O Cavalheiro da Esperança*, by the novelist (and PCB member) Jorge Amado. In the words of U.S. Ambassador Adolf Berle, Prestes was "a ready made hero."[29] He drew much larger crowds than either of the two presidential candidates at two *comícios* (political meetings) that took the form of popular celebrations. Fifty to seventy thousand gathered on 23 May at the Estádio de São Januário (the home of the Vasco da Gama football club) in Rio de Janeiro where a sea of Red flags was as much evidence of the postwar prestige of the Soviet Union, with which Brazil had recently established diplomatic relations, as support for the Communist Party. Over one hundred thousand gathered on 15 July at the Pacaembú Stadium in São Paulo. This second meeting was attended by the Chilean poet (and leading member of the Partido Comunista de Chile) Pablo Neruda, who read a poem he had written in honor of Prestes. Neruda has provided a vivid description of the occasion:

I was stunned when I saw the crowd packed into Pacaembú Stadium, in São Paulo. I'm told there were more than 130,000 people. Their heads looked very tiny in the vast circle of the stadium. Small of stature, Prestes, who was at my side, seemed to me a Lazarus who had just walked out of the grave, neat and dressed up for the occasion. He was lean and so white that his skin looked transparent, with that strange whiteness prisoners have. His intense look, the huge violet circles under his eyes, his extremely delicate features, his grave dignity, were all a reminder of the long sacrifice his life had been. Yet he spoke as calmly as a general after a victory.[30]

The UDN had made overtures to Prestes on his release from prison, hoping to persuade him to join the anti-Vargas democratic front now that the war was virtually over. At his first press conference (26 April) Prestes, however, had made it clear that he had confidence in neither Dutra and the PSD ("fascist") nor Gomes and the UDN ("reactionary"). Thus, in contrast to Argentina, where the Communist Party joined the Unión Democrática against Perón, the PCB refused to join the UDN. Most individual Communists now left the UDN, as did some elements on the non-Communist Left. For example, Paulo Emilio Sales Gomes of the Frente de Resistência left in July to form the independent União Democrática Socialista (UDS), whose ideal was "democracy without

29 Berle, no. 1153, 26 April 1945, RG 59, 832.00/4–2645.
30 Pablo Neruda, *Memoirs* (London, 1977), pp. 313–4

classes."[31] In August, however, the UDS merged with the Esquerda
Democrática (ED), which became the left wing of the UDN until it broke
away to form the Partido Socialista Brasileiro (PSB) in 1947.

Prestes looked toward a broad coalition of class forces – the proletariat,
the petite bourgeoisie, and progressive sections of the bourgeoisie – for
support in the construction of what he called *democracia genuina*. Eventually
it became the Communist position that this could best be achieved not
through the presidential and congressional elections planned for December, but through the election of an Assembleia Geral do Povo or Constituinte (Constituent Assembly) that would elaborate a democratic
constitution for Brazil. The implication, of course, was that Vargas meanwhile would continue in the presidency.

For his part, Vargas had soon lost what little confidence he had in
Dutra's capacity to win an election in which, for the first time in Brazilian
politics, the working-class vote would be decisive. He publicly endorsed
Dutra only once: at a political meeting in the Estádio de São Januário on
1 May attended by only four thousand people. At the same time, Vargas
was concerned about the rapid advance of the PCB, and more especially
of the MUT inside the labor movement. He saw the PTB (a Brazilian
version of the British Labour Party whose election victory in July was to
make an enormous impression on Vargas) as the only effective *anteparo*
(barrier) to communism and he urged Brazilian workers to join it.[32] Union
affiliation to a political party remained illegal, but the PTB soon claimed
250,000 individual members. Of the three new political parties only the
PTB had failed to nominate a candidate for the presidency. Vargas encouraged public debate of the idea of a third candidate, an alternative to
Dutra and Gomes and a "civilian candidate of the people." As João Batista
Luzardo, who had reason to know, assured Dutra's biographer thirty years
later: "Vargas só tinha uma *tertius:* ele mesmo" ("Vargas had only one
third candidate in mind: himself").[33]

As early as 1 May there had been indications that a new political
movement might be formed around the slogan "Queremos Getúlio."
Comités-pro-Getúlio sprang up in a number of cities throughout Brazil
during May, June, and July. The *queremistas* formally established *sedes* in
Rio de Janeiro on 31 July and in São Paulo on 2 August. Soon they were

31 Dulles, *São Paulo Law School*, p. 184.

32 The most recent expression of the view that the PTB was created to act as a barrier between the
   Brazilian people, and especially the organized working class, and the Communist Party can be
   found in an interview with Alzira Vargas de Amaral Peixoto (Vargas's daughter) in *Jornal do
   Brasil*, 20 April 1988.

33 Quotation from an interview (August 1978) in Osvaldo Trigueiro do Vale, *O General Dutra e a
   Redemocratização de 1945* (Rio de Janeiro, 1978), p. 135.

in every state.[34] Behind the movement were government ministers like Alexandre Marcondes Filho (Labor) and Agamenon Magalhães (Justice), leading officials of the Ministry of Labor, the National Department of Labor, and the social welfare institutions, government-appointed union leaders (the *pelegos*), national and state leaders of the PTB, and some "progressive" or maverick businessmen, notably the industrialist, banker, and commodity speculator Hugo Borghi (sometimes referred to as *o lorde trabalhista*) – the "fascist gang," the British embassy liked to call them. The key questions to which there are no satisfactory answers for lack of evidence concern Vargas's own involvement in the movement and its objectives. It is scarcely credible, as is sometimes claimed, that he knew nothing of it. Did he actually promote or merely tolerate it? Certainly he did nothing to stop it. Was Vargas's nomination – and electoral victory – the aim? Or were they (was he) preparing the ground for a populist coup? Both were impossible without the approval of the military. There was some indication that the *queremistas* might go along with the Communist idea of a Constituent Assembly. That way, Vargas would at least remain in power beyond December 1945. And a Constituent Assembly might elect him president for another term as had happened in 1934. There are no definitive answers to these questions.

After smoldering for months, *queremismo* burst into flames in mid-August. Comícios were held in São Paulo on 15 August, in Recife on 17 August, and in Rio de Janeiro and Belo Horizonte on 20 August. Banners appeared carrying the slogan "Getúlio diz não ser candidato, mas o povo o quer" ("Getúlio says he is not a candidate, but the people want him"). During the last week of August the Rio daily *O Globo* listed thousands of telegrams (each with thousands of signatures) from factories, unions, and neighborhood associations in favor of the presidential candidacy of Getúlio Vargas.[35] The British ambassador, Sir Donald St. Clair Gainer, who at the beginning of August had described the *queremistas* as "something of a mystery but . . . not at present . . . a political force of importance," reported three weeks later that they had become "a nuisance . . . of some magnitude."[36]

Mass demonstrations on a scale never before seen in Brazil were organized in Rio de Janeiro during the last ten days of August. The thirtieth of August was to be Vargas's *dia do fico* (*fico* meaning "I stay" – a reference

34 On the emergence of *queremismo* there is a wealth of material in Rowell's labor reports, in U.S. embassy reports, and in British embassy reports. The *Diario Oficial* published on 10 September the statutes of the União Queremista do Brasil dated 30 August 1945. The full history of the *queremista* movement remains to be written. But see Elza Borghi de Almeida Cabral, O Queremismo na redemocratização de 1945 (Master's thesis, Universidade Federal Fluminense, 1984).

35 *O Globo*, August 1945, Biblioteca Nacional, Rio de Janeiro.

36 Gainer, no. 156, 1 August 1945; no. 169, 21 August 1945. FO 371/44808.

to a famous declaration by the Portuguese Prince Regent Dom Pedro in
1822 that he would remain in Brazil and lead the movement for Brazilian
independence). Instead, Vargas told a huge crowd that had marched on
the Catete Palace that he was not a candidate for the presidency and that
he intended to leave office after the elections. Candidates had to resign
public office at least three months before the election. The second of
September passed without Vargas's resignation. The immediate crisis was
over, but although Vargas continued to insist that he was not a candidate
(again, for example, on 7 September), there remained a good deal of
ambiguity in his attitude toward the *queremistas,* who now adopted the
slogan "Constituinte com Vargas" and planned a further mobilization of
popular forces for 3 October, the fifteenth anniversary of the Revolution
of 1930 that had brought Vargas to power.

The PCB, at first disturbed by the rise of *queremismo* and fundamentally
antagonistic toward it, decided on a policy of *aproximação,* or *frente comun,*
with what it regarded as *a força menos reacionaria* (less reactionary than
either the UDN or the PSD). For this further "betrayal" of the working
class, following the MUT's curbing of labor militancy earlier in the year,
the PCB has been bitterly criticized by non- and anti-Communists over
the years.[37] Prestes's decision was based on the following: the relative
weakness of the PCB, only recently semilegalized; the relative weakness
of the labor movement dominated for so long by the "fascist" state; the
strength – and profound anti-Communism – of the forces of reaction (represented by both the UDN and the PSD); and, most important, the
evident popularity of Vargas – and his economic and social project – with
broad sectors of the working class. The Communists redoubled their efforts
in September to secure a Constituinte, a "Constituinte com Getúlio."

Political mobilization by the Communists and *queremistas* in August
and September – for a Constituent Assembly, for Vargas as presidential
candidate, for a "Constituinte com Getúlio" – produced an inevitable
conservative backlash. Elite and middle class supporters of the UDN,
frightened by the prospect of a *república populista,* a *república sindicalista,*
or even a *república comunista,* moved significantly to the Right. Despite
the attachment of the Esquerda Democrática in August, the UDN looked
less than ever like, in the words of Virgílio de Melo Franco, "um partido
de centro inclinado para a esquerda" ("a Center party inclined to the
Left"). It had never really believed that the regime would permit free

---

37  The question of a Communist *traição* of the working class in 1945–6 was at the heart of an early
and famous exchange of views on the nature of the postwar conjuncture in Brazil: Francisco
Weffort, "Origens do Sindicalismo Populista no Brasil (A Conjunctura do Após-Guerra)," *Estudos
CEBRAP* 4(April–June 1973):65–105, and Carlos Estevam Martins and Maria Hermínia Tavares
de Almeida, "Modus in Rebus: Partidos e Classes na Queda do Estado Novo" (unpublished paper,
Centro Brasileiro de Análise e Planejamento [CEBRAP], [1973]).

elections in December and had long demanded the transfer of power from Vargas to the judiciary before the elections. Now it was openly encouraging military intervention to guarantee democracy, which is always a risky undertaking whose consequences are uncertain. At the same time, within the PSD representatives of the rural oligarchy, the bureaucracy, and especially the industrialists, previously some of Vargas's strongest supporters, began to exhibit their concern at the turn of events. Important sections of the press demanded Vargas's resignation or a military coup to overthrow him.[38] Finally, the Catholic church – and especially Catholic archbishops of Rio de Janeiro and São Paulo, openly and fiercely anti-Communist – added its voice to the growing demand from the Right that elections should take place in December as originally scheduled. There was thus widespread upper- and middle-class *desconfiança em Vargas*. The slogan "Lembrai-vos de 37" ("Remember 1937") made its appearance (a reference to the cancellation by Vargas and the military in November 1937 of the presidential elections due to take place in January 1938).

There were, however, two major differences between 1945 and 1937, apart from the fact that in 1937 Vargas had justified his *manobras continuistas* on the need to avert a Communist-led mass insurrection (the evidence for which was entirely fabricated by the regime), and in 1945 he appeared to be deliberately mobilizing popular support and, yet more dangerous, accepting the support of the Communists. In the first place, the military high command (including Dutra and Góes Monteiro, the architects of the 1937 coup, and General Osvaldo Cordeiro de Farias and other leaders of the Força Expedicionária Brasileira (FEB), which returned to Brazil from Europe in July and August) now saw itself as not only the defender of national security (especially against the threat of communism) but also the guarantor of democracy. Góes, who replaced Dutra when he resigned as minister of war in August as he was legally obliged to do, reiterated (for example, on 3 September and again on 7 September) the military's commitment to the December elections.[39] Secondly, the United States was now committed to democratic transitions in Latin America and risked open intervention in Brazilian domestic politics for the first time in an attempt to guarantee the December elections.[40]

38 On the UDN demand for military intervention, see Lourival Coutinho, *O General Góes Depõe* (Rio de Janeiro, 1955), pp. 404–9; on the press, see Alfred Stepan, *The Military in Politics: Changing Patterns in Brazil* (Princeton, 1971), pp. 102–3.

39 Stanley E. Hilton, "The Overthrow of Getúlio Vargas in 1945: Diplomatic Intervention, Defense of Democracy, or Political Retribution?" *HAHR* 67(1987):13. By far the best account of the Brazilian military and its role in politics during the 1930s and the Second World War is José Murilo de Carvalho, "Armed Forces and Politics in Brazil 1930–45," *HAHR* 62(1982):193–223.

40 There is an extensive literature on the controversial actions of the U.S. ambassador in Brazil,

Adolf Berle, a progressive New Dealer who had served as assistant secretary of state from 1938 to 1944, had been persuaded by Roosevelt in January 1945 to go to Rio de Janeiro as U.S. ambassador until at least the end of the war. For six months he had quietly encouraged the dismantling of the Estado Novo. Unlike Spruille Braden after his arrival in Buenos Aires in May, Berle did not feel that it was necessary to adopt a more active role in favor of democratization. Presidential and congressional elections had been promised as early as February, and a date had been set in May. The two candidates for the presidency were too "politically conservative and economically reactionary" for Berle's taste but they were running in a democratic election and were both satisfyingly pro-United States. It remained Berle's view that if Vargas, "far and away the most popular individual in the country," had offered himself for election, he could have been expected to win. But Vargas had not run. Berle did not share Gainer's (and the UDN's) skepticism of Vargas's intention to preside over free elections and then relinquish power. Even with the rise of the *queremistas* in August and pressure early in September from the UDN to adopt a tougher stance ("as Braden has attacked Perón") Berle chose to maintain his faith in Vargas. The Brazilian dictator, he insisted, and both President Truman and the State Department agreed, was not to be compared with Perón, not least because he had always been "our friend." Truman also agreed with Berle that U.S. interference at this stage was not only unnecessary but could prove disastrous. "As long as Brazil travels towards democracy with a definite date on 2 December," Berle wrote on 4 September, "we are happy. We will be happier still when the job is complete."[41]

In the middle of September, however, Berle came to believe that there was a real danger that Vargas might be tempted to postpone or cancel the elections and retain power on a wave of popular mobilization. This

---

Adolf Berle, in late September 1945. Berle's own published diaries and correspondence are an indispensable source: B.B. Berle and Jacobs, eds., *Navigating the Rapids*. See also McCann, *Brazilian-American Alliance;* Bryce Wood, *The Dismantling of the Good Neighbor Policy* (Austin, TX, 1985), pp. 122–31; C. Neale Ronning, "Adolf Berle in Brazil, 1945–6" in *Ambassadors in Foreign Policy: The Influence of Individuals on U.S. Latin American Policy,* ed. Neale Ronning and Albert P. Vannucci (New York, 1987), pp. 74–94; Jordan A. Schwarz, *Liberal: Adolf A. Berle and the Vision of an American Era* (New York, 1987), pp. 254–78; and Stanley E. Hilton, *O Ditador e o Embaixador: Getúlio Vargas, Adolf Berle Jr. e a Queda do Estado Novo* (Rio de Janeiro, 1987). Some of the correspondence between Berle and the State Department was reprinted in Paulo Sérgio Pinheiro, "Os EUA agem em 45," *Isto E,* 27 September 1978, pp. 34–41.

41 A. Berle, 3 September 1945, RG 59, 832.00/9–345; A. Berle to Truman, Private, 4 September 1945, Biblioteca Harry Truman (henceforth BHT) 45.09.04 (copies of Truman correspondence relevant to Brazil held in the Centro de Pesquisa e Documentação de História Contemporânea [CPDOC], Fundação Getúlio Vargas, Rio de Janeiro); Truman to A. Berle, 13 September 1945, BHT 45.09.13.

could lead to one of two equally unpalatable developments. Either Vargas would establish a populist-nationalist dictatorship, possibly with Communist support (which raised for the first time in some minds in the State Department the danger of Soviet penetration of Brazil).[42] Or there would be a preemptive military coup, ironically by U.S.-trained troops using U.S. equipment, and the establishment of a military dictatorship, possibly followed by an approximation with Argentina and the strengthening of the Peronist bloc against the United States. Without firm instructions, but with the encouragement (albeit lukewarm) of the State Department to make contingency plans for action short of intervention to discourage any moves by Vargas to postpone the elections as planned,[43] and stiffened by Ambassador Braden, who having (or so he thought) brought democracy to Argentina passed through Rio de Janeiro on 23 September on his way to Washington to take up the post of assistant secretary of state, Berle decided on a public expression of opinion in favor of democracy in Brazil. "After much sweating," Berle came to the conclusion that "the only way to have democracy was to have it." In a speech to the government-controlled journalists' union, which was shown in advance to Vargas (although it is not clear whether he understood the import of what was put before him), at a "small and dull luncheon" at the Hotel Quitandinha in Petrópolis on 29 September, Berle declared that any disruption of the existing election timetable and any "continuance of the dictatorship" in Brazil would be regarded by the United States as "tragic."[44] The speech was soon being referred to by the opposition as "the atomic bomb that ended Queremismo." This was, of course, an exaggeration and as things turned out a little premature. But Berle's speech was an undoubtedly important, perhaps decisive, factor in defusing the second political crisis caused by the rise of *queremismo.*

On 3 October Vargas again declared that he was not a presidential candidate. However, he emphasized his respect for the will of people, his support for a "genuinely democratic process" (in which the election of a Constituent Assembly might perhaps be the best way forward), and the need to defeat "powerful reactionary forces" threatening to undermine the transition to democracy. "His speeches," reported Sir Donald Gainer, had become "masterpieces of obscurantism." And on another occasion Gainer wrote, "I see nothing but trouble ahead for Brazil for a long time to

---

42 State Department, Division of Brazilian Affairs, office memorandum, 18 September 1945, RG 59, 832.00/9–1845.

43 A. Berle, 18 September 1945; State Department, 21 September 1945: RG 59, 832.00.

44 A. Berle, 29 September 1945, 1 October 1945, RG 59, 832.00; A. Berle to Truman, Secret, 1 October 1945, BHT 45.10.01; A. Berle diary (1 October, 6 October), B.B. Berle and Jacobs, eds., *Navigating the Rapids,* pp. 549–53. Berle's intervention was subsequently approved by both the president and the secretary of state.

come. . . . In moments of despair I sometimes wonder if democracy is really a suitable system of government for this illiterate, vain, venal but charming people."[45] In an important speech in Santa Cruz on 14 October Vargas again urged Brazilian workers to affiliate with the PTB (which had still not nominated a presidential candidate) and declared his continued interest in the idea of a Constituent Assembly. By this time the Communists were having second thoughts and were promoting the idea of a "Constituinte sem Getúlio."

Meanwhile, for the third time, the *queremistas* and the Communists were mobilizing their support for mass meetings, to be held on 26 and 27 October. In a significant parallel development in Buenos Aires, on 17 October mobilization of the working class was successful in restoring Perón to power following his arrest by the military. The Brazilian military, to some extent prompted by the UDN, had by now lost all confidence in Vargas. It was generally believed that the December elections would be called off and that a decree for the election of a Constituent Assembly was being drafted. Berle, too, was thoroughly alarmed. When he returned to Rio from a vacation in the south of Brazil on 22 October, however, plans for a *golpe* were already well advanced. Meetings of senior military officers took place almost daily in late October. "The stage seems set for fireworks," Gainer reported.[46]

In the event, the authorities cancelled the *comícios* set for 26 and 27 October. Nevertheless on 29 October after he had, in an extraordinary move, appointed his brother Benjamín ("the worst thug in Brazil" in the view of the British embassy) as Rio police chief, Vargas was presented with an ultimatum by the military (delivered personally by Cordeiro de Farias) and forced to relinquish power. It was the third intervention by the military in Brazilian politics in fifteen years.[47] There was no resistance from Vargas himself, from pro-Vargas factions in the military, from the *queremistas,* from the Communists, or from the people. Hardly a shot was fired. Berle commented: "As a revolution, if it is that, this was the quietest thing I have yet seen."[48]

The October *golpe* did not lead to military dictatorship as many, in-

---

45  Gainer, 23 October 1945, 9 October 1945, FO 371/44808.

46  Gainer, 23 October 1945.

47  On the 29 October 1945 *golpe*, see Coutinho, *O General Góes Depõe*, pp. 441–69; Stepan, *Military in Politics*, pp. 116–17; and Hilton, "The Overthrow of Getúlio Vargas," *HAHR* 67(1987):1–37. Hilton challenges what he calls the "liberal-military thesis" that Vargas was maneuvering to perpetuate his personal rule and therefore had to be removed forcibly to ensure free elections. He argues forcefully (as always), but in the end unconvincingly, that Vargas's public and private declarations that he had no intention of remaining in power deserve to be taken entirely at face value (not least because he knew the military would not allow him to remain in power) and that therefore the 29 October *golpe* was unnecessary.

48  A. Berle diary (30 October 1945), in B.B. Berle and Jacobs, eds., *Navigating the Rapids*, p. 556.

cluding Berle, had feared. There were a number of arrests (Prestes, union leaders affiliated to the MUT, Benjamin Vargas, and some PTB/*queremista* leaders like former Ministers Magalhães and Marcondes Filho). The post-coup repression was, however, limited and short lived; most detainees were soon released, not least thanks to Berle's intervention.[49] In accordance with the UDN slogan "All power to the judiciary," the interim presidency went to José Linhares, the president of the Federal Supreme Court. His cabinet was drawn mostly from the UDN. Most state *interventores* and many *prefeitos* were replaced, weakening PSD control of the forthcoming presidential and congressional elections that were confirmed for 2 December. It was determined that the newly elected Congress would meet as a Constituent Assembly, ending in Berle's view a "famous (and false) issue." Antitrust legislation (*a lei malaia*), introduced by Vargas in June but never implemented and directed more at domestic than foreign capital, was revoked (prompting the British ambassador to comment, "Excellent. Even the most futile revolutions are occasionally useful").[50] A measure of pluralism was reintroduced into the union structure. The PCB, which had behaved prudently so as not to provide the military with an excuse for its proscription and which had given its full support to the interim government, was formally registered and permitted to participate in the elections. (It would not, however, under any circumstances be allowed to win, as the commander of the first military region made clear to the British military attaché.)[51] The PCB chose as its presidential candidate not Luis Carlos Prestes (that would have been too provocative) but Yedo Fiuza, a non-Communist engineer, former mayor of Petrópolis, and director of the National Department of Highways.

The elections of 2 December 1945 constituted the first relatively free, democratic elections (albeit without universal suffrage) in Brazilian history. The electorate was 7.5 million, four times that of 1930 (1.9 million). It represented approximately 35 percent of the adult population compared with only 10 percent in 1930. Half the electorate consisted of individual voter registrations, half ex-officio group registrations. Almost two-thirds of the electorate was concentrated in four areas (all in the Center-South): São Paulo (1.7 million); Minas Gerais (1.2 million); the Federal District and the state of Rio de Janeiro (1 million); Rio Grande do Sul (900,000). In all, 6.2 million Brazilians voted. Adolf Berle expressed himself "delighted with the democratic spectacle."[52]

Against all forecasts and expectations, the UDN, the broad coalition

---

49 "I am taking some steps to try and see that the political liberty and rights of the Communist Party are respected." Berle diary (30 October 1945), ibid.
50 Gainer, 14 November 1945, FO 371/44809.
51 Top secret memorandum, 28 November 1945 in Gainer, 15 December 1945, FO 371/44810.
52 Berle quoted in Schwarz, *Liberal*, p. 272.

of Right, Center, and non-Communist Left opponents of the Estado Novo, was defeated in the elections. Dutra won the presidency with an overwhelming 55% of the vote (3.25 million votes). A decisive factor was the eleventh hour (27 November) appeal by Vargas to the Brazilian workers on behalf of the PTB to vote for Dutra against Gomes ("O general Dutra merece vossos votos" ["General Dutra deserves your vote"]). Gomes came in second with 35% (2.04 million votes). Fiuza was third with 10% (570,000 votes – a third of them in São Paulo). The congressional elections were won by the PSD (42% of the vote: 151 federal deputies, 26 senators), with the UDN second (26% of the vote: 77 deputies, 12 senators), and the PTB, which only ran in fourteen states, third (10% of the vote: 22 deputies, 2 senators, including Marcondes Filho in São Paulo). The PCB came in fourth with 9% of the vote, electing 14 federal deputies (4 in São Paulo) and one senator (Luis Carlos Prestes for the Federal District). The PCB had some striking local successes. It won in Santos, for example, with 28% of the vote, and tied with the UDN for second place in the Federal District. It also performed well in the industrial areas of São Paulo and in Campinas, Sorocaba, Recife, Olinda, and Natal. The two politicians who accumulated the most votes were Vargas, who gathered 1.3 million votes and was elected senator for São Paulo and Rio Grande do Sul (he chose the latter) and federal deputy for the Federal District and six other states, and Prestes, who was not only elected senator but federal deputy in the Federal District, Pernambuco, and Rio Grande do Sul as well as *suplente* (alternate deputy) in three other states. João Neves da Fontoura, a prominent *gaucho* politician and future foreign minister, had no doubt that the chief credit for Dutra's victory – "essa verdadeira bomba atómica" (the most popular metaphor of 1945) – as well as the victory of the PSD and the PTB over the UDN – and the Communists – belonged to Vargas, *o grande eleitor*.[53]

Following the elections of 2 December 1945 there was a resurgence of labor unrest throughout Brazil that reached a peak during February and March and again in May 1946. Since May and June 1945 when an earlier upsurge of labor militancy had been brought to an end, or rather had been suspended, the wages of most Brazilian workers, which remained in real terms below their prewar level, had again failed to keep up with inflation. However, the establishment of a democratic political system and, more particularly, the crucial role the workers themselves had played in the election of Dutra as president raised their expectations. During the first six months of 1946 there were more than 70 major strikes involving

53 João Neves da Fontoura to Vargas, 7 December 1945, Vargas papers, Centro de Pesquisa e Documentação de História Contemporânea (CPDOC), Rio de Janeiro.

more than 100,000 workers. The most notable were: a national bank strike (24 January–12 February); a strike in the coal mines of Butiá and Arroio dos Ratos in Rio Grande do Sul, which lasted for thirty-four days (1 February–7 March), longer than any previous strike in Brazilian history; strikes with almost 100 percent support in the São Paulo metallurgical and textile factories in mid-February; a strike on the Leopoldina railway in May; various stoppages in the "Light" (the Canadian owned Light, Power, and Telephone Company) in May, which threatened to paralyze transport, light, and power services in Rio and São Paulo; and persistent strikes by both dockers and stevedores in the ports of Rio de Janeiro and, more particularly, Santos (now known as Prestesgrad).[54]

Big business had no doubt that the Communists were behind this renewed labor militancy. A telegram sent by Francisco Pignatari, president of Laminação Nacional de Metais S.A., to President Dutra on 16 March 1946 is instructive:

We await . . . the most energetic steps [against] strikes which menace the national interests, strikes which have as an objective only the triumph of exotic doctrines and criminal ideologies always condemned by the population of Christian sentiments. Your Excellency will know . . . how to repress the action of the agitators which, at the service of Communist totalitarianism, attempts to subvert order and disorganize labor.[55]

In fact the role of the PCB remains unclear. It seems to have begun by opposing many of the strikes as "adventurist"; then they were tolerated; finally, after some hesitation, it was decided that the MUT could not afford not to lead them. At the same time the MUT pursued its policy of taking control of the unions away from the *pelegos* and the PTB. Local groups of union leaders, Communist or sympathetic to the PCB, were organized into "permanent commissions" in the main industrial centers (over forty of them in the state of São Paulo alone). The two main bodies were the União Sindical dos Trabalhadores do Distrito Federal (USTDF) and the União Sindical dos Trabalhadores de São Paulo (USTSP).

54 The most detailed description and analysis of the labor unrest during the period December 1945 to May 1946 can be found in Rowell's Monthly Labor Reports: no. 15 (December 1945), 23 January 1946; no. 16 (January 1946), 28 February 1946; no. 17 (February–March 1946), 30 April 1946; no. 18 (April 1946), 31 May 1946, and no. 19 (May 1946), 10 July 1946: RG 84/850.4/55/152/280/341/445 – together with numerous special reports on particular strikes like, for example, the Rio Grande do Sul coal strike (RG 84/850.4/204, 21 March 1946). But also see Arnaldo Spindel, *O Partido Comunista na Gênese do Populismo: Análise da Conjuntura de Redemocratização no Após-Guerra* (São Paulo, 1980), anexos, pp. 95–107; Ricardo Maranhão, *Sindicatos e Democratização (Brasil 1945–50)* (São Paulo, 1979), pp. 43–4; and Silvio Frank Alem, Os Trabalhadores e a "redemocratização:" Estudo sobre o estado, partidos e a participação dos trabalhadores assalariados urbanos na conjuntura da guerra e do pósguerra imediato 1946–48 (Master's thesis, Universidade Estadual de Campinas, 1981).

55 *O Jornal*, 16 March 1946, quoted in Rowell, Monthly Labor Report no. 17.

From the outset General Dutra, who was inaugurated as president on 1 February 1946, declared war on the more independent sectors of organized labor and on the Communists. In this he had the full support of Brazil's employers and especially the industrialists who were anxious to control labor (and eliminate Communist influence over labor) in order more effectively to curb wage demands and create a more favorable climate for foreign (that is, U.S.) direct investment in Brazilian industry.[56] New and severe antistrike legislation (Decree-law 9070, 15 March 1946) was introduced. Strike leaders, especially those linked to the MUT, were arrested by troops and police. It was made clear (for example, by the police chief of the Federal District on 12 March and the minister of labor on 10 April) that the MUT had no legal status and that its activities would no longer be tolerated. Individual unions were purged of their Communist leaders. A counteroffensive against the MUT in May was particularly effective. Brazil was in effect under what the *Estado de São Paulo* called "um estado de sítio branco" ("a white [or 'soft'] state of siege"). An uneasy peace descended on the labor front.

By September, sufficiently confident that it had reestablished its influence and control over the unions, and recognizing the strength of demands for a national confederation of labor, the government decided to permit, somewhat surprisingly nevertheless, Brazil's first National Labor Congress – to be held in Rio de Janeiro under the aegis of the Ministry of Labor. In advance of the congress the "independents" (Communists and fellow travelers who had a strong presence in some 150 of Brazil's 800 or so *sindicatos,* but also independent-minded union leaders who belonged to the *queremista* wing of the PTB) secured one important concession: each *sindicato* would send two delegates, one appointed by the union's directorate, the other chosen or elected by the members in general assembly.

56 The dispute over Brazil's place in the new, postwar international economic order and especially the future growth of Brazilian industry, including the economic role of the state and the role of foreign capital (see, for example, the famous exchange of pamphlets between Eugênio Gudin and Roberto Simonsen at the end of the War: Instituto de Planejamento Econômico e Social (IPEA), *A Controvérsia do Planejamento na Economia Brasileira: Coletânea da Polêmica Simonsen x Gudin* [Rio de Janeiro, 1978] was not yet, however, resolved and would not be finally resolved in favor of import substitution industrialization (ISI) until the 1950s. On the economic policy of the Dutra administration (1946–51), see Pedro S. Malan et al., *Política Econômica Externa e Industrialização no Brasil (1939–52)* (Rio de Janeiro, 1977); Pedro S. Malan, "Relações Econômicas Internacionais do Brasil (1945–1964)" *História Geral da Civilização Brasileira,* vol. 3, pt. 4, ed. Boris Fausto (São Paulo, 1984), pp. 53–106; Sérgio Besserman Vianna, "Política Econômica Externa e Industrialização: 1946–51" in *A Ordem do Progresso: Cem Anos de Política Econômica Republicana, 1889–1989,* ed. Marcelo de Paiva Abreu (Rio de Janeiro, 1989), pp. 105–22 and Fausto Saretta, O elo perdido: Um estudo da política econômica do governo Dutra (1946–1950) (Ph.D. diss., Instituto de Economia, Universidade Estadual de Campinas, 1990), which came to my attention after this chapter was written.

The U.S. labor attaché estimated that in the Federal District, for example, independents did not lose a single contested election.[57]

After the official opening on 11 September presided over by Minister of Labor Octacilio Negrão de Lima, the congress met in the Vasco da Gama Stadium. In defiance of the known government position the overwhelming majority of the 1,500–1,700 delegates, only 200–300 of whom were members of the PCB or fellow travelers, supported the main objectives of the MUT: union autonomy, that is to say, freedom from Ministry of Labor intervention and control; the unrestricted right to strike; the foundation of a General Confederation of Labor; and international affiliation to the CTAL and the WFTU. The fragile unity maintained for ten days was shattered, however, at the third plenary session on 21 September when a dissident ministerial group of 200 or so withdrew, alleging Communist domination of the proceedings. The minister then closed the congress. The remaining delegates, however, voted to conclude the business of the congress and, at a crowded meeting held at the premises of the hotel workers' union, agreed among other resolutions to establish for the first time a Confederação dos Trabalhadores do Brasil (CTB). The representative council of the CTB with the Communist leader Roberto Morena as its general secretary met for the first time in December.[58]

The U.S. labor attaché Edward Rowell, who wrote some outstanding reports on the National Labor Congress, offered in November this considered assessment of what he had witnessed:

It may be regrettable from a democratic point of view that the vanguard role in the Brazil labor movement fell by default to alleged Communist elements. However it can hardly be denied that the Communist elements, which successfully framed the major resolutions, scrupulously avoided outward manifestations of partisan interests. Nor can it be denied that the Congress itself represented the maximum attainable in representative character and democratic action.

The congress was, he emphasized,

representative of the organized workers of Brazil . . . its resolutions accurately reflected the current aspirations of a substantial representative majority.

The outside observer found himself caught in a dilemma, he added a few months later:

57 Rowell, no. 594, 17 September 1946, RG 84/850.4.
58 On the National Labor Conference, see Rowell, no. 778, Monthly Labor Report, no. 22 (September 1946) 16 December 1946; Rowell, no. 594, 17 September 1946 and no. 739, 27 November 1946 (two-part special report): RG 84/850.4.

[It] involves the unquestioned participation and influence of Communist labor leaders on the one hand and a trade union program which is sympathetic to trade union status and activities as recognized by Western Democracies on the other.[59]

The Ministry of Labor refused to accept the validity of any of the resolutions of the National Labor Congress, never recognized the CTB, and withdrew official recognition from any union that affiliated. From the beginning, therefore, the CTB operated outside the law. On 24 October President Dutra hurriedly signed a decree establishing an alternative Confederação Nacional dos Trabalhadores (CNT) based on the official state federations and national confederations, but the decree was never published and the CNT was stillborn. Members of Congress had protested against this exercise of executive power in violation of the Labor Code that prohibited a single national confederation of labor. Instead – as permitted under the Labor Code but never implemented – first a Confederação Nacional dos Trabalhadores Industriais (CNTI) and then a Confederação Nacional dos Trabalhadores no Comércio (CNTC), based on existing and approved official union hierarchies, were established.

During the same week in September 1946 that the Dutra government closed down the National Labor Congress, the Constituent Assembly, which had been in session since February, completed its work.[60] The Constitution that it produced incorporated most of the Labor Code of the Estado Novo with all the restrictions it imposed on the autonomy and, above all, financial independence of unions, free collective bargaining, the right of workers to strike (especially in essential services and basic industries), and the right of unions to form a national confederation of labor and to affiliate with international labor organizations. Although in most other respects the Constitution of 1946 was broadly democratic, suffrage was, as before, restricted to those Brazilians who were literate (less than half the adult population at the time), and the power of the popular and especially the working-class vote was curbed. For example, the experiment with group voter registration was abolished; registration to vote became, once again, the responsibility of the individual. Furthermore, seats in the Chamber of Deputies were distributed in such a way as to leave the more heavily populated, urban and economically developed states of the federation underrepresented. And although state governors were to be elected, no provision was made for the direct election of mayors of either the Federal District or state capitals. Finally, under

59  Rowell, no 739, 27 November 1946; no. 152, Monthly Labor Report; no. 25 (February 1947), 28 April 1947: RG 84/850.4.
60  The most recent study of the 1946 Constituent Assembly is João Almino, *Os Democratas Autoritários: Liberdades Individuais, de Associação Política e Sindical na Constituinte de 1946* (São Paulo, 1980).

Article 114 of the Constitution, the Tribunal Superior Electoral (TSE) could cancel the registration of any political party whose program was deemed to be contrary to democratic principles or whose political orientation and funding could be said to be drawn from outside the country. The writing was on the wall for the PCB, the principal party (virtually the only party) of the Left, after only eighteen months of de facto legality.

Since its strong showing in the December 1945 elections the PCB had maintained its growth in all regions of Brazil. In August 1946 William D. Pawley, Berle's successor as ambassador in Rio de Janeiro, sent to Washington a top secret document that offered the secretary of state "a complete picture" of Communist Party activities in Brazil:

Hardly a town . . . of over 1,000 inhabitants . . . does not have a Communist office openly displaying the hammer and sickle . . . [and] actively engaged in trying to poison the minds of the peasants and workers against the United States principally and the Brazilian government to a lesser degree.[61]

The party by now claimed 180,000 members, making it by far the largest Communist Party in Latin America.

There had been rumors as early as March 1946 that Dutra, always intransigently anti-Communist, was preparing a decree outlawing the PCB. During the following months Communists were systematically purged not only from the leadership of labor unions (as we have seen) but also from federal and state bureaucracies. The military and the police, especially the political police, had party leaders under close surveillance. On 23 May at a Communist meeting in the Largo de Carioca in Rio, police mounted a cavalry charge and fired on the crowd wounding over a hundred people. In July congressional leaders were summoned to the presidential palace to receive a report on the "Communist threat." In August Ambassador Pawley was told by a senior official in the Rio police that the closure of the party by presidential decree was imminent.[62] There were still, however, members of the cabinet (possibly including Minister of War Góes Monteiro) who felt a move against the PCB was inopportune: the Constituent Assembly was still in session; a second round of elections was due to be held in January 1947; domestic opinion was not yet prepared. On the international front, it should be remembered, the Cold War was still in its preliminary stages. At the beginning of January 1947, on the eve of the elections, at a meeting with the Rio chief of police and a member of Dutra's *gabinete militar,* Pawley warned that in his view

61 Pawley, 16 August 1946, Top Secret, RG 59/832.00B/8–1646.
62 Ibid.

precipitate action could force the PCB underground and make martyrs of its leaders.[63]

The supplementary congressional, state gubernatorial, state assembly, and municipal elections held in January 1947 – which represented a further stage in the democratization of Brazil at the end of the Second World War – were won by the PSD (30% of the vote) with the UDN second (21%) and the PTB third (14%). The PCB did not increase its share of the vote, but nor did it lose ground. As in December 1945 the PCB polled around 9% of the vote, though on a lower turnout (only 460,000 votes compared with 570,000 in December 1945). Two more Communists (Pedro Pomar and Diógenes Arruda Câmara in São Paulo) were elected to the Chamber of Deputies. In the contest in São Paulo for an additional Senate seat the industrialist Roberto Simonsen defeated the Communist candidate, Brazil's greatest painter Cândido Portinari, by less than 4,000 votes. The Communists captured a total of 64 seats in fifteen state legislatures. The PCB became the largest single party in the assembly elected for the Federal District (the city of Rio de Janeiro) with 18 out of 50 seats. Eleven Communists, including Brazil's leading Marxist historian Caio Prado Júnior, were elected to the São Paulo state assembly and nine to the state assembly in Pernambuco. The party had a strong presence in a number of municipal councils, including that of Recife. Perhaps most significant of all, Communist support was decisive in the election of Adhemar de Barros as governor of São Paulo, Brazil's most populous and industrialized state. Industrialist, coffee *fazendeiro,* and politician, Barros was the candidate of the Partido Social Progresista (PSP), the party he had created as a vehicle for himself in June 1946. Instead of putting up its own candidate, the PCB, which was particularly strong in the industrial cities and suburbs of São Paulo – it had 60,000 members and had secured 180,000 votes in 1945 – endorsed Adhemar de Barros two weeks before the election. Barros won 35% of the vote, narrowly defeating Hugo Borghi of the Partido Trabalhista Nacional (PTN), a dissident wing of the by now deeply divided PTB, and Mário Tavares of the PSD to become São Paulo's first democratically elected governor.[64]

During the early months of 1947, with the new Constitution (including Article 114) in force, with the elections safely out of the way, and with the international climate of the Cold War reinforcing domestic anticommunism (the Truman Doctrine had been unveiled in March 1947), the Dutra administration brought intense pressure to bear on the Tribunal

---

63 Pawley, 3 January 1947, RG 59/832.00B/1–347.
64 Antônio de Almeida Prado of the UDN came in fourth with only 8.3% of the vote. On the election of Adhemar de Barros in São Paulo, see John D. French, "Workers and the Rise of Adhemarista Populism in São Paulo, Brazil 1945–47," *HAHR* 68(1988):1–43.

Superior Electoral (TSE) to rule against the PCB. Significantly, there were now no words of caution from the U.S. embassy. On 7 May the TSE voted (though narrowly, by 3 votes to 2) to cancel the legal registration of a party that had secured about 10% of the vote in two successive democratic elections. There followed a wave of anti-Communist repression during which the authorities in São Paulo, under instructions from Governor Adhemar de Barros (who himself came under direct pressure from President Dutra), were especially zealous in their efforts to put a stop to the activities of the Communist Party, which was once again proscribed.[65] Hundreds of Communist cells in São Paulo were closed down as were hundreds more in Rio de Janeiro where in August and September the conference was held (actually it took place in the Hotel Quitandinha, Petrópolis) that led to the signing of the Inter-American Treaty for Reciprocal Assistance (the Rio defense pact, sometimes called the first Cold War pact). In October Brazil broke off diplomatic relations, only recently established, with the Soviet Union.

On the day the TSE pronounced the PCB illegal by a majority decision, the Dutra administration promulgated what Clifford German, the British labor attaché, called "a quite unexpected and totally unheralded decree" imposing severe restrictions on the freedom and independence of Brazil's labor unions.[66] For some time, as we have seen, big business had been urging the government to eliminate Communist influence (real and alleged) in the unions once and for all. In September 1946, following the fiasco of the National Labor Congress, Morvan Dias Figueiredo, a *paulista* industrialist, had been appointed minister of labor. Interventions in union affairs by Ministry of Labor officials and by the police had significantly increased. In a private conversation on 1 February 1947, Roberto Simonsen had said to German, "The Communists in the unions are not a real danger, the police can deal with them."[67] In May more than two years of hesitation and uncertainty on the labor front came to an end. Compromise solutions were finally abandoned; the decision was taken to impose 100 percent state control once again. No new legislation was necessary. Existing laws that had been partially relaxed but not abolished in the transition from Estado Novo to democracy had simply to be enforced.

Under Decree 23.046 (7 May 1947) the Confederação dos Trabalhadores do Brasil (CTB), always illegal, was finally closed down. Leaders (*elected* leaders) and officials of unions affiliated with or even sympathetic to the CTB were removed. Within three weeks all Communists, Communist sympathizers, and independents (including some leaders belonging to the

65 Ibid.
66 German, Labour Report no. 23 (May 1947), 18 June 1947, LAB 13/498.
67 Ibid.

PTB) had been purged from 93 unions (27 in São Paulo state, including 10 in Santos, 19 in Rio de Janeiro state, 14 in the Federal District, 12 in Recife).[68] By the end of July, 170 unions representing 300,000 workers had been "intervened."[69] Intervention on this scale was unprecedented – even during the Estado Novo. German was impressed:

> For a West European democratic government to try and sack a single trade union official would be somewhat of a national event, but on this occasion approximately 800–1,000 leaders have been dismissed with the greatest of ease and without stirring up any real interest amongst the general public or press.[70]

At a private meeting in Rio in September Serafino Romualdi, the roving ambassador of the American Federation of Labor (AFL) and scourge of Communist labor leaders in Latin America, told German that he had it on good authority that if free elections had been permitted (as redefined, for example, by the International Labor Organization in 1947), Communists would have won control of 80 percent of Brazil's unions. German agreed.[71] It was at the banquet given to mark Romualdi's visit to Brazil, at which both Rowell and German were also guests of honor, that the minister of labor announced that the CNTI and CNTC would be allowed to send delegates to Lima in January 1948 for the founding of the AFL-sponsored Confederación Interamericana de Trabajadores (CIT) in opposition to the "Communist" CTAL.

In October 1947 Congress approved the dismissal of all public functionaries suspected of belonging to the PCB. There remained, however, the problem of Communists who had been *elected* to public office in December 1945 and January 1947. Beginning in September 1947 the Dutra government pressed Congress to revoke their mandates. Finally, on 7 January 1948 the PSD secured enough support from the UDN and some of the smaller parties to push through the *cassação* of the one Communist senator (Prestes), the sixteen Communist federal deputies, and all Communist state deputies and municipal councillors. The PTB, the PSB, and half of the UDN voted against the measure. Gregório Bezerra, federal deputy for Recife and a participant in the attempted Communist putsch in 1935, was chosen to speak for the *cassados* a week later in the last session of Congress attended by the elected representatives of the PCB.[72] At the Ninth International Conference of American States held in Bogotá

---

68 Ibid.

69 Rowell, no. 306, Monthly Labor Report no. 30 (July 1947), 26 August 1947, RG 84/850.4.

70 German, Labour Report no. 23 (May 1947), 18 June 1947, LAB 13/498.

71 German, Labour Report no. 27, 10 September 1947, LAB 13/498.

72 See Helio Silva, *1945*, pp. 383–457; Paulo Sérgio Pinheiro, "Um Livro Sobre a Cassação do PC: Gregório Bezerra, o Presidente Dutra e o Brasil de 48," *Isto E*, 20 June 1979, pp. 53–4.

in March–April 1948, Brazilian delegates had no difficulty supporting resolutions against international communism.

The democratization of Brazil at the end of the Second World War was real. But since the transition from dictatorship to democracy had been controlled in the end, despite some alarms, by the forces that had sustained the Estado Novo, Brazil's newly constituted democracy was restricted in scope and fundamentally antipopular in nature. The price of democracy was state control of organized labor, restrictions on political participation, and the elimination of the Communist Left. Democracy of this limited kind survived beyond the immediate postwar years, not least because the military, which in many other Latin American countries was instrumental in its overthrow, had in Brazil, through the election of Dutra, retained the political power it had exercised during the Estado Novo, indeed since the Revolution of 1930. Dutra served his full five-year term as president. In October 1950 Vargas was finally – and for the first time – elected president. His suicide on 24 August 1954 under pressure from the military to resign threatened to end Brazil's first experiment with democracy after less than a decade. But the crisis of 1954–5 was resolved and democracy was consolidated under Juscelino Kubitschek (1956–61). It was the economic crisis and political turmoil of the early sixties, which brought a resurgence of labor militancy and a renewal of the Left, including the Communist Left, that finally led in 1964 to the overthrow by the military of postwar Brazilian democracy.

# 2

## Chile

*Andrew Barnard*

Cold War tensions began to have a noticeable impact on the political climate in Chile in late 1945 and early 1946 when Cold War rhetoric and postures helped to precipitate confrontation between the Chilean government and the Partido Comunista de Chile (PCCh) and division in the country's most powerful trade union confederation, the Confederación de Trabajadores de Chile (CTCh). However, it was not until late 1947 that Chile's Cold War struggles reached their climax in a coal miners strike that led, a year later, to the passage of the Ley de Defensa Permanente de la Democracia through Congress, a law that formally excluded Communist party members from participation in Chile's political and trade union life for more than a decade.

Because the PCCh was not an isolated sect on the margins of Chilean politics, but a major working-class party with deep roots in the political and trade union life of the country, the processes of confrontation and exclusion had traumatic repercussions. By the time the Ley de Defensa Permanente reached the statute book, the Center–Left coalition that the PCCh had done so much to create and sustain and that, since 1938, had helped to elect three successive presidents of the republic from the centrist Partido Radical (PR) – Pedro Aguirre Cerda, Juan Antonio Ríos Morales and Gabriel González Videla – was irrevocably destroyed. By that time too, the split inside the CTCh had become permanent and the trade union movement as a whole was cowed and contained. Finally, the issue of Communist exclusion helped to precipitate divisions and fractionalization in almost all the major political parties in Chile, not excluding those of the Right.

But why should spiraling tensions between the superpowers in the period following the Second World War have such a devastating effect on the politics of what was, after all, a relatively minor power on the periphery of the world stage? Part of the answer to that question clearly lies in the closeness of the economic ties that linked Chile to one of the major protagonists in the Cold War, the United States. It also lies in the severe economic and financial difficulties that faced Chile in the postwar period, difficulties that made Chilean governments particularly concerned about U.S. reactions to events in Chile and, on the infrequent occasions it was formally exercised, vulnerable to U.S. governmental pressure. Part of the answer can also be found in the nature of the Chilean working-class movement and, in particular, in the intense rivalry for working-class support between the Partido Socialista (PS) and the PCCh, a rivalry that had always drawn strength and color from the PCCh's international ties and from the changing international climate.

Even before the Second World War, the United States was Chile's most important trading partner; U.S. companies controlled the vital copper industry, dominated the nitrate industry, and were important in banking and commerce; U.S. nationals owned the greater part of Chile's foreign debt. Cut off by the war from its other markets in Europe, the importance of the United States to Chile, as a consumer of those mineral exports that were the mainstay of Chile's prosperity, as a supplier of goods essential for the regular functioning of the economy, and as a source of credits for development purposes, was correspondingly magnified.

During the war years Chile thus became increasingly dependent on its economic and financial ties with the United States. However, that increased dependence did not translate into a crude increase in the power of Washington to determine Chilean government policy – rather it helped to create conditions for complex diplomatic games of pressure and counterpressure, games in which Chilean governments were by no means without leverage. Increased dependence – and the recognition of that fact by successive Radical presidents of Chile – did mean, however, that the U.S. government's wishes usually prevailed where Chilean foreign policy was concerned – in the long run at any rate.

The closer economic and financial relationship between Chile and the United States was accompanied by a closer U.S. concern with any development inside Chile that could affect its economic or strategic interest. Equally, Chilean governments became concerned about U.S. reactions to events in Chile since these could affect the prospects of obtaining much needed aid. One manifestation of the increased U.S. concern was the appointment to the U.S. embassy in Santiago of labor reporting officers, who between 1944 and 1946 kept Washington informed about industrial disputes and the trade union movement. Another manifestation was the increased activities of the Federal Bureau of Investigation (FBI). Intermittently active in Chile from 1941, by the time the war was drawing to a close there was a resident FBI agent in Chile who held the appointment of legal attaché at the U.S. embassy and who was specifically concerned with monitoring the activities of the Left in general and the PCCh in particular. During 1945 the legal attaché organized a network of informants that included civil servants, police and politicians, together with ex-Communists and even some active PCCh members. With their help he collected a great deal of information about PCCh members, organization, training, and finance, which was duly relayed to the State Department in Washington.

The FBI network, which was apparently only concerned with gathering information, was disbanded in mid-1947 – to the regret of some Chilean Foreign Ministry officials – and its functions taken over by the Central Intelligence Agency (CIA). Whether the CIA went beyond information gathering to engage in some form of executive action – and there is some evidence, as we shall see, that suggests U.S. operatives either advised or observed in President González Videla's confrontation with the coal miners in 1947 – cannot be established with any certainty since the CIA files on that episode remain closed.

What can be established is that the American Federation of Labor (AFL) was involved in Chilean Cold War struggles even before the election of González Videla. Serafino Romualdi, the AFL organizer for Latin America who had helped the Office of Strategic Services (OSS) to reorganize Italian trade unionism in the closing stages of the war, has stated that he was channeling funds into the Socialist section of the CTCh from 1946 onward, probably, though he does not say it, from the early months of that year.[1]

Whatever the precise nature and role of the various U.S. interests, governmental and otherwise, in the development of Cold War struggles in Chile, that country was made particularly sensitive to the concerns and wishes of the United States by the state of its economy.

Despite some bright spots, the Chilean economy did not flourish during the war years. Production in the copper mining industry reached record levels, not least because U.S. government agencies contracted to purchase the entire output between 1942 and September 1945. However, most commentators agree that the price paid for copper was artificially low, so Chile did not make massive windfall profits from its most important export industry. Other sectors of the mining industry did not perform so well. Indeed, the record of the economy as a whole was generally rather

---

1 On the CIA's taking over the functions of the FBI in Chile, see U.S. National Archives, Washington, D.C., Department of State Records (henceforth USNAW), 825,00B/6–2047, Ambassador Bowers to State, 20 June 1947. The British ambassador in Santiago reported to London that he thought it likely that the FBI had played a "considerable part" in the episode. See British Foreign Office Records (henceforth FOR), FO 371/61232, AS 6026/32/9, Leche to American South Department, 20 October 1947. On Romualdi and the CTCh, see Serafino Romualdi, *Presidents and Peons* (New York, 1967), pp. 37–42, 332.

patchy. That was true of agriculture, where despite significant expansion in the production of some cereals like rice, Chile was importing increasing amounts of wheat and cattle to feed its population by the end of the war. It was also true of the manufacturing sector, which, helped by the processes of import substitution, achieved remarkable growth rates between 1939 and 1945. Nonetheless, Chilean industry was still not able to meet all its domestic demand for manufactured goods and much of the foreign exchange earned by Chile's mining industries was spent in purchasing manufactured imports from Brazil and Argentina. Moreover, during the war, Chile was unable to import much of the machinery and capital goods it needed, had to contend with adverse terms of trade, and sometimes experienced shortages of vital commodities like gasoline.

But perhaps the single most important economic problem for Chile during the war years was that of inflation, caused, according to one expert observer, by the Central Bank's foreign exchange dealings, by increased spending of successive governments, and by credit inflation by the banks.[2] Whatever the precise nature of the causes of inflation, the cost of living more than doubled between 1939 and 1945, and since wages rarely kept pace with inflation, living standards for most workers fell during the war years. The decline in the purchasing power of wages was not the only consequence of inflation for the average Chilean household. As the inflationary spiral took hold, speculation by merchants and retailers in basic necessities became increasingly common. Merchants used cheap bank credit to purchase goods at official prices that they then hoarded until inflation gave them windfall profits.[3] Genuine bottlenecks in supply, caused by scarcity or transportation difficulties, were thus exacerbated and made the business of day-to-day living more arduous and frustrating for many Chileans both during and immediately after the war.

Because of inflationary pressures there was an undercurrent of industrial unrest during the war years that surfaced every now and then in a spate of illegal strike actions, which reached their high point in 1943 when 46,832 workers took part in 101 illegal strikes.[4] Generally speaking, in the vital mining and transportation sectors, such actions were contained by the government ordering the workers back to work and decreeing minimal wage increases – a practice that was accepted with varying degrees of reluctance by both Socialist and Communist trade unionists. Prolonged stoppages were usually avoided. With the ending of the war, however, workers were less inclined to postpone or moderate their demands for improved wages and conditions and less ready to accept government

---

2 FOR, Annual Economic Report, 1939–45, FO 371/52006, Leche to Bevin, 1 June 1946.
3 FOR, Larkins to Bevin, 11 December 1946, FO 371/52007.
4 Brian Loveman, *Chile: The Legacy of Hispanic Capitalism* (New York, 1979), p. 266.

methods of dealing with labor disputes. At the same time, with the Axis
now defeated, the PCCh and the PS were less ready to use their influence
to curb or contain industrial unrest whereas employers, uncertain of their
prospects in the postwar world, were less inclined to make placatory
concessions to their work forces.[5] All in all, it was not surprising that
strike activity, both legal and illegal, reached record levels in the months
that followed the end of the war. In 1945, 98,946 workers took part in
148 strikes, more, incidentally, than in the politically turbulent years of
1946 (90,737 in 176 strikes) and 1947 (69,531 in 164 strikes).[6]

Chile's economic and financial situation did not improve during 1946
and 1947. Indeed, with the ending of the war, the purchasing agreements
with the United States lapsed and the world demand for copper slumped.
Although the effects of this were partly offset by a sharp increase in copper
prices and by increased demands for nitrates, the fall in copper production
and exports inevitably had adverse consequences for the economy and the
Chilean exchequer. The reserves of hard currency built up by Chile during
the war – which in any event were not immense – were soon dissipated
and indeed, by mid-1946, Chile had insufficient hard currency to meet
its immediate needs. During 1945 and 1946 bank note issue and easy
bank credit continued to add fuel to the inflationary spiral as did government spending. As a result, increases in the cost of living index rose
from 8 percent in 1945 to 15.9 percent in 1946 to 33.5 percent in 1947.
In March 1947, President González Videla announced an accumulated
budget deficit of 1.55 billion (American billion) pesos, a Treasury deficit
of 1.3 billion pesos, and a foreign exchange deficit of $45 million.[7]

As these figures might suggest, the first year of González Videla's
administration was one of severe financial and economic difficulty as well
as one of sharpening political and social tensions. Despite governmental
efforts to bring inflation under control by imposing credit restrictions in
December 1946, the cost of living still rose by 20 percent between October
1946 and May 1947, while its efforts to stop price speculation and ensure
an adequate supply of articles of first necessity had little initial success.[8]
In September 1947, just as González Videla was shaping up for his final
confrontation with the Communists in the coal zone, the British ambassador reported from Santiago that despite serious government efforts to
keep food prices down and stop profiteering, prices had continued to rise,

---

5  USNAW, Bowers to State, 27 March 1945, 825.504/3–2745, report for February–March 1945
   by the labor reporting officer, Daniel L. Horowitz.
6  Loveman, *Chile,* p. 266.
7  *El Mercurio,* 1 March 1947.
8  FOR, Larkins to Combs, 18 August 1947, FO 371/61237, AS 5050/33/9.

more food stuffs had become scarce, gas was rationed, electricity had been cut off for one day a week, and coal and coke were in short supply.[9]

This, then, was the economic and financial background against which Chile's Cold war battles were fought. But whereas Chile's economic and financial problems made that country particularly sensitive to the susceptibilities and concerns of both U.S. government and U.S. business, U.S. agencies, governmental or otherwise, had little to do with Chile's early Cold War struggles. Indeed, Cold War tensions began to have an impact on Chilean politics a year before the State Department was showing much concern with the Communist threat in Chile, and some months before the FBI or the AFL became preoccupied by it. The main agency by which the Cold War made its early entrance into Chilean politics was through the intense rivalry between Chilean Communists and Socialists for working-class support and, in particular, through their battles for dominance in the trade union movement.

Since its foundation in 1922, the PCCh had faithfully attempted to follow the policies endorsed by the Moscow-based Comintern. In 1935 the PCCh duly abandoned hard-line, revolutionary Third Period analysis and tactics for the Popular Front strategy and scored a great success in helping to create and sustain the Center–Left coalition that secured the election of Aguirre Cerda as president in 1938. Favorably disposed toward the United States and the Western democracies in the Popular Front years, the attitude of the PCCh changed drastically after the signing of the Nazi–Soviet pact and, just as drastically and rather more rapidly, after the Nazi invasion of Russia in June 1941. Emphatically pro-Allies during the war years, the PCCh again became increasingly critical of the United States and its allies as the international climate deteriorated during the second half of 1945.

While the PCCh was characterized by its loyalty to Moscow, the PS was characterized by its anticommunism. Indeed, anticommunism was one of the root causes of the creation of the PS in 1933; it helped to give the new party much of its distinctive identity and was used by party leaders to bolster their positions and rally their supporters in times of difficulty. Although the two parties shared revolutionary goals and a Marxist ideology, the founders of the PS were united by their rejection of what they saw as the PCCh's subservience to Moscow and, in particular, by their rejection of the Comintern's hard-line Third Period tactics, which

9 For example, see FOR, Leche to Bevin, 22 September 1947, FO 371/61237; Leche to Bevin, 21 April 1948, FO 371/68200, AS 2856/3/9.

they thought to be inappropriate to Chilean conditions and actively destructive of the possibilities for revolutionary change.

The Socialists attacked, with hostile contempt and considerable gusto, the various shifts in policy that the PCCh undertook in compliance with policy changes adopted by the Comintern. And although the PS and the PCCh found themselves cooperating in political coalitions and in the trade union movement between 1936 and 1940, and between 1942 and 1945, they did so with wariness and barely concealed antagonism. These antagonisms surfaced in a ferocious fashion in late 1940 and destroyed the Popular Front coalition. They receded, however, after the Nazi invasion of Russia in June 1941, and again after August 1944 when the PCCh refashioned its policies and actions to make them consistent with Earl Browder's concept that class collaborationism rather than class conflict would be the motor force for fundamental change in the postwar world.[10] In late 1945 hostilities again broke out as the PCCh began to distance itself from the Browderist heresy and move toward more aggressive policies and, indeed, in the early months of 1946 something like a civil war ensued in the working class movement.

Apart from Congress and the hustings, the trade union movement was perhaps the most important arena for competition between Socialists and Communists. By the 1940s only something like 10 percent of the Chilean work force was unionized, but the union movement was stronger than that percentage might suggest because of the strategic importance in the economy of the unionized sectors, which included the vital mining and transport industries. Although most trade unionists belonged to legal trade unions (that is, unions organized according to the Código del Trabajo, which had been specifically designed to depoliticize and fractionalize the union movement), by the 1940s 90 percent of unionists belonged to the country's largest trade union confederation, the highly political and technically illegal CTCh.[11]

Although rivalry between Socialists and Communists in the union movement sometimes had a momentum of its own, the activities of trade unionists from both parties were strongly conditioned by the policy decisions of their respective leaderships. Indeed, it is quite likely that the CTCh would not have come into existence when it did – or survived its First National Congress in August 1939 – had the Popular Front strategy not been in place,[12] Similarly, political differences over a range of issues

---

10 This took place at the Fifteenth Plenum of the Central Committee of the PCCh in August 1944. For an account of the Fifteenth Plenum, see *El Siglo,* 5, 6, and 7 August 1944.
11 Alan Angell, *Politics and the Labour Movement in Chile* (London, 1971), pp. 108–12.
12 For an account of those difficulties, see *Frente Popular,* 7 August 1939, 26th October 1939.

not directly connected with trade unionism could quite easily find expression in an explosion of hostilities in the union movement. Such was the case in late 1940 when foreign policy differences and electoral imperatives combined to destroy the Popular Front coalition and unleash violent conflict in the union movement – a conflict that only ended when the Nazi invasion of Russia abruptly changed the PCCh's stance.

In terms of relative strength, the Socialists were probably the stronger force in Chilean trade unionism from the early 1930s to the mid–1940s. However, during the war years the PS suffered two important splits, giving birth to the Partido Socialista de Trabajadores in 1940 and to the Partido Socialista Auténtico in 1944, and both these divisions helped to fractionalize its union support. Since the PCCh avoided fractionalization and eventually absorbed the remnants of both schismatic Socialist parties, it emerged from the war years in a relatively stronger position. Even so, it is not altogether clear that the PCCh had overtaken the PS in terms of union support by that time; the PCCh had to face a vexatious "apolitical" challenge from a series of unions in the North in early 1944, and its efforts to maintain industrial peace, especially after August 1944, cannot have helped the party to consolidate its advantage.[13] Nonetheless, by the time the war had ended, the Socialists had lost their preeminence on the Consejo Directorio Nacional (CDN) of the CTCh and it was clear that they could not expect to control the office of secretary general for very much longer.

The roots of Chile's first Cold War crisis lay in the sharpening hostilies between the PCCh and the PS and the adjustments each made in the immediate postwar period, in the accelerating pace of industrial unrest, and in the presidential politics of the Partido Radical (PR).

After the war, both the PCCh and the PS rediscovered an active interest in fundamental reform and adopted a more aggressive policy in favor of labor. To an extent these changes were merely a reassertion of those concerns and attitudes that had been sacrificed to the world crusade against fascism. But they were also a response to more particular pressures, most notably the defeat of the Alianza Democrática de Chile (ADCh) parties in the March 1945 congressional elections (a defeat that cost the coalition control over the Chamber of Deputies) and the rising tide of industrial unrest, which became pronounced in the last months of 1945. The PS had an additional reason for readjusting its policies – the fractionalization and decline that it had experienced during the war years and that had

13 For details of this challenge, see *El Popular*, Antofagasta, Chile, late February to early March 1944; *El Chileno*, 4 March 1944; and *El Mercurio*, 7 March 1944.

been painfully demonstrated in the March elections.[14] For the PCCh, the need for readjustment was reinforced by events abroad, most notably, Jacques Duclos's denunciation of the Browderist heresy in June 1945.

Both parties began the formal process of readjustment in July 1945. During that month the PS held a congress in which it placed a large share of the blame for the ADCh's electoral defeat in March on the National Unity policies of the PCCh. After an unsuccessful attempt to pressure the ADCh into either persuading the PCCh to drop its National Unity policies or to exclude the PCCh altogether, the PS left in August 1945, declaring its independence of both the government and the coalition.[15] For the PCCh the process of readjustment was rather more gradual. Starting in July, however, and culminating in December 1945 at its Thirteenth National Congress, the PCCh elaborated a program of reforms designed to speed Chile through its "bourgeois democratic revolution," and adopted a tougher policy on labor disputes.[16] Even so, the PCCh continued to express its commitment to National Unity – the idea that the progressive Right as well as centrist groups could be drawn into a broad popular movement dedicated, in this instance, to fundamental change.

The PCCh's shift leftward, a move that also entailed becoming more critical of the shortcomings of the Ríos administration, was not welcomed by either the Radicals or the Socialists in late 1945. The PR, which since May 1945 was once again represented in cabinet, did not appreciate the PCCh's more critical stance toward government, was not happy at the PCCh's failure to control Communist-led unions in a copper miners strike at Chuquicamata in October 1945, and was angered by the PCCh's policy of seeking to prevent the export of coal and nitrates to "fascist" Argentina and Spain by unleashing regional general protest strikes.[17]

If relations between the PCCh and the Radicals grew cooler in late 1945, those between the PCCh and the PS approached open warfare. Although the burgeoning of hostilities was, in part, a natural product of the Socialists' efforts to revive their fortunes by, among other measures, seeking to outflank the PCCh in the union movement, they also owed much to the increasingly tense international climate. Indeed, as relations between the Soviet Union and the West deteriorated, the PCCh became increasingly critical of the United States, accusing it of seeking world hegemony. For its part, the PS rushed to defend the United States from

---

14 See Germán Urzúa Valenzuela, *Los partidos políticos chilenos* (Santiago, 1968), pp. 86–7, for the March 1945 election results. The PS lost 9 of its 15 seats in the Chamber of Deputies.

15 *La Opinión*, 7 August 1945.

16 For the official account of the Thirteenth National Congress, see *El Siglo*, 9 December 1945.

17 USNAW, Bowers to State, 27 November 1945, report by Horowitz, 825.504/11–2745. See also Partido Radical *Cuenta de la actuación del CEN del PR a la XVI Convención Nacional Ordinaria, enero 1944–enero 1946* (Santiago, 1946), p. 48.

such charges, accusing the PCCh of being the agents of Soviet imperialism. Although there was nothing particularly novel about these exchanges, passion was injected into them when, in January 1946, the PCCh made a series of personal attacks on the Socialist leader, Bernardo Ibáñez. The attacks were precipitated by reports that Ibáñez, who had just returned from a trip to London where as secretary general of the CTCh he had attended the World Trades Union Congress, had been trying to drum up support for a non-Communist, regional labor confederation to rival the Confederación de Trabajadores de América Latina (CTAL).[18] In response to these attacks the PS issued a statement accusing the PCCh of converting Chile into a battleground between the Great Powers and of fomenting indiscipline and disorganization in the trade union movement; it declared that henceforth it would have no political relations with the PCCh or any of its allies.[19] At the same time the PS warned the PR, then holding a national convention in Valdivia, that unless it adopted a belligerent attitude toward the PCCh, it could expect no help or support from the PS.[20]

The sharpening of hostilities between the Communists and Socialists came at the precise time that the government decided to do something about the rising tide of industrial unrest. On 9 January 1946 President Ríos, reacting to an illegal regional strike in the coal zone that had found resonances in other parts of the republic a few days earlier, declared that any union that went on illegal strike in future would have its *personalidad jurídica* removed.[21] And on 22 January Vice-President Alfredo Duhalde Vásquez, who had just taken over from what proved to be the mortally ill Ríos, removed the legal status of two nitrate unions for precisely that offense.[22]

The measures taken against the nitrate unions set in motion a chain of events that led to confrontation between the government and the PCCh, to open division in the CTCh, and to bitter and bloody struggles between Socialists and Communists. Initially, however, Duhalde's action produced unity in the working-class movement. The PS set aside its animosity toward the PCCh in order to cooperate with the ADCh parties and the CTCh in a national movement of public protest, culminating in a general

18 Henry W. Berger, Union diplomacy: American labor's foreign policy in Latin America, 1932–1955 (Ph.D. diss. University of Wisconsin, 1966), 273–6.
19 See *El Mercurio*, 17 January 1946, for the official PS declaration.
20 Agustín Alvarez Villablanca, *Objetivos del Socialismo* (Santiago, 1946), p. 1.
21 See *El Mercurio*, 10 January 1946, for Ríos's declaration and for an account of the illegal strike wave that preceeded it. See also USNAW, Bowers to State, 31 January 1946, 825,504/1–3146, report by Horowitz.
22 *El Siglo*, 23 January 1946. For a report on the significance of this particular illegal strike, see USNAW, Hoover to Lyon, 6 May 1946, 825.5045/5–646.

strike called for 30 January. Two days before the general strike was due to take place an already tense situation was made worse when police opened fire on demonstrators in Plaza Bulnes, close to the presidential palace in Santiago, killing five and wounding many more.[23] Duhalde immediately imposed a state of seige and invited Armed Services chiefs to join his cabinet – actions that caused the PR, the Falange Nacional, and the PSA ministers to resign. Despite the state of seige, the general strike was successful and in order to have it lifted Vice-President Duhalde agreed to a number of conditions put before him by the CTCH. Although Duhalde had commenced to honor some of those conditions, the CDN of the CTCh, with its Socialist members in attendance, decided to reimpose the strike for 4 February.[24] But on 2 February the PS accepted an offer of cabinet office from Duhalde and instructed its supporters not to respond to the second strike call. The result was that the second strike, less effective than the first, was called off after forty-eight hours. Even so, in some industries where workers were in dispute for their own reasons, the strike continued, and in others reinitiation of production was a slow process because employers were encouraged by the government to dismiss strikers and recruit new labor.[25] It was not until the end of February that a semblance of industrial peace was restored – and even that was shattered in early March when Communist coal miners initiated a brief regional protest strike against the slow implementation of an arbitration award.[26]

The defection of the Socialists caused the CTCh to split and unleashed a bitter, bloody, and protracted civil war in the union movement that lasted for much of 1946. Socialist ministers and other members of the government used their powers to harrass the PCCh, and by April 1946 there were over one hundred Communist activists in jail, including the director of the party newspaper, *El Siglo*.[27] During these struggles both sides made use of Cold War language and analysis. Vice-President Duhalde accused the Communists of following international instructions designed to undermine the national economy and the democratic regime; the PCCh's recent conduct had been openly subversive and revolutionary, he declared.[28] The PCCh, for its part, accused the United States of plotting with the Chilean oligarchy in order to install a dictatorship that would

23 *El Siglo*, 29 January 1946.
24 *El Siglo*, 5 February 1946.
25 USNAW, Bowers to State, 19 March 1946, 825,504/3–1946, report by Horowitz.
26 Ibid. See also *El Siglo*, 1–8 March 1946.
27 *El Siglo*, 15 April 1946.
28 See *El Siglo*, 22 February and 8 March 1946, for key speches by Duhalde in which he made these charges.

ensure that Chile remained in its underdeveloped state.[29] How much truth was there in these allegations?

Although it is perfectly clear that the PCCh did follow the Soviet lead in attacks on U.S. imperialism, it is just as clear that the PCCh had no subversive or revolutionary intention in early 1946. Certainly since 1938, and arguably earlier, the PCCh had set its face against extraconstitutional attempts to oust elected authority and had rallied to Aguirre Cerda when he was threatened by a right-wing military coup in 1939, and to Ríos when rumors of a Socialist-inspired coup were circulating in November 1945.[30] Moreover, it is difficult to see how a revolutionary movement in the circumstances of early 1946 could have been consistent with the National Unity concept that, if nothing else, stood for multiclass alliances designed to attract mass popular support and orderly, constitutional change.

If the PCCh was not engaged in a revolutionary or subversive attempt, what considerations were guiding its actions in early 1946? In the first strike on 30 January, the PCCh like the PS was determined to show that the government could not embark on an offensive against labor with impunity. In the second general strike, other motivations were probably also at work. Ever since late 1944 the PCCh had been trying to emulate the Communist Parties of recently liberated Europe and to participate in government at a ministerial level. According to the labor reporting officer at the U.S. embassy in Santiago, that particular consideration had been in the forefront of the PCCh's preoccupations, conditioning its conduct during the labor conflicts of late 1945 and early 1946.[31] If that analysis is correct, one of the reasons why the Communists persisted with the second strike may have been that they wanted to demonstrate that they were now the dominant force in the CTCh and that the government had chosen the wrong partner in selecting the PS.

If the PCCh was not guilty of the most serious charge leveled against it, namely, that it was plotting revolution at the behest of Moscow, there is, similarly, no evidence to suggest that the Chilean government was acting on the orders or suggestion of any branch of U.S. imperialism. Duhalde, it is true, did take the classic first step of all Radical presidents when expecting or planning a confrontation with the Communists – he asked the U.S. State Department to arrange for the shipment of coal to Chile. However, although the State Department responded willingly

29 See articles by Humberto Abarca and Galo González in *Principios*, February–March 1946, and *El Siglo*, 24 January, 4 April, and 8 May 1946, for expressions of this viewpoint.
30 *El Siglo*, 18 November 1945. USNAW, Hoover to Lyon, 19 December 1945, 825.00/12–1945.
31 USNAW, Bowers to State, 31 January 1946, 825.00/5054, report by Horowitz; see also Hoover to Lyon, 19 December 1945, 825.00/12–1945.

enough to Duhalde's urgent requests for coal, those requests were made after, and not before, his confrontation with the Communists.[32] Moreover, while Ríos claimed to the Communists that he was under strong national and international pressures to outlaw the PCCh, there is absolutely no indication in State Department archives that any such pressure emanated from Washington. Indeed, State Department officials attributed rumors that the United States was involved in efforts to outlaw the PCCh, which had first surfaced in *Ercilla,* a Santiago newsmagazine, to *aprista* propaganda since the editor of that magazine was a prominent *aprista* exile.[33]

In short, there is no indication in State Department records that the U.S. government or any of its intelligence agencies played any role in the confrontation between the government and the PCCh in early 1946. It may be, however, that the AFL's Latin American organizer, Serafino Romualdi, did play some part in bolstering Bernardo Ibáñez's resolve to take on the Communists. The AFL had been assiduously cultivating Ibáñez since 1943 when he showed himself to be a serious rival to Vicente Lombardo Toledano for the leadership of the CTAL.[34] Even so, it would probably be an error to deduce from this that the breach in the CTCh was engineered by Ibáñez because of any direction or suggestion from the AFL. It is more likely that Ibáñez took the action he did for domestic political and career reasons, and although he may have been fairly sure that the AFL would come to his assistance once he had joined battle with the Communists, the balance of probabilities remains that he did not begin to receive financial and other practical aid from the AFL until after February 1946.

In spite of the Cold War rhetoric that larded the public pronouncements of all sides in the clashes of early 1946, the battle between Communists and Socialists and the confrontation between the PCCh and the government can be explained in purely Chilean terms, that is to say, in terms of a PS intent on recouping its fortunes after the fractionalization and decline of the war years, and in terms of a government intent on stemming the rise of industrial unrest. Ríos's illness and the probability of presidential elections in the near future undoubtedly also had some bearing on the development of events. The national convention of the PR in January had confirmed the dominance of the party's left wing and the likely candidacy of González Videla as the left-wing Radical standard-

---

32 USNAW, Byrnes to Embassy, 8 February 1946, 825.5045/2–846; Bowers to State, 11 February 1946, 825.6363/2–1146; Memo, 9 March 1946, 825.6362/3–946.

33 USNAW, Office of the American Republics Memo, 9 March 1946, RG 59. In the 1940s, APRA was a Peruvian left-wing, populist party with an antiimperialist ideology and a revolutionary past that earned it the hostility of the Peruvian military.

34 See Henry W. Berger, Union diplomacy, pp. 273–6. See also Romualdi, *Presidents and Peons,* p. 7.

bearer. Vice-President Duhalde, however, was a right-wing Radical who had presidential ambitions of his own and it is difficult to believe that his actions during January and February 1946 were not, to some extent at least, geared to undermine left-wing Radicals associated with the Radical–Communist alliance. Similarly, the PS, caught short by the prospect of presidential elections two years before they were due, probably found the temptation of government office irresistable because access to the machinery of state seemed the only way to a rapid restoration of party fortunes and to electoral advantage as well as a means of chastising Communist rivals.

While Cold War rhetoric was evident enough in the political crisis of early 1946, Cold War pressures were not sufficiently strong to prevent the "Communist" candidate from winning the presidential elections that took place in September 1946 after President Ríos had died in office. The successful candidate, González Videla, a left-wing Radical who had the support of the PCCh, fought the election on a program that promised firm state action to encourage industrial development, the nationalization of some public utilities, a modest but not insignificant land reform, and a series of constitutional and social reforms, including unionization rights for the peasantry and the extension of suffrage to women.[35] It was, in sum, a program designed to advance political democracy and improve conditions for working people. It was also a program intended to finally realize those expectations for change and improvement that had been promoted by the crusade against world fascism but that had not been fulfilled since the end of the war. Even so, González Videla could hardly claim that his program had received the overwhelming endorsement of the electorate; in a four-cornered contest he received just over 40 percent of the vote; his two right-wing rivals, 57 percent between them.[36] No candidate having an absolute majority, a Congreso Pleno was summoned to choose the victor and despite last minute maneuvers by the Conservative candidate, González Videla was confirmed in office with the help of votes from the right-wing Partido Liberal (PL).

If Cold War pressures were not yet strong enough to persuade most Chileans to join a crusade to stop the "Communist" candidate, neither was the U.S. State Department prepared to act in order to secure the election of a candidate more to its liking. Thus, although the State Department and the U.S. ambassador Claude G. Bowers clearly identified

---

35 *El Siglo*, 16 July 1946.
36 González Videla polled 192,207 votes; Eduardo Cruz Coke, the Conservative candidate, 142,441; Fernando Alessandri, Liberal, 131,023 votes; Bernardo Ibáñez, Socialist, 12,114. See Germán Urzúa Valenzuela, *Los partidos*, p. 88.

González Videla as the candidate most hostile to U.S. interests, they refused to interfere. Indeed, Ambassador Bowers, approached for financial support by representatives of all the candidates, including González Videla's, rejected all such requests and instructed U.S. business interests to follow suit.[37]

But if Cold War tensions were not sufficiently strong to prevent González Videla from becoming president, they were clearly very much present. So much so that González Videla thought it advisable, between being elected and taking office, to reassure both the U.S. and the British ambassadors that though he might find it necessary to invite the PCCh into government, he would get rid of them as soon as was possible (indicating to the U.S. ambassador that this would take two to three months).[38] Furthermore, Cold War considerations helped to shape his first cabinet, the so-called tricolor cabinet, which included Radicals, Liberals, and Communists. Given that González Videla was apparently determined to invite the PCCh to share government office, he needed the Liberals in his cabinet to counterbalance the Communists and to allay the Cold War fears of the Chilean Right, Western governments, and, most particularly, the Chilean armed forces, which although dominated by constitutionalists at this time, could not be expected to remain neutral if it really seemed Chile was "going Communist."[39]

That having been said, the Cold War was by no means the only factor involved in the shaping of González Videla's first cabinet. He himself made much of the country's dire economic and financial position, which, he claimed, necessitated the cooperation of all parties across the political spectrum. But there were other considerations. First, González Videla had to repay specific political debts: the Liberals had demanded cabinet office as their price for supporting him in the Congreso Pleno; he owed the PCCh for the support it had given him in two presidential election campaigns. Second, González Videla needed Liberal support in order to secure working majorities in Congress and, moreover, it made excellent sense to involve the Liberals in government in order to prevent the emergence of a united right-wing opposition of the sort that had made President Aguirre Cerda's first years of government so difficult. Third, Communist involvement was made attractive, even necessary, by its strength in the labor movement. With the Socialists in disarray and decline, the Com-

37  USNAW, Bowers to Braden, 5 August 1946, 825.00/8–546.
38  USNAW, Bowers to Braden, 18 November 1946, 825.5045/11–1846; FOR, Leche to Bevin, 21 October 1946 and 4 November 1946, FO 371/52003.
39  The dominance of the constitutionalists was demonstrated when the army refused to countenance Conservative maneuvers in the Congreso Pleno designed to prevent the ratification of González Videla's victory in the presidential elections. See Elías Laferte, *Vida de un comunista*, (Santiago, 1957), p. 336.

munists were certainly the more cohesive and possibly the stronger force in the trade union movement even after the difficulties of the earlier part of 1946. González Videla thus looked to the party for its influence to help maintain industrial peace at a time of sharpening social tensions; he probably also felt that the PCCh would be easier to control inside rather than outside of government.[40] Although subsequent events make González Videla's commitment to the reform program on which he was elected somewhat suspect, he began his presidency as a man of the left wing of the PR with at least a degree of emotional commitment to reform and, for that reason, probably had no wish to be overdependent on right-wing parties.

However sound the reasons for incorporating the antagonistic Communists and Liberals in cabinet, it was not a formula designed to produce harmonious or long-lasting government. The Liberals, for their part, claimed to have accepted office only as a gesture of patriotic self-sacrifice and openly announced their intention to actively combat the spread of Communist influence inside and outside government.[41] They not only did what they could to prevent the appointment of Communists to positions in government and semiofficial agencies but, from the first, acted more like an opposition than a government party. They publicly attacked government economic policy, backed a restrictive law on peasant unionization without consulting or informing the president, and supported opposition candidates in congressional by-elections.

Neither was the PCCh the pliant partner for which González Videla had hoped. Before coming to office, the PCCh made it perfectly clear that its main aim was to secure the implementation of the reform program on which González Videla had been elected. To this end the PCCh announced that it was not part of its role to curb the legitimate struggle of the workers for improved pay and conditions. On the contrary, popular mobilizations for that struggle, for peasant unionization, and for campaigns against speculators and the rising cost of living were to be the means by which González Videla's reform program would be realized.[42] Although such declarations seemed to indicate that the PCCh was in no mood for any attempt by the government to step back from its reform program, in practice the party was more flexible. Thus, despite misgivings, the PCCh accepted the credit restrictions imposed by Finance Minister Wachholtz in December 1946 and, after supporting an initial wave of strike

---

40 Whatever the relative strengths of the Communist and Socialist CTChs at the beginning of González Videla's administration. U.S. embassy officials estimated that the Communist CTCh encompassed anything from 55 to 70 percent of organized labor by October 1947. USNAW, Bell to State, 2 October 1947, 825.5043/10–247.

41 *La Hora,* 19 December 1946.

42 See *El Siglo,* 17 November 1946, for Galo González's speech to the PCCh's national conference.

actions, the party did use its influence to contain industrial unrest and increase production, publicly unveiling a program to those ends in February 1947.

Even so, the PCCh's initial unwillingness to clamp down on industrial unrest, its campaigns to unionize the peasantry under the existing Código del Trabajo, and its insistence on getting its proper share of administrative appointments strained relations with the PR. By the time the municipal elections took place in April 1947, the PCCh was not only at loggerheads with its Liberal colleagues but with the Radicals as well. That election, in which the PCCh polled 90,000 votes (some 17 percent of the total cast and its best electoral showing to date), was used by the Liberals as the pretext for their withdrawal from government, arguing, rather perversely in light of the PCCh's record poll, that the election results demonstrated the massive rejection of communism by the electorate.[43] The Radicals promptly followed suit as was customary when a major component of a governing coalition withdrew. After some hesitation, the PCCh also resigned, having been assured by González Videla that, should circumstances permit, they would be invited to return to government in the near future and that, in the meantime, Communist officeholders other than ministers would remain in place.[44]

Despite this evidence of González Videla's goodwill toward the PCCh – a goodwill that may have been sincere at that moment – relations between the president and the party rapidly grew cooler after April 1947. In late May at a national PCCh conference, Secretary General Ricardo Fonseca delivered a trenchant attack on the United States in which he accused that country of supporting corrupt and reactionary regimes throughout the world, poured scorn on the idea that a Third World War was imminent, and denounced U.S. economic and military plans for Latin America as inimical to Chile's sovereignty and independence.[45] Perhaps even more ominous for social peace, Fonseca went on to predict that the capitalist world would soon be experiencing an economic crisis more devastating than that of 1929; he urged workers to mobilize against rising prices and evictions, and for the implementation of the electoral program.

Barely two weeks later, a bus strike, which led to bloodshed, caused González Videla to issue his first public broadside against the PCCh, angrily accusing the party of duplicity for trying to blame the government for the bloodshed while continuing to enjoy the fruits of office, and for failing to acknowledge its own responsibility for the violent acts of its

43 La Hora, 11 April 1947.
44 El Siglo, 17 April 1947; Luis Corvalan, Ricardo Fonseca: Combatiente ejemplar, 2d ed. (Santiago, 1971), p. 196.
45 El Siglo, 24 May 1947.

members in the strike movement.[46] Moreover, while the bus strike was in progress, the Radicals, at their national convention, adopted a political resolution that prevented the PR from serving in government with any party whose social and economic doctrines were antagonistic to its own.[47] Although the PCCh professed itself not be alarmed by this development, in fact the resolution ruled out any possibility of a Communist return to government in the near future and, in retrospect, formally marked the end of a decade of Radical–Communist cooperation.

González Videla began his major offensive against the PCCh on his return from a trip to Rio de Janeiro where, on the eve of the conference of American States on regional security, he had endorsed U.S. plans for military cooperation in Latin America. In early August, after lengthy consultations with all political parties except the PCCh, González Videla formed a cabinet that included the heads of the armed services. The new cabinet immediately announced a program of economic stabilization that included a sharp cutback in public spending, steps to deal with illegal strikes, and a price policy that could only lead to rises in the cost of living.[48] The PCCh reacted vigorously to the formation of the new government and to its plans. Stating that the country was now faced with the choice between popular democracy and dictatorship, the PCCh urged the masses to mobilize to the maximum in order to influence the course of events, giving popular solutions to Chile's problems.[49] In the weeks that followed, the party supported a series of illegal actions called by coal and rail workers to protest against price rises in basic foodstuffs. González Videla, for his part, accused the party of obstructing his plans to combat price speculation and, worse still, of launching revolutionary strikes. On 19 August, González Videla declared all government posts held by PCCh members to be vacant and called for special powers to deal with the situation that was caused, he claimed, by the Communists' revolutionary demagoguery and by the unscrupulous machinations of speculators. These special powers were granted, a state of emergency was imposed on the coal zone, and, equally ominous, the PR issued instructions for its trade union members to withdraw from the Communist-led CTCh.[50]

The PCCh's reaction to these developments was to argue that the strikes were caused by the rises in the cost of living and obeyed no revolutionary plan – pointing to the fact that the miners had returned to work once special powers had been approved by Congress. The party also declared that whereas it would not support any extraconstitutional attempt to oust

46 *El Mercurio*, 15 June 1947.
47 *La Hora*, 9 June 1947.
48 *El Siglo*, 5 August 1947.
49 *El Siglo*, 11 August 1947.
50 *El Siglo*, 22 August 1947.

legitimate authority from office, it would not give up its defense of the
rights and interests of the workers or their struggle for better wages and
conditions.[51] In effect the PCCh tried to step back from the confrontation.
Without fundamentally changing its position, it softened its attacks on
the government and called for a regrouping of popular forces. But by that
time it was already too late – the PCCh was completely isolated from its
old allies. González Videla, however, was not content with isolating the
party and rooting it out of government. He was looking for an excuse to
launch a national offensive against the PCCh. That excuse came in early
October when coal miners on legal strike rejected government orders to
return to work.

In what was already an emergency zone under military rule, the strike
leaders were arrested; miners on the reserve list were recalled to the colors;
and those who refused to work were deported from the region, the government accepting offers from Bernardo Ibáñez to provide replacements.[52]
Even so, the strike was not broken rapidly; the military authorities found
it necessary to seize food stocks and prohibit fishing in an effort to ensure
that those who did not work did not eat. After two weeks, the strikers
began to drift back to work, and after 21 October, when miners staged
a final protest by refusing to surface after their shifts were over, the strike
ended.

González Videla claimed that the coal strike was part of a Communist
attempt to overthrow the democratic regime mounted in obedience to
instructions from Moscow, and during October he ordered the arrest of
PCCh leaders, closed *El Siglo,* the party's principal newspaper, and broke
off diplomatic relations with Yugoslavia, Czechoslovakia, and the USSR.[53]
It seems highly unlikely, however, that the PCCh had any such revolutionary plans. Indeed, isolated as it was from its customary allies, the
PCCh can have had little illusion that Chile was ripe for revolution or
that the party had the resources and support necessary for mounting a
successful revolutionary attempt. It is also clear that the party, which had
reluctantly accepted government orders ending strike actions during the
war years, had this time supported the miners in their resistance. But
that support did not obey any revolutionary plan; rather the swift and
drastic measures taken by the government on 4 October gave the PCCh
the choice of abject capitulation or acceptance of confrontation on the
government's terms. Given the prevailing Cold War climate, and given

---

51 Ibid.
52 *La Hora,* 16 October 1947. For a detailed and comprehensive description of the strike and its
   ramifications, see the lengthy report prepared by James Bell, second secretary at the U.S. embassy
   in Santiago, in USNAW, Bowers to State, 23 December 1947, 825.5045/12–2347.
53 *La Hora,* 9 and 22 October 1947.

the legal and legitimate nature of the miners' conflict and the importance of that body of workers to the Communist-led CTCh, the party had little alternative but to accept the government's challenge. Indeed, by that time the party leadership may well have felt that the only choice before it was the issue on which the PCCh was to be forced into clandestinity – and that the miners' case was a better issue than most.

The PCCh, for its part, alleged that González Videla, acting under pressure from the United States, had engineered the confrontation with the precise intention of launching a national offensive against the party and the working-class movement. That González Videla did engineer the confrontation seems clear enough. Although there was some justice in the government's claim that the dangerously low state of coal stocks demanded swift action, its handling of the conflict was little short of provocative. No attempt was made, as was customary, to persuade the miners to return to work; no opportunity was given for the government's terms to be considered by the miners in their assemblies. Instead, a decree that set out new, improved wage scales and empowered the commander of the emergency zone to recruit new personnel was peremptorily issued.[54] Despite decreeing wage increases, the government effectively disregarded the strikers' legal and constitutional rights and treated their conflict as if it were illegal. No trade union could be expected to accept such treatment without protest.

But was González Videla under U.S. pressure to move against the Communists? State Department records show that he was. They also show that the principal instrument of pressure was Chile's increasingly desperate need for U.S. credits and financial assistance. Although González Videla had told the U.S. ambassador that he would break with the Communists as soon as possible, his actions and behavior during a legal strike of Communist copper miners at Sewell during late 1946 gave State Department officials deep suspicions as to his true motives and feelings toward the Communists. As a result of those suspicions, Assistant Secretary of State Spruille Braden placed an informal embargo on all new credits for Chile in November 1946 and did his best to ensure that neither the Export–Import Bank nor the International Bank for Reconstruction and Development responded favorably to Chilean requests for aid.[55] Although some State Department officials were deeply critical of Braden's use of economic sanctions in the Sewell dispute, which they regarded as being neither effective nor proper, the embargo remained in force even after the

54 *El Siglo*, 6 October 1947; *La Hora*, 7 October 1947.
55 USNAW, Braden to Clayton, 6 November 1946, 825,5045/11–646; Memo, 10 December 1946, 825,51/12–1046.

dispute had been settled to the satisfaction of the Kennecott Corporation in January 1947.[56]

By April 1947, as Chile's economic and financial situation continued to deteriorate, its need for U.S. credits became even more pressing. By that time as well, González Videla had been advised by a number of U.S. sources, official and otherwise, that if he wanted U.S. aid, he would first have to put the economy in order and break with the Communists. And on the eve of sending a high-level economic mission led by Guillermo del Pedregal to Washington, González Videla apparently took note of that advice and eased the PCCh out of his cabinet.

If González Videla thought that the departure of the Communists from his cabinet would be sufficient to placate the State Department and open the way for new credits, he was soon disabused of that notion. Braden swept aside del Pedregal's efforts to justify González Videla's collaboration with the Communists and told him that the State Department regarded the Communists as a worse threat than the Nazi Fifth Column and that it was incumbent on all American republics to take a firm stand against the Communists.[57] Braden went on to say that Chile would get no further credits until it regularized its debt situation and advised the Chilean delegation that Chile's best hope of solving its economic difficulties lay in attracting foreign capital investment − investment that would not be forthcoming if the copper companies continued to be subjected to discriminatory taxation or until exchange regulations had been satisfactorily adjusted.

Even while del Pedregal was in Washington, González Videla appeared to give another indication that he was preparing for a break with the Communists − or at least expecting serious trouble from them − when he asked the State Department to secure twenty thousand tons of coal in anticipation of a strike in the coal mines.[58] But in May, State Department officials rejected the request on the grounds that such a small shipment would only enable González Videla to temporize with the Communists. These officials argued that only an "economic tie up" would discredit the Communists and persuade the president to break with them and only then would coal shipments be of real and lasting benefit to Chile and the United States.[59] But while the State Department pondered, González Videla approached the head of the Kennecott Corporation, told him of

56 USNAW, Memo, 15 November 1946, 825.5045/11−1546; Bowers to Braden, 2 January 1947, 825,5045/1−247.
57 USNAW, Memo, 18 April 1947, 825.00/4−1847.
58 USNAW, Bowers to Braden, 21 April 1947, 825.00/4−2147.
59 USNAW, Memo, 5 May 1947 RG 59.

his determination to break with the PCCh, and persuaded him to underwrite the costs of the coal shipments he needed.[60]

In June and July, González Videla, who had now convinced Ambassador Bowers that he was definitely going to break with the PCCh, began to explore the possibility of meeting some of the financial and other requirements needed to regularize Chile's credit standing. Despite Bowers's support, however, he found that the doors of the international financial institutions were closed against him. And although he broke with the Communists in August 1947 and immediately sought and obtained State Department approval of that action, there was no change in the State Department's attitude toward Chile's creditworthiness.[61]

The breakthrough came only after González Videla had made his irrevocable commitment to the anti-Communist cause in October. A week after González Videla had joined battle with the coal miners, the State Department agreed to arrange for the shipment of coal to Chile.[62] The State Department also agreed to approach the Exim Bank on Chile's behalf in order to obtain credits to pay for the coal shipments; the bank responded favorably and, on the condition that news of the transaction was to remain absolutely secret, provided $4 million against an existing steel mill credit to pay for the coal.[63] After the coal strike, other matters also began to improve rapidly. With State Department help Chile was able to regularize its foreign debt situation. And early in 1948 Chile began once again to receive credits from the international financial institutions.[64]

It seems clear, then, that the U.S. State Department pressured González Videla into breaking with the Communists and pressured him also into a national offensive against them. Yet how important was that pressure? It was not, after all, the only factor involved. Chile's parlous economic and financial situation, the rising tide of industrial and social unrest, and the logistics of party strengths in Congress all played their part. Even if the State Department had not exerted the pressure it did, it seems highly likely that González Videla, like his two Radical predecessors in the presidency (Aguirre Cerda in 1940 and Ríos in 1946), would have had to break with the Communists at some point. As on both prior occasions, although international considerations of one sort or another were not

---

60 In October Kennecott was complaining that it had not been paid for the coal shipment it had arranged. See USNAW Memo, 23 July 1947, 825.5019/7–2347; Memo, 10 October 1947, 825.5019/10–1047.

61 USNAW, Memo, 2 August 1947, 825.00/8–2247.

62 USNAW, Memo, 14 October 1947, 825.5045/10–1447.

63 USNAW, Memo, 17 October 1947 825.5045/10–1747.

64 USNAW, Memo, 25 March 1948, 825.51/3–2548; Memo, 13 April 1948, 825.51/4–1348; Memo, 16 August 1948, 825.51/8–1648; Memo, 21 December 1948, 825.51/12–2148.

entirely absent, it was clearly domestic imperatives that were the key causes of the breach with the PCCh.

Although González Videla was a left-wing Radical who owed the PCCh a greater debt of personal gratitude than either of his predecessors, by August 1947 he faced a stark choice between left-wing economic and social policies and continued cooperation with the PCCh – a course that could only have led to constitutional deadlock and extraconstitutional attempts to oust him from office – or a conservative economic program and cooperation with the Right. By that time, with Cold War tensions affecting practically all Chilean parties, there was, in reality, no feasible middle course. Once having made his choice, González Videla's decision to seek confrontation with the PCCh, the strongest and most aggressive working-class party, can be seen as an attempt to cow and contain a labor movement whose quiescence was necessary for the success of his now conservative economic program.

Even if domestic factors alone would have resulted in a breach between González Videla and the PCCh, it seems clear that the October confrontation in the coal zone and the eventual proscription of the PCCh were primarily designed to convince the U.S. government of González Videla's commitment to the anti-Communist crusade. And, ironically enough, González Videla himself helped to create the need for such a demonstration of commitment by his efforts if not precisely to remain loyal to his Communist allies, at least to keep them in the political game long after it was wise in either domestic or international terms. Had he been able to convince the State Department of his "reliability" in the first months of his administration, and, above all, had he not continued to send out contradictory signals as to his real attitude toward the PCCh until well into 1947, he might well have saved Chile and the PCCh much of the trauma they subsequently experienced. However, the very qualities that had enabled him to rise to the front ranks of the Partido Radical and to become president hardly helped him in the task of convincing U.S. officials of his trustworthiness. An adept manipulator in love with the mechanics of the political game, he appeared to Ambassador Bowers, as late as July 1947, to be an opportunist who chose expediency before principle, seeking to appease the Communists for fear of provoking serious political and industrial disturbances.[65] Given such reports, it was not surprising that Washington withheld its help until it was impossible for González Videla to turn away from the anti-Communist crusade.

The October confrontation between González Videla and the PCCh was not the end of the story. Between November 1947 and September 1948, the party was allowed a slender legal existence although its newspapers

---

65 USNAW, Bowers to State, 11 July 1947, 825.00/7–1147.

were censored and its leaders were detained in an internment camp at Pisagua or were under police surveillance. In April 1948, however, the government presented a bill to outlaw the PCCh and exclude it from the country's political and trade union life. Although the bill was opposed by congressmen belonging to the Falange Nacional, most Socialists and a scattering of members from other parties – not excluding the Partido Conservador and including, of course, those Communist congressmen who were still sitting – it was passed by 93 to 20 votes in the Chamber of Deputies and by 31 votes to 8 in the Senate.[66]

Under the Ley de Defensa Permanente de la Democracia, dubbed the Ley Maldita by the PCCh, some 23,000 Communists were eventually struck off the electoral roll and hence excluded from holding public or trade union office.[67] Unions were purged of their Communist officials both before and after the passage of the Ley Maldita and, partly as a result, strike activity fell sharply during 1948 (only 1,203 workers involved in six illegal strikes) – although that probably owed more to the uncertainties generated by the general climate of repression and to wage increases generally in excess of rises in the cost of living than it did to the removal of the Communist officials. Union officials were not, of course, the only ones to suffer. During 1949 several hundred public servants, teachers, telegraphists, and postmen lost their jobs because of their party membership.[68]

The PCCh was not the only casualty of the Ley Maldita. The issue of the legal exclusion of the Communists caused fractionalization in all the major political parties except the Partido Liberal. Thus, right-wing Conservatives, who had long been resentful of the social christian proclivities of some of their party's leaders, broke away to found the Partido Conservador Tradicionalista; the left wing of the PR broke away to form the Partido Radical Doctrinario; and the bulk of the Socialists rejected the anti-Communist stance and tactics of Bernardo Ibáñez and founded the Partido Socialista Popular. Even the PCCh was not immune to divisive tendencies. Once the Ley Maldita had come into force, the question of the tactics to be used in the new circumstances caused a serious division; proponents of the armed struggle, including two Central Committee members, were expelled in 1949.[69]

Before concluding, perhaps a word should be said about the impact of the Cold War on Chile's foreign policy. During the presidential election campaign, González Videla had adopted a somewhat independent stance,

66 *La Opinión*, 13 May and 14 August 1948.

67 La Dirección del Registro Electoral, *La Ley de Defensa de la Democracia* (Santiago, 1950).

68 USNAW, Bowers to State, 25 August 1949, 825.00B/8–2549.

69 Carmelo Furci, *The Chilean Communist Party and the Road to Socialism*, (London, 1984), pp. 46–52.

advocating the strengthening of Latin American economic and cultural
ties and a Latin American unity that would enable the continent to deal
with the Great Powers on an equal footing.[70] At the same time, however,
he had also made the usual commitments to the maintenance of friendly
relations with the United States and to the principles of hemispheric
solidarity. It could be argued, then, that when González Videla duly fell
in line behind the United States, endorsing U.S. military plans for the
continent and severing recently established relations with the Soviet Union
and the Soviet bloc countries, he was merely fulfilling his campaign
commitments. And it does seem to be true that in breaking off relations
with the Soviets, he was not responding to any direct pressure or request
from the State Department. Similarly, despite Chilean expectations, State
Department pressure was not exerted to torpedo the commercial treaty
with Argentina that González Videla had pursued in the early months of
his administration when Argentina (under Perón) was still the bête noire
of the United States in Latin America.[71] In fact, while the Cold War
obviously did have an impact on Chile's foreign policy, González Videla
was not responding to specific directions or suggestions from the State
Department so much as to his own perceptions of the realities of Chile's
situation. As he himself put it when explaining his breach with the
Communists to Socialist workers in January 1948: "El Jefe del Estado
veía claramente que Chile, república incrustada en el continente ameri-
cano, con una economía débil y dependiente, no podía salirse de la órbita
en que la geografía la había clavado."[72]

In the final analysis, it is still rather difficult to give a precise weighting
to the Cold War factor in the development of Chilean politics in the
immediate postwar period. Clearly it had an impact on the sharpening
antagonisms between Socialists and Communists in late 1945, but given
the deep-seated rivalry between the two parties, the deteriorating international climate was as much an excuse for the reinitiation of customary
hostilities as it was a cause. However, it may well be that the division
of the CTCh would not have been sustained for very long without the
Cold War and the resources that it made available to the Socialist faction.
Clearly, too, the Cold War was partly responsible for the exclusion of the
PCCh from González Videla's cabinet and for its eventual proscription.
Yet even here it could be argued that the exclusion of the Communists

---

70 For an expression of these views, see González Videla's letter to the PS printed in *El Siglo*, 16
   July 1946.
71 For the reaction of State Department officials to the prospect of the Argentine treaty, see USNAW,
   W.E. Dunn to State, 12 February 1947, 825.50/2–1247; Memo, Wells to Lyon, 18 December
   1946, 825.51/12–1846.
72 *El Mercurio*, 1 February 1948.

from the cabinet was primarily a consequence of the country's sharp economic difficulties and the logistics of party strengths in Congress. And there is no need to look outside Chile for the origin of the move to proscribe the party. Such an objective had long been the ambition of some sectors of the Chilean Right, which had tried to outlaw the PCCh in the 1930s and which had actually succeeded in 1941 only to have the bill vetoed by Aguirre Cerda. More recently, the paramilitary Acción Chilena Anti-Comunista (AChA) had made its appearance in 1946 and a national campaign to outlaw the PCCh, which drew support from anti-Communists from across the political spectrum, was launched in June 1947.[73]

In essence, then, in Chile the Cold War had the effect of exacerbating existing factionalisms and encouraging already established tendencies rather than that of initiating novel departures. Perhaps because of that, the actual process of excluding the PCCh from Chile's political and trade union life, though traumatic at the time, was, by more modern standards, a relatively mild affair.

73 For an account of AChA by one of its founders, see Arturo Olavarría Bravo, *Chile entre dos Alessandri* (Santiago, 1962), vol. 2, pp. 41–53. For a fuller and more recent account, see Carlos Maldonado, *AChA y la proscripción del Partido Comunista en Chile* (Santiago, 1989), FLACSO Documentos. no. 60. AChA approached U.S. ambassador Bowers for help in obtaining arms but was given a dusty refusal (USNAW, Bowers to Wright, 4 August 1947, 825.00/8–447). Even so, AChA did acquire arms and embarked on a sporadic campaign against the Communists that claimed some lives. After the passage of the Ley Maldita, AChA's involvement in an aborted military coup plot earned it governmental hostility and hastened its disbandment in early 1949.

# 3

# Argentina

## Mario Rapoport

The 1929 world crisis had an impact on Argentina different in many aspects from the rest of Latin America. The reasons for this can be found not only in the specific effect of the crisis itself on the Argentine economy and society but also in the changes that had occurred in Argentina's political system and in Argentina's international relations since the First World War.

In 1916 the leader of the Partido Radical (PR), Hipólito Yrigoyen, became president in the first truly democratic elections in Argentine history, putting an end to the succession of ideologically liberal but oligarchic governments that had run the country since the mid-nineteenth century. In September 1930, however, a coup d'état led by General José Félix Uriburu led to the restoration of the old conservative oligarchy to power. Thus in Argentina in the 1930s the process of import substitution industrialization did not occur within the framework of democratic or populist politics as in many Latin American countries, but under the auspices of conservative governing elites and a repressive, authoritarian political regime, even though democratic institutions were formally preserved.

Although the essentially agro-export structure of Argentina's economy had not changed, since the First World War a triangular system of foreign trade had been established whose major axes were the United States, the major exporter of goods to Argentina, and Great Britain, the major importer of Argentine goods, and increasingly the United States had displaced Britain in the financial field.[1] Nevertheless, contrary to what occurred in the rest of Latin America in the 1930s, the British recovered ground in Argentina, because the interests of the landowning sectors,

---

1 See Mario Rapoport, *Gran Bretaña, Estados Unidos y las clases dirigentes argentinas, 1940–1945* (Buenos Aires, 1981); Mario Rapoport, "El triángulo argentino, las relaciones con EE.UU. y Gran Bretaña," *Todo Es Historia* (henceforth *TEH*) 154 (March 1980).

which had regained political power in 1930, were more closely linked to Britain and the rest of Europe than to the United States. On the contrary, Argentine and U.S. interests clashed. In spite of its economic penetration of Argentina, the United States could never establish a lasting alliance with a sector of the ruling classes, as the British had done. This was of vital importance during the Second World War and in the immediate postwar years and favored the tendency toward neutral and nationalist stances that predominated in Argentina at that time.

The Depression years witnessed substantial changes in Argentina's industrial development, including the growth of certain branches of manufacturing (textiles and light metallurgy in particular) and the massive absorption of wage-earning labor.[2] These new factories produced for the domestic market and took over from foreign, particularly British, interests. Many were medium and small enterprises based on intensive use of labor with only very limited incorporation of new machinery or technology. A characteristic of the 1930s and the Second World War was the serious lack of capital and the rapid obsolescence of existing capital goods.

It was not under Juan Domingo Perón, but under the conservative governments of the 1930s, with their liberal economic ideology, that the state began to intervene systematically in the Argentine economy. The regulation and centralization of the banking system through the establishment of the Banco Central, the implementation of exchange control and income tax, and the setting up of a large number of control boards, advisory commissions and so forth, which covered almost all the country's productive activities, marked the beginning of a new type of economic policy that Perón would continue to pursue, though for different purposes. As in the case of the industrialization process, these governments used economic interventionism as a temporary device to deal with the world crisis and to protect their own interests, but they were unable or did not have the time to retrace their steps.[3]

These years also saw the start of the participation of the military in the economy and their interest in the development of basic sectors connected with the war industry. Strategic concerns, particularly due to the military buildup of Brazil; nationalist ideas, reinforced by the refusal of the United States to supply armaments; and a more active interest in Argentine politics, strengthened this tendency. The development of Yacimientos Petrolíferos Fiscales (the state oil company), the installation of Fábrica Militar de Aviones in Córdoba, General Manuel Savio's attempts

2 See Adolfo Dorfman, *Evolución industrial argentina* (Buenos Aires, 1942); Javier Villanueva, "El origen de la industrialización argentina," *Desarrollo Económico* (henceforth *DE*) 47 (October–December 1972); and Jorge Schvarzer, "Los avatares de la industria argentina," *TEH* 124 (September 1977).

3 Alejandro Bunge, *Una nueva Argentina* (Buenos Aires, 1984), pp. 286–96.

to implement an iron and steel industry, and, in the early 1940s, the setting up of Fabricaciones Militares are the main landmarks indicating the increased military presence in the economic sphere.[4] To some extent this explains the fact that the military was able to act as proxy for a weak, local industrial bourgeoisie and participated, through Perón, in a political undertaking to which they would in fact give only limited support.

Meanwhile, the political system was proving to be extremely fragile and was to show an increasing decline, which would culminate in the military coup d'état of June 1943. After the initial predominance of nationalist and corporativist elements during the brief presidency of Uriburu (1930–2), the liberal oligarchy was able to return to political power under the government of General Agustín P. Justo (1932–8), through the so-called Concordancia coalition that included Conservatives, "anti-personalist" Radicals, and right-wing Socialists. But their chances of staying in power constitutionally were based on fraudulent elections and political repression, an anachronism that held up the above mentioned economic and social transformations.[5]

The international situation did not favor these governments either. The predominance of the pro-British sectors, symbolized by the signing of the Roca–Runciman Pact in 1933 and by confrontations in international forums with the United States, which with its Good Neighbor Policy was seeking to consolidate its hegemony throughout the Americas in view of the possible outbreak of war in Europe, produced tensions and splits within the ruling classes. On the one hand, there appeared pro-American sectors; on the other, there developed right-wing, nationalist tendencies that had much in common with fascism and nazism.[6]

The reestablishment of a genuinely democratic system and later the policy of neutrality in the war were to become the hub of serious disagreements. President Roberto M. Ortiz, who took over from Justo in 1938, encouraged changes in both domestic and foreign policies that he was unable to see through because of ill-health and attacks from his adversaries; Ramón J. Castillo, his vice-president, who replaced him in 1940, was on the contrary determined to maintain the existing political system and the policy of neutrality in the war, despite pressure from the United States. The situation then became intolerable. The power vacuum could not be filled by the opposition political parties, particularly not by the PR, discredited by its performance during this period and lacking any outstanding leader. It was the military initially, and Perón later, who

4  See Robert Potash, *El ejército y la política en la Argentina, 1928–1945* (Buenos Aires, 1981); Alain Rouquié, *Poder militar y sociedad política en la Argentina* (Buenos Aires, 1981); María del Carmen Angueira and Alicia del Carmen Tonini, *Capitalismo de estado (1927–1956)* (Buenos Aires, 1986).
5  See Alberto Ciria, *Partidos y poder en la Argentina moderna 1930–1946* (Buenos Aires, 1985).
6  See Rapoport, *Gran Bretaña;* Cristián Buchrucker, *Nacionalismo y Peronismo* (Buenos Aires, 1987).

filled this vacuum and initiated a new stage in Argentine history. At the same time, changes "from below" were also taking place, and it is necessary to bear in mind the extent of these changes if we are to understand the subsequent course of events in the immediate postwar period and the possibility that it might have turned out differently. Consequently, it is necessary to make a detailed analysis of the role of the labor movement and of the political parties of the Left.

Despite the description "infamous decade" acquired by the period 1930–43 because of its political corruption, fraudulent elections, and repressive policies, for the labor movement this period was a significant stage in its development, and for the left-wing parties, a culminating point in their participation in Argentine political and trade union life. External events undoubtedly contributed to this. While these years saw the high point of fascism and the rise to power of nazism, they also witnessed the Popular Fronts and hopes for the outcome of the Spanish Civil War. The consolidation of Soviet power, when Stalinism still enjoyed a halo of prestige, and the political changes in the United States under Roosevelt and the New Deal reformist initiatives, were also a powerful encouragement to the development of the Argentine Left.

Nevertheless, developments on the domestic front were decisive. The trade unions and left-wing parties began to occupy a space in public life that had hitherto been denied them or that, for ideological reasons, they themselves had refused to fill. In the first place, the final ousting of the anarchists from the leadership of the labor movement strengthened the reformist tendencies and the bureaucratization of the trade union leadership and gave the trade union organizations a stronger institutional profile. Secondly, in September 1930, the same month in which Uriburu carried out his coup d'état, the Confederación General del Trabajo (CGT) was founded, providing temporary unity for the labor movement. Within a few years, the CGT was to divide into two main groupings the CGT-1 and the CGT-2. However, the founding of the CGT indicated a desire for unity that Peronism would develop and consolidate. This was also evident in the setting up of single unions for each branch of industry, a principle upheld by Socialists and Communists and that Peronism would later use to consolidate its control over the labor movement. Thirdly, the 1930s meant the decline of "syndicalism," which had predominated in the Radical period and which rejected the identification of the working class with a political party.[7] In 1935 the syndicalists lost control of the

---

7 The "syndicalist" line in the Argentine labor movement, originally "revolutionary" and then predominantly "reformist," was a "purely worker trend" and "not political," so that "union unity"

CGT, which from then on was controlled by Socialist trade union leaders. Socialists, and to a lesser extent Communists, led the labor movement until 1943, although, as we shall see, two opposing tendencies soon appeared within Socialist trade unionism, which led to the split in the CGT. Fourthly, while the traditional trade unions – particularly the unions of railwaymen, commercial workers, and municipal workers, all connected with the agro-export economy and the transport and services sector – continued to predominate in this period, workers in new branches of industry began to organize and hitherto unknown trade union leaders came to play a leading role in many of the toughest conflicts of the 1930s and early 1940s.[8]

Academic discussion on the origins of Peronism has tended to minimize the importance of these processes, preferring to emphasize the continuing low level of unionization among the workers. It was, it is argued, Perón himself who won over the inexperienced and unpoliticized mass of workers recently arrived from the rural areas via the internal migrations that accompanied the industrialization process. Criticism by historians of this sociologically based, rather simplistic view has shown the importance of the "historic" trade unions and trade union leadership in the formation of Peronism.[9]

And for the first time, Marxists had entered the leadership of the labor movement, although for many leaders this Marxism was somewhat superficial. They differed little from the syndicalists of an earlier period; many of them had in fact themselves been syndicalists. The issue is significant because the responsibility for the actions of the labor movement in the 1940s lay partly in the hands of the trade union leadership of the parties with which it was connected. If Perón was able to win many of these leaders and the workers they represented over to his cause, it was not only because of his social policy, which satisfied old trade union and left-wing political party claims, nor simply because of the repression of those sectors that obstinately opposed him. The reasons for the Peronist

was above ideological disputes. See Hugo del Campo, El "sindicalismo revolucionario" (1905–1945) (Buenos Aires, 1986), pp. 9–20.

8 For a detailed analysis of the history of the Argentine labor movement during the 1930s and 1940s, see Hiroschi Matsushita, Movimiento obrero argentino, 1930–1945 (Buenos Aires, 1983); Hugo del Campo, Sindicalismo y peronismo (Buenos Aires, 1983). For the approach, from different ideological viewpoints, of leaders of the labor movement, see Alberto Belloni, Del anarquismo al peronismo (Buenos Aires, 1960); Rubens Iscaro, Historia del movimiento sindical, vol. 2 (Buenos Aires, 1973); Alfredo López, Historia del movimiento social y la clase obrera argentina (Buenos Aires, 1971).

9 Matsushita, Movimiento obrero; del Campo, Sindicalismo; M. Murmis and J.C. Portantiero, Estudios sobre los orígenes del peronismo, vol. 1 (Buenos Aires, 1972); Walter Little, "La organización obrera y el estado peronista, 1943–1955," DE 75(1979); Joel Horowitz, "Ideologías sindicales y políticas estatales en la Argentina, 1930–1943," DE 94(1984); Louise Doyon, "La organización del movimiento sindical peronista, 1946–1955," DE 94(1984).

success, and therefore the defeat of the Left, must also be sought in the social base and ideology of the Left itself, and in the political errors committed by both Socialists and Communists during this period.

The Partido Socialista (PS), founded at the end of the nineteenth century, was led from the start by men such as Juan B. Justo, Nicolás Repetto, and others, whose Marxism was influenced more by Bernstein than by Marx himself. Their vision of social change was reformist, not revolutionary. The "mission" of the proletariat, according to Justo, was to "ask for" and to obtain improved living conditions from the bourgeoisie, not to take power. On the other hand, the Socialist leader despised "national politics" and the inorganic parties, which led him to fight primarily against the Radicals rather than the Conservatives, of whom "Justoist" socialism came to consider itself a kind of "loyal opposition," along the lines of the British Labor Movement.[10]

With regard to the "national issue" and the question of imperialism, Justo attached no real importance to them, and in the economic field he upheld liberal ideas because he found a justification for free trade in the lower cost of living this policy meant, according to him, for the working classes. Justoist socialism also placed great emphasis on the effectiveness of parliamentary action for achieving its political objectives and did not conceive of the party as class-based – from its viewpoint the social base of such a party should include other sectors as well as the proletariat.

In the course of its history up to the advent of Peronism, the PS experienced several splits, two of which stand out clearly: that of the left-wing group that set up the Partido Socialista Internacional, later the Partido Comunista (PC) in 1918; and the right-wing group that in 1927 established the Partido Socialista Independiente, which joined the Conservative Concordancia coalition in the 1930s.[11] The PS was weakened by these and other splits or separations, although the new political sit-

10  For an overview of the history of socialism by one of its leaders, see Jacinto Oddone, *Historia del socialismo argentino,* 2 vols. (Buenos Aires, 1983). For a critical view from the Left, see José Ratzer, *El movimiento socialista en Argentina* (Buenos Aires, 1981). The ideas of Juan B. Justo can be found in his book *Teoría y práctica de la historia* (Buenos Aires, 1909), and the progress of the PS's newspaper can be followed in Roberto Reinoso, comp., La Vanguardia: *Selección de textos (1894–1955)* (Buenos Aires, 1985).

11  The most important leaders of independent socialism, Federico Pinedo and Antonio de Tomaso, took an active part in the military coup of September 1930 and were ministers in the Conservative governments that developed from it. Together with a number of brilliant technocrats of Socialist origin such as Raúl Prebisch, Ernesto Malaccorto, and others, they were in fact the main instigators of the economic policy of those governments. Pinedo boasted of having been one of the few Argentines to have read Marx's *Das Kapital* in German. Pinedo's testimony regarding his performance during those years can be found in Federico Pinedo, *En tiempos de la República* (Buenos Aires, 1946). An analysis of independent socialism can be found in Horacio Sanguinetti, *Los socialistas independientes* (Buenos Aires, 1982).

uation resulting from the coup d'état of September 1930 was, paradoxically, to operate in its favor. On the one hand, the ban on and later
absenteeism of the PR, the major political force, and the lack of other
alternatives were to allow PS to triumph in the elections of 1931, winning
43 seats in the Chamber of Deputies and 2 in the Senate (compared with
only 4 deputies in 1929 and 1 in 1930). In the presidential elections,
the main opposition political grouping had a Socialist as candidate for
vice-president. Keeping to the rules of the game, despite the fact that
the democratic system was a mere fabrication due to fraudulent elections,
proscriptions, and political repression, the PS proposed a large number
of projects, questioned ministers, protested against government policy
and methods, denounced the rise of fascism in Europe, and, later on
during the war, supported Argentine participation in the conflict on the
side of the Allies. Many laws in favor of the workers and other types of
law, such as suffrage for women, that were subsequently passed under
Peronism, originated in Socialist initiatives. But practically none of them
managed to win approval at the time, and the futility of the work of the
Socialist deputies and senators became evident toward the end of the
1930s when the party lost a considerable amount of its electoral support.
Its position was made worse by the return of the PR to active politics.
The Socialist electoral successes were due, in fact, to temporary support
from middle-class sectors and were restricted to the city of Buenos Aires,
since the party lacked a presence in the provinces.[12]

At the same time, as we have seen, the Partido Socialista also had some
success in the labor movement as syndicalism and anarchism, which had
predominated during the period before 1930, lost influence and followers.
However, the involvement of the PS in the labor movement suffered from
certain inherent weaknesses that, as happened at the electoral level, were
later reflected in a rapid loss of influence. In the first place, the ideological
base of the Socialist leaders was very poor or fragile. Many of them, such
as the long-time head of the CGT, José Domenech, hardly differed in
their conduct or viewpoints from the old syndicalist leaders. They tried
not to involve the labor movement in politics and, save for rare exceptions,
based their struggle on union claims.[13] Secondly, the leadership of the
PS consisted mainly of middle-class intellectuals and their attitude toward
the labor movement was distant and paternalistic. They seemed to be
afraid of the influence of trade union leaders within the party since most
of the latter, some enjoying considerable prestige or in control of large

---

12 Ciria, *Partidos y poder*, pp. 175–82; Nicolás Repetto, *Mi paso por la política: De Uriburu a Perón*
   (Buenos Aires, 1957), pp. 88–98. Repetto, one of the main leaders of the PS, besides the
   testimony he provides regarding his party's policy during those years, defends its reformist
   character and states his personal differences with Marxist thought.
13 Matsushita, *Movimiento obrero*, pp. 136–7.

unions, such as Domenech himself or the commercial union leader Angel Borlenghi, played no part in the running of the party. There was thus a gap between politicians and trade unionists of which Perón took full advantage, winning over important Socialist trade union leaders in a short space of time.[14] By separating the unions from the broader political action or subordinating them to it, the PS was thus unable to meet the challenge from Peronism in the struggle to win over the union leaders and their supporters.

The subsequent loss of Socialist influence in the labor movement can also be explained by the fact that the trade unions controlled by the PS were the most traditional ones connected with the old agro-export structure: for example, railway workers, commercial employees, municipal workers, and so forth. Due to its ideology – basically subscribing to free trade and unquestioning as to the foundations of the country's economic development – and to its overwhelming concern with its political and parliamentary tasks, the PS failed to understand the far-reaching effects of the industrialization process and consequently did not develop a specific policy with regard to the new labor sectors joining it. Socialist trade unionism was a more faithful reflection of the country prior to 1930 than of the one emerging as a result of the industrialization process that took place during the 1930s.

Like the Partido Socialista, the Partido Comunista developed into a respectable political force during the 1920s and 1930s.[15] Of the initial founders of the new party, two leaders finally stood out from among the rest after various internal struggles similar to those that occurred in all international Communist movements: Victorio Codovilla and Rodolfo Ghioldi. Codovilla became an outstanding leader of the Comintern in Latin America and Europe and, up to the Second World War, spent many years abroad. He was an intimate of Stalin's, and in Spain, for example, he was one of the leading advisers to the Spanish Communist Party during the 1936–9 Civil War. Ghioldi, brother of the Socialist leader, Américo, though less important, played a decisive role in the negative profile of Peronism and during his life led the party's anti-Peronist line. One characteristic of both these men, and of the PC's leadership in general, was their unconditional support of the Soviet Union.[16]

14 del Campo, *Sindicalismo*, p. 61; Matsushita, *Movimiento obrero*, pp. 63–5, 104–8.
15 See Emilio J. Corbiere, *Orígenes del comunismo argentino* (Buenos Aires, 1984), pp. 50–6; José Ratzer, *El movimiento;* Partido Comunista, *Esbozo de historia del Partido Comunista de la Argentina* (Buenos Aires, 1947); Otto Vargas, *El marxismo y la revolución argentina* (Buenos Aires, 1987).
16 There are no biographies of Codovilla and Ghioldi, but their careers can be followed in the books cited in note 15 on the origins and history of the PC, as in the critical works of Jorge Abelardo Ramos, *El Partido Comunista en la política argentina* (Buenos Aires, 1962); Rodolfo Puiggrós, *Las izquierdas y el problema nacional* (Buenos Aires, 1973), and *El peronismo, sus causas* (Buenos Aires,

Two events provide the key to the Partido Comunista's behavior in this period – indeed throughout its history: the Seventh Congress of the Comintern in 1935 and the Second World War. Until the mid-1930s the PC had followed an erratic path, shaken by similar faction fighting as other Communist Parties and with expulsions or splits of left-wing or right-wing groups. It was only in 1928 that the party's leadership began to clarify more precisely its profile of the country and the nature of the revolution that should take place, giving up the old slogans of struggle against capitalism in general and locating the main enemies of the working class among the landowning oligarchy and imperialism. [17] However, the conclusions of the Fifth Congress of the Comintern and the description of social democracy as "the moderate wing of fascism," which in Germany contributed to the advent of nazism, were also to permeate the policy of the PC. Besides isolating the party from the other left-wing forces, this line would lead it to describe Yrigoyen's Radical government, a month before its fall to the conservative military coup d'état, as a "government of the capitalist reaction," pointing out its "repressive, reactionary, fascistic policy against the struggles of the proletariat," and accusing it of applying "terrorist methods." As a result of these standpoints, the PC was to have great difficulty in establishing itself within the working class and other popular sectors, as is recognized in the party's own "official history." [18]

The 1930s opened with governments much more inclined to suppress communism and persecute its militants, many of whom were detained, tortured, and sent to remote prisons. In spite of this, the PC began to

1969); Juan José Real, *Treinta años de historia argentina,* (Buenos Aires, 1976). (Puiggrós and Real were ex-leaders of the PC.) See also Robert Alexander, *Communism in Latin America* (New Brunswick, N.J., 1957), where he shows the important role played by Codovilla as representative of the Comintern in the organization of the Latin American Communist movement. A brief description of Codovilla can also be found in U.S. National Archives (henceforth USNA), Hoover to Lyon, 18 March 1946, 835–00B/3–1846. With regard to Rodolfo Ghioldi's well-known anti-Peronism, a State Department document shows how at a party congress after Perón's 1946 election victory, Ghioldi still held a hard line position with regard to the new president: see USNA, State Department (DOS), O'Donoghue to DOS, Buenos Aires, 29 May 1947, 833–00B/5–2947. Codovilla, and most of the leadership of the PC, adopted a more conciliatory position, though several leaders who proposed greater rapprochement with Peronism were removed. Among Ghioldi's international activities, we should remember his collaboration with Prestes in Brazil, for which he spent several years in prison: see Partido Comunista, *Esbozo de historia,* p. 90.

17 Partido Comunista, *Esbozo de historia,* pp. 64–6. The change took place at the Eighth Congress of the PC. A year later the Conference of Latin American Communist Parties was held in Buenos Aires, where the same theses were reaffirmed.

18 For an analysis of the general line of the international Communist movement, see Fernando Claudin, *La crisis del movimiento comunista,* (Barcelona, 1978), pp. 118–19. On the PC's position with regard to Yrigoyen, see Partido Comunista, *Esbozo de historia,* p. 70; and Rodolfo Puiggrós, *Las izquierdas.*

establish itself more firmly within the labor movement and to set up parallel organizations, such as International Red Aid, which would play an important role in subsequent years. But sectarianism continued to predominate among the leadership, preventing participation by Communists in Argentine political life.[19]

The Seventh Congress of the Comintern and the Popular Front policy in 1935, later encouraged by the movement to aid Republican Spain, enabled the PC to consolidate, however, and gave it a certain amount of influence among the workers and the lower classes. It also began to establish links with political and economic sectors, including Conservative leaders who would be useful to it during the Second World War.[20]

The PC carried out its activities in the labor movement between 1930 and 1935 through the Comité de Unidad Sindical Clasista, helping to set up and create several unions that undertook various actions and strikes during this period, for example, the meat workers and timber workers strikes.[21] After the trade union "coup d'état" of December 1935, through which the CGT acquired a majority Socialist leadership, the Communists, who since the middle of the year had adopted the new Popular Front strategy, began to support the CGT, from which they had previously remained aloof. In the construction guild, one of the most combative of the period, the Communists organized a new union and led several important strikes in 1935. A year later they set up the Federación Nacional de Obreros de la Construcción (FNOC), thus triggering the introduction of single trade unions per industry. It was due to this struggle by the construction workers and other conflicts that, in January 1936, the CGT declared its first general strike, which had considerable repercussions on the public.[22]

19 See Partido Comunista, *Esbozo de historia,* which is, of course, biased, but contains valuable information, particularly in the notes.

20 Later we shall see some actual cases that exemplify these relations, but in his memoirs the son of the famous journalist of the period, Natalio Botana, director of the newspaper *Crítica,* tells how Conservative politicians such as Huberto Vignart or Manuel Fresco, the pro-fascist governor of Buenos Aires, and Communist leaders such as Victorio Codovilla or the "aristocratic" Rodolfo Aráoz Alfaro, used to lunch "elbow to elbow" at his father's house. See Helvio Botana, *Memorias, tras los dientes del perro* (Buenos Aires, 1977), p. 115.

21 Iscaro, *Historia del movimiento,* pp. 219–22.

22 The name "trade union coup d'état" was given to the forcible takeover of the CGT by Socialist leaders after a serious conflict with the syndicalists, who had been running the trade union central office until then. The leaders of the deposed CGT set up another, minority, organization, the CGT Catamarca. From then on, the Socialists, allied with the Communists, ran the original CGT, which included the great majority of the existing trade unions. See Matsushita, *Movimiento obrero,* pp. 141–7. For the construction strike, the role of that union and of the Communists, see Iscaro, *Historia del movimiento,* pp. 222–5. Iscaro, Communist construction leader, was one of the agitators of the struggles during this period. Matsushita (*Movimiento obrero,* pp. 163–6)

In spite of the fact that the syndicalist sector split away, as a result of the trade union coup d'état, the leadership of the CGT, now called the CGT Independencia from the place where it had its headquarters, led the majority of the labor movement until the beginning of the 1940s. However, there followed new confrontations of great significance for the future course of events, this time between the Socialists themselves, a sector of whom allied with the Communists. The dividing line was now the degree of participation workers should have in political action and the links between the trade unions and the political parties. José Domenech, who from 1937 would be general secretary of the CGT, accepted collaboration with the political forces and had confidence in parliamentary activity, but he refused to go any further and advocated trade union independence in relation to the parties. The leader of the Unión de Obreros Municipales (UOM), Pérez Leirós, and the Communists wanted closer relations between politics and trade unionism.

One example of these differences was the degree of support the CGT gave to the Republican cause in the Spanish Civil War. Although the CGT at once expressed its solidarity with that cause and set up an aid commission headed by Pérez Leirós, no delegate was sent to Spain. The attitude toward fascism and toward government policy would provoke similar discrepancies, which would lead in 1942 to the final split in the CGT in the pre-Perón period.[23]

In short, the participation of the Communists in the labor movement during those years had a considerable influence. This influence was felt particularly in trade unions in the newly developing industries, such as textiles and metalworking, and in such important sectors for the country's economic activity as the construction industry, meatpacking, and the timber industry. After their incorporation into the CGT, they exerted a strong influence in the overall trade union leadership, obtaining as many as 15 of the 47 seats on the Central Committee. Among other things, they promoted the setting up of a university for workers in which outstanding left-wing intellectuals participated.[24]

and del Campo (*Sindicalismo* pp. 94–8) make detailed analyses of the advance of the Communists in the trade union movement and their change of tactics after 1935.

23 See Matsushita, *Movimiento obrero*, pp. 166–77; López *Historia del movimiento social*, pp. 335–6, 353–61; Iscaro, *Historia del movimiento*, pp. 239–43.

24 See del Campo, *Sindicalismo*, pp. 95–8. José Peter, Communist leader of the meat union, describes in his memoirs the participation of the Communists in this union, which they organized and developed (José Peter, *Crónicas proletarias* [Buenos Aires, 1968], pp. 140–7, just as Rubens Iscaro relates what happened in the construction union. On the Universidad Obrero Argentina (UOA), see *Universidad Obero Argentina* (Buenos Aires, 1940), where there is a description of its history and activities. The UOA was set up in May 1938 by a group of university students and was to be "a workers' school where workers may: a) acquire general culture; b) improve their skill in their trades; c) train to present union claims, and d) become educated to participate in national

The Communists also benefited from the appearance of a leftist movement within socialism that in 1937 founded the Partido Socialista Obrero whose main leaders, such as Benito Marianetti, ended up joining the PC.[25]

Aid to Republican Spain was another important field of activity and expansion for the Communists and would later serve as experience for the setting up of similar movements during the Second World War. Some important Communist leaders even took part in the International Brigades or collaborated with the Republican government or with the leadership of the Spanish Communist Party, as in the case of Juan José Real, José Belloqui, and Victorio Codovilla. When the Republicans were defeated a number of Communists took refuge in Argentina and established a branch of the Spanish Communist Party that was active in subsequent years both in Argentina and in Spain.[26]

The 1930s also saw a great development among the left-wing intelligentsia. The phenomenon of the publishing house Editorial Claridad, which published widely read books and magazines and had the collaboration of Socialists and Communists, the participation of left-wing writers (several of them Communist leaders), in such newspapers as *Crítica,* and in general the mobilization of the intelligentsia in aid of the Spanish Republic and against fascism, were all unprecedented in Argentina and have not been much studied by historians.[27]

civic progress." Its first board of directors included, among other, the Socialist Carlos Sanchez Viamonte, the Radical Arturo Frondizi, and the Communist Rodolfo Aráoz Alfaro. The instructors and lecturers included well-known intellectuals, politicians, and trade unionists such as the Communists Rodolfo Puiggrós, Manuel Sadovsky, Haymes Duncan, (Jr.), Samuel Schmerkin; the Socialists Sergio Bagú, Juan Atilio Bramuglia, Rómulo Baglioli, Jacinto Oddone, and other well-known figures such as Adolfo Dorfman and Mario Bunge.

25 See Partido Comunista, *Esbozo de historia,* p. 84; Ratzer, *Movimiento socialista,* pp. 171–4; Benito Marianetti, *Argentina, realidad y perspectivas* (Buenos Aires) pp. 380–4. After joining the PC, Marianetti was immediately appointed as a member of the party's Central Committee.

26 On the attitudes of public opinion, government, and political parties toward the Spanish Civil War, see Mark Falcoff, "Argentina," in *The Spanish Civil War, 1936–1939: American Hemispheric Perspectives,* ed. Mark Falcoff and Frederick B. Pike (Lincoln, NB, 1982), pp. 291–348. On the role of the Communists, see Partido Comunista, *Esbozo de historia,* p. 85; Iscaro, *Historia del movimiento,* p. 238; Real, *Treinta años,* pp. 68–71. Víctor Alba in *El Partido Comunista en España* (Barcelona, 1979) shows the importance of Codovilla in the running of the Spanish Communist Party during the war, where he was one of the major figures sent by the Comintern: "They clung to 'Fatty' or the 'Banker,' as they used to nickname Codovilla," says Alba, "and they followed all his indications" (pp. 134–5). But in the 1920s, Codovilla had already belonged to a commission charged by that body to reorganize the party (p. 94). With regard to the branch of the Spanish Communist Party organized in exile in Buenos Aires, see USNA, Hoover to Lyon, 2 May 1946, Spanish Communist Activities in Argentina, 835–00B/5–246.

27 On Editorial Claridad, see the articles on its influence during the 1920s and 1930s by José Barcia, " 'Claridad' una editorial de pensamiento"; Ernesto Giúdici, " 'Claridad' en la década del 30"; Saúl N. Bagú, "La revista 'Claridad' "; Elías Castelnuovo, "Antonio Zamora"; Sergio Bagú, "De

Thus the Left progressed during these years in Congress, in the labor movement and among the intelligentsia. From the more general perspective of its influence on Argentine politics, however, its efforts did not achieve a great deal. In the case of the Socialists, some of the reasons for this failure have already been indicated. In the case of the Communists, it was even more striking. Their political decline occurred when the prestige of the USSR and the international Communist movement was at its height, during the Second World War, and at a time when they had managed to build up a solid core of around 20,000 members and 50,000 supporters, according to U.S. government estimates.[28]

In 1938 a new president, Roberto M. Ortiz, took over the government of Argentina. Ortiz, like Roque Saenz Peña at the start of the century, realized that there was a dangerous power vacuum and that the system's economic foundations could be at risk unless its political structures were changed "from above." And to do so meant giving up fraudulent electoral practices, thus giving the main opposition party, the Partido Radical, the chance of becoming the government and, in a more general sense, making political life more democratic.[29] But Ortiz was ill and was soon criticized and attacked by his own conservative supporters. He very soon had to leave the government, which was left in the hands of Vice-President Castillo, a traditional conservative willing to uphold the existing political customs and the system of repression.

There were also considerable differences between Ortiz and Castillo on the question of international politics. Whereas the former seemed to be prepared to reach a better understanding with the United States and to endorse Pan-Americanism, the latter kept to the traditional anti-American attitude predominant among the traditional oligarchy that always leaned more toward Great Britain and Europe. When the Second World War broke out, Argentina was to face the paradox of having a nominal president, Ortiz, who supported the Allies and adopted an attitude of active support for them; and a vice-president, Castillo, acting as president, who

'Claridad' a 'Eudeba' "; Héctor F. Miri, "Un libro de 0,50"; and Emilio J. Corbiere, "Un templo de la cultura popular"; all published in the magazine *Todo Es Historia* 172 (September 1981). The founder and prime mover of Claridad was the Socialist Antonio Zamora. This publishing house published a large number of Marxist works, including Lenin and other Russian authors. It also published a magazine. Around this time, the PC set up other minor publishing companies, such as Editorial Problemas and Editorial Lautaro. Two American reports give details on the organization and operation of these two publishing companies, see USNA, Hoover to Lyon, Washington, 17 June 1946, 835–OOB/6–1746. On *Crítica*, several well-known Communists, such as Paulino González Alberdi, Ernesto Giúdici, and Héctor Pablo Agosti, worked on the newspaper. See Botana, *Memorias*, p. 102.

28 USNA, Hoover to Lyon, Washington, 2 May 1946, 835.OOB/5–246.
29 See Félix Luna, *Ortiz, reportaje a la Argentina opulenta* (Buenos Aires, 1978).

was in favor of neutrality and determined to keep the country out of the war. But Castillo held the reins of power and, furthermore, in July 1942, Ortiz finally succumbed to his illness. Argentina adopted a neutral position with regard to the two sides at war and was thus involved in a serious conflict with the United States up to the immediate postwar period.

Ortiz's brief period in power was also one of illusions for the Left, particularly the Partido Comunista, which decided to support him in all measures intended to regain constitutional normality and to criticize him in those that might mean reconciliation with the oligarchy and imperialism. This meant a change in the party's policy of some considerable significance. It initiated a position of "critical support" for certain governments, which would later be repeated, but above all it meant a favorable attitude toward a conservative ruler from the oligarchy whom they were supposed to be combating and who had been fraudulently elected. In fact, for the PC it was the start of an open policy that included collaboration with "democratic" oligarchic sectors and that was designed to combat the main enemy, the "fascist" oligarchic sectors and, after the 1943 military coup, the "fascist" military dictatorship.[30] Since the introduction of the new tactics of the Popular Front, the PC had begun to make contacts and to undertake activities together with other political forces: the rally held on 1 May 1936 as part of the anti-fascist struggle in which the CGT, the Socialists, the Communists, the Radicals, and the Partido Democrático Progresista participated, was the first example of shared political action. It was not repeated in the immediately subsequent period and would only gather force during the war.[31] Shortly before the outbreak of war, despite many disagreements and arguments, unity between Socialists and Communists, particularly within the labor movement, strengthened considerably; at its First Ordinary Congress, the CGT, controlled by the two parties, outspokenly condemned nazi-fascism and committed itself, in the case of conflict or threat from the totalitarian countries, to "cooperate for the victory of the defenders of peace, democracy and social justice."[32]

The German–Soviet Pact, however, brought a new change of tactics on the part of the Communists and a period of acute confrontation between them and the Socialists that was to continue for two years and would mean a serious setback in the process of unifying the Left. The war was now considered interimperialist, and within Argentina the main enemy was the Anglo-Saxon powers, particularly Britain. This period, which has

---

30 Partido Comunista, *Esbozo de historia*, pp. 86–7.
31 Partido Comunista, *Esbozo de historia*, p. 84; Matsushita, *Movimiento obrero*, pp. 168–9; Iscaro, *Historia del movimiento*, pp. 235–6.
32 Iscaro, *Historia del movimiento*, p. 240. The congress was held on 13, 14, and 15 July 1939. See also del Campo, *Sindicalismo*, pp. 98–9.

been very much neglected, and which the PC has almost entirely disowned (there is no reference to it in the party's official history published in 1947), paradoxically might have had consequences that would have profoundly affected the subsequent course of events.[33] By identifying British imperialism as the main enemy, the Communists adopted a similar line to the Fuerza de Orientación Radical de la Juventud Argentina (FORJA) group (a left-wing nationalist group with Radical origins) and to other nationalist sectors that would later come together under Peronism. Nazism constituted a threat, but the significance of British interests in the country's economy, with a history of nearly one hundred years, was a reality that was difficult to disguise for a political party that called itself anti-imperialist. The railway and meat packing workers would not forget it and this would later provide the basis for Peronist nationalism. Had the PC continued with this policy, its subsequent relationship with Peronism would undoubtedly have been different.[34]

Meanwhile, the immediate result of the PC's brief "neutral" period was to make enemies of its main allies, the Socialists, which was reflected mainly in the CGT, where militants from the two parties embarked on a heated controversy. Unlike the Communists, the Socialists adopted a clearly pro-Allied attitude from the start of the war. This forced the Socialist leaders to redefine the nature of imperialism, though they had never been very clear in this respect. Thus, for example, Nicolás Repetto, in an article entitled "British Imperialism," stressed how important British capital had been for Argentine economic development and argued that although this imperialism existed, it was not "our enemy" and was in no way a threat to Argentina. On the contrary, Britain was fighting "only for the freedom of everyone." The leaders of the PS also praised the United States and the Good Neighbor Policy and exalted the virtues of Pan-Americanism. It is not surprising that the PS was one of the founders

33  In the PC's *Esbozo de historia* there is not a single line on this period, which, as well as the historical distortion by omission this represents, reflected in 1947, the date of its publication, the Communists' need to avoid recalling the period. References to this episode in the PC's history can be found in Abelardo Ramos, *El Partido Comunista*, pp. 136–44.

34  See Ernesto Giúdici, *Imperialismo inglés y liberación nacional* (Buenos Aires, 1984), pp. 8–9. This book was written by a member of the PC's leadership. The book, which had been withdrawn from circulation in 1941 after the party's new change of tactics, was republished by Giúdici himself, who was expelled from the PC in 1973, undoubtedly for political purposes. Giúdice says in the new 1984 prologue that "those who only saw the war did not understand what was going on within and those who were suffering oppression here in sometimes semi-feudal conditions were unable to comprehend a 'democracy' that would come thanks to London or Washington." Giúdici later maintains that "the important thing, what was really new at the time of the book, was what was developing among the mass of peasants and workers who, misunderstood by a dogmatic left, gave rise to a political change that was obvious to some, unexpected for others." See also, Abelardo Ramos, *El Partido Comunista*, pp. 436–44.

and promoters in June 1940 of Acción Argentina, along with leading members of the conservative elite, including many politicians who had held high posts in recent governments, and leaders of the PR and other parties. Acción Argentina was possibly the first step toward what would later be the Unión Democrática.[35]

The invasion of the Soviet Union by the Germans in June 1941 brought about a new, definitive change in PC policy (the party's first priority was, after all, the defense of the USSR). From now on, Socialists and Communists had a common purpose in the defeat of the Axis. (At least the party leaderships were united; the labor movement was soon to divide again.) The Communists' new policy coincided with the return from abroad of their main leader, Victorio Codovilla, who launched the slogan "unión nacional" (against fascism), which governed the party's actions up to the 1946 elections. If Acción Argentina was a precursor of the Unión Democrática, the "unión nacional" was the first announcement thereof by a political leader. At its party congress in October 1942, the PS also formulated a similar slogan in its attempt to establish an electoral alliance in the presidential elections of September 1943.[36]

However, major difficulties arose in the first instance in the union sphere. There was serious disagreement in the CGT between a group of Socialist leaders, headed by General Secretary José Domenech, a railway union leader, and the Communists and other Socialist leaders, such as José Pérez Leirós of the UOM. This was not related to their attitude toward the war; both factions were pro-Allies and opposed President Castillo's neutralist policy. But there their ways parted. Whereas Domenech continued trying to keep politics and union matters separate and based his pro-Allies attitude on economic reasoning (according to him Argentine workers suffered from shortages because of Allied displeasure at the Castillo government's attitude), the other group stated the need for the labor movement to pronounce itself clearly against nazi-fascism from an ideological standpoint. It also pointed out the close connection between trade union and political struggles, stressing in this respect the importance of worker participation in the Unión Democrática. The con-

35  Mario Rapoport, *Política y diplomacia en la Argentina, las relaciones con EE. UU. y la URSS* (Buenos Aires, 1987), pp. 80, 87. See also Nicolás Repetto, *Mi paso por la política*, pp. 209–11.

36  Rapoport, *Política y diplomacia* p. 88; Partido Comunista, *Esbozo de historia* pp. 92–6; Matsushita, *Movimiento obrero* p. 239. Victorio Codovilla said, "Those who refuse to occupy their posts and fulfil their duty within the National Union in defence of their country against the nazi-fascist aggressor will exclude themselves from the Democratic National Front." Natives or foreigners, Conservatives or Socialists, Catholics or Protestants, proletarians or members of the bourgeoisie, whether or not they are active in a party or a trade union, all should be prepared "to give their lives," to defend "the country's traditions and freedoms against foreign aggression and domination." From these slogans, the country seemed to be on the brink of war. On the other hand, this political line presaged the communist alliances of 1945–6 (*Esbozo de historia*, p. 99).

troversy between Domenech and his group and the Communists was
particularly tough, the former accusing the latter of being a "sterile,
disruptive branch of Argentine social life," and of wanting to take over
the labor movement. It is interesting to point out that Angel Borlenghi,
Socialist leader of the commercial workers, who would later join the
Peronist movement, was a member of the Pérez Leirós group.[37]

Despite this setback, in early 1943 Communists and Socialists began
negotiations with other political forces, particularly with the Partido
Radical, to achieve the long-desired Unión Democrática and offer a common platform at the forthcoming elections. But here there emerged further
differences between the parties of the Left because, although both were
in agreement over the nomination of a Radical for the presidency, the
Communists preferred a Progressive Democrat as candidate for vice-
president, whereas the Socialists proposed one of their own members.[38]

One of the main factors assisting the negotiations for unity was the
common criticism of the government's international policy, which was
generally seen as pro-fascist. In the PC's opinion, "All those who favour
victory by the USSR and its allies are our friends. All those who are
against them, openly or underhandedly, are our enemies."[39] The Socialists
had already closely questioned the minister for foreign affairs Enrique
Ruiz Guiñazú, in Parliament in June 1942, criticizing his position at the
Rio Conference, and denouncing him and Castillo for "their unshakeable
conviction that a military victory by the Axis powers was a certainty."
In this judgment on the government's foreign policy an important part
was played by the Congressional Commission on Anti-Argentine Activities, set up in mid-1941 at the request of both Radicals and Socialists,
which published a number of reports showing the extent of nazi-fascist
penetration in Argentina and urging the authorities to take measures
against it. The country's position on the war became an increasingly
important factor in the domestic political struggle.[40]

In the midst of the unity negotiations the military coup d'état of 4
June 1943 took all political parties by surprise, including those of the
Left. There was disagreement over the nature of the coup. Whereas the
Communists accused its leaders of being fascists, the Socialists were more
hopeful and felt confident there would be a change in foreign policy. The
former stuck to its categorization and failed to notice the changes that
subsequently occurred within the military government; the latter were

37 Matsushita, *Movimiento obrero,* pp. 236–49; del Campo, *Sindicalismo,* pp. 102–8; Iscaro, *Historia
del movimiento,* pp. 244–54. Iscaro gives a detailed account of the official Communist position.
38 Rapoport, *Política y diplomacia,* pp. 93–4.
39 Partido Comunista, *Esbozo de historia,* p. 94 ff.
40 Nicolás Repetto, *Política internacional* (Buenos Aires, 1943), pp. 147–89; Rapoport, *Política y
diplomacia,* pp. 88–9.

soon to be disappointed and would embark on a stubborn opposition to the government.[41]

The military government's first measures were indeed ambiguous. On the one hand, it wanted to save the country from the political corruption and disrepute rife during the conservative regime; on the other, because the political parties as a whole were involved in this disrepute, all their activities were banned in December 1943. The PC, which had been illegal during almost its entire existence and had built up a clandestine organization, was less affected by such measures than the Socialists and the Radicals, though it and some of its main leaders, including Codovilla, who later went into exile, were the major victims of subsequent repression. In other spheres, such as education, in which right-wing nationalists and groups close to the church predominated, the ideological speeches and the actual measures taken seemed to confirm the reactionary direction the new regime was taking.[42] As for foreign policy, political parties held some illusions regarding a prompt break with the Axis and the country's entry into the Allied camp until the resignation in October of several members of the cabinet who were willing to accept a change of policy. The economic and diplomatic sanctions imposed by the State Department to force Argentina to change its policy hindered, rather than facilitated, the possibility of changes.[43] Toward the end of the year a large number of political leaders went forcibly or voluntarily into exile, and most of the parties, except for the PR, which for a long time waited to see what would happen, began an open struggle, at home and from abroad, against the military regime, which they now described as nazi-fascist.[44]

Colonel Juan Domingo Perón, one of the leading figures in the military movement (the Grupo de Oficiales Unidos [GOU], which came to power in 1943), had a different strategy from that of his comrades-in-arms. It was no coincidence that he took over responsibility for the old, disreputable National Labor Department and turned it into the Labor and Welfare Secretariat. He also seemed to differ from his colleagues when he began to negotiate with political leaders, particularly Radicals, offering himself as future president of a constitutional government.

The labor movement had been seriously affected by the coup d'état. Although at the beginning leaders of both labor confederations made

41 The position of the political parties with regard to the military coup is dealt with in Rapoport, *Política y diplomacia*, pp. 97–109. For the Socialists, see particularly, Américo Ghioldi, *Palabras a la nación* (Buenos Aires, 1943), pp. 14–31; for the Communists, Partido Comunista, *Esbozo de historia*, pp. 108–10 and Ernesto Giúdici, "El surgimiento de una nueva realidad social argentina (1943–45)," *TEH* 193 (June 1983).

42 Partido Comunista, *Esbozo de historia*, pp. 112–19.

43 Rapoport, *Gran Bretaña*, pp. 261–3.

44 Rapoport, *Política y diplomacia*, pp. 106–7.

friendly approaches to the new government, the CGT–2, dominated by
the most politicized elements of the PS in the union sector and by the
Communists, was dissolved by force and many of its chief leaders were
persecuted and imprisoned. The railway unions, the most important in
the country, which belonged to CGT–1, had also been brought under
government control. But under Perón's management, a much more skill-
ful, flexible policy began to be implemented. Perón began to fly the
banner of social justice, hitherto unknown to the military. And he tried
to gain ground in the union movement and to attract its leaders, regardless
of the sector or party to which they belonged. Thus, for example, in
September 1943 he had the Communist José Peter released in the midst
of a violent meat workers strike despite the fact that he was one of the
main opponents of the military regime.[45]

By early 1944, Perón had established solid bases among the workers,
centered on the two government-controlled railway unions, which were
under the provisional management of Colonel Domingo Mercante, son of
a railway worker. He undertook feverish political activity alternating
between public speeches and daily contact with union leaders and militants. It was around this time that Domenech referred to Perón as "number
one worker," which the latter was later to use as his slogan.[46]

Meanwhile, in January 1944, there occurred a political event of paramount importance; as a result of its own mistakes (including a dishon-
orable negotiation for the purchase of arms in Germany through the
influence of pro-Nazi sectors – the Helmuth affair) and pressure from the
U.S. State Department, the military government was obliged to break
off relations with the Axis countries. This provoked deep unease in the
army and shortly afterward General Pedro P. Ramírez, head of the junta,
was forced to resign. The assumption of the presidency by General Edelmiro J. Farrell and of the Ministry of War by Colonel Perón, who also
retained the Labor and Welfare Secretariat, triggered off a wave of concern
at home and abroad about the fascist leanings of the regime. The State
Department, together with Great Britain and other Latin American countries that were forced to follow the same line, decided not to recognize
the new government and initiated the toughest ever period of political
and economic harassment against "fascist" Argentina.[47]

The parties of the Left essentially agreed with the State Department's
view of the regime. The Partido Comunista, for example, gave an interpretation of these events some years later, pointing out that the Ramírez
government had been under pressure from the most fascistic sectors of

45 del Campo, *Sindicalismo*, pp. 127–35; Matsushita, *Movimiento obrero*, pp. 257–61.
46 Matsushita, *Movimiento obrero*, p. 268.
47 Rapoport, *Gran Bretaña*, pp. 265–6.

the GOU, and "when it tried to resist this pressure" (through the break with the Axis), it was ousted "violently from power by the Farrell-Perón combination." "This event," continued the party's account, "served to show even more clearly the pro-fascist reactionary nature of the coup d'état of 4th June, 1943." The military regime was turning into a "bridgehead" for Hitlerism in Latin America. Thus the Soviet and U.S. governments held similar views on Argentina at this time.[48] For their part, the Socialists had been denouncing the regime's totalitarian and pro-fascist nature and strongly criticizing its foreign policy through their paper *La Vanguardia*. They now asked the new government to consider "their political and administrative task at an end," and the members of the government to return to the barracks to devote themselves "patriotically to the execution of their specific onerous, delicate tasks."[49]

But the military regime was not prepared to give up power. Nor had Perón in particular, who became vice-president in July 1944 while retaining the Ministries of War and Labor, any intention of setting aside his social policy, which would eventually attract the bulk of the working class.

During 1944 the conflict between Perón and the Left grew steadily more serious, both in the political and the trade union spheres. In mid–1944 the PC still detected some differences, however, among members of the military government, particularly between Perón, whose nationalism was seen as moderate and pragmatic, and General Luis Perlinger, the minister of the interior, who made no attempt to hide his right-wing nationalist ideas, pointing out in a document that Perón, "the official demagogue," tried not to appear to be "directly abetting the Axis," unlike Perlinger and his group.[50] Even in March 1945, an editorial in *La Vanguardia* by Américo Ghioldi stressed as a "positive attribute of the Vice-President the fact that he was a man who [had] not publicly given in either to the Catholic Church or to the manipulations of the policies of a fanatical government line," and that "with regard to his so-called social justice efforts," it could be recognized that "Colonel Perón has carried out a not uninteresting task" regardless of his motives and the circumstances in which he conceived it. However, the editorial stated that Perón's plan had been prepared hurriedly in order to gain popular prestige for a revolution that had been a total failure.[51]

Nevertheless, the predominant political attitude among Socialists and Communists was a stubborn opposition to the regime. Since the party

---

48 Partido Comunista, *Esbozo de historia*, p. 109.
49 Ghioldi, *Palabras*, p. 189.
50 Rapoport, *Política y diplomacia*, p. 105.
51 Ghioldi, *Palabras*, p. 258.

apparatus in Argentina had far fewer chances of expression, the tone was set above all by the political groupings set up by exiles in Montevideo, particularly the Asociación de Mayo, dominated by the Socialists, and Patria Libre, in which Conservatives like Rodolfo Moreno, ex-governor of Buenos Aires, and progressive Democrats and Communists led by Rodolfo Ghioldi, were active. From the end of 1944, the Communists promoted a single line whose major points were: the characterization of the government as nazi-fascist; the need to overthrow it by force (there was talk of a "popular rising to overthrow the military-fascist dictatorship as soon as possible" with the help of civilian and military sectors); united democratic forces, ranging from Communists to Conservatives; and the close connection between the domestic and international situations, the struggle between the democracies and nazi-fascism having been extended to Argentina where the same principles were in play as on the field of battle.[52] In an interview given in Chile while in exile, Victorio Codovilla expressed this view clearly: the capitalist countries that made up the anti-Hitler coalition now had a "democratic, progressive policy" and the Second World War had become a struggle for "the liberation of peoples and the removal of all kinds of political and social oppression." Collaboration between the two systems, the capitalist democracies and socialism, would make it possible to set up "a new kind of democratic regime" in which the Communist Parties would be recognized as national parties par excellence and would occupy an important position in political life. Codovilla's view reflected, of course, the line of Earl Browder, the general secretary of the U.S. Communist Party.[53]

This understanding – as expressed, for example, in pro-Allied organizations like Patria Libre and the Junta de la Victoria, a women's organization – between liberal Conservatives and Communists, and between the Communists and the representatives of the capitalist Allies, had deep roots, as we have seen, going back to the period before the 1943 coup.[54] Thus, for example, José Peter, the Communist trade union leader, stressed years later, in order to show the political importance the Communists had acquired before the military coup, that the Federación de Obreros de la Industria de la Carne (FOIC), which he was leading at that time, had

---

52 See Partido Comunista, *Esbozo de historia*, pp. 108–26, and the pamphlets by Victorio Codovilla (*Hay que derrocar a la camarilla nazi del G.O.U.* [Buenos Aires, Dec. 1944]; *En marcha hacia un mundo mejor* [Buenos Aires, April 1945]; and *Cómo ganar las próximas elecciones* [Buenos Aires, 1946].

53 Victorio Codovilla, *En marcha hacia*, p. 5; Rapoport, *Diplomacia y política*, p. 127.

54 See Partido Comunista, *Esbozo de historia*, p. 94, where there is a list of several pro-Ally organizations in which the PC had influence. On the Junta de la Victoria there is an extensive report by the U.S. embassy in Buenos Aires (USNA, Messersmith to Braden, Buenos Aires, 21 June 46, 835.00B/6–2146).

held a public meeting in January 1943 with the participation of Governor Rodolfo Moreno, his minister, Vicente Solano Lima, the director of the National Labor Department (the same post Perón was to hold after the coup), national senators and deputies, and the ambassadors of Brazil, Great Britain, and the United States. The Communist newspaper *La Hora* stated that, "the solidarity of the people was joyfully in evidence at the FOIC celebration."[55] Thus it is no surprise that the State Department should invite to Washington to work for a time in the Office of Inter-American Affairs, the cultural and propaganda body run by Nelson Rockefeller, María Rosa Oliver, a writer from an upper-class Argentine family who was very close to the PC and who had been among the founders of the Junta de la Victoria.[56] In the final stages of the political drama that developed in Argentina at the end of the war, the political alliances were both domestic and international.

Meanwhile, between late 1944 and mid-1945, Perón was advancing in his attempts to win over the labor movement. The measures taken by the military government in favor of the workers were of various types; some of a general nature, others intended to favor certain unions or sectors. They ranged from wage increases to the implementation of the annual bonus, from the Rural Workers Statute to pension laws, and so forth. All these measures had a considerable impact among the workers, who for the first time saw how, in a short space of time, many claims they had struggled to achieve for decades began to materialize.

The support for Perón from important trade union leaders such as the Socialist Angel Borlenghi, who had shortly before publicly declared himself to be anti-fascist and in favor of the setting up of the Unión Democrática, had to do in the short term with significant advantages that his union, the commercial workers, had obtained, and that had to be acknowledged. But it also, as Borlenghi himself declared, reflected a greater desire on the part of the unions to have some influence in Argentine politics.[57] This ran counter both to the policy of the PS, for which trade union matters and politics should be dealt with separately, and to the policy of the PC, which ended up subordinating the former to the party's

---

55 Peter, *Crónicas*, p. 198.

56 Oliver has left in her memoirs a rich testimony of her time in Washington (María Rosa Oliver, *Mi fe es el hombre* [Buenos Aires, 1978]). The PC also recruited some other members from the Argentine upper classes who were to play an outstanding role in the party, such as Rodolfo Aráoz Alfaro. A large number of well-known intellectuals also joined the PC at this time, see Partido Comunista, *Esbozo de historia*, p. 119.

57 Matsushita, *Movimiento obrero*, pp. 280–1; del Campo, *Sindicalismo*, pp. 189–90. Juan Atilio Bramuglia, leading Socialist and adviser to the Railway Union, later minister of foreign affairs to Perón (Borlenghi became minister for home affairs), was one of the first to "jump the fence" and switch to Peronism (*Sindicalismo*, p. 201). See also Puiggrós, *El peronismo*, pp. 126–7.

political objectives, as can be seen clearly in the case of Peter, who attempted to stop a significant conflict in the meatpacking industry because it involved firms belonging to the Allies and continuity of work affected supplies to these countries. Giving up workers' claims in favor of the struggle for more general objectives could not be acceptable to the workers, as the PC itself was to recognize later, in a moment of self-criticism.[58]

On the one hand, the policy of the Left was incomprehensible to those same workers; its description of Perón as nazi-fascist was inaccurate, and unity was promised with economic and political sectors that had governed the country undemocratically in the past and reflected the oligarchic and imperialist forces that had for so long been singled out as the main enemies of the working class. Other Communist parties, such as that of Brazil, through its leader Luis Carlos Prestes, reproached the Argentine PC for its attitude toward Perón, whom they did not consider to be a fascist, and for its strange alliances; in Latin America the main enemies were still the United States and the local oligarchies, not a "populist" colonel with a certain similarity to Getúlio Vargas.[59] There is no doubt that the establishment of "parallel" trade unions by those who opposed the government, particularly the Communists, and the persecution they underwent, was connected with Perón's success and the loss of worker support for the left-wing parties. On the other hand, in the case of the Communists, their unions, which were relatively new, did not have a large number of members and the loss of their main leaders contributed to their disappearance as institutions or their takeover by Peronist leaders.[60]

The fact is that the workers supported Perón's political project, based ideologically on his concept of class harmony under state arbitration. First, the Argentine working class was mostly reformist, as was reflected in their preferential support for syndicalism and socialism, and Perón's ideas contained an essentially reformist message. Second, the workers could not understand why Perón's class harmony was very different from the alliance proposed by the left-wing parties, which included policies and institutions representing the main employers' sectors, both Argentine

58 On the Peter case, see Puiggrós, *El peronismo*, pp. 46–50, and the Foreign Office documents that acknowledge Peter's attitude quoted in Rapoport, *Gran Bretaña*, pp. 202–3. On the PC's "self-criticism," see Partido Comunista, *Esbozo de historia*, p. 140, where reference is made in this sense to the participation by the general secretary, Arnedo Alvarez, in the Eleventh Congress of the PC, held in 1946. But the official history itself, published in 1947, is written with no sense of self-criticism and basically reasserts the party's earlier positions, as we have already seen in many quotations from this history.

59 Rapoport, *Política y diplomacia*, pp. 24–5, 129. This book shows the role played by Prestes in the establishment of diplomatic relations between Perón's government and the Soviet Union.

60 Matsushita, *Movimiento obrero*, p. 285.

and foreign. Third, the accusation by these parties regarding the demagogic nature of Perón's measures not only ran counter to concrete benefits the workers received, but clashed with the recognition that this policy had found its inspiration in old Socialist and Communist proposals. All in all, Peronism offered more advantages than the Left in the short term, and in the medium term, the dubious alliances of the latter offered no more guarantees than Perón's military origins or the nature of the regime from which he had arisen. When a nationalist element was added, in reaction to direct U.S. interference in the political process in Argentina in 1945–6, Perón was able to take up other banners discarded by the Left.

Following the resignation of Secretary of State Cordell Hull (November 1944), the appointment of Nelson Rockefeller as under secretary of state (December 1944), and the conference of American states at Chapultepec (February–March 1945) as the Second World War came to an end, Argentina was finally persuaded to declare war on the Axis (21 March 1945) in return for U.S. recognition and a place at the United Nations conference in San Francisco at the end of April (against the opposition of the Soviet Union). But Argentina was still widely regarded in the United States as "fascist"; the decline of Rockefeller's influence in the State Department due to the death of Roosevelt, the onset of the Truman administration in April (Rockefeller was eventually dismissed in August), and the appointment of Spruille Braden as U.S. ambassador to Argentina (also in April) led to a renewal of U.S. hostility toward the Farrell–Perón military regime, which in turn reactivated the opposition to the regime in Argentina. On his arrival in Buenos Aires on 19 May, Braden embarked on a personal crusade to rid Argentina of fascism and to restore democracy.[61] He actively rallied the Unión Democrática, the broad front of Conservatives, Radicals, Socialists, and Communists, which as political tension mounted, secured in July the promise of presidential elections and in August the lifting of the state of seige. On 19 September the opposition

---

61 Braden's period in Buenos Aires (May–September 1945) and the events of September–October 1945, culminating in first the arrest and then the release of Perón and the victory of Perón in the elections of February 1946, have received a great deal of scholarly attention. See, for example, Félix Luna, *El'45* (Buenos Aires, 1971); Mario Rapoport, *Gran Bretaña, Estados Unidos y las clases dirigentes argentinas, 1940–45* (Buenos Aires, 1981); Carlos Escudé, *Gran Bretaña, Estados Unidos y la declinación argentina, 1942–1949* (Buenos Aires, 1982); Callum A. MacDonald, "The Politics of Intervention: The United States and Argentina, 1941–1946," *Journal of Latin American Studies* 12 (November 1980), and "The Braden Campaign and Anglo-American Relations in Argentina, 1945–6" in *Argentina between the Great Powers, 1939–46*, ed. Guido di Tella and D. Cameron Watt (London, 1989); David Tamarin, *The Argentine Labor Movement, 1930–45* (Albuquerque, NM, 1985); Daniel James, "October 17th and 18th, 1945: Mass Protest, Peronism and the Argentine Working Class," *Journal of Social History* 2(Spring 1988); Juan Carlos Torre, *La vieja guardia sindical y Perón: Sobre los orígenes del peronismo* (Buenos Aires, 1990).

mounted a massive demonstration of perhaps two hundred thousand people, the March for Constitution and Liberty, in Buenos Aires. This was followed a week later by an abortive attempt at a coup d'état by General Arturo Rawson. Although Farrell retained power, he was forced to make concessions, including a firm commitment to elections in April 1946 and the dismissal of Perón. The arrest of the former minister of labor on 9 October provoked an immediate response from the workers of Buenos Aires. Perón's supporters and collaborators launched a campaign for his release. After some internal debate the CGT called on its members to demonstrate on 18 October. The union leadership, however, was overtaken by an upsurge of rank-and-file militancy. As 17 October dawned, somewhere between two and three hundred thousand workers from the industrial suburbs of Avellaneda and Berisso poured into downtown Buenos Aires and filled the Plaza de Mayo. Faced with this show of strength, Farrell backed down and Perón was brought from imprisonment to the Casa Rosada. From this moment on, the momentum of Perón's rise to power was unstoppable.

In the presidential elections, brought forward to February, José P. Tamborini, the candidate of the Unión Democrática, was opposed by Perón, who was backed by the bulk of the unions in Buenos Aires and its suburbs (now organized politically in the Partido Laborista [PL]), by nationalist sectors in the army and outside, by a minority of the PR, by some local political bosses, and by elements within the Catholic church. On the eve of the election at the instigation of Spruille Braden, now assistant under secretary of state, the State Department attempted to discredit Perón by publishing a Blue Book in which the evidence, such as it was, that he had been linked to the Nazis was rehearsed in some detail. Instead it crippled the Unión Democrática. Perón immediately launched a highly effective – possibly decisive – campaign slogan, "Perón or Braden." The elections gave Perón a clear victory with 52.4 percent of the vote.

Thus in Argentina it was not the Cold War but the Second World War – and particularly the Grand Alliance policy, which was reflected domestically in a kind of broad front of the traditional political parties of Left, Center, and Right against the Peronist coalition (or "nazi-Peronism," as Codovilla put it) – as well as the Left's own weaknesses and shortcomings that laid the foundation for the defeat of the Left. Despite an adverse political climate and indeed repression, the Left had consolidated itself as a respectable force in the Argentine labor movement and in Argentine politics in the 1930s and early 1940s. After 1946 the Partido Socialista practically ceased to exist in the labor movement, and the Communists never regained the position they had once held. Politically, the PS, after a succession of divisions, ceased to carry any weight, but paradoxically the PC maintained a presence based on its influence amongst the bourgeoisie and the intellectuals, the roots of which lie in part in the prestige it acquired during the period of the Unión Democrática.

There were only two alternatives open to the Left in its defeat: the Partido Socialista chose stubborn opposition to Perón (except for a small faction that became reconciled with the Peronist movement in 1952); the Partido Comunista accepted the rules of the game, ordering its members to join the Peronist trade unions, and attempted to implement a policy of critical support for the government, the results of which were not very favorable but did make it possible for them to come through the Peronist regime relatively unscathed and maintain a small but organized force. Some sectors within the PC went so far as to fight for a greater rapprochement with the Peronists and even for militants directly to join the Peronist Party. Rodolfo Puiggrós, a prominent intellectual, had set up a small pro-Peronist PC in 1946, and in 1952 no less a figure than the general secretary of the PC, Juan José Real, was expelled from its ranks because he headed a line that wanted to bring about a merger between Communists and Peronists.

The Left was largely defeated in Argentina as it was in many other Latin American countries in the aftermath of the Second World War (although in Argentina the defeat came earlier and in different circumstances). Labor, however, was not demobilized in Argentina as it was elsewhere in Latin America. On the contrary, organized labor, which had been largely responsible for bringing Perón to power, remained one of the pillars of the regime until Perón's downfall in 1955. Once in power Perón in fact supported a further rapid expansion of unionization – between 1945 and 1949 union membership rose from 530,000 to 1.9 million – and delivered substantial wage increases.[62] At the same time, Perón consolidated his hold on organized labor by moving to disarticulate the independent forces within the unions. And those labor leaders who had set up the Partido Laborista (PL) in the belief that it was possible to have an independent working-class party, supporting Perón but with its own political agenda, were proved mistaken. Shortly after Perón's investiture as president, the PL was dissolved (and replaced in January 1947 by the Partido Peronista [PP]). Leaders of the PL, such as Cipriano Reyes, were harrassed.[63] Reyes was arrested in mid-1947 and again in September 1948, when he was accused of plotting to assassinate Perón. He spent the next several years in prison. Perón also moved to crush Communists and independent figures within the unions, such as meatpacking workers' leader

62 David Rock, *Argentina 1516–1987* (Berkeley, 1987), p. 283.
63 See Elena Susana Pont, *Partido Laborista: Estado y Sindicatos* (Buenos Aires, 1984).

José Peter. A key target was Luis Gay, who was elected general secretary of the CGT in November 1946. Gay was a former president of the PL who indicated clearly to Perón that he wished to preserve a certain measure of autonomy. In January 1947 the arrival of a delegation from the American Federation of Labor on an inspection visit was manipulated by Perón to force Gay's resignation on the grounds of collaboration with unacceptable foreign interference in Argentine politics. He was replaced with an unconditional supporter of the regime.[64] Although industrial unrest continued to manifest itself in a variety of unions in the years up to 1950, this was never organized as a coherent challenge to government control over the labor movement, and these isolated actions were contained or repressed by the Ministry of Labor or by the CGT itself.[65] The exact point at which Perón achieved unchallenged control over labor will, no doubt, remain a matter of dispute, as will the possibility that any other outcome was conceivable. But certainly by the end of 1947, if not earlier, all hope of a union movement independent of Perón had collapsed.

Despite a decline in real wages beginning in 1949, Perón managed to retain the support of organized labor. Strike activity, which peaked in the years 1946–8, fell off in the late 1940s and early 1950s. (And the anti-union policies of non-Peronist governments in the period after 1955 did much, of course, to cement the historical alliance between Perón and the unions and to reinforce the nostalgic perception of the Peronist government as a golden age for Argentina's workers.) Nevertheless, as Daniel James has argued,

much of the Peronist state's efforts between 1946 and its demise in 1955 can be viewed as an attempt to institutionalise and control the heretical challenge it had unleashed in the earlier period and to absorb this challenge within a new state-sponsored orthodoxy.[66]

The election of Perón in 1946 had been a defeat for the United States. As the other countries of Latin America consolidated their Second World War alignment with the United States in the new conditions of the Cold War and adjusted their domestic and international policies accordingly, Perón's Argentina, though never denying its affiliation with the West in international politics and remaining strongly anti-Communist at home, continued to represent a challenge to U.S. hegemony in the hemisphere.

64  Juan Carlos Torre, "La caída de Luis Gay," TEH, 89 (October 1974).
65  See Walter Little, "La organización obrera y el Estado Peronista" in La formación del sindicalismo peronista, ed. Juan Carlos Torre (Buenos Aires, 1988).
66  Daniel James, Resistance and Integration: Peronism and the Argentine Working Class, 1946–1976 (Cambridge, 1988), p. 34.

The period from 1950, however, witnessed a growing rapprochement between Perón and Washington, so that even before the fall of Perón in 1955, Argentina was much less out of line with the rest of Latin America. In this respect, too, Argentina's exceptionalism was short-lived.

# 4

# Bolivia

*Laurence Whitehead*

Few corners of the world were more physically isolated from the military conflagration of the Second World War, and from the near-military conflict of the ensuing Cold War, than the landlocked Andean republic of Bolivia. Yet, spurred by the insatiable external demand for strategic products such as tin, wolfram, and quinine, these global conflicts penetrated into the remotest mining camps and up the most inaccessible headwaters of the Amazon. Local political conflicts, with their own longstanding logic and structure, were thereby transmuted into extensions of the world struggle for ascendancy. External analysts with no previous knowledge of or interest in Bolivian political history were particularly prone to misleading simplification and prejudicial labeling of the contending forces (in some cases even engaging in willful falsification), but many Bolivians also threw themselves with relish into the game. After all, whereas a provincial movement to shore up the privileges of the landlord class might merit scant respect, this same movement, by adopting the "Falangist" label in 1938, could hope to ride on the prestige of Franco's victorious armies in Spain, and perhaps obtain some lucrative foreign sponsorship in the process. Similar considerations inspired the upsurge of pro-Nazi rhetoric in 1941, the regrouping of Left and Right under the banner of "democracy" in 1945, and the shattering of that alliance after 1947 as the deepening of the Cold War offered displaced economic elites a hope of restoring the old order.

Thus Bolivian political struggles of the 1940s came to be judged through the prism of international alignments, equating incipient nationalists with the Axis powers, Marxists with the USSR, and the traditional Right with Anglo-American democracy. The year 1946 witnessed the culmination of this trend, with Marxists and conservatives allying against the nationalists to "liberate" Bolivia from alleged nazism (a replication of the international events of 1945). Political groupings that owed their origins to internal factors nevertheless took sides in the world conflict, borrowed from the competing ideological models, and saw the varying fortunes of the war reflected in their own varying fortunes. However, the strength of these international influences should not be exaggerated; the three main groupings that crystallized into organized forces during the war originated from local circumstances and continued their rivalries long after the Allied victory. Indeed it would not be long before the "Nazis" were being reclassified as "Communist" revolutionaries,[1] after which the "democrats" would be reclassified as feudalistic landowners only concerned with resisting agrarian reform.

Certainly there had been an international dimension to Bolivian politics long before 1939. The "liberal" politics of 1900–20 had derived its limited coherence from an international economic and political order (which entered into crisis with the World Depression of the 1930s). And as a producer of strategic raw materials, Bolivia's wartime significance had already been made apparent to the Great Powers during the First World War. In 1914 Germany supplied about one-third of all Bolivia's imports and purchased about a sixth of its exports. The first effect of the war was to interrupt transatlantic shipping – affecting not only trade with Germany but indeed all European trade. Many Bolivian mines were paralyzed, the railways ran empty, and in 1915 the value of imports fell to two-fifths the level of 1913. "Liberal" President Ismael Montes declared a state of siege and blamed all social unrest on a subversive conspiracy. He also introduced various price controls and emergency taxes, and suspended the gold standard. An impressive roll call of influential German-owned mining houses, banks, and trading companies were placed on the British and American blacklists.

The temporary eclipse of German economic influence in 1915 was quickly followed by an upsurge in trade with the United States. Once Wilson declared war on the Central Powers, Bolivia (unlike Argentina, Chile, or Paraguay) severed diplomatic relations with Berlin. In the last two years of the First World War, demand soared for Bolivia's strategic products (tin, wolfram, quinine, rubber, etc.), and in 1918 the country's exports reached a never to be repeated fivefold excess over imports (182 million bolivianos to 35 million). This export bonanza persisted during the commodity boom of the immediate postwar period. But boom was followed by collapse in 1921, with exports falling back to the nominal values of 1914. (The year 1921 saw Bolivia's only merchandise trade deficit between 1895 and 1930.) The internal counterpart to this boom

---

1 It is a revealing if depressing exercise to trace the successive reclassifications of such prominent Bolivian leaders as Juan Lechín and Víctor Paz Estenssoro through the archives of the U.S. government.

and bust cycle was a great upsurge in labor organization and social protest at the end of the war, which had much to do with the overthrow of the Liberals and the installation of a more broadly based government in 1920 – a government whose verbal radicalism was soon drowned out, however, by the exigencies of the postwar slump.

Thus after the First World War, Bolivia emerged with quite different (but no less onerous) international alignments; with a greatly enriched and internationalized mining sector; with a more mobilized and politicized working class (but not one whose material aspirations could easily be satisfied); and with a half-formed liberal regime that seemed to ride on the surface of events rather than control them.

As in many parts of Latin America, the 1929 Depression abruptly terminated Bolivia's cycle of *desarrollo hacia afuera* and undermined the facade of transplanted liberalism. Indeed, the substantial "delinking" of Bolivia from the international economy in the early 1930s weakened the political ascendancy of the old upper classes (mineowners, bankers, land-owners, and merchants, who could broadly be labeled the "oligarchy") and permitted the emergence of two new and relatively unstructured sociopolitical forces – the nationalists and the Left. The impetus for these internal changes was provided by the long and futile ordeal of the Chaco War (1932–5). The tragic loss of life, territory, and treasure in the course of Bolivia's defeat by Paraguay generated the search for a scapegoat. The prewar oligarchical system seemed to require sweeping reform if the nation was to survive the war. This was the central belief unifying the nationalists, a heterogeneous coalition in which Chaco veterans and frontline soliders occupied symbolic positions of honor. (Many others also rallied to the nationalist banner, often opportunistically, in order to disguise their less than creditable war records.) The Left, a grouping that was loosely Marxist in orientation, allied with the nationalists against the oligarchy, but was to some extent in bitter competition with them. For example, nationalists and socialists would readily combine forces to denounce the most privi-leged sectors of the oligarchy (the *rosca*), and to promote state intervention, primary education, and the organization of an urban labor movement. But when the fruits of office came within reach, these two groupings became rivals for power.[2] Moreover, they were divided over the future role of the armed forces, particularly since many on the Left had evaded military service during the war.

In this way the Chaco War both accentuated the break with the past

---

2 Both these groupings still seemed insubstantial to many outside observers in the late 1930s. A British embassy report of 26 February 1938, for example, opined that "the term 'socialism' here, as used by the government today, is simply a cloak under which the ruling classes can pursue their own political and private interests." Public Records Office (henceforth PRO), London, A 2392/984/5.

and sowed the seeds of new dissension, turning Bolivia even further inward, and creating a new social climate born of mass conscription and defeat. Successive "military socialist" governments between 1936 and 1939 failed to establish a stable new order. Five days before the Nazi invasion of Poland, President Germán Busch dramatized that failure by committing suicide after clashing with the mining companies.

If Europe had pulled back from war in September 1939, what course would Bolivian affairs have taken? Realignment with the United States, which came almost immediately, would have been less urgent – and less easy (it was only because of the war that Roosevelt was able to resolve the friction between Bolivia and the Standard Oil Company over the oil nationalization of 1937). Relations with Europe would have bulked larger, with Britain and Germany pursuing their rivalry by peaceful means. The "tin barons" would have continued to conduct their affairs on the assumption of world oversupply and the need for a cartel. Their relations with the government of Bolivia would have remained uneasy and strained (it was only the prospect of sharing in a wartime bonanza that dissolved preexisting suspicions). On the other hand, a conservative restoration, relying on the loose and broad-based alliance of the old parties and forces (the *concordancia*), would probably have taken charge, much as it did in March 1940, if only because the sole alternative had been temporarily exhausted and discredited. And over the longer run, this conservative restoration would have had to contend with some form of serious radical challenge as the political and social forces unleashed by the Depression and the Chaco War gathered momentum, and as the heirs to Busch regrouped. The final outcome need not have taken the precise form that it did, the National Revolution of 1952, but it would probably have displayed many of the same basic characteristics.

Busch's successors were, however, obliged to contend with the local consequences of global conflict. Their first step was to close ranks (as much against the insecurities of domestic militarism as against the traumas of world war). The *concordancia* that carried General Enrique Peñaranda to the presidency in March 1940 was broader based than that supporting Montes during the First World War. The decision to align unconditionally with the United States crystallized well before Washington entered the war (a decree of 10 May 1940 stipulated that for so long as the war continued in Europe, the boliviano would be pegged at 40 to the U.S. dollar),[3] and was carried through with great vigor by Foreign Minister

---

3 But see John Hillman's careful reassessment of Anglo–Bolivian economic relations during the war. In particular he notes the continuing British stranglehold over the world tin market until well into the war. Hillman, "Bolivia and British Tin Policy, 1939–1945," *Journal of Latin American Studies* (henceforth *JLAS*) #22(May 1990): 289–315.

Alberto Ostria Gutiérrez. Prosperity arrived quite rapidly for the major exporters, and, at least initially, the distribution of burdens and benefits was less inequitable than in 1914–15. But three days after the attack on Pearl Harbor, Bolivia froze the funds of all German, Italian, and Japanese subjects resident in Bolivia. A major concern of U.S. diplomats in Bolivia was to enforce a blacklist modeled on those of the First World War against Axis enterprises.[4]

Once again the German trading network was threatened. In May 1941 the German airline Lloyd Aéreo Boliviano was nationalized. In 1942 the British embassy in La Paz identified Cochabamba as both the logical capital for Bolivia, and the main center of Nazi activity. "The Germans found themselves thoroughly at home there (from Cochabamba it [was] possible to maintain contact with and control over Eastern centres such as Trinidad, Todos Santos and Santa Cruz, Vallegrande and even Sucre infinitely more closely than it [was] possible from La Paz). . . . The military connection (most provincial authorities being army officers) and the air network were used to their full value and a close knit and well-organised politico-commercial domination of almost the whole Eastern part of Bolivia was built up with Cochabamba at the centre of the web."[5] Notwithstanding Jerry Knudson's recent defense of *La Calle* and the Movimiento Nacionalista Revolucionario (MNR),[6] it seems clear that German government and business interests exerted considerable leverage – some of it financial – over the nationalist opposition to Peñaranda. The German influence within the military was also important, particularly when it looked as if Hitler's forces would prove unstoppable in Europe.

However, the nationalist movement in Bolivia was far from being just a direct product of Axis influence. In fact, Berlin took only a fairly distant

4  Indeed, Spruille Braden asserts as early as 1935 that he began drawing up a blacklist of German enterprises the moment he took up his ambassadorship in Colombia. "My extensive experience in Chile during World War One in composing blacklists *and* making their prohibitions stick was of much value in World War Two. . . . I think there was no-one else in Washington who could have done it, because no-one remained in the State Department who had played an important part in handling blacklists in World War One." Braden, *Diplomats and Demagogues* (New York, 1971), pp. 58–9.

5  Memo to British ambassador from Mr. Howell, second secretary at the British embassy in La Paz, 20 October 1942, which reached foreign secretary level. Howell added that "there are many influential elements that are friendly to our cause and would readily respond to a little 'pressure' or encouragement. These even include some of the most respected Germans themselves, besides the numerous and wealthy Yugoslav colony; large numbers of refugees; a Francophile section of educated Bolivians; and quite a lot of decent Bolivians . . . [but] . . . the Palestinians and Syrians, a very high proportion of whom are disloyal and an easy tool for the Nazis must be made to tow the line "or else." PRO, London, A 1069/3017/5.

6  Jerry W. Knudson, *Bolivia: Press Revolution 1932–64* (Langham, MD, 1986), contains two informative chapters on *La Calle* (1936–46) and a useful discussion of the "Nazis versus nationalists" debate concerning the MNR during the war.

interest in Bolivian affairs, and such pro-Axis influence as did reach Bolivia was mainly filtered through Argentina, which had objectives of its own to promote. Viewed from the Altiplano, it seemed that Germany and Italy had found a formula for national reconstruction after the collapse of liberalism that was also applicable to post-Chaco Bolivia. Senior officers like General Peñaranda (commander of the Chaco forces after December 1933, who remained in office when the military overthrew the civilian president near the end of the war) spoke of democracy and kept Bolivia on the path laid down by the Allies, but were resented by those below them. The next generation of officers had served on the frontlines of the Chaco, and their secret societies (like Colonel Gualberto Villarroel's Razón de Patria [RADEPA]) bore some apparent resemblance both to Hitler's SS and Perón's Grupo de Oficiales Unidos (GOU). (The resemblance was heightened in November 1944 when, with Villarroel in the presidency, *radepistas* executed a number of prominent opposition figures in cold blood.) And in 1941, when the MNR was founded with a Nazi-style policy statement, Hitler looked likely to win the European war. But the driving force of nationalism came from elsewhere − the hostility toward the so-called *rosca* of the large mining companies, who profited from tying Bolivia as tightly as possible into the Allied war effort. Nationalist struggles against the power of the mineowners, combined with their competition with the Marxists for labor support, progressively radicalized these groups.

Opposition to Peñaranda also came from the Marxist Partido de la Izquierda Revolucionaria (PIR), newly organized from Chile, at a time when the Nazi–Soviet pact was still in force. The Marxists drew inspiration, of course, from the Soviet Union, but were not subject to much Comintern control. The main international influences on them filtered through the Chilean Left, and since this was the period of Popular Front tactics, Bolivia's Marxists attempted a similar approach. They had established positions in the student and labor movements in the mid-thirties, but their opposition to the Chaco War had created deep enmity, and under Busch all Communist and anarchist activities had been prohibited (a ban only reluctantly lifted by the *concordancia*). Thus the restored conservative regime could present itself, like the Liberal oligarchs, as a loyal partner in the Western democratic alliance against Central European tyranny. It could claim diplomatic and economic support from Washington, and it stood ready to delegitimize its domestic critics as agents of international subversion.

But the fortunes of war fluctuate unpredictably. President Peñaranda soon had to contend with the new situation created by the Nazi invasion of the Soviet Union and the Japanese attack on Pearl Harbor. The five years from July 1941 to July 1946 (the overthrow of President Villarroel) derive a certain unity from the fact of Allied–Soviet cooperation, which transformed both international and internal patterns of political alignment.

However, domestic events in Bolivia did not immediately reflect the international situation. Thus, for example, it took some time after Hitler overturned the Nazi–Soviet pact for relations between the nationalists (the MNR) and the Marxists (the PIR) to deteriorate. For about eighteen months (until the Catavi Massacre of December 1942), there was a degree of wary tacit cooperation between the two rival opposition parties, both of which were subject to intermittent persecution by the Peñaranda government. The PIR may have drawn gradually further away from the MNR, and may have edged slightly closer to the conservative "democratic" government, but its possibilities were distinctly limited. The propertied classes would never forget it was Marxist, the army would never forgive its opposition to the Chaco War, and the lower classes were all too easily susceptible to the demagoguery of its rivals in the MNR. It was only after the Villarroel government had come to power in December 1943, and the MNR had begun to use its access to the state apparatus to build a mass base, that the PIR and the oligarchy were really driven together in an "anti-fascist" alliance. It was not until about the middle of 1944 (perhaps when PIR leader José Antonio Arze narrowly escaped assassination) that the PIR's breach with the MNR became unbridgeable. Indeed it was only after antifascism had become the legitimizing orthodoxy of governments all around the world (in mid-1945) that this improbable Bolivian alliance really gained momentum. Its triumph (the overthrow of the Villarroel government and the lynching of the president by an angry mob in July 1946) came well after such movements had begun to fragment in most other countries.

Although externally the Villarroel regime was perceived as blatantly pro-Axis and antidemocratic, this was a war-distorted simplification. Had President Peñaranda remained faithful to the Constitution, he would have faced a difficult election in 1944; his opponents had good reason to doubt his intentions. After he was overthrown, Bolivia remained technically at war with the Axis powers and indeed continued to supply the Allies with quantities of strategic raw materials. The congressional elections of June 1944 were by no means more undemocratic than those that preceded them, indeed rather to the contrary.

Similar distortions colored international perceptions of the July 1946 "revolution" that overthrew Villarroel. It was generally heralded as a belated Allied victory over fascism, although the few foreign observers with sufficient background to make a serious assessment (such as Philip Bonsal at the State Department) had their doubts from the start. Certainly the domestic actors soon had other concerns on their minds. The strongest component of the anti-fascist coalition was the Marxist PIR, whose leaders considered it their top priority from the outset to reassure the propertied classes and their foreign backers of their extreme moderation. Thus the PIR chose to field no candidate in the 1947 presidential elections; it offered no resistance to the reestablishment of old military structures; and it failed to defend even the patchy social reforms of the Villarroel period. By early 1947 the domestic meaning of July 1946 was thus clear to all currents of Bolivian opinion: it had not been a popular antifascist uprising, but rather a conservative restoration.

This loose fit between domestic and international perceptions can also be demonstrated from another angle. When Axis prospects of world domination looked most favorable (i.e., from mid-1940 to early 1943), the MNR's prospects of success within Bolivia looked quite doubtful. But as Hitler's fortunes faded, the MNR went on from strength to strength, reaching its high point around the middle of 1945. Something similar could be said of the GOU in Argentina. However, whereas after 17 October 1945 Perón successfully consolidated his regime, the MNR (and above all its nationalist military allies in RADEPA) failed to achieve this transformation. This apparent Bolivian counterpart to Peronism therefore foundered in July 1946, defeated by a self-styled antifascist front that gained cohesion from its mimicry of the dominant international consensus, despite the inaccuracy of its account of the internal issues at stake within Bolivia.

Precise conclusions about the war's impact on the internal distribution of forces are difficult to reach, given the looseness of fit between domestic and international variables, and the false labeling of domestic forces to reflect the (imperfectly understood) world conflict. However, the war's impact was undoubtedly considerable, as the Belmonte letter forgery of July 1941 illustrates. At this time the United States was still out of the war, but officials in Washington were already closely monitoring reports of German activity in Bolivia, fearing a Nazi-sponsored putsch that might interrupt the flow of wolfram needed for the aircraft industry. In May 1941 the director of the Federal Bureau of Investigation (FBI), Edgar Hoover, informed British Security Coordination (BSC) that the White House wanted evidence on the activities of the Bolivian military attaché in Berlin, Major Elías Belmonte. A British intelligence officer was sent to La Paz, where he concluded that Belmonte was involved in a pro-Nazi military conspiracy, and would in due course dispatch a plan for a coup by diplomatic courier to the German legation in Bolivia. The British officer then decided to anticipate this contingency by arranging for a forged letter from Belmonte to be supplied to the FBI, as if there were a genuine coup threat. On 19 July 1941 President Roosevelt broadcast the contents of this forgery to the American people. Peñaranda declared a nationwide state of siege, expelled the German minister, and arrested a number of MNR leaders and the chief of the Cochabamba military zone. Four nationalist periodicals, including *La Calle,* were suspended.

Suppose the British secret service had *not* forged the Belmonte letter, attempting to incriminate the MNR as the instrument of a German conspiracy to take power in La Paz? Suppose the State Department had *not* repeated these false charges in its Blue Book of February 1946, which was, after all, aimed against Perón rather than Villarroel? Not much of any significance would have changed in the course of the global conflict, but much might have been different within Bolivia.

H. Montgomery Hyde, the author of the Belmonte forgery, concluded his discussion of the episode as follows:

This BSC operation must be judged by its result. It probably averted a revolution in Bolivia; it certainly caused the expulsion of the German Minister and the closing of the German Legation in La Paz, as well as the arrest of a number of dangerous men; it denied Germany further exports of wolfram, while continuing them to the United States; and finally it prepared the climate for the Pan-American conference at Rio six months later, when Bolivia and eighteen other Latin American states broke with the Axis Powers.

But this self-vindicating conclusion was accompanied by the following reservations:

That the Germans were engaged in subversive activities in Bolivia at this time there can be no doubt, although the precise extent to which Major Belmonte was engaged in them must remain a matter of conjecture. Two and a half years later the Germans got their own back in some measure when they helped to engineer a military revolution which overthrew President Peñaranda.[7]

If this forgery had not been perpetrated, is it really likely that Belmonte would have succeeded in carrying through a pro-German coup in Bolivia, with or without the MNR? (Before British intelligence came on the scene the Peñaranda government was already denouncing its opponents using just this kind of language, but of course the Bolivian public discounted such rhetoric so long as it came from Peñaranda's ministers.) R. A. Humphreys found "little reason to doubt that the Peñaranda regime . . .

7  H. Montgomery Hyde, *Secret Intelligence Agent: British Espionage in America and the Creation of the OSS* (New York, 1982), pp. 159–60. The denial of wolfram to Germany may suffice to justify the operation from a British standpoint, although Bolivians are entitled to a different view.

feared a totalitarian-minded *coup d'état* in 1941,"[8] although it was certainly convenient for Peñaranda to smear the opposition. If Peñaranda had really believed in this threat, would he have appointed Víctor Paz Estenssoro the leader of the MNR, to his cabinet in June 1941? A more sober assessment would be that so long as the United States remained out of the war, pro-German elements in Bolivia might have had the opportunity of hampering the British war effort, but would not have been able to seize power. This, at least, is what the German archives appear to indicate.[9] After Pearl Harbor, any Bolivian government would surely have clamped down on alleged German sympathizers, whether or not British intelligence had engaged in black propaganda. In fact, but for this forgery, the prodemocratic and reformist elements that existed within the MNR from its inception[10] might well have weaned the party away from its flirtation with nazism more quickly, and more easily. The party's relations with the Marxist PIR might also have remained somewhat more cordial, and the Villarroel government might therefore have achieved a more broadly based and more internationally respectable reformism, with less reliance on the secret military society (the RADEPA).

This judgment follows partly from the belief that the December 1943 coup was largely an internal affair, not essentially the product of German or Argentine machinations.[11] Admittedly, the intense partisanship that characterizes Bolivian political rivalries might in any case have produced considerable polarization and mutual suspicion. But it is difficult to avoid

8 R. A. Humphreys, *Latin America and the Second World War: 1939–42* (London, 1981), pp. 127–33. Humphreys provides a clear, concise account of the episode, viewed from a Foreign Office perspective. John Hillman's recent research leads him to the conclusion that "had there been a real Axis coup in Bolivia in July 1941 which succeeded in blocking tin supplies it is unlikely that the military history of the war would have been at all different." Hillman, "Bolivia and British Tin Policy," p. 313.

9 Ferrán Gallego reports that the Potsdam Archive indicates German subsidization of *La Calle* and other opposition papers, but that otherwise Berlin's links with Bolivia appear "escasísimo," at least compared to those with Argentina, Brazil, and Mexico. Gallego, "Notas sobre el gobierno de Enrique Peñaranda en Bolivia (1940–43)," *Ibero-Amerikanisches Archiv* (1987):244.

10 Founders of the MNR (such as Hernán Siles Suazo) had long, subsequent careers, which lends credence to their claims to have been reformist democrats from the beginning. Likewise, as Knudson shows in some detail, journalists on *La Calle* subsequently became well-known writers and intellectuals, some of whom also fit that description. Undoubtedly, they kept some questionable company in 1941, and their flirtations with antisemitism seem particularly objectionable in view of the Holocaust. However, Bolivian understanding of European politics was inevitably incomplete. The local situation was highly confused, with the "pro-Axis" *La Calle*, for example, consistently supporting Republican Spain (not something London could claim). Similarly, Villarroel broke Bolivia's relations with the Franco regime.

11 Carlos Salamanca was one of the MNR's first national deputies to condemn the party's decision to defend Belmonte. He became Villarroel's ambassador in Buenos Aires. "If I find any evidence of Peronist involvement in your coup I'll resign," he told the president. "That's why I appointed you," came the reply. (Interview with Carlos Salamanca, New York, 26 March 1978.)

the conclusion that Montgomery Hyde, with almost no knowledge of or interest in Bolivian internal politics, injected an additional element of venom that destabilized the domestic competition for popular support. It is also important to remember that Hyde's aim was to deceive a still technically neutral Washington – an objective he achieved all too well. His forgery contributed in no small measure to the U.S. policy of non-recognition carried out against Villarroel for the first six months of 1944, and subsequently to the denunciation of his government in the State Department's Blue Book of February 1946.

Suppose, finally, that in February 1946 the section on Bolivia had been omitted from the Blue Book. Analysts in the State Department warned of the likely consequences of pushing the Villarroel regime into a corner,[12] but unless they could prove that the Belmonte letter was a forgery, it was hard to argue against a public indictment of the Bolivian government. In any case, it seems likely that by early 1946 the process of internal polarization had already gone so far that the Villarroel administration would have been short-lived whether or not the State Department sought to bring it down. But the publication of the Blue Book may well have contributed to the tragic and extreme form of the denouement. The legacy of British wartime disinformation may go some way toward explaining why Villarroel not merely lost power, but was martyred.

From the British point of view, these may seem unimportant consequences by comparison with the great issues at stake in the global conflict. However, the point at issue in Bolivia was precisely whether Bolivian national interests and aspirations were to be given consideration, or whether Great Power definitions of the issues were all that would matter. Some nationalists may have succumbed to the dictates of Berlin, some Marxists were no doubt willing to do Moscow's bidding without question, and quite a few traditionalists were accustomed to the idea of sheltering under the sponsorship of a metropolitan power. But the new social forces emerging in Bolivia during the thirties and forties demanded a more autonomous stance and greater responsiveness to internal concerns. This was the tendency that was finally to impose itself in the National Revolution of 1952, but it was present for at least a decade before that. To understand why it clashed with the interests of the warring alliances, we have to consider Bolivia's strategic role in the Second World War.

---

12 "What the reaction will be in Bolivia to the publication of this information can only be speculated upon. The following three alternatives are suggested: 1) The overthrow of the Villarroel government by revolution. 2) The present regime . . . turning the Junta into a 'fortress' ready to take on all comers in 'a battle to the death.' . . . 3) The reforming of the government." State Department Memo, 12 February 1946, National Archive 824.00/2–1246. The memo was noncommittal on the relative probabilities.

During the Second World War, tin was regarded as a vital strategic raw material. Neither the United States nor Germany possessed significant domestic supplies. More than half of world production originated in Malaya, Indonesia, Siam, and China. With the fall of Singapore in February 1942, the Allies were cut off from these supplies. Bolivia, Nigeria, and the Congo remained the residual producers of ore, and the only available smelters were in Bootle, Lancashire, with a new plant opening in Texas City in 1941. Several other Bolivian minerals were equally strategic, and in similarly short supply. Producers of wolfram, antimony, and lead, together with rubber and quinine, faced unlimited Allied demand. Moreover, Japan put up a spirited contest with the United States for Bolivia's wolfram in April–May 1941.

At the end of 1939 the United States had already established a small strategic stockpile of around 4,000 tons of tin. In November 1940 the United States contracted to purchase all Bolivian output of concentrate (other than that pledged to Britain) for the next five years. The price was set at 49.50 cents a pound in 1942–3, and was somewhat increased in 1944–6. A speech in June 1940 by the future founder of the MNR, Víctor Paz Estenssoro, deserves attention here:

Because the tin industry is more profitable than other economic activities in Bolivia, almost all tax and foreign currency obligations fall on it. Consequently its relationship with the state has become one of the gravest national problems, characterised by a pendular movement, swinging from extreme liberality towards the industry to severe fiscal rigour, and back.[13]

Instead of shifting all the burden of cyclical adjustment onto the wage bill, he advocated more flexibility in the mining industry's railway rates and electricity charges. For one week in June 1941, Paz Estenssoro even served as Peñaranda's minister of economy, but when he learned that his assignment was to preside over a devaluation of the boliviano from 40 to 46 to the dollar – thus boosting the profitability of exports and reducing real wages – he resigned (immediately after which the Belmonte scandal erupted).

Toward the end of the war Bolivia was supplying about half of free world tin consumption. William Fox estimates that at the end of 1945, total tin stocks held in the United States were 120,000 tons of metal and 33,000 tons of concentrate – three years output for Bolivia, or the equivalent of twelve months' requirements for the United States in time of war.[14] Thus one consequence of the war was that market power had shifted decisively from producers to consumers, that is, from the *rosca* to the U.S.

13 *La Patria*, 29 June 1940.
14 William Fox, *Tin: The Working of a Commodity Agreement* (London, 1974), p. 230.

government, and in particular to the Senate Committee that supervised procurement policy.

To many Bolivian nationalists this outcome seemed to confirm what the MNR had been saying, notably its claim in November 1942 that under Peñaranda's presidency the country had become a virtual colony of the United States. Notwithstanding these criticisms, in April 1943 Bolivia became the second South American state (after Brazil) to declare war on the Axis – another reason why nationalist critics accused Peñaranda of subservience to Washington. Although he received aid from the United States, nationalists countered (quite unjustly in the view of John Hillman) that it was Bolivia that was really dispensing the aid, by supplying its vital tin at an unduly low set price.

The State Department's initial plan for long-term economic cooperation between Bolivia and the United States was put forward in August 1941, in the wake of the Belmonte forgery, which no doubt heightened nationalist animosity. Eleven million dollars in armaments was allocated to Peñaranda's government in December 1941 under Lend–Lease. The conflict with Standard Oil was amicably settled (with help from the U.S. taxpayer) in January 1942. An economic expert, Merwin Bohan, produced a report in 1942 that provided the basis for Bolivia's long-term economic planning for years to come. He envisaged a total investment package of $80 million, of which the Eximbank provided an immediate $10 million. Under this plan the Corporación Boliviana de Fomento was created, with a Bolivian president, an American general manager, and capital of $25 million.

Striking evidence of arguably excessive U.S. intervention in the internal affairs of Bolivia during the war came in the wake of the December 1942 miners strike and the ensuing repression, which became known as the "Catavi massacre." However, this was "Good Neighborly" intervention, rather than dollar imperialism. Since the U.S. government was the main purchaser of Bolivia's tin, and since labor peace in the mines was a matter of urgent concern for those in charge of Allied procurement, a public outcry over the Catavi massacre gave rise to a Joint Bolivian–U.S. Labor Commission, headed by Judge Calvert Magruder. Martin Kyne of the U.S. Congress of Industrial Organizations (CIO) made sure that the trade union viewpoint received a thorough airing before the Commission. Labor clauses were then written into the U.S. tin contract. The mineowners might well have regarded this as an unwarranted U.S. government intrusion into an area that had formerly been under their exclusive control, but neither they nor the Peñaranda government were in a position to object publicly. The MNR benefited most from this American intrusion into Bolivia's affairs, for Martin Kyne's testimony lent special authority to Paz Estenssoro's denunciations of Peñaranda's misgovernment.

Table 4.1. *Tin output and mine employment*

| | Share of world tin production (%) | Tin exports (metric tons) | Mining work force (all metals) |
|---|---|---|---|
| 1935 | 18.4 | 25,403 | 16,000 est |
| 1940 | 16.4 | 38,531 | 33,595 |
| 1943 | 29.6 | 40,960 | 52,937 |
| 1945 | 49.4 | 43,168 | 43,466 |
| 1947 | 30.1 | 33,810 | 31,440 |
| 1950 | 19.0 | 31,714 | 26,632 |

*Sources*: Eduardo López Rivas, *Esquema de la historia económica de Bolivia* (Oruro, 1955), pp. 83, 110, 165; Ricardo Anaya, *Nacionalización de las minas de Bolivia* (La Paz, 1952), pp. 83, 93.

From the standpoint of the mining companies, there was a big contrast between the profitability of the First World War, and that of the Second. Simón I. Patiño's biographer, Charles Geddes, writes that "during the Second World War the Bolivian tin-mining companies made only reasonable profits on their high production . . . as the price of tin was stabilized by the buyers. . . . It should be taken into account, however, that the prices of most of other metals were also controlled, as well as the prices of machinery and supplies produced by mining companies."[15] What Geddes means by "only reasonable profits" is not made clear, but he denies that production costs were as low as 30 cents a pound. By comparison with what the mining companies may have hoped for in such exceptionally favorable circumstances, their returns were perhaps disappointing. However, by comparison with the situation they had faced throughout the 1930s, or would face again from 1946 until June 1950 (the Korean War), they undoubtedly prospered.

How much of this wartime surplus would be captured by the Bolivian state, or retained for local factors of production? This subject deserves serious examination, for there are many myths about it. Table 1 shows how much output and employment rose in the tin sector.

The December 1942 Catavi massacre was a response to miners' demands for higher wages to compensate for the inflation, overcrowding, and scarcities that accompanied the wartime expansion of output. This episode fatally weakened the Peñaranda government, and gave the MNR leadership of the increasingly active mining proletariat.

Four days after the coup of 20 December 1943 that brought Villarroel to the presidency, and the MNR to the cabinet, all the Western Hemi-

15 Charles F. Geddes, *Patiño: The Tin King* (London, 1972), p. 276.

sphere governments that had broken relations with the Axis resolved not to recognize any government in their region that had been instituted by force. This policy of nonrecognition was to apply for the duration of the war, subject of course to regional consultations. In practice, Washington would decide whether or not the outcome of any coup in Latin America would receive recognition. Villarroel had already expressed unreserved support for the United Nations, and Bolivia remained technically at war with the Axis, and practically dependent on U.S. government contracts. Nevertheless, the policy of nonrecognition was sustained for six months. Economic sanctions were not imposed, but Lend–Lease was suspended, and contracts for secondary minerals (copper and antimony) were not renewed. In order to secure recognition, Villarroel was obliged to exclude MNR nominees from his cabinet, to proclaim an amnesty and convoke a Constituent Assembly, and to detain and expel all Axis nationals. On 23 May 1944, eighty-three German and Japanese subjects were deported by air to the United States. According to Paz Estenssoro, Villarroel was also required to give the United States assurances that the MNR would not be allowed to win many seats in Congress. In any event, however, the party waged a vigorous electoral campaign. It broadened its popular base, and secured a much better result than many observers had expected. Thus it might be argued that the U.S. policy of nonrecognition galvanized the MNR into a more vigorous and radical mobilization. It may also have intensified interparty sectarian feeling. As with various other limited political interventions from Washington, both before and since, it seems not to have added in any lasting way to the U.S. capacity to control or manage domestic politics.

After December 1943 the Villarroel government took a series of measures intended to consolidate the support of wage earners, and to symbolize the downgrading of managerial power. The MNR was responsible for organizing the Federación Sindical de Trabajadores Mineros de Bolivia (FSTMB), which was created in June 1944 under the leadership of Juan Lechín. In 1944–5 a pent-up demand for redistributive measures was allowed free expression. The mining companies (and also the landowners) saw their political security coming under threat as wartime excess demand and political populism opened the way for new social groups to enter onto the political stage. The mining companies were also alarmed by renewed official attempts to regulate their finances. In particular, they may have resented an April 1945 decree requiring them to deposit 100 percent of their export revenues with the Central Bank. This question of security for propertied interests was, evidently, the principal issue at stake in the confrontation between Villarroel and the so-called antifascist alliance.[16]

---

16 The principal issue, but not of course the sole one. It must also be recognized that opposition

In most of Latin America the main effects of the Allied victory over the Axis powers was felt in 1945, or at the latest in early 1946. In Bolivia, there was a time lag until mid-1946. In May 1946, Villarroel held elections on schedule, but they were boycotted by the antifascist parties, and they conferred no postwar legitimacy on his government. The transition therefore took the form of a violent rupture.

The United States certainly played a role in bringing down the Villarroel government, in particular, as we have seen, by publishing the February 1946 Blue Book. It may suffice to add that the MNR's main rival for lower-class support, the Marxist PIR, was one of the immediate beneficiaries of this initiative. In fact, the PIR emerged as much the strongest force, certainly in the streets of La Paz, after the lynching of Villarroel. The PIR leaders naturally looked toward Washington with some misgivings. Their initial strategy was to emphasize the extreme moderation of their program (the Marxist "stage theory," which was used to demonstrate that Bolivia would have to experience capitalist development before taking any steps toward socialism), and they constantly reiterated their commitment to democracy. It is fascinating to follow the switch in official U.S. attitudes toward this party as the memory of the Villarroel regime began to fade. In July and August 1946, the PIR was still greeted at the U.S. embassy in the spirit of liberation day. (However, the FBI was already beginning to show a somewhat different attitude.) But within less than twelve months, and regardless of all the best efforts of the party's leadership, Washington had completely reversed its attitude toward Marxists masquerading as antifascists.[17] The Cold War had arrived in force.

We have already seen that after Hitler invaded the Soviet Union, the Marxist PIR found itself outshone by the MNR as a spokesman for the lower classes, particularly during the protests over the Catavi massacre. The PIR attached a high priority to supporting the Soviet Union in its resistance to Hitler's invasion. This implied labor discipline, or at least self-restraint, whenever the production or transportation of war material was at stake. One reason why Trotskyism achieved a substantial foothold in Bolivia during the 1940s, was that Marxists who put the social question before the international question had a natural appeal for many Bolivian

to Villarroel was galvanized by its excesses, and in particular by the nonjudicial execution of four prominent individuals in the wake of a failed rebellion (November 1944). The military secret society, the RADEPA, appears to have been directly responsible, rather than either the president or the MNR.

17 Until April 1948 the full weight of American bureaucracy was still directed against "Axis collaborators" in Bolivia. Then on 28 April in the wake of the Berlin blockade, the State Department told the U.S. ambassador it would "be content for the time being to see the Embassy relax its efforts" (*Foreign Relations of the United States {FRUS}*, 1978, vol. 9 of *The Western Hemisphere* [Washington, 1972], p. 347). By April 1951, after the outbreak of the Korean War, the U.S. Counter Intelligence Corps was assisting Gestapo officer Klaus Barbie, "the Butcher of Lyons," to start a new and also unsavory career in Bolivia.

workers. Nationalists, who saw the war as a dispute between distant countries that had no special concern for the well-being of the Bolivian masses, were even better placed. In some ways, then, it is surprising that the PIR retained a mass base of any kind, particularly once it allied with the local upper classes to bring down the Villarroel regime. By all accounts this conventional Left did, nevertheless, hold on to a substantial quota of working-class and popular support throughout the period of mass mobilization and radicalization at the end of the war. Distrust of the MNR, dislike of the military, and the hope of material rewards after the Allied victory must all have contributed to this continuing strength. Yet it was patchy, it was contingent, and it could not long survive the evident bankruptcy of the party's leadership once the Cold War had taken hold.

The mobilization of the miners at the end of the war, under the leadership of Lechín and the FSTMB, was, as we have seen, largely in alliance with the MNR,[18] as was the equally important mobilization of some sectors of the peasantry, under the paternal guidance of the RADEPA military. These mobilizations could only begin because the Villarroel administration provided a certain limited and ambivalent official cover, and even intermittent protection. But once such a mobilization was underway, it tended to escape the limits set by its originators and indeed began to pose problems of control for a party in government. This was all the more so considering that when the MNR returned to the cabinet in January 1945, it was confronted with an extremely difficult economic situation. Paz Estenssoro, who took the office of economy minister, was obliged to face up to some unpalatable realities.

The Allies' voracious demand for a variety of Bolivian strategic exports had much to do with the war. U.S. stockpiles were bulging when peace came. (Tin price controls would be terminated in November 1946.) Moreover, the return of peace meant the return of Bolivia's Far Eastern competitors to the world market. If Bolivia had been a high-cost producer of tin before the war broke out, it was a higher cost producer now. Whether or not, as some argue, the "eyes had been picked out" of the mines, the average grade of tin ore continued to fall. At Llallagua it was 2.45% in 1938, and only 1.61% in 1946. Only the most essential repairs and investments had been possible during the war years, with the result that the physical plant of the export sector was increasingly decapitalized. (Bolivia's share of world tin production, which was almost 50% in 1945, would fall to 30% in 1947, and to under 20% in 1950; see Table 1.)

Paz Estenssoro adopted a policy of fiscal austerity intended to prepare the country for postwar economic hardship. His refusal to award more

18 Laurence Whitehead, "Miners as Voters: The Electoral Process in Bolivia's Mining Camps," *JLAS* 13(November 1981):333–8.

than a modest pay rise to the (PIR-led) teachers' union provided the anti-fascist front with its most potent rallying point during the last months of the Villarroel regime. Signs of estrangement between the MNR and the FSTMB, led by Lechín, can be traced to the same cause. Thus, in Bolivia, perhaps more than in other parts of Latin America, there was a very pronounced *desfase* (slippage) between the strategies and calculations of the educated political class (including the nationalists and the Left), and the untutored impulses of the newly mobilized social forces.

It is important to remember that in 1946 neither Villarroel nor the MNR was advocating the nationalization of the mines, and only very timid steps toward agricultural reform were in the offing. If the government's lower-class supporters remained relatively well-fed in the first half of 1946, this was due to wheat deliveries on concessional terms from Perón in Argentina, rather than the buoyancy of domestic production. With luck and skill, a broad-based reformist government might have managed to ease the process of adjustment to straitened postwar circumstances, but there are many examples from both other parts of Latin America, and from Bolivia, of how limited the room to maneuver tends to be.

The disintegration of the Villarroel regime must therefore be seen as the product of two simultaneous processes of equal importance. The anti-fascist campaign coincided with a loss of cohesion within the ruling alliance, attributable to disagreements about the nature and pace of the social reforms it was sponsoring. In the view of the radicals, Villarroel had only just begun to address historical grievances and unjust property relations that would require far-reaching initiatives from below. Union membership had soared and local *sindicatos* had gained confidence and experience as the war drew to an end, but all these gains would be lost (as they had been at the end of the First World War) if the beneficiaries relied on those in power to act on their behalf. From the Villarroel government's, point of view on the other hand, inexperienced and unrealistic activists were sabotaging the prospect of sustainable reform, and were playing into the hands of their worst enemies. This tension was disguised due to the conflict with the so-called antifascists, until the martyrdom of Villarroel provided a way to obscure its existence. After July 1946, the various currents that had supported his government faced persecution and the prospect of political oblivion. It was not until the antifascists held their first election in January 1947 and elected Enrique Hertzog to the presidency, that attention shifted to *their* internal differences, or that the continuing strength of the MNR and the FSTMB became apparent.

It is important to analyze what the Villarroel regime had meant to previously unorganized popular sectors, in particular, what it (as distinct from the union) had achieved for the miners. In February 1944 the *fuero sindical* (protection from dismissal for union leaders) was established, although this did not prevent the government from persecuting labor leaders whom it regarded as guilty of subversion (i.e., supporters of the PIR). In November 1944 employers were instructed to deduct union dues at source,[19] thereby greatly improving their finances. In December the *aguinaldo*, or Christmas bonus, was enacted, by which all employees were to receive a thirteenth month's salary every December (calculated on the average of the previous three months' earnings).

Nevertheless, the miners did not achieve great economic gains during the Villarroel administration. In fact, considering the exceptionally favorable situation of the world tin market in 1944–5, and the noisy anticapitalist rhetoric of the party prior to December 1943, the workers might have felt that they fared rather badly. The FSTMB secured a substantial pay rise in February 1945, but from then until the downfall of the MNR sixteen months later, there were no further general wage rises for its members, despite accelerating inflation.[20] Indeed, Luis Peñaloza (who was engaged in economic policy making at the time) shows that Paz Estenssoro pursued a very conservative economic policy, emphasizing price stability and the accumulation of reserves. He admits that the policy "may have been sound in economic terms, but it was a political error."[21]

Thus the MNR's high prestige was probably due to the party's stand on the Catavi massacre and its challenges to the mining companies, rather than to the precise balance of its wage policies. In government, engaged in the inevitable political maneuvers and the undramatic implementation of reforms, its popular momentum flagged and others, recommending more dramatic methods of direct action, gained an audience. Later, in opposition again, the MNR regained its reputation by manipulating the symbol of a martyred President, rather than by pointing to its record of governmental achievements.

It is hardly surprising that Lechín drifted away from the MNR in the course of 1945 (during which time his party membership appears to have lapsed). After all, the party affiliation was a handicap to labor unity; it provided only limited support in industrial conflicts; and it offered no

---

19  The scale of dues was determined by an open vote in union assemblies. There was probably rather little dishonesty at this stage. The system collapsed in September 1947 when, as part of its campaign to break the union, the government froze it assets in the Central Bank.

20  Patiño Mines and Enterprises, *Los conflictos sociales de 1947* (La Paz, 1948), p. 360. This text quotes the Siglo XX management report for 1946: the average wage rate rose only 7 percent in money terms compared to 1945.

21  Luis Peñaloza, *Historia del MNR*, (La Paz, 1966), pp. 80–1.

real redistribution of income or authority. The successes of the FSTMB were mostly a consequence of the MNR's weakness – but that weakness was also a danger for the future. With the wartime boom ending, the union would need a strong protector, or considerable strength of its own, to resist the imminent economic contraction. The MNR was too weak and too cautious to provide such protection; indeed, it was in need of protection itself. Its "nazi" reputation and its intolerance of opposition had led to acute isolation, and it could only cling to office through repression and uncontested elections. The FSTMB had little to gain from continued subservience to such a party, and much to lose if the party fell from power before the union had broken free. When in July 1946 the MNR finally lost power, after a week of strikes and riots in La Paz that caused the regime's confidence and effectiveness at repression to crumble, the FSTMB played no effective role in the defense of the Villarroel government. The miners' behavior demonstrated that the FSTMB had acquired a genuine local power base and did not merely exist through the protection of Villarroel's minister of labor. The new regime, united only in its antinazism and commitment to "democracy," continued to recognize the union.

In July 1946 Bolivia had ostensibly overturned "nazi-fascism" and returned to the liberal democratic fold. The MNR was, of course, outlawed and largely excluded from the "democratic" elections scheduled for January 1947. The army and the state bureaucracy were vigorously purged. Indeed, a powerful element of antimilitary sentiment affected the new regime in its early months. It was not long, however, before the armed forces reemerged as a decisive component of the power structure, simply refashioned to suppress both the MNR and the parties of the Left as well as the social forces they had sought to mobilize. The widespread peasant protests of 1947 were fiercely suppressed, and landowner dominance was generally reestablished. It took longer to demobilize the miners, and another year passed before the PIR-led trade unions of La Paz felt the full force of "democratic" repression. But the class character of the post-1946 regime was apparent almost from the start. If this was what the Allies meant by liberal democracy, then many disfranchised Bolivians were liable to forget their earlier disappointments and conclude that so-called fascism (the Villarroel–MNR regime) was not so bad.

The miners strike of May 1947 was a decisive turning point. The FSTMB's principal demand was a new pay scale, which would have raised the Patiño Mines' wage bill by 55 percent in money terms. (Since the previous pay settlement over two years earlier, the cost of living had risen about 30 percent.) When the issue was sent to official arbitration (the findings of which were supposedly binding on both company and unions), the labor inspector ordered a new pay scale, conceding half the rise demanded by the union. The company refused to accept this award on technical grounds, and insisted that the problems of the enterprise stemmed not from unsatisfactory pay scales, but from union interference in the affairs of management. This position contained a clear threat to FSTMB privileges, which could perhaps have been blocked if the union had accepted the official award and thereby compromised the government on its side. But instead, believing that their claim was just, that they could defeat the company on their own,[22] and perhaps wishing to embarrass the government (or perhaps simply unable to disappoint the hopes they had raised among their members), the FSTMB rejected the award and ordered a general miners strike on 8 May in support of their full claim. This was the union's first full-scale trial of strength with the employers, and they had chosen a period of relatively low demand in which their members were already engaged in work-sharing to avoid redundancy. After ten days, violent incidents caused a number of senior personnel (all Anglo-Saxons) to quit the camp, and within two weeks the situation had become so bad that the government was able to intervene and order an unconditional resumption of work. The management, having established its strength, now refused to pay wages to employees who had returned to work by mere ministerial order. The company's conditions for a resumption of work were now the calling in of all the arms that had been distributed in the mining camps, and the dismissal of 400 named workers. The FSTMB had therefore exhausted its resources and credibility during the strike, had forfeited even the compromise pay award offered by the labor inspector, and had left itself defenseless in the face of company retaliation.

At this point the crucial consideration for FSTMB leaders was whether or not the government was willing to use force against them. The events of July 1946 had given them armed supremacy in key mining camps,[23] and they were prepared to defend this power base with violence if necessary. They knew that the big companies would use all the resources

---

22 The founder of the company, Simón I. Patiño, died on 20 April 1947, and some union leaders may have believed that his departure would leave the management weakened and uncertain about future policies. Lechín commented on his death as follows: "The life expectancy of the mineworker is lower than that of any worker (on average about 27 years, whereas Señor Patiño died at the age of 76). This shows that the balance is unjust between the effort he expends and the salary he receives. . . . Furthermore, higher wages for the workers would mean that a higher proportion of Bolivia's mining production would remain in the country, benefitting the overall economy." Patiño Mines, *Conflictos sociales,* p. 153.

23 For example, according to the vice-president of Patiño Mines, in Siglo XX trade unionists had disarmed and dispersed the Mining Police and even a fraction of the regiment stationed in Uncia. The region was left virtually in the hands of the Policía Sindical Obrera. Patiño Mines, *Conflictos sociales,* pp. 342–3.

they could muster to persuade the government that "law and order" had to be restored in the camps, but the experiences of 1923 and 1942 had demonstrated the disastrous political consequences that could befall a government believed by the public to have "massacred" workers. President Hertzog was in a worse position than his predecessors in terms of carrying out such a policy: he was committed to free elections; boastful of the nonviolence of his government; dependent on support from the pro-Soviet PIR; and uncertain of the army, which had been badly humiliated in the July revolution and then drastically purged.

After the failure of the May strike, the military was considered to be a crucial element in any assessment of the government's capacity to intervene. This is demonstrated by the instructions Lechín gave to other FSTMB leaders on 5 July 1947:

> I consider it very urgent for you to interview all the officers and commanders in Oruro and explain our situation to them, asking them in particular whether they would, if the circumstances arose, fire on a demonstration of workers. It is urgent to hold such conversations tomorrow or Monday. Something very interesting should emerge.[24]

At this point, the Hertzog government came down firmly on the side of the employers. To justify its shift in policy, the government accused the FSTMB of conspiring with the MNR to subvert the established government and of sacrificing the interests of the ordinary workers to the ambitions and appetites of a clique of union leaders. It insisted that the authorities were not acting as a passive instrument of the companies, but as an active arbitrator, and were scrupulously avoiding unnecessary bloodshed. The charge of subversion was difficult to deny entirely, considering the union's explicit commitment (expressed in the Thesis of Pulacayo of November 1946) to the promotion of a workers revolution. Furthermore, according to the minister of the interior, spies had acquired very specific information about the details of a subversive plot that was discussed in a secret session of the Colquiri Conference in June 1947. Although the details may be inexact, the general accusation is highly plausible, and in any case must have been taken rather seriously by the rest of the cabinet, even if they were skeptical of the way the minister embellished his evidence. For example, none of the evidence he produced actually proved his charge that the FSTMB was preparing to take power. On the contrary, it all suggested that the FSTMB was engaged in contingency planning for self-defense. Also, the accusation of union subservience to the exiled MNR was rather unconvincing. The MNR's official historian states that

---

24 Ibid., p. 198. The then minister of the interior, Enrique Ponce Lozada, read this text to Congress on 25 September 1947, stating that it was the transcript of a telephone conversation.

until September 1947 the party was too weak and disorganized to attempt any conspiracy.[25] The party's first public demonstration was on 21 July 1947 (the anniversary of Villarroel's death), at which time it did succeed in circulating leaflets in the Catavi and Llallagua areas,[26] as well as in the major cities. However, the government was probably both mistaken and unwise in identifying the FSTMB as a mere tool of the *revanchistes*, even if some union leaders did invite such misrepresentation. Roberto Arce, a former personnel manager of Patiño Mines, pointed out the long-run risks of this political strategy in a speech to Congress on 2 October 1947:

> The government has blamed worker unrest entirely on the MNR, without pausing to consider the consequences of this statement. The mass of poor people who set out their demands, and believe that justice is on their side, will end up believing if they are accused of acting on behalf of a political party, that only that party is capable of dealing with their problems; and in due course, as always, the temporary advantage gained by distorting the truth will be paid for, not by the original instigators of the falsehood, but by the government itself.[27]

Once charged with fomenting subversion, the union was inevitably exposed to increasingly drastic reprisals by the government. Accusations of illegal arms purchases and corruption led naturally to the freezing of union funds; charges of politically inspired leadership foreshadowed a campaign to rally workers against the militants. Whereas the government itself possessed the power to carry out the first part of this program, only management had the means to isolate the union leaders from their followers. In consequence, despite their somewhat divergent interests, government and management had to coordinate their policies against the union, and it is not surprising that many people (not only committed revolutionaries) concluded that Hertzog was being used by Patiño Mines. The truth was that the company was united, clear-sighted, and resolute in the pursuit of its aims, and to a large extent it dragged a confused and myopic administration in its tow. On 5 September the whole cabinet (including members of the PIR) authorized Patiño Mines to dismiss the entire work force and then rehire 95 percent, in this way ridding the

---

25 Peñaloza, *Historia*, p. 144. Peñaloza states that 17 September 1947 was the first time the MNR decided to use force in an attempt to seize power.

26 The text of the leaflet, *Manifesto No. 5*, is reproduced in Patiño Mines, *Conflictos sociales*, pp. 211–2. It reads in part as follows: "Hertzog, sus Ministros y los dueños de las grandes empresas saben que tenemos preparada una gran revolución con el pueblo y para el pueblo. El Ejército está de acuerdo con nuestros postulados.... Entonces ¡ay!... de los traficantes con la dignidad de la patria... ¡ay!... de los TRAIDORES OBREROS, entonces será el crugir de dientes y el arrepentimiento."

27 Quoted in Patiño Mines, *Conflictos sociales*, p. 231. Arce had been personnel manager in Catavi in 1940. He organized a short-lived political party in 1946–7.

company of all the principal "troublemakers." To the accusation that the government's decision was a "betrayal of the interests of the working class," the then minister of the interior replied:

> I also consider it a betrayal of interests, but not exactly those of the working class. The interests are those of the miners' leaders who are determined to continue this conflict, and create others, in order to maintain their influence over the working classes, and thereby maintain their generous salaries, extravagant lifestyles, luxury cars and pretty girls. Public opinion knows it is true.[28]

The FSTMB popularized the term "White Massacre" to describe the policy of mid-1947. All permanent staff (workers and employees) of Patiño Mines were discharged with compensation according to the law, and the company then rehired only those who were not known for their trade union or political activities or sympathies. Thus managerial control over the mining camps (broken since some time between December 1942 and June 1944) was decisively reasserted. Whether the government appreciated it or not, the destruction of union power in the mines led to a restoration, not so much of national authority, but of the prerogatives of Patiño's management. The company used these gains to promote the total destruction of its enemies, urging the government to use violence against them, where forced redundancy proved insufficient.

By 1949 the company had fully achieved the aims it set itself in 1946. The government, on the other hand, had abandoned the objectives of democracy and national reconciliation, and was locked in a struggle to the death with a revolutionary opposition that grew more popular with every upheaval. One consequence of the events of 1947 was, in fact, the growing belief (widespread ever since the suicide of President Busch in 1939) in a mining superstate that, behind the facade of Bolivian politics, manipulated all crucial decisions. The PIR's minister of labor, Alfredo Mendizábal, responsible for the government's union policy right up to and including the decree of 5 September, further contributed to this belief (and to the discrediting of his own party) when he resigned, an-

---

28 Ibid., pp. 217–8. Roberto Arce predicted in Congress in his speech of 2 October 1947 that the distribution of $200 per worker in the rehiring exercise would only bring the company a temporary advantage. "Having squandered their redundancy payments they [the workers] will find themselves confronted by the new (more disciplined) work regime, and they will begin to see the real scale of their losses under the new plan. In these conditions, the sacked workers, those regarded by the company as agitators, will maintain their influence over the masses, and will set about convincing people that the new arrangements worsen the workers' situation. Immediately there will arise a feeling of open discontent with the company, and new labour leaders will arise from the re-contracted workforce, who will have a good platform for their attacks on the management," ibid., p. 227.

nouncing that he was "leaving because [he did] not wish to continue in the employment of Patiño Mines."[29]

The restoration of landowner ascendancy and of the political persecution of labor activists in Bolivia after the Second World War may have been contingent, that is, avoidable by better or much fortunate political management. There was, however, an unmistakable and critical element in the postwar demobilization that was "structural" – almost unavoidable, given Bolivia's economic endowments and its geopolitical location. Similar experiences in a variety of other Latin American countries at the same time point to the same conclusion. In some ways the Cold War might be considered a fortuitous external event that aggravated the problem. From another standpoint, however, if the Cold War had not existed, ruling groups throughout Latin America would have tried to invent it; they desperately needed a legitimizing device of this kind to excuse the policies of economic adjustment that were, in any case, bound to be implemented.

However, in the case of Bolivia, any overall assessment of the domestic consequences of global conflict must take into account the 1952 Revolution. In a sense this was the postponed (and perhaps distorted) outcome that "should" have taken place five or six years earlier. The successive failures of Villarroel, of the PIR, and of the restored oligarchy to formulate and carry through sustainable reforms paved the way for a much more sweeping and uncontrolled form of adaptation to the postwar world.

Was there a lost opportunity for reform after 1945? Historical "might-have-beens" are notoriously subjective and unprovable, but every description of what was contains implicit assumptions about the alternatives that did not materialize. It might have helped if the military socialism of 1936–9 had survived in some form after the war began. Instead, the traditional parties achieved their comeback just as excess demand appeared in all of Bolivia's export markets. Boosted by this unexpected good fortune, the parties of the *concordancia* monopolized responsibility for the realignment with the Allies, an accommodation that Busch or Colonel David Toro might have made more hesitantly in the same circumstances. This contributed to an exaggerated identification of oligarchical interest with Anglo-American democracy, and of social redistribution with pro-Axis sentiment. It also foredoomed Villarroel (who was in essence another military socialist in the 1936–9 mold) to more ostracism than his – admittedly sometimes vindictive – regime would otherwise have earned for itself. The Belmonte forgery greatly reinforced this distortion, although the MNR contributed by the reckless way some party leaders

29 Ibid., p. 353.

courted identification with the Nazis in the darkest moments of the war. The PIR was unwise to join so wholeheartedly in the well-tried oligarchical practice of slandering social reformers as mere instruments of foreign subversion. This method had been used most unscrupulously against the Marxists before they helped turn it against the MNR (which is why some PIR leaders showed awareness of the fraudulence of the Belmonte letter from the beginning). It should have been no surprise that it would again be used against them, from 1947 on, as soon as the MNR had been outlawed. By 1944 or 1945 their theoretical analyses should also have told them that any alliance with the *rosca* and the United States would probably end in much the same way as the Nazi–Soviet pact.[30]

Thus a "better outcome" would have required some form of cooperation or fusion between the military reformers, the civilian nationalists, and the Marxist intellectuals in order to 1) strike a better bargain with the U.S.; 2) open the channels for increased popular participation within Bolivia; 3) domesticate the old upper classes and the mining superstate; and 4) maintain such control over the process that the transition to adverse postwar economic conditions would not be ruinous. This is certainly a tall order, but then all the alternative strategies were at least as farfetched, and it should be recalled that Mexico accomplished much of this in the 1940s.

In contrast to this "best case" counter-factual, the traditional rulers sought a subservient alliance with the United States, whereas the Marxists and the nationalists polarized the forces of reform over irrelevant questions of international ideology. At the same time, the popular movement burst anarchically onto the scene, and the forces of reaction staged a comeback based on a false prospectus of democracy. Finally, the Cold War was invoked to justify (or magnify) postwar measures of austerity, demobilization, and social exclusion. The immediate outcome was thus fairly disastrous to the causes of modernization, participation, and reform.

However, what makes postwar Bolivia so atypical is not the immediate failure of reformism or the harshness of the subsequent backlash, but the subsequent denouement. In April 1952 Paz Estenssoro and the MNR returned to power after an urban revolution. The PIR dissolved itself, the tin mines were nationalized, a radical land reform swept away the *hacendado* class, the army and the state apparatuses were drastically reshaped, and

---

30 Paz Estenssoro provided a measured rebuttal of PIR allegations that his party was subjecting Bolivian workers to "Nazi type" forced labor, and pointed out the historic error of their decision to ally with the Right: "What has happened is that the PIR with its eye on a very immediate and concrete objective, the coming elections, and fearful of some persecution which it might suffer after the Revolution, has lost its sense of historical perspective. . . . [I]ts strongly reactionary attitude reflects the fear that its own programme may be carried into effect by the MNR." Speech to Congress, 23 October 1944, quoted in Whitehead, "Miners as Voters," p. 337.

universal suffrage was established. After a short period of hesitation, the U.S. government embraced the MNR and poured in economic aid. By the mid-fifties Bolivia was being held up as a demonstration that the United States was not opposed to social revolution in Latin America, but only to (supposed) Soviet-directed totalitarianism (as in Guatemala).

The 1952 Revolution exposed the vulnerability of the post–1948 regional status quo, a vulnerability not revealed in various other parts of South America until the late 1950s. It demonstrated the resilience of the popular movements that had begun to emerge in the mid-forties. Although the peasant movement seemed to have been decapitated and disarticulated by the repression of 1947, it reemerged with considerable breadth and vigor as soon as the urban correlation of forces shifted in its favor. Similarly, the antilabor measures adopted between 1947 and 1951 proved ineffective, and even counterproductive. Above all, the Revolution demonstrated the irrepressibility of a multiclass nationalist party, better organized and more resolutely led than any of Bolivia's traditional parties. Neither charges of nazism nor of communism (nor even of both together) succeeded in denting the MNR's popular appeal to a society in which these labels meant little, and in which the bankruptcy of the ancien régime was so glaringly evident.

# 5

# Venezuela

*Steve Ellner*

In the aftermath of the Second World War, the military coup of 18 October 1945 altered the course of Venezuelan history in fundamental ways. Because of its far-reaching significance – and because its main actors continued to dominate the political scene for decades to come – the coup is surrounded by controversy. In the first place, was the October coup "democratic"? The coup's critics argue that it broke a "constitutional thread" that had extended over the decade since the end of the long dictatorship of Juan Vicente Gómez (1908–35); both President Eleazar López Contreras (1936–41) and President Isaías Medina Angarita (1941–45) had accepted a gradual implantation of democratic structures and liberalization, while at the same time the military was removed from decision-making authority. The October coup, it is argued, thrust the military back into politics. The restlessness and activism that 18 October engendered in the armed forces would come to haunt the new government and its civilian leaders. The coup of 24 November 1948, which led to the dictatorship of General Marcos Pérez Jiménez (1948–58), was spearheaded by a military clique that consisted mostly of the same officers who had conspired against Medina three years before. Thus even though 18 October was carried out in the name of democracy, in effect it set back the cause of democracy in Venezuela.[1]

The coup's defenders deny the validity of the constitutional thread thesis. They characterize the López and Medina administrations as pro-oligarchic and antidemocratic. In spite of the democratic winds that were sweeping over Latin America following the defeat of fascism in the Second World War, presidential elections in Venezuela remained indirect and excluded illiterates and women. Not only did the government of the *trienio* (1945–8) correct these shortcomings, but it fortified democracy in other

---

1 See, for example, Arturo Uslar Pietri, "El 18 de octubre" in *Isaías Medina Angarita: Democracia y negación,* ed. José Eduardo Guzmán Pérez (Caracas, 1985), pp. 263–8.

ways – in its sponsorship of a constitutional assembly, legalization of political parties, and active encouragement of labor unionization. Furthermore, the decision to overthrow Medina was vindicated at the polls; Acción Democrática (AD) led by Rómulo Betancourt, the party that came to power in October 1945, triumphed in all three elections held during the *trienio* (including presidential elections in December 1947) by over 70 percent of the vote.[2]

There is a second controversy over whether the *trienio* government should be considered "leftist." AD's evolution from a leftist party, whose founding leaders had been committed to socialism and some of whom had been linked to the Communist movement, to one that has occupied a center position on the political spectrum in more recent years, is undeniable. At what point did AD cease to be a party of the Left? Those who criticize the 18 October coup see the reforms of the *trienio* as timid and no more radical or far-reaching than those sponsored by the Medina administration.[3] The contrary view holds that AD belonged to the democratic Left: it boldly challenged the privileges of the oligarchy and the church; it reduced the profits of the foreign oil companies; and it introduced reforms favoring welfare and economic development, initiating import substitution policies based in part on the program of loans and subsidies extended by the Corporación Venezolana de Fomento (CVF) to agriculture and industry.[4] The *trienio* was, in Betancourt's words, "Venezuela's second war of independence." This debate has focused on education, labor, agriculture, and the oil industry, and seeks to determine whether the reforms carried out by AD represented a thorough break with the past. The party's role in organized labor is particularly relevant in that its main rival was the Partido Comunista de Venezuela (PCV), and thus it was here that AD's relationship and differentiation from the Marxist Left was made most evident.

The attitude of the United States toward the coups of October 1945 and November 1948 and toward the AD government has been a third

---

2  Robert Jackson Alexander emphasizes the reformist thrust of the AD *trienio* government and gives it credit for initiating import substitution policies, based in part on the program of loans and subsidies extended by the Corporación Venezolana de Fomento (CVF) to agricultural and industrial sectors. Among the more radical and controversial measures of the *trienio* that will not be discussed in this essay were the establishment of a merchant fleet for Venezuela, Colombia, and Ecuador, known as the Flota Mercante Grancolombiana (which was to be the first step toward a customs union) and a deal with Nelson Rockefeller whereby his International Basic Economic Corporation created four subsidiaries, which at a future date were to be turned over to the CVF. Alexander, *The Venezuelan Democratic Revolution: A Profile of the Regime of Rómulo Betancourt* (New Brunswick, NJ, 1964), pp. 22–36.

3  See, for example, Luis Cordero Velásquez, *Betancourt y la conjura militar del 45* (Caracas, 1978), pp. 214–20.

4  Alexander, *Venezuelan Democratic Revolution*, pp. 22–36.

source of contention. Some of those who argue against the revolutionary thrust of the *trienio* maintain that the State Department supported, if not actually encouraged, the 1945 coup, and deplored the overthrow of the government in 1948.[5] Betancourt, on the other hand, in an article published in 1975, attempted to demonstrate the neutrality of the United States and the outright hostility of Britain toward the October coup.[6] Some of the defenders of the *trienio* government, including Rómulo Gallegos who was elected president in 1947, and overthrown after he had been in power less than twelve months, have accused the U.S. government and multinational oil companies of having consorted with the military conspirators at the time of the 1948 coup.[7]

Few if any historians have maintained that the U.S. government endorsed both the 1945 and 1948 coups. Those who have written on the period generally assume that the U.S. attitude toward the *trienio* government – whether it was favorable or unfavorable – remained essentially the same throughout the three years. Such an assumption fails to take into account the profound political changes on the world scene and in U.S. foreign policy at the time of the outbreak of the Cold War. This study will place the *trienio* period in an international setting; a broader perspective is essential for explaining the mounting pressure that was exerted on the Venezuelan government from both internal and external sources.

It is also necessary to place AD in a theoretical framework that can shed light on the conflicting internal currents of opinion and vague objectives that characterized the party, and at the same time explain the reaction of powerful groups to the *trienio* government in November 1948. AD can be considered "populist" in that 1) although its program was far-reaching, its ideology suffered from indefinition; 2) its maximum leader, Rómulo Betancourt, displayed charismatic qualities; 3) its style was grounded in popular culture; and 4) its greatest support came from the popular classes, both rural and urban. AD leaders, Betancourt and Gallegos in particular, gave repeated assurances to business interests and to the U.S. State Department of their total rejection of communism and their respect for private property. Nevertheless, the reforms that AD implemented, although in no way undermining capitalism and foreign investments in Venezuela, had far-reaching implications. Some of the popular measures, especially benefits granted organized labor, set a dangerous precedent in that they infringed on sacred principles in the area

---

5 See, for example, *Antecedentes del revisionismo en Venezuela* [documents of the Partido Revolucionario Progresista (Comunista)] (Caracas, 1973), p. 98; Juan Bautista Fuenmayor, *Historia de la Venezuela política contemporánea: 1899–1969*, vol. 5 (Caracas, 1979), p. 405.

6 "Hubo ingerencia extranjera en el derrocamiento del Presidente Medina Angarita?" [interview with Betancourt], *Resumen* 9(26 October 1975):45–6.

7 *Documentos para la historia: El golpe contra el Presidente Gallegos* (Caracas, 1982), pp. 321–7.

of "management prerogatives." The unpredictability and revolutionary
potential that are salient features of populism – the possibility that AD
would go beyond its stated objectives, either deliberately or as a result
of circumstances the party could not control – produced uncertainty,
skepticism, and hostility toward AD in conservative quarters. Discussion
of the reforms promoted by the *trienio* government, AD's relationship
with the PCV, the growth of the labor movement and the demands it
put forward, and the behavior of the loyal and disloyal opposition explain
the November 1948 coup and, specifically, AD's failure to retain the
support of the diverse sectors that had originally applauded and, in some
cases, actively participated in the coup of October 1945.

In many ways, the *trienio* years were marked by continuity rather than
change. In 1936, following the death of Gómez, the government began
to play an active role in promoting development and guaranteeing general
welfare. Many of the institutions that would underpin the economic
policies of AD during the *trienio,* such as the Central Bank and the
Industrial Bank, were created between 1936 and 1945.[8] In addition, the
Law of Hydrocarbons of 1943 was the first nationalist oil legislation
enforced by the Venezuelan government. Although AD harshly criticized
the law for not going far enough and refused to vote for it in Congress,
AD leaders in government pledged themselves to abide by it.[9] Perhaps
AD's most celebrated accomplishment in oil policy, the principle of "50–
50" (government oil revenue = company profits), was first devised by
the framers of the 1943 law as a means of roughly calculating the taxes
that the petroleum companies were forced to pay.[10] Finally, the agrarian
reforms, promulgated by both Medina and AD in the last months of their
respective governments, were to have left large productive estates mainly
intact while distributing public land to the peasantry. Both laws were
dubbed "socialist" and "revolutionary" by landowning interests and some
conservatives, and were criticized by progressives for being excessively
mild.

  During the years 1936–45, moreover, the groundwork was laid for the
fully fledged democracy that the *trienio* government would later pride
itself on achieving. The López administration discontinued the use of
torture and the ruthless persecution of government opponents, both prominent features of the Gómez regime. Equally impressive was the toleration
of the Medina government, as demonstrated by the absence of political

---

8 Winfield Burggraaff, "Democracy and Development in Venezuela, 1936–1948" [in press],
  p. 190.
9 Stephen G. Rabe, *The Road to OPEC: United States Relations with Venezuela,* (Austin, TX, 1982),
  p. 97.
10 AD takes complete credit for the "50–50" policy and denies that it dates back to the 1943 law.
  See Rómulo Betancourt, *Venezuela: Política y petróleo* (Mexico, 1956), pp. 153–161.

prisoners and the legalization of AD at the outset of the administration and of the PCV one month before its overthrow. Furthermore, Medina implemented direct elections for the Chamber of Deputies and granted women the right to vote at the municipal level. While discarding the advice of prominent members of the governing Partido Democrático Venezolano (PDV) who favored direct elections for president in 1946, he did agree to use his influence to introduce such a system before the 1951 presidential contests.

Two marked differences between the Medina and AD governments, however, go far in explaining the intransigent behavior of the adversaries of both administrations. In the first place, Medina developed close ties with members of the Unión Popular (UP), which was the legal front of the PCV. The UP formed a coalition with Medina's PDV that swept the municipal elections of Caracas in 1944, winning 19 of the city council's 22 seats. The legalization of the PCV and the legitimacy arising from its association with the mainstream PDV opened promising possibilities for the Communists in the elections due to be held in 1946. These prospects were a source of consternation for Venezuelan conservatives, as well as for the U.S. State Department. The fervently anti-Communist AD, on the other hand, boasted of being the main bulwark against Communist penetration in Venezuela, and during the *trienio* spurned formal agreements with the Communists.[11]

In the second place, Medina's reforms were enacted in the absence of mass social pressure, whereas those of the *trienio* were carried out in a climate of unrest and popular expectation. Medina, who as an ex-military officer upheld a paternalistic view of the underprivileged classes, failed to institutionalize his support. The *medinista* PDV was mainly a party of government bureaucrats that did not attempt to exert influence over labor, peasant, and student organizations. In contrast, AD dominated all three movements during the *trienio.* The possibility that AD would mobilize its popular base in order to deepen the reforms carried out by the government loomed as a major threat to the privileged classes. AD's program, in itself, was not designed to produce radical changes in socioeconomic relations. Nevertheless, certain provisions of the reforms in oil policy, labor relations, agriculture, and other areas could have served as stepping stones to profound structural transformation at a future date. Thus, uncertainty and fear regarding the implications of policy changes, rather than the policies themselves, moved conservatives to assume a position of hardened opposition to the AD government.

Distrust of AD leaders and skepticism regarding their true intentions also stemmed from the socialist strategy designed by AD's precursor parties

---

11 *El País*, 18 June 1946, p. 1.

headed by Betancourt in the 1930s. As a political exile during the Gómez regime, Betancourt adhered to Marxism–Leninism but discarded the dictum formulated in the *Communist Manifesto* that Communists have no reason to conceal objectives. Betancourt pointed out that the industrial working class, which was the vehicle for socialist transformation, was of minuscule size in Venezuela. Due to the Left's weak position, it should subordinate its ultimate goals to a "minimum program" of democratic and economic reforms. According to Betancourt, Communists should establish a tight-knit leadership, equivalent to an "army staff of leaders who are in perfect agreement," and at a given moment in the revolution effect a "turn to the radical [L]eft." Up until that point, however, Communists should masquerade as "bourgeois democrats."[12]

Betancourt's pragmatism manifested itself several years later when his followers petitioned the government for legalization of the projected AD. For this purpose, they decided to bury their program of revolutionary nationalism and avoid any reference to socialism.[13] Many AD members presumed that AD's modified program, far from reflecting the party's basic objectives, was a ruse designed to allay the fears of conservatives. These leftists inherited Betancourt's notion that as long as AD leaders were firm in their commitment to far-reaching change, it was unnecessary and even ill-advised to broadcast the party's true goals. As testimony to the continued acceptance of this Machiavellian strategy, scores of interviews with AD and ex-AD leaders reveal that it was widely assumed within AD during these years that the party was committed to covert objectives.[14] Further evidence of the prevalence of this strategy can be found in the three divisions of AD in the 1960s. Leaders of different age groups left the party as a result of its failure to live up to its socialist and antiimperialist goals, and founded left-wing parties based on a more explicitly formulated program and ideology.

By the time of the October 1945 coup, Betancourt himself had completely abandoned his previous ideological beliefs, and had convinced most conservatives of the sincerity of his rejection of communism. Nevertheless, they were well aware of the strategy based on concealment and duplicity adhered to by AD leftists in the previous decade. During the *trienio,* ex-president López Contreras and other ardent anti-Communists made frequent reference to, and even republished, Betancourt's private correspondence, which had been captured by Gómez's secret service, in order

---

12 *Libro Rojo del General López Contreras 1936: Documentos robados por espías de la policía política,* 3d ed. (Caracas, 1975), p. 179.
13 Betancourt, *Venezuela,* p. 133.
14 Ramón Quijada, interview in Cumaná. 15 October 1977; Jesús Paz Gallarraga, interview in Caracas, 26 November 1986; Steve Ellner, "The Venezuelan Left in the Era of the Popular Front, 1936–45," *Journal of Latin American Studies* 11 (May 1979): 176–9.

to remind the public that AD could not be trusted in power. One of the major complaints of military plotters, which was expressed in declarations following the November 1948 coup, was that "extremist elements" in AD threatened the stability of the nation and enjoyed great influence in the party and the *trienio* government.

The October coup took most Venezuelans, including AD members, (with the exception of a dozen or two party leaders who conspired with the military rebels) completely by surprise. Indeed, at first it was generally assumed that the coup was the work of ex-president López Contreras, who had broken with President Medina in 1942. The rebels were confident that they would be able to count on the blessing of the U.S. government, and at one point in the uprising, when the tide appeared to be turning against them, they considered calling on the U.S. embassy to act as mediator.[15] Although the U.S. ambassador was not informed of the plot against Medina, the rebels had apparently received prior assurances from other diplomats that prompt U.S. recognition would be extended – as indeed it was.[16] AD's commitment to democracy was in harmony with U.S. policy at the time, and the party's strident anticommunism was a welcomed contrast to Medina's rapport with the PCV. The amicable relations prior to the coup between certain AD leaders and the audacious president of the Venezuelan subsidiary of Standard Oil of New Jersey – the largest oil company in the country – must have also been reassuring to the State Department.[17]

One of the first important decisions of the AD-led provisional government, and perhaps its most controversial, was the creation of a Tribunal of Civil and Administrative Responsibility to judge López, Medina, many of the leading members of their administrations, and other ex-government functionaries – 172 in all. They were accused of graft and the more nebulous charge of misuse of public funds. The Tribunal could not be considered nonpartisan since it consisted of four AD leaders, one Communist, and two military officers who had participated in the coup. Government critics pointed out that the Tribunal supplanted the established legal system and that appeal procedures were lacking. More important, the trials were denounced as a form of political reprisal. Betancourt later admitted that the creation of the Tribunal was a fatal error in that many of the indicted ended up conspiring against his government.[18]

---

15 Rodolfo Luzardo, *Notas histórico-económicas* (Caracas, 1963), p. 119.
16 Fuenmayor, *Historia de la Venezuela*, p. 405.
17 "Creole Business Embassy," *Fortune*, February 1949, pp. 92–5.
18 Sanin [Alfredo Tarre Murzil], *Rómulo: Cuenta su vida*, 2d ed. (Valencia, 1984), p. 232.

AD's zeal in prosecuting ex-government functionaries dated back to 1931 when in a famous manifesto Betancourt and his followers proposed a "Tribunal of Public Health" to bring to justice members of the Gómez regime for their appropriation of public funds.[19] Following Gómez's death, Betancourt and his followers continued to see the López and Medina administrations as *gomecista,* and thus failed to acknowledge the obvious improvement in the ethical conduct of government officials. The Tribunal and the controversy it generated led many AD members to think along personalistic rather than class lines. Thus, for instance, AD peasants were encouraged to believe that the land confiscated from *gomecistas, lopecistas,* and *medinistas* would form the basis of the agrarian reform, instead of thinking in terms of destroying latifundism as an institution.[20] Equally important, the charges brought against *medinistas* and *lopecistas* alienated those who had identified with these governments and set the tone for a personalistic and sectarian style, which predominated during the *trienio* at the expense of sober analyses of political issues.

Another government measure that provoked heated public debate shortly after the October coup was Decree 321 on educational reform, which discriminated against students in private (Catholic) schools taking public examinations.[21] Although President Betancourt bowed to pressure by eliminating the discriminatory provisions of Decree 321, the church and conservatives in general feared the possibility of a complete takeover of religious educational institutions by the state. Some AD leaders, including the future minister of education, Luis Beltrán Prieto Figueroa, had called for the nationalization of private schools in the 1930s, a demand that continued to be upheld by the AD-controlled Federación Venezolana de Maestros (FVM) and the Colegio de Profesores. Furthermore, on 10 June 1946 at some of the largest rallies ever held in Caracas, Valencia, and Maracaibo, AD and PCV leaders spoke in support of Decree 321. The Caracas demonstration was replete with PCV but not AD banners because, although it was sponsored by the AD-controlled Federation of Workers of the Federal District, AD as a party refused officially to endorse it.[22] In fact, the issue produced serious strains in AD, as some party leaders favored maintaining Decree 321 intact at a time when Betancourt had decided to revise it in an attempt to diffuse the issue before the

---

19 "Plan de Barranquilla" in *Libro Rojo,* p. 294.
20 FCV [Federación Campesina de Venezuela], *La cuestión agraria venezolana: Tesis política y programa de la Federación Campesina de Venezuela* (Caracas, 1948), p. 12: Valmore Rodríguez, *Discurso radiado por el Sr. Valmore Rodríguez, encargado del Ministerio de Relaciones Interiores* (Caracas, 1945), p. 13.
21 The other provisions of the decree are discussed in Donald L. Herman, *Christian Democracy in Venezuela* (Chapel Hill, NC, 1980), p. 32.
22 Juan B. Fuenmayor, interview in Caracas, 11 February 1987.

national elections, and concentrate on other "central tasks of the nation and the government."[23]

Three aspects of the controversy involving Decree 321 alarmed conservatives: the possibility that a relatively minor reform could set a precedent, undo long-held, virtually sacred principles, or serve as a stepping stone to far-reaching structural change; the influential role played by the PCV that, in spite of the government's policy of anticommunism, was able to close ranks with AD in a moment of crisis and polarization; the division in AD that pitted "extremist" party leaders against "responsible" government members, such as Betancourt, whose authority and prestige were consequently undermined.

The student disturbances that shook several university campuses in early 1948 also led conservatives to question the government's ability to guarantee stability. The Gallegos administration acceded to student pressure at Caracas's Universidad Central de Venezuela (UCV), and allegedly requested the resignation of the university's rectoral authorities, including Vice-Rector Luis Manuel Peñalver, a prominent AD leader and former president of the main student federation. UCV's University Council responded by ordering the suspension of classes for the rest of the semester. Gallegos failed in his effort to act as mediator between students and professors while avoiding overt government intervention that would have compromised the university's recently granted autonomous status. The incident, one biographer wrote, "reinforced Gallegos' image as a politician of good will but inefficacious, incapable of dealing with the rivalries which afflicted the country."[24]

The structural implications of oil policy were also a source of preoccupation for conservatives and powerful economic groups. Historical studies have differed widely on the immediate economic consequences of the reforms during these years. While pro-AD writers exalt the "50–50" policy, some leftists have argued that under the arrangement the government's true share was less than 50 percent.[25] In addition, some historians claim, as did the PCV and other parties at the time, that the policy of "no more concessions" was designed to strengthen the position of the

---

23 Sanin, *Rómulo*, p. 244; José Rivas Rivas, *Historia gráfica de Venezuela: La Junta Revolucionaria de Gobierno y el régimen de Rómulo Gallegos* (Caracas, 1972), p. 86. Internally, Betancourt argued that the decree's supporters displayed anticlerical attitudes that were a throwback to the nineteenth century, an accusation (directed largely at Prieto Figueroa, who in 1967 led a socialist split in AD) that one prominent AD historian subsequently made. See Rubén Carpio Castillo, *Acción Democrática, 1941–1971: Bosquejo histórico de un partido* (Caracas, 1971), p. 78.

24 Harrison Sabin Howard, *Rómulo Gallegos y la revolución burguesa en Venezuela*, 2d ed. (Caracas, 1984), p. 301.

25 This position was upheld by Salvador de la Plaza. See William Rísquez Iribarren, Víctor Guerere Añez, and Salvador de la Plaza, *Breve historia del petróleo y su legislación en Venezuela* (Caracas, 1973), p. 124.

three large oil companies in Venezuela (subsidiaries of Gulf, Standard Oil, and Shell), which had an abundance of proven and nonproven reserves, by shutting the door on potential competitors.[26] This view contrasts with pro-AD accounts that view the policy as a challenge to all oil companies, both large and small.

Regardless of whether the immediate interests of the petroleum companies were well served by oil policy during these years, their long-term prospects were placed in doubt. The big three oil companies obviously had no pressing need to acquire more concessions, but government policy implied that the concession system itself was being scrapped in favor of a new, yet to be determined, mode of operation. The plans for the creation of a national oil company and a state-run refinery left open the possibility that the government would compete with the private sector and follow an incremental strategy of gaining control of the industry. In 1948 the multinationals reacted strongly against the government's decision to sell royalty oil on the international market, rather than accept all of it in cash as was the custom. The government's intention was to ascertain the true price of oil for tax purposes.[27] Nevertheless, the companies were not convinced that once this objective was achieved the government would withdraw from the international market. The prospect of competition at this level was especially disturbing since international sales, more than production, had always been the major locus of oligopolistic control of the industry.

The key role played by Venezuelan oil in the Second World War after the elimination of the German submarine threat in coastal waters, enabled Venezuela to double its exports between 1943 and 1945. As in Argentina, foreign reserves that had been accumulated during the war when imports were reduced to a minimum financed improvements in the standard of living and benefits for labor during the early postwar period. Thus, Venezuela largely avoided the acute social clashes that became generalized throughout the world as the result of the rising expectations due to the triumph of democracy over fascism and the end to the war-imposed postponements of wage increases.[28] Real wages in Venezuela rose 31 percent in 1946, and another 5 percent in 1947. Some historians maintain that these higher production costs weighed heavily on local businessmen, with their limited economic capacity, who as a result applauded, if not actively

---

26 Comisión Ideológica de Ruptura, *El imperialismo petrolero y la revolución venezolana: Las ganancias extraordinarias y la soberanía nacional* (Caracas, 1977), p. 188.

27 Luis Lander [AD's second vice-president in 1948], interview in Caracas, 20 October 1981.

28 For a discussion of the relationship between Venezuela's status as an oil exporter and the absence of intense social conflict, see Terry Lynn Karl, "Petroleum and Political Pacts: The Transition to Democracy in Venezuela," *Latin American Research Review* 22 (1987):63–94.

supported, the November 1948 coup. The capital-intensive oil companies, on the other hand, were riding the crest of a spectacular expansion in the industry and were thus less burdened by structural changes in the national income.[29]

Nevertheless, changes that altered the relationship between workers and management, and enhanced the role of unions in the shaping of the destiny of the nation, were threatening to both foreign and local capitalists. The centralization of the labor movement, its extension to hitherto unorganized sectors, and contractual and legal provisions, which granted unions an input into decisions that were previously the exclusive preserve of management, stood out among the most significant gains of the period. The outstanding achievement was the fourfold increase in the number of unions and the sixfold increase in the number of organized workers, a trend that was fostered by the Ministry of Labor.

The oil workers, who had always played a vanguard role in the Venezuelan labor movement,[30] were the most forceful in demanding changes in the postwar period. Fedepetrol (the Federation of Petroleum Workers) drew up a proposed contract in 1948 that contained a host of provisions the companies rejected on the grounds that they infringed on "management prerogatives." They included: union consultation as a prerequisite for modifying the workday; management's obligation to supply unions with reports on all information relating to union members; union supervision of company stores; union participation in the hiring of workers (the *cláusula sindical*); checkoff of union dues for all workers; removal of supervisors who engaged in antiworker conduct; and management's obligation to ensure that benefits were applied to workers who were employed by firms contracted by the oil companies.[31] The most important demand was *estabilidad absoluta,* which would have prohibited all unjustified dismissals. The companies adamantly rejected *estabilidad absoluta* on the grounds that it would have limited their flexibility in reducing overhead in accordance with market conditions. This demand, which became the central issue in the negotiations, was resolved by company acceptance of *estabilidad indirecta,* whereby costly severance pay obligations discouraged layoffs.[32]

Unions in other industries made similar demands, although not as

29 Rabe, *Road to OPEC,* p. 103; the same opinion was expressed to this author by José Antonio Mayobre, interview in Caracas, 15 July 1976.

30 On the history of the Venezuelan oil workers' movement, see Charles Bergquist, *Labor in Latin America: Comparative Essays on Chile, Argentina, Venezuela, and Colombia* (Stanford, 1986), pp. 191–273.

31 *El Nacional,* 6 February 1948, p. 8.

32 Steve Ellner, *Los partidos políticos y su disputa por el control del movimiento sindical en Venezuela, 1936–1948* (Caracas, 1980), pp. 124–5.

militantly or consistently as did Fedepetrol. In the majority of the 203 cases involving union petitions introduced in the Ministry of Labor in 1947 as a prerequisite for legal strike activity, automatic checkoff of union dues was conceded by the management.[33] A special severance pay called *cesantía* was created by law in 1947 for the purpose of achieving *estabilidad indirecta*. Some AD trade union leaders unsuccessfully attempted to introduce a series of far-reaching provisions in the 1947 Constitution for the stated purpose of spreading the benefits enjoyed by oil workers. These clauses included company-sponsored schools and scholarships for the children of workers, obligatory *cláusula sindical*, a forty-four-hour work week, reduction of the ratio between foreign professionals and native-born professionals in each company from 25 percent to 10 percent, and the circumscription and definition of the government's authority in settling worker conflicts.[34]

The *trienio* witnessed a significant increase in strikes, though AD's policy of "labor peace," as well as rising real wages, helped avoid the confrontations that racked other nations in the years immediately following the Second World War. Some commentators play down the incidence of labor conflict and the number of workers involved.[35] Nevertheless, the number of work stoppages increased from 4 in 1944 to 32 in the period October 1945–December 1946 and 55 in 1947. Some of these strikes took place in important sectors such as the textile industry, which had the only labor federation controlled by the PCV. In these struggles, rank-and-file AD trade unionists closed ranks with Communists, a trend that worried conservatives and was a source of considerable preoccupation to Rómulo Betancourt.[36]

Throughout the *trienio* the Venezuelan Communist movement was weakened by factional conflict, which partly accounts for its poor showing in the presidential elections of December 1947 when PCV candidate Gustavo Machado received a mere 3.2 percent of the vote. Nevertheless, the Communists had been the dominant force in organized labor until as late as 1944 and continued to enjoy considerable backing, especially in the strategic oil workers movement. The party's relative strength in the labor movement as well as the discipline of PCV members were not taken into account by Betancourt when he argued that AD had nothing to gain

33 Ministerio del Trabajo, *Memoria y cuenta* (Caracas, 1947), p. 50.
34 *El País*, 11 March 1947, p. 5. These constitutional proposals resembled those put forward by Communist labor leader Jesús Faría. See Dorotea Melcher, "Estado y movimiento obrero en Venezuela (Represión e integración hasta 1948)" (Universidad de los Andes, Department of Economics, 1984), p. 141.
35 Burggraaff, "Democracy and Development," p. 231.
36 Ministerio del Trabajo, *Memoria y cuenta*, 1944, pp. 56–89; 1946, pp. 80–107; 1947, p. 50; Betancourt, *Venezuela*, p. 816.

and everything to lose from reaching an understanding with the Communists.[37] In conversations with AD toward the end of the *trienio*, PCV representatives proposed a joint effort to mobilize the general populace in opposition to the threat of a coup, a plan that several AD leaders were willing to consider.[38]

Relations between the PCV and AD were tense in the months following the 18 October coup as the provisional government made preventive arrests of *medinistas* and their Communist allies. AD and the PCV engaged in sharp polemical interchanges regarding the emergency measures that prohibited strikes; the Communist attitude toward the government was also shaped by the appointment of Rafael Caldera, the nation's leading conservative spokesman, as attorney general. Some writers dwell on AD–Communist relations during these early months and draw the conclusion that the PCV's position toward AD throughout the *trienio* was one of outright hostility.[39] In fact, by early 1946, following Caldera's resignation and the revocation of the provisional decrees, the PCV had toned down its initial rhetoric and upheld a position of qualified support for government policies. Indeed an unwritten understanding existed between the two parties regarding the desirability of maintaining friendly relations.[40]

The Communists put forward radical demands for structural changes and reforms that were designed to benefit workers and strengthen the labor movement. Some of their proposals met a favorable response from AD labor leaders, especially at the middle and lower leadership levels. Thus, for instance, the PCV supported mandatory checkoff of union dues for both union and non-union members. Although Augusto Malavé Villalba, secretary general of the AD-dominated Confederación de Trabajadores de Venezuela (CTV), criticized the practice as illegal,[41] the AD-dominated Fedepetrol incorporated it in the proposed oil workers contract of 1948. The Communists also advocated the transformation of the FVM into a union with the right to strike, a proposal that AD opposed,[42] and the granting of social security benefits to all workers.

37 Steve Ellner, *Venezuela's Movimiento al Socialismo: From Guerrilla Defeat to Innovative Politics* (Durham, NC, 1988), p. 96. For an analysis of the relative strength of the Communist movement during these years, see Margarita López Maya, "Las elecciones de 1946–1947," *Boletín de la Academia de la Historia*, 70 (April–June 1987):445.

38 Communist labor leader Eloy Torres wrote that in November 1948 the PCV sent him to the state of Falcón where he called for armed resistance to the coup: "We decreed a general strike and if we did not face the [military] insurgency with arms in our hands as I proposed it was because the Adecos backed down." Torres, "Soy hijo de la clase obrera y a ella he permanecido fiel durante toda la vida" in *Clarín*. 26 September 1962, p. 12.

39 Sanin, *Rómulo*, p. 263.

40 Juan Bautista Fuenmayor, *1928–1948: Veinte años de política*, 2d ed. (Caracas, 1979), p. 337.

41 *El País*, 11 January 1946, p. 22.

42 *Acción Democrática*, 9 February, 1946, p. 12.

Most important, the PCV called for the centralization of the labor movement and the elimination of parallel unions. The PCV argued that the industrial federations (such as Fedepetrol) should be replaced by national unions that would consist of individual locals or "sections." Since the national unions would have more authority than the federations had, they would be able to eliminate "parallel" organizations within their fold, which had often developed along party lines. Thus the Communists questioned the need to have two oil tanker workers unions, one for maritime workers who traveled abroad and another for those who did not, as well as the white-collar workers union, Asociación Nacional de Empleados (ANDE), in the oil industry alongside Fedepetrol. The Communists pointed out that parallel unionism made the "revolutionary practice" of the *cláusula sindical* virtually inoperative since two competing unions would never agree on the hiring of the same worker.[43] The PCV national leadership criticized both AD and Communist local trade unionists for being resistant to the dissolution of their own unions which lacked strength in order to join rival ones which had a larger number of workers.[44] These positions were accepted, at least in theory, by AD labor leaders who were also committed to combating parallel unionism, and who had made efforts to promote centralization in the form of the CTV and the industrial federations that were founded during the period.

The polarization of the hemispheric labor movement along ideological lines created tension between AD and the PCV. After some initial criticism, leaders of the CTV sympathized with the efforts of the American Federation of Labor (AFL) to form a rival to the allegedly pro-Communist Confederación de Trabajadores de América Latina (CTAL). However, they refused officially to take sides in the dispute, unlike, for example, the Alianza Popular Revolucionaria Americana (APRA) in Peru. AD peasant leader Ramón Quijada attended the CTAL convention in Mexico in April 1946 where the AFL attempted to gain recruits for a projected splinter group. Quijada was criticized by Venezuelan Communists for his support of various pro-AFL propositions. Nevertheless, he sponsored a resolution designed to maintain unity, and even called CTAL's president Vicente Lombardo Toledano a "great Mexican patriot."[45] The AFL's efforts finally came to fruition in January 1948 with the founding of the Confederación Interamericana de Trabajadores (CIT) in Lima. The CTV delegation, headed by its president, Pedro Bernardo Pérez Salinas, announced its decision to assume a mere observer status, much to the dismay of the

43 *El Popular*, 11 April 1947, p. 3.

44 *El Popular*, 4 January 1947, p. 3; Steve Ellner, "Factionalism in the Venezuelan Communist Movement, 1937–1948," *Science and Society* 45 (Spring 1981):66.

45 *El País*, 1 May 1946, p. 2.

host APRA representatives at the convention.[46] In fact, the disgruntled
*apristas* attempted to bar the Venezuelans from participating in the convention, although this proposal was overruled.[47] The incident demonstrated that, in spite of the ardent anticommunism of many AD labor
leaders, the AD-controlled labor movement was less anti-Communist and
more autonomous with reference to the polarities of the Cold War than
its ideological counterparts in other countries.

In contrast with other important sectors of organized labor, such as
oil, where only at the time of the October 1945 coup did AD eclipse the
PCV, AD's strength in the peasant movement had been overwhelming
since the foundation of the party in 1941. During the *trienio*, the Ministry
of Labor actively encouraged unionization in the countryside, and in doing
so undermined the paternalistic relations between peasants and landowners
as well as the latter's recourse to the use of force.[48] The *trienio* saw a
tenfold increase in the number of peasant organizations, most of which
were grouped in the Federación Campesina de Venezuela (FCV), which
in turn was affiliated with the CTV. Thus the AD government was
something of an exception in Latin America; elsewhere radical populist
regimes prohibited the organic integration of worker and peasant movements (as Lázaro Cárdenas did in Mexico, for example), and stopped short
of encouraging organizing activity in the countryside.

AD's agrarian reform of 1948, which has often been compared with
that of the government of Medina Angarita, has generated sharp debate
among scholars. D. F. Maza Zavala, for instance, has stated that the *trienio*
reform was timid in that its main objective was to promote colonization
schemes in which peasants were to settle on infertile or inhospitable land
owned by the state; he concludes by saying that while Medina's reform
was based on the principle of "land for the peasants," that of 1948 was
"peasants for the land."[49] Those who defend the AD *trienio* government
argue that the 1948 reform was more far-reaching and radical than that
of Medina.[50] The fact is that the main thrust of both reforms was the
distribution of state land rather than the breaking up of *latifundios*. This
was made possible by the state's possession of large extensions of land
that had been abandoned as a result of the decline in agriculture in the
1920s, as well as its confiscation of *gomecista* property after Gómez's death

---

46 See Steve Ellner, "Populism in Venezuela, 1935–48: Betancourt and Acción Democrática" in
  *Latin American Populism in Comparative Perspective*, ed. Michael Conniff (Albuquerque, NM, 1982),
  p. 144.

47 Pedro Bernardo Pérez Salinas [CTV president, 1947–8], interview in Caracas, 21 October 1986.

48 Armando González [ex-president of the FCV], interview in Caracas, 29 January 1987.

49 Agustín Blanco Muñoz [interviewer], *Venezuela: Historia de una frustración: Habla D. F. Maza
  Zavala* (Caracas, 1986), p. 68.

50 *El Popular*, 13 June 1947, p. 8.

in 1935.[51] Both reforms were ratified only after having been watered down from their original versions due to pressure from conservative sectors. Moreover, the two reforms were followed within weeks by the 1945 and 1948 coups, suggesting that powerful economic interests were in some way responsible for the overthrow of Medina and Gallegos.

The Communist leader Gustavo Machado used the same arguments against the agrarian reform of 1948 that he had used three years earlier against the reform sponsored by the Medina administration. He criticized AD's agrarian policy for stopping short of the takeover of large productive estates, and for offering part of the compensation for expropriated uncultivated land in cash, instead of paying for all of it in twenty-year bonds. Machado also attempted to refute statements by Ramón Quijada that the breakup of large estates could transform the countryside into autarchic *minifundios*. Machado pointed out that the peasants were so shackled by semifeudal obligations that they were unable to produce a surplus on their own land. Thus the elimination of latifundism would stimulate peasant production and do away with small nonexporting units in the countryside.[52]

Although conservatives had qualms about certain features of the 1948 agrarian reform, their major fear was not the reform per se, but the possibility that it would set off a process of agitation and mobilization that would be difficult to contain and would lead to more drastic changes. Conservatives took apprehensive note of the vacillations and contradictions in the positions assumed by the FCV and its president, Ramón Quijada, some of which went counter to AD's respect for private property. The FCV published a pamphlet in 1948 that called for "agriculture without latifundism," "the socialization of agricultural production," and the expropriation of large estates without compensation. The federation went on to proclaim that the revolution in the countryside was the most pressing task facing the government: "The latifundist system . . . has been the principle cause of the decadence of our economy and [explains why] the stabilization of our democratic regime has not been possible."[53] These statements were especially significant because the FCV was to play a major role in the administration of the agrarian reform. In short, FCV leaders represented a vanguard within the governing party, which threatened to propel relatively moderate reforms to a leftist extreme.

Prominent members of the opposition who took a wait-and-see attitude, and refused initially to condemn the coup of 24 November 1948, have

---

51 Manuel Caballero, *Rómulo Betancourt* (Caracas, 1977), pp. 74–80.
52 *El Popular*, 13 June 1947, p. 8.
53 FCV, *La cuestión agraria*, pp. 3–4.

justified their behavior by saying that the new regime did not truly define itself until several years later.[54] Although it is true that the military junta was not homogeneous, the coup from the very outset was reactionary in that its primary objective was to undo the reforms of the *trienio* government. At the time of the coup, Junta President Carlos Delgado Chalbaud assured the U.S. ambassador that the new military rulers felt AD's oil policy was too radical, especially the policy of "no more concessions," as was its educational policy and the agrarian reform.[55] The Junta returned distributed land to its original owners and it outlawed most labor organizations.

The main target of the military rebels was AD, particularly its "extremist" wing, rather than the PCV. López Contreras, who had attempted to rally military support to overthrow the *trienio* government on the basis of its alleged ties with the Communist movement, was not held in high regard by the young officers who had plotted first against Medina, and then against Gallegos. The new military rulers immediately outlawed AD, but gave public assurances to the PCV that it would retain its legal status – as indeed it did until May 1950 when the Communists participated in a national oil workers strike with insurrectional overtones.

In the days prior to the November coup, the military rebels presented Gallegos with an ultimatum that called for the exile of Rómulo Betancourt and the replacement of all but four AD cabinet members with military officers and independents. The conspirators defended these demands as necessary in order to free the presidency of the control of AD and its "extremist elements." In lashing out at AD "extremists," the military insurgents were referring to two distinct sources of danger. In the first place, AD extremists were those who promoted agitation over reforms, land distribution, and wage benefits, and whose real aim was to achieve a social revolution, if not socialism. Betancourt, who invariably attempted to moderate party stands and had clearly renounced his former socialist beliefs, was not included in this version of extremism.

In the second place, the military rebels viewed the AD extremists as those who were bent on restricting the decision-making power of the military and submitting it to government and even party dictates. Despite the naive assumptions of many of the supporters of the *trienio* government,[56] the young officers who participated in the October coup remained unsatisfied with the military's original representation in the cabinet, and

---

54 Martín Marval [leading dissident Communist labor leader], interview in Anaco, 19 May 1976.

55 "Documentos para la historia: La crisis del 48 y el derrocamiento de Gallegos" in *El Nacional*, 13 April 1980, p. C–4.

56 Jorge Eliécer Gaitán, *La revolución venezolana en la opinión extranjera: Declaraciones del ilustre Dr. Jorge*, (Caracas, 1946), p. 18; "Documentos para la historia: La política venezolana entre 1945 y 1948" in *El Nacional*, 25 May 1980, p. C–1.

chafed at the erosion of its influence in the course of the *trienio*.[57] The discontented officers recognized that AD, with its vocation for power and its mass base, would inevitably encroach on the authority of the military and would be in a stronger position to overcome military resistance than were previous governments. Many officers took seriously the threat (which turned out to be a mere bluff) made by Betancourt in public – and again by AD's Secretary of Organization Alberto Carnevali to the military plotters in private – of calling a general strike to halt the conspiracy against Gallegos.[58]

The military was not only apprehensive of the institutionalization of the Armed Forces – an integral part of the modernization process – but of AD interference in military appointments, and the party's efforts to carve out a sphere of influence within the officer corps.[59] Thus the military exerted pressure on the government to replace its minister of the interior, Valmore Rodríguez, whose brother was a high-ranking military officer.[60] In the days before the November coup, the rebels also insisted on the exile of Lieutenant Colonel Jesús Manuel Gámez and General Mario Vargas, who were two leading AD *adictos,* and demanded a pledge that AD would not influence military appointments.[61] The Military Junta that took over on November 24 declared: "The extremist faction that controlled AD initiated a series of maneuvers designed to dominate . . . the Armed Forces, trying to sow discord and disunion within it."[62] Within this institutional context, the rebels considered Betancourt to be AD's leading extremist.

In addition to acting on the basis of its own concerns, the military in November 1948 was a barometer of the attitudes of other powerful economic and political sectors. This is not to say that the Armed Forces acted at the behest of these groups, or that their outlook and interests completely coincided, as some interpretations of the November coup have stated or implied.[63] Pressure was exerted by landowning and business

---

57  Cordero Velásquez, *Betancourt y la conjura militar, p. 189;* Andrés Stambouli, *Crisis política: Venezuela, 1945–58* (Caracas, 1980), p. 83.

58  "Documentos para la historia: La política venezolana entre 1945 y 1948 vista por los embajadores y agregados militares de Estados Unidos en Venezuela" in *El Nacional,* 14 April 1980, p. C–2.

59  Robert J. Alexander points to the military's fear of the "institutionalization of civilian control" without referring to the danger of party control of the armed forces. Alexander, *Rómulo Betancourt and the Transformation of Venezuela* (New Brunswick, NJ, 1982), p. 314.

60  "Documentos para la historia: El derrocamiento del general Medina Angarita" in *El Nacional,* 12 April 1980, p. C–2; Ramón J. Velásquez, "Aspectos de la evolución política de Venezuela en el último medio siglo" in *Venezuela moderna: Medio siglo de historia, 1926–1976* (Barcelona, 1979), p. 92.

61  Fuenmayor, *Historia de la Venezuela,* vol. 7, p. 567.

62  *SIC* 11 (December 1948):486.

63  See, for example, Harvey O'Connor, *World Crisis in Oil* (New York, 1962), p. 145.

sectors and the conservative opposition, the Copei party in particular, all of which were hostile to the *trienio* government. Whereas industrialists and their representatives talked of "aggressive and authoritarian trade unionism,"[64] landowners lashed out, not so much at the agrarian reform itself, as at the peasant movement that the reform stimulated and encouraged. One article in the conservative *El Universal* ominously stated: "There is a new war cry in the peasant movement – 'Long live the [agrarian] reform and destruction to the abhorrent *haciendas*.'"[65] Copei, in its newspaper *El Gráfico*, attempted to incite the Armed Forces by warning of the danger that the *trienio* government posed to its interests and of the existence of a pact between AD and the PCV.[66] Like the Armed Forces, powerful economic groups were apprehensive of the institutionalization and further strengthening of AD's mass support and the possibility that, at a given point, the party would move significantly to the Left. Concessions that the government offered these interest groups and modifications in its policies were not sufficient to temper these fears.

Conflicting opinions have been expressed regarding the role of external forces in the November coup. One AD historian implied that the oil companies were partly responsible for the overthrow of Gallegos,[67] whereas Gallegos himself blamed both petroleum interests and U.S. diplomats, although he subsequently retracted his statement after receiving a letter from President Truman disclaiming involvement.[68] Betancourt and Domingo Alberto Rangel, who represented a leftist current in AD at the time, adamantly denied that the United States was behind the coup. Betancourt claimed that the military rebels were closely linked to Argentine president Juan Domingo Perón, an assertion that has been reinforced by ex-PCV secretary general Juan Bautista Fuenmayor,[69] but denied by Betancourt's biographer and friend, Robert Jackson Alexander.[70]

64 *El Universal*, 29 October 1948, p. 4.
65 *El Universal*, 19 October 1948, p. 4.
66 *Documentos para la historia*, p. 6. Copei historians have denied that their party belonged to the disloyal opposition or played a role in the overthrow of Gallegos. This thesis is based on Copei's program during the *trienio*, which coincided in large part with that of the government, and on the party's less intransigent posture during its early months of existence. See Naudy Suárez F., "Los socialcristianos en el trienio 1946–1948" in *Los Copeyanos* (Caracas, 1982), pp. 75–113; José Rodríguez Iturbe, "Los socialcristianos y la década 1949–1958" in *Los Copeyanos*, pp. 123–4. Rodolfo José Cárdenas, *Copei en el trienio populista, 1945–1948: La tentación totalitaria de Acción Democrática* (Madrid, 1987). Some AD members claimed that Copei leaders conferred with the military rebels prior to the 24 November coup. See Alberto Carnevali, "Itinerario de una traición" in *El Cuartelazo del 24 de November 1948* (Caracas, 1980), p. 58.
67 Carpio Castillo, *Acción Democrática: Bosquejo histórico de un partido, 1941–1974*, 2d ed. (Caracas, 1983), p. 89.
68 *Documentos para la historia*, pp. 301–47.
69 Fuenmayor, *Historia de la Venezuela*, vol. 7, p. 579.
70 Alexander, *Rómulo Betancourt*, p. 299.

Gallegos's original accusation against the United States was based on eyewitness accounts of the presence of the U.S. military attaché, Colonel E. F. Adams, alongside the rebel leaders at the time of the coup. Those who deny U.S. involvement point out that Adams represented only himself, and that in conferring with the military rebels, he was disobeying orders from U.S. Ambassador Walter Donnelly who, along with other embassy officials, maintained cordial relations with the *trienio* government. U.S. diplomatic papers, however, demonstrate that Adams's animosity toward AD was shared by various military attachés who preceded him in Caracas and who accused Betancourt of being a Communist, even suggesting the necessity of a coup. These officials were especially concerned that the militant oil workers unions, some of which were dominated by the PCV, could endanger the steady supply of oil, a concern that Donnelly himself shared and expressed to President Gallegos in private. One military diplomat wrote to the Defense Department in 1946: "There is evidence that AD is secretly providing support to the Communists in favor of greater demands to the [oil] companies in order to create a crisis which would lead to greater government intervention and participation in the petroleum industry."[71]

In addition, an ex-U.S. military official in Caracas was apprehended in the United States for his participation in a plot to steal weapons from the U.S. army to finance the overthrow of the Venezuelan government.[72]

The differences among embassy officials in Caracas reflected internal fissures in Washington where Acting Secretary of State Dean Acheson attempted to refute charges formulated by the Defense Department that the *trienio* regime menaced U.S. economic and strategic interests.[73] The detractors of the *trienio* regime in the Truman administration were more than just mildly critical: their hostility toward AD was sufficiently aggressive as to suggest that they were in contact with the military rebels and expressed support for their plans at the time of the November coup. Most likely, Colonel Adams, far from acting on his own, was a courier who carried out instructions from higher levels.

The negative attitude of an important current of opinion within the Truman administration toward the *trienio* government can be explained in terms of international trends. In 1945, the cornerstone of Truman's foreign policy was the defense of pro-U.S. democratic governments, whereas with the outbreak of the Cold War, this objective was eclipsed by anticommunism. The tremendous power that the United States enjoyed

71 Fuenmayor, *Historia de la Venezuela*, vol. 7, pp. 486, 491.
72 *Documentos para la historia*, p. 159.
73 Fuenmayor, *Historia de la Venezuela*, vol. 7, p. 487; "Documentos para la historia: El derrocamiento," 12 April 1980, p. C-2.

following the defeat of fascism meant that this change of priority in Washington was strongly felt throughout Latin America. Military regimes came to power in several countries and were more forcefully anti-Communist than their democratic predecessors. At the same time, the democratic governments of Brazil and Chile outlawed the Communist Party, while the president of Cuba publicly announced his determination to destroy Communist influence in organized labor. In contrast, the PCV retained its legal status and maintained relatively cordial relations with important leaders in the governing party. Furthermore, the *trienio* government devised the "Betancourt Doctrine" whereby diplomatic relations with military regimes were severed at the same time that aid was apparently extended to antidictatorial insurgents.[74] These moves, by 1948, were clearly out of tune with the times and at odds with U.S. foreign policy objectives.

U.S. businessmen and diplomats as well as conservative Venezuelan leaders expressed fears that AD had allied itself with the Communist Party: they stated or hinted that the Venezuelan government should outlaw the PCV.[75] Conservatives noted that the Venezuelan delegation to the Ninth Inter-American Conference in Bogotá (which was headed by Betancourt), in contrast to that of other nations, was "lukewarm in everything that referred to repression of Communism."[76] Communist influence in organized labor, and particularly among oil workers, was an additional cause for alarm. During these years the United States was greatly concerned about how the Latin American labor movement would react in the eventuality of a Third World War. This preoccupation was especially pronounced in the case of Venezuela due to the strategic importance of oil and the militant tradition of the oil workers' unions.

Betancourt and Gallegos were not oblivious to the mounting pressure from conservative and anti-Communist circles. They were wary that the efforts to dub the *trienio* government "pro-Communist," or "soft on Communism," could endanger foreign assistance programs and, in the words of Betancourt, "reach the extreme of convincing the United States [government] to cancel licenses for the export of machines and food to Venezuela."[77] Both Gallegos and Betancourt went to great pains to assure the United States that Venezuela was willing to take stringent measures to contain communism. President Gallegos accepted Ambassador Donnelly's proposal, made in private, to invite foreign counterinsurgency specialists to train Venezuelans for the purpose of counteracting the Com-

74 Charles D. Ameringer, *The Democratic Left in Exile: The Antidictatorial Struggle in the Caribbean, 1945–1959* (Coral Gables, FL, 1974), pp. 65–6.
75 *El Gráfico*, 15 June 1948, p. 8; Alexander, *Rómulo Betancourt*, p. 288.
76 *SIC* 11 (May 1948):241.
77 *El Nacional*, 25 May 1948, p. 14.

munist threat. At the Bogotá conference, Betancourt discussed similar ideas with Secretary of State George Marshall.[78]

Betancourt made an additional effort to confront the problem of the alleged Communist menace shortly after his meeting with Marshall. In a private gathering in his house with the presidents of the Venezuelan subsidiaries of Standard Oil, Shell, and Gulf, along with the president and vice-president of Fedepetrol, Betancourt argued that in the event of a world war, or a further deterioration in the international situation, the task of repressing the Communists should be shared by the government, the oil industry, and Fedepetrol. The response of the Fedepetrol leaders did not at all please the company executives. The Shell president later jotted down his impressions of the encounter: "It was unfortunate that the worker leaders expressed the opinion that the best way to fight against the Communist threat was for the companies to give in on everything that Fedepetrol asked for, not only to strengthen the federation but so that the Communists would not have anything left to demand." The head of Shell went on to say that he and his two colleagues attempted to explain the unfeasibility of this strategy, and that their arguments were well received by Betancourt.[79]

The basic danger to U.S. interests was not posed by Betancourt, Gallegos, or other top AD leaders, but rather by the party's mass base and the workers themselves, who were flushed with confidence as a result of labor's organizational gains and the government's recently enacted reforms. Even the most realistic and well-informed conservatives who projected into the future could not help but see the following scenario: AD, squared off against powerful economic forces and conservative adversaries, would discard its anti-Communist rhetoric, ally itself with the PCV, and move further to the Left. Conservative distrust of populist parties like AD stemmed from the fact that with their ideological ambiguity, popular makeup, radical program, and antiestablishment rhetoric, they could move to the far Left, renege on their guarantees to private property, and even abandon their anticommunism. Betancourt's gestures of good intentions were not enough to dispel these fears and convince AD's critics that the *trienio* government did not jeopardize U.S. and business interests.

During the 1940s, AD occupied a middle ground on the Latin American democratic Left.[80] On the one hand, AD's pragmatic strategy of sub-

---

78 "Documentos para la historia: El derrocamiento," p. C-2.

79 Nora Bustamante, *Isaías Medina Angarita: Aspectos históricos de su gobierno* (Caracas, 1985), p. 581; Ismael Ordaz [vice-president of Fedepetrol, 1946–8], interview in Maracaibo, 5 August 1976.

80 AD maintained close historical ties with the leaders (or future leaders) of the Renovación Nacional of Guatemala, the Partido Socialista of Chile, and the Partido Revolucionario Dominicano (PRD) of the Dominican Republic. Alexander notes AD's "particularly close relationship" with the

merging long-term goals placed it to the Right of Chile's Partido Socialista, which was more straightforward about its structural objectives. On the other hand, AD was reluctant to arrive at understandings with political movements to its right, which it viewed as the major threat to its government. In contrast, APRA, which has often been considered identical to AD, was willing to form alliances with forces to its right in order to get close to the sources of power, a policy that would later earn it the reputation of being "opportunistic" due to its pact with right-wing military figures. The contrast between AD and APRA was noted by Jorge Eliécer Gaitán, himself a leading member of the leftist current of the democratic Left, when he wrote shortly after the October coup: "Contrary to what happened to Aprismo, when it reached power and found itself burnt out and lacking vitality as a result of a struggle which had lasted many years, the members of Acción Democrática came to power fresh and dynamic with all the potential for the execution of its ideas."[81] Another important difference between APRA and AD was that the former worked hand in glove with the Conservative AFL in setting up the CIT for the purpose of dealing international communism a blow. In contrast, AD identified more with the left-leaning Congress of Industrial Organizations (CIO). Moreover, in spite of AD's strident anticommunism, the *trienio* government did not succumb to the anti-Communist furor of the period by outlawing the PCV or openly declaring war on it in the labor movement, as did the government of another party of the democratic Left, Cuba's Partido Auténtico (PRC–A). The AD government was aided in its bold approach to reforms and its refusal to cede to Cold War pressures by the oil boom, which translated itself into increased government revenue. Unlike Venezuela, many other Latin American nations faced bleak economic prospects and were thus more vulnerable to pressure from foreign sources. Undoubtedly, the political differences between AD and its counterparts in Peru, Cuba, and elsewhere were noted by those members of the Truman administration – particularly in the Defense Department – who used the epithets "extremist" and "pro-Communist" only against AD among the parties of the democratic Left. These officials viewed AD as a threat to U.S. interests and applauded the coup of 24 November 1948 that removed it from power.

government of Juan José Arévalo, which came to power in 1944 in Guatemala. Alexander, *Rómulo Betancourt*, p. 282; Betancourt, "Discurso de Rómulo Betancourt" in *Acción Democrática: Primeros años: Oposición y poder, 1941–1948* (Caracas, 1987), p. 154.

81 Gaitán, *La revolución venezolana*, p. 18.

# 6

## Peru

*Nigel Haworth*

Peru enjoyed a unique political opening between 1945 and 1948. In June 1945 José Luis Bustamante y Rivero, the candidate of the Frente Democrático Nacional (FDN) (a broad popular front formed in 1944) was elected president in Peru's first free elections with the support of the Alianza Popular Revolucionaria Americana (APRA), Peru's one large, popular, mass-based political party, which had been forced to operate illegally for more than a decade. The Bustamante administration replaced the explicitly pro-oligarchic regime of Manuel Prado (1939–45). The transfer of power seemed to herald an era of freedom for popular political organization and debate, trade union development, economic restructuring, and social change. However, in October 1948, only three years after his electoral success, Bustamante was overthrown by a military coup and replaced by the dictatorship of General Manuel Odría (1948–56). The window of opportunity was firmly closed – and remained closed until the early 1960s. The failure of the Bustamante experiment (1945–8) was due to a variety of factors. The political liberalization was premature and unsustainable, primarily because traditional political elites were unwilling to concede power to a popular mandate, and the representatives of popular political power – APRA especially – were unable to seize political control or negotiate a stable, long-term political opening. The lack of a significant industrial bourgeoisie able to counter the demands of the traditional agro-export elite contributed to the resilience of the status quo. At the same time, Peru's political opening received no support from the United States. The U.S. State Department was primarily concerned with Argentina and the broader issues of hemispheric security. Only economic issues associated primarily with the servicing of U.S. bondholders' debts attracted the attention of the United States. In the eyes of U.S. foreign policy makers at the end of the Second World War, and at the beginning of the Cold War, Peru remained a marginal concern.

However, this simple picture of failure and marginality obscures a number of facets of the Peruvian postwar *apertura* that provide a fascinating insight into the longevity of the Peruvian oligarchy, the role of APRA in Peruvian politics, and the role of the Peruvian labor movement in carrying Cold War ideologies into the international labor movement.[1]

Four factors dominated the political process prior to the election of Bustamante in 1945: the ability of the agro-export elite to establish an accommodation with the Leguía, Benavides, and Prado governments that dominated Peru between the wars; the failure of a popular opposition to consolidate a constituency in either the incipient middle classes or the working class within a democratic order; the tenuous hold of democratic principles and practices of the Peruvian polity; and the continuing domination of the economy by traditional agro-export and mining sectors at the expense of an effective industrialization policy. Each of these factors became simultaneously a target for Bustamante's reform and a challenge to his ability to wrest power from the established oligarchy.

The 1895 civil war set the agenda for Peruvian politics until the mid–1950s. A small, coastal agro-export elite – often termed the "oligarchy" or, in Carlos Astiz's phrase, the "coastal plutocrats" – brushed aside a challenge from the Sierra landlords who consequently went into political and economic decline. Content with their control of the dominant agro-export sectors, and able usually to control directly or indirectly the state, the elite manifested little interest in a coherent strategic development policy for Peru. Industrialization opportunities around the turn of the century were missed, reform of a notoriously weak and unsophisticated state apparatus was not undertaken, and democratic political reforms, for example, the extension of the franchise, were rejected.

In terms of popular opposition to the established political order, little organizational headway was made until the 1920s when APRA – formed in Mexico in 1924 and formally constituted in Peru in 1928 – and the Partido Comunista Peruano (PCP) – formed in 1930 from the Partido Socialista that had been founded in 1928 – came into existence. APRA and the PCP were at loggerheads when the crucial opportunity for popular mobilization arose after the fall of the Leguía dictatorship in 1930.[2] The byzantine twists of Peruvian politics between Augusto B. Leguía's fall and the taking of power by Oscar Benavides in 1933 are of relevance only insofar as they offered little opportunity for democratic political processes

---

1 I would like to express my thanks to the Institute of Latin American Studies, University of London, for the support that enabled me to complete archival research in Washington, D.C. My thanks also to the staff of the U.S. National Archives, who greatly aided me in the concentrated perusal of their records.

2 On the clash between the PCP and APRA in the early 1930s, see C. Balbi, *El Partido Comunista y el APRA en la crisis revolucionaria de los años treinta* (Lima, 1980).

to take root and provided neither the PCP or APRA with an opening to power. The PCP, weak in numbers and organization, was quickly driven from the political scene by repression. APRA had a sufficiently broad following in the urban population, labor movement, and regional centers of the country to pose a serious threat. But defeated in the elections of 1931, and compromised by insurrections leading to the bloody events in Trujillo in 1932, APRA was also driven underground by Benavides in 1934. The experience of popular mobilization in Peru up to 1945 was, therefore, substantially colored by this major defeat in the early 1930s, which caused the dislocation of organizations with popular bases. Equally important, the established political order was not forced by events to reform its structures in order to permit popular democratic participation. Rather, the antidemocratic rigidities fostered by Leguía were continued under Benavides's dictatorship (1933–9) and Prado's oligarchical administration (1939–45) – with clear consequences for the 1945–8 opening.

The populist, later explicitly pro-fascist, tradition launched by Luis M. Sánchez Cerro in the aftermath of the collapse of the Leguía dictatorship merits some attention at this point. *Sanchezcerrismo* offered an alternative populist option to that purveyed by APRA.[3] Based on a broad, if fragile, coalition of urban workers, peasants, and the *sierra* population of the Center and South, its focus was the personal status of Sánchez Cerro and, rapidly, an explicit anti-APRA position. The political base built up around Sánchez Cerro actively provided support for the Benavides government and, in the form of the Unión Revolucionaria, supported General Eloy Ureta's candidacy in the 1945 elections. The U.S. embassy reported to Washington in May 1945 that the Unión Revolucionaria constituted "the APRA of the Right,"[4] and in its reporting of Peruvian politics in the preelection period, emphasized the continuing tradition of support for *sanchezcerrismo* from the extreme, even fascist, Right. The presence of this tradition had one crucial effect on Peruvian political life – APRA was deprived of some popular sectors that might otherwise have been drawn to its own opposition to the oligarchy.

Notwithstanding the eclipse of the PCP, the repression of APRA, and the dissipation of political opposition to the oligarchy, pressures for political change grew under both Benavides and Prado (1933–45). Benavides

3 On *sanchezcerrismo*, see B. Loveday, *Sánchez Cerro and Peruvian Politics, 1930–33*, Institute of Latin American Studies, Occasional Paper no. 6 (Glasgow 1973), and S. Stein, *Populism in Peru* (Madison, UW, 1980).

4 U.S. National Archive 823.00 5–1145, No. 3265. These files are drawn from the 823.00 series, which brings together embassy reports with some U.S. State Department documentation. The details appended to the 823.00 file number relate to individual document identification – date and report or telegram number if available. Much of the key material in the 823.00 series is not available for use due to FBI and CIA vetting.

came to power with a twofold project: firstly, to establish order after the turmoil of 1929–33 – his slogan "Paz, Orden, Trabajo" captures this aspect of his rule; secondly, to create circumstances for an effective transition to civilian power in the 1936 elections. Manuel Prado was the chosen individual to succeed Benavides, and the 1936 electoral process seemed set to achieve the handover of power to a Center–Right democratic coalition. However, this "National Front" fragmented quickly; APRA, though legally barred from the elections, appeared as an electoral threat to Benavides's planned process, and a variety of other candidatures were quickly presented. Benavides responded vigorously by annulling the October election, setting up a military government, and biding his time until he could be certain of a Prado victory, as was to be the case in 1939. Nevertheless, the plurality of political projects exhibited in the 1936 electoral process demonstrated the burgeoning pressure for the creation of an open, democratic political system. Under Manuel Prado (1939–45), this demand would become an imperative.

Manuel Prado was successfully elected in 1939 with the backing of Benavides, the explicit constraining of a more conservative oligarchic candidate, José Quesadas Larrea, and the continuing exclusion of APRA from the political process. The Prado administration, however, heralded policy changes on a number of fronts. In a general sense, the issue of social change emerged as urbanization, ideas associated with liberal democracy counterposed to fascism (and Bolshevism), and perceptions of the bankruptcy of the oligarchic model became more widespread. Politically, working-class and middle-class pressure grew and posed the issue of accommodation rejected in the 1930–3 settlement.[5] Economic policy changed too, particularly with regard to the role of the state and the role of industrial promotion.

State economic policy in the 1930s had responded to the Depression in distinctive style. The oligarchy, confirmed in power by the outcome of the crisis of 1930–3, rejected the state-led, import-substitution model frequently employed elsewhere in Latin America. Popular pressure was disarmed by the defeats of 1930–3, and there was little effective challenge to an economic policy that continued to promote the traditional export orientation. Equally, the diversity of the export sector and the relatively sound performance of some export products gave the oligarchy a degree of economic security, which obviated the need for a strong protectionist, interventionist state. Prado's economic policies after 1939 appeared to be very different. In particular, state expenditure grew from revenues gen-

5 N. Haworth, "Restoring Disorder: Problems in the Analysis of Peruvian Industrial Relations" in *Region and Class in Modern Peruvian History,* ed. R. Miller, CLAS Monograph no. 14 (Liverpool, 1987).

erated by taxation of exports, and investment funds expanded due to increased enterprise profitability. Despite this, large-scale industrialization based on national capital did not emerge, though a degree of sectoral diversification was achieved.

Perhaps the key issue in the late 1930s and early 1940s was the growth of a new base for trade unions, legally registered under Benavides's 1936 legislation. Between 1940 and 1945, 118 unions were registered (compared with 33 between 1936 and 1939).[6] Food processing, brewing, transport, commerce, leather working, and service sectors experienced a degree of union expansion in this period. The focal point for these new union organizations was the cost of living. Prado sought to keep the cost of living index stable by freezing the prices of basic goods, in the process disturbing elements in the oligarchy who feared such a strategy might compromise the "sound money" strategy of the 1930s. However, pressure mounted from the union movement after 1943, culminating in the 1944 formation of the Confederación de Trabajadores de Peru (CTP). The CTP focused attention on the rise in the cost of living (83 percent between 1939 and 1945) and the willingness of some labor leaders to cooperate with the Prado government in an attempt to defuse wage demands.[7] Certainly the September 1944 general strike in Lima was a breakthrough in terms of independent union action after the defeats of the early 1930s. The CTP was at the forefront of the September action, and a national union presence became a possibility.

The marginalization of the PCP in the early 1930s resulted in the CTP falling firmly into the hands of APRA.[8] Although formally illegal until the 1945 election campaign, APRA's search for power looked to electoral alliances as the way forward. As the rejection of the traditional insurrectionism gained ground in APRA's ranks, so did the fear that too militant a labor movement might prejudice APRA's chances of legality and its participation in the 1945 elections. Consequently, the leadership of the CTP found itself in an ambiguous position, on the one hand enjoying the support of a newly energized and militant constituency, on the other, under guidance not to undermine the electoral process. In any event, APRA opted to support the liberal Bustamante in return for preelection legality and postelection favors.

Before turning to the Bustamante government of 1945–8, it is important to understand the relationship between the United States and Peru before 1945. Under Leguía, the United States enjoyed close contact with the

6 D. Sulmont, *Historia del movimiento obrero peruano 1890–1977* (Lima, 1977).
7 Ibid., pp. 81–2.
8 Ibid., pp. 84–5.

Peruvian state. There is some suggestion that Leguía's coup in 1919 enjoyed overt support from the U.S. representative in Lima and from U.S. weapons manufacturers. U.S. firms and U.S. citizens enjoyed privileged access to Leguía. It is therefore interesting to note that the United States did little to help Leguía when he fell from power in 1930, the corruption that marked his later years in office playing some part in determining U.S. reactions to his fall.[9]

The lasting consequence of Leguía's link with the United States was the debt burden built up on extensive borrowing, especially in 1927 and 1928. In these two years, securities to the value of $100 million were issued in the United States and in Europe.[10] The problem of debt servicing and debt settlement would haunt all Peruvian governments until a settlement was reached in the 1950s. During the Bustamante government, for example, conversations between Peru and the United States about aid were constantly inconclusive. U.S. Ambassador Prentice Cooper maintained that only when an acceptable debt settlement package had been established, would U.S. aid for Peru be a serious proposition.[11]

On the surface of things, the 1930–3 crisis seemed to lead to a decline in the role of the United States in Peru. The Depression caused a fall in the levels of U.S. investment and, potentially, a decline in influence, whereas political instability made it necessary to remove the previously powerful naval mission in 1933. However, contemporary commentaries point to the continuing domination of large parts of the export sector, external finance, communications, and transport by U.S. capital, and a continuing relationship between families in the oligarchy, the U.S. embassy, and U.S. enterprises.[12] There is little doubt that, just as the resolution of the crisis in Peru brought a high degree of continuity in the structure of political power, there was a similar continuity in the indirect influence enjoyed by the United States and its representatives up to the outbreak of the Second World War, if not with the same degree of closeness as that enjoyed under Leguía.

The war brought Peru and the United States into a much closer relationship. Although Peru was to make a declaration of belligerency only as late as 1945, and then primarily in order to be permitted to attend the conference of the United Nations in San Francisco, economic contacts

9 On U.S.–Peruvian relations in the first half of the twentieth century, see J. Carey, *Peru and the United States 1900–1962* (Notre Dame, IN, 1964).

10 Ibid., p. 73.

11 823.00 12–3146, No. 1296, Prentice Cooper to Secretary of State Telegram, 31 December 1946.

12 It is again worth emphasizing the constant links, both formal and informal, between embassy officials and representatives of the oligarchy. Much tittle-tattle was relayed to Washington in the 1945–8 period based on these contacts, much of which proved to be wrong.

were maintained throughout the war. In 1941 discussions were held between Peru and the United States about closer military ties, harking back to the close ties up to 1933. In 1942 Peru agreed to guarantee the sale of surplus rubber to the U.S. government; throughout the war key metals (copper, vanadium, molybdenum) were sold to the United States on the basis of a 1941 agreement, as was cotton after 1942. Peru cooperated with the U.S. government in the removal of Axis nationals from positions of authority in the Peruvian air transport network. Japanese – but not German – property in Peru was expropriated and distributed as a bonus to the government's allies. During the war Peru received $18 million of Lend–Lease aid – an amount exceeded only by that given to Brazil, Mexico, and Chile. There was indeed an ever-deepening relationship through cultural exchanges, health aid, and personal contacts, reinforcing the economic links.[13] Peru even accepted price controls on export goods, which substantially reduced export earnings on the open market.

This increasingly close relationship between Peru and the United States developed despite occasional differences. Chief among these was the war with Ecuador in 1941, which the United States wished to see brought to an end as rapidly as possible. Although the United States sought to direct Latin America's attention toward the larger conflict then in full flow, such a policy did not find favor with all Peruvians. Felipe Barreda Laos, the Peruvian ambassador to Argentina, strongly attacked U.S. insistence that Pan-American neutrality be rejected in favor of an anti-Axis position, arguing that such a policy would permit the United States to divide and rule in Latin America. Perhaps surprisingly, this argument found little favor with the erstwhile strongly anti-United States APRA. Víctor Haya de la Torre himself spoke forcefully in favor of actions in alliance with the United States, and downplayed the traditional APRA critique of U.S. imperialism. There was apparently a good deal of elite support for Barreda's analysis, implying that the closeness between Prado and the United States was not well regarded by all sections of the oligarchy.[14] Certainly, in popular political circles, fears about U.S. intervention, which had existed since the 1920s, played a minor part in the anti-Prado labor movement, but this was complicated by the changing position of the PCP, which in 1941 moved to all-out support of the Allies.

APRA's attitude toward the United States had changed markedly; from its formation in 1924, APRA had seemingly abhorred it. "Yankee imperialism" was a prime target for Haya's oratory. However, by the early 1940s, circumstances had created a new climate in which U.S.–APRA relations might be reassessed. On APRA's side, the decade in the "cat-

---

13 Carey, *Peru.*
14 A. Whitaker, *The United States and South America: The Northern Republics* (Harvard, 1948), p. 148.

acombs" had introduced a growing pragmatism into the *aprista* ideology. To gain legality and make use of its massive popular base in elections, APRA was willing to concede ideological ground in political alliance building. The Second World War also brought APRA closer to the Allies than to the Axis, and Luis Alberto Sánchez, a leading *aprista,* argued that it was Haya's anti-Axis, pro-Roosevelt position that led to the establishment of relations between U.S. Ambassador John Campbell White and APRA in late 1944 and early 1945.[15] It should also be added that APRA's strategists looked to the United States to provide the foreign capital that would be needed to initiate economic growth in the postwar era.[16] On the eve of the 1945 elections, the U.S. embassy believed that "little doubt remained that victory for Dr. Bustamante spells government in Peru by APRA."[17] The United States continued, however, to be reassured by APRA's evident popular power, its avowed commitment to democracy and inter-American cooperation, and its explicit anticommunism. Indeed it has been argued that Ambassadors Pawley and Cooper remained fundamentally sympathetic to APRA throughout the period 1945–8.[18]

The life of the Bustamante government may be analyzed in four phases: the period immediately after the election, June–December 1945; the formal involvement of APRA in the government, January 1946–January 1947; the dropping of APRA from the government, January–July 1947; and the constitutional stalemate, July 1947 to the coup in October 1948. Throughout, the government faced three adverse factors – political instability, economic weakness, and the presence of a newly confident urban working class.

The political instability that dogged Bustamante's government was signaled in the politicking during the election itself. The Frente Democrático Nacional (FDN), which supported Bustamante, was a very pragmatic and fragile coalition of regionalist, constitutionalist, and democratic political elements united solely by their opposition to Prado, Benavides, and the candidate of the oligarchy, General Eloy Ureta, supported by the Unión Revolucionaria. Tacit support for the FDN was also forthcoming from APRA (after much negotiation) and from the PCP. It was apparent that the 1945 election had created, or drawn on, few new forces in Peruvian political life.[19] Many of the pro-Bustamante groups had been pro-Prado in 1939 and had simply shifted allegiance to the more

15 Carey, *Peru,* p. 117.

16 G. Portocarrero, *De Bustamante a Odría* (Lima, 1983), p. 138.

17 823.00 5–2945, No. 3777, Embassy Dispatch to Secretary of State, 29 May 1945.

18 Carey, *Peru,* p. 118.

19 G. Bertram, "Peru 1930–1960" in *The Cambridge History of Latin America Volume VIII: Spanish South America since 1930,* ed. L. Bethell (Cambridge, 1991), p. 425–9.

explicitly democratic FDN, but, with the obvious exceptions of APRA and the Unión Revolucionaria, no large-scale, relatively homogeneous mass party organizations were present in the 1945 campaign.

The instability of the political process attracted U.S. embassy attention. The overriding concern in the embassy was the presentation of "an acceptable civilian candidate . . . who [would] in due course receive the blessing of President Prado and thus remove the shadow of the armed forces from the scene."[20] U.S. observers were concerned about the "obscure and unpredictable" nature of the incipient democratization process, and, in particular, were worried that Benavides would increase the political presence of the PCP on the basis of a campaign for social justice. A fear existed that APRA, already displaying a pragmatic approach to electoral politics, was seeking an alliance with Benavides since Prado seemed to have lost control of the reelection bargaining process.[21] U.S. commentators harbored grave fears for the successful completion of the June 1945 elections, as the army, APRA, and Prado were all viewed as likely conspirators. The sudden death of Benavides in July represented the demise of a bulwark against unrestrained APRA power and further raised the prospect of military intervention.[22]

The electoral program of the FDN was seen as posing a threat to foreign investment in Peru. Edward G. Trueblood, first secretary of the embassy, described it as "a mixture of APRA political philosophy heavily diluted with *Benavidismo*," and as "reflect [ing]. . . . an awareness of the trend of political and economic thinking in the world today."[23] Trueblood's comment displays the mixed signals that permeated many U.S. embassy reports at that time. The appropriateness of the FDN's economic policies in both national and regional terms contrasted with their origins in ideologies with which the United States had previously found itself in conflict. In the case of Peru, it was precisely during the period of 1943–5 that the United States made a pragmatic step toward an accommodation with the massed popular forces represented by APRA. As the Council on Foreign Relations put it in 1947:

The trend towards the Left was also apparent in Peru where the conservative and semi-dictatorial government of Manuel Prado allowed a free election in June 1945, and thus opened the gates to a democratic coalition including the *Apristas,* who for years had preached the need for fundamental social reform and an appreciation of the Indian element in Peruvian society. . . . In Peru the *Aprista* party led by Haya de la Torre. . . . had finally

20 823.00 1–945, No. 2353, Edward G. Trueblood to Secretary of State, 9 January 1945.
21 823.00 1–1945 No. 2426, Edward G. Trueblood to Secretary of State, 19 January 1945; 823.00 1–3045, No. 2506, Edward G. Trueblood to Secretary of State, 30 January 1945.
22 823.00 7–645, No. 3573, Edward G. Trueblood to Secretary of State, 6 July 1945.
23 823.00 3–2645, No. 2911, Edward G. Trueblood to Secretary of State, 26 March 1945.

been allowed to come out into the light of day to campaign for the place in the councils of government to which its popular support entitled it.[24]

By April 1945, U.S. opinion felt that if anybody other than Bustamante were to be elected in June, there would be considerable doubt as to the freedom and legitimacy of the elections. On the other hand, the FDN ticket on which Bustamante stood was portrayed as a broad alliance of APRA, the PCP, and supporters of Benavides and the liberal tradition arrayed against the reactionary and conservative traditions represented by Unión Revolucionaria. Thus, democratization implied, to some extent at least, a potential success for the PCP in Peru in the eyes of the U.S. observers. They were therefore primed to expect PCP expansion as a consequence of Bustamante's victory in June.

The economic prospects of the Bustamante government were bleak as it plunged into comprehensive crisis in the wake of difficulties already evident in the last years of the Prado government.[25] A frozen exchange rate in the face of a growing black market for hard currencies destroyed confidence in the government's financial strategy, which was already weakened by declining import tax revenues levied in the context of an incoherent import control strategy. Inflation, up 35 percent in 1947, could not be controlled and food prices in particular rose, ensuring immediate popular reaction. Legislation to guarantee wage levels merely reinforced the inflationary spiral. Tight controls, exacerbated by the need to continue social subsidies in order to avoid unrest, imperiled nationally owned enterprises as the government sought to control inflation, alienating investors who in other circumstances might have gone along with modernizing policies.

The U.S. embassy noted the importance of economic instability in its assessment of Bustamante's future. As early as June 1945, Trueblood noted the depreciation of the sol, the growth of black markets, and the poor government revenue position, amongst other economic woes, and called into question Bustamante's economic abilities.[26] Similar fears were expressed throughout Bustamante's period in office. In October 1946, for example, food shortages, strikes, transport disruption, and exchange problems were highlighted; in June 1947, wheat imports were reported to be

---

24 Council on Foreign Relations, *The United States in World Affairs, 1945–47* (New York, 1947), pp. 234, 239.

25 On the Peruvian economy in this period, see R. Thorp and G. Bertram, *Peru 1890–1976: Growth and Policy in an Open Economy* (London, 1978).

26 823.00 6–2945, No. 3549, Edward G. Trueblood to Secretary of State, 29 June 1945.

disrupted, with private credit expansion and a sol under pressure compounding the economy's woes.[27]

The relationship between democratization and political and economic stability led to discussions in the U.S. embassy about a possible U.S. aid effort for Peru, which would be couched explicitly in terms of the need to safeguard the democratic process. In September 1945 Rafael Belaúnde, Bustamante's prime minister, expressed his concern to Ambassador William D. Pawley about economic prospects and defined which sorts of U.S. aid would be acceptable to the Bustamante government. These included inputs into fishing, metal processing, the auto industry, and petroleum development.[28] In September, the exercise of U.S. economic muscle was proposed by Pawley to be the means by which APRA disruption of Bustamante's early months could be controlled. Pawley and his colleagues were entering the phase in which they came closer to APRA in the anti-Communist crusade in Peru, but in late 1945 Pawley believed U.S. economic influence would "avoid a premature assumption of power by the APRA party which many think would lead to military intervention."[29] Washington was very much against this policy, stressing APRA's popular support and the destabilizing effects of Pawley's proposed action.[30] Unabashed, Pawley continued to press for the explicit use of U.S. aid to support the democratization process. In October 1945, he described aid as the "honorable" way to provide support to Bustamante and Belaúnde and praised their "sincerity of purpose."[31]

Notwithstanding this view, the United States was willing to flex its economic power to pressure the Bustamante government about the treatment of the debt settlement package under negotiation throughout the 1945–8 period. For example, in December 1946 the embassy argued that U.S. power should be used to obstruct loans to Peru until the settlement

---

27  823.00 10–2446, No. 8546, Prentice Cooper to Secretary of State Telegram, 24 October 1946; 823.00 6–1647, No. 1701, R.H. Ackerman to Secretary of State, 16 June 1947.

28  823.00 9–1945, No. 306, William D. Pawley to Secretary of State, 19 September 1945.

29  823.00 9–2845, No. 336, William D. Pawley to Secretary of State, 28 September 1945.

30  823.00 9–2845, Butler to Braden and Briggs Memo. The perception of U.S. intervention in Peru's internal politics was a constant worry for the embassy. On a number of occasions, press campaigns were mounted criticizing embassy actions in Peru. For example, in November 1945, Pawley was hauled over the coals in La Prensa for what was seen as an improper and pro-APRA public comment on APRA's support for Bustamante (823.00 11–2345, No. 621). In December, anti-Pawley comments were made in the Peruvian Senate due to what were seen as moves to meddle in Peruvian politics by the embassy. In this case, it concerned petroleum legislation and the abrogation of the Salt Tax (823.00 12–745, Telegram). By 1947, it was evident that the embassy was taking great care not to be seen to be intervening in Peru's internal affairs (823.00 5–2347, No. 1630).

31  823.00 10–545, No. 357, William D. Pawley to Secretary of State, 5 October 1945.

was reached.[32] In any event, there was some aid offered to Peru in agriculture, health, education, and other areas, especially the military, but there is no evidence that the aid effort was organized in terms such as those laid down by Pawley.[33]

The U.S. view of Bustamante and his government upon his victory in June 1945 was clouded by the ambiguity of Bustamante's own personality and politics. Perhaps the most interesting insight into the new president was provided in a report by Trueblood in May 1945. In this report, clearly begun in an attempt to assess whether Bustamante was in any way pro-Axis, Argentine reports of his pro-Axis sentiments were brushed aside in favor of his portrayal as a church-influenced, conservative *arequipeño* who had adopted relatively progressive social attitudes and a reformist stance, and who had, by dint of his opposition to Leguía, shown himself to be a firm supporter of democratic government. He was portrayed as not so much anti-United States, as singularly lacking the contact with the United States upon which to make an informed policy.[34] In this context, Bustamante's appointment of Belaúnde as his prime minister was seen as a positive step. Ambassador Pawley, speaking of Belaúnde, put it this way: "It is desirable to have a man who knows our country as well as he does and who professes to be genuinely friendly to us."[35]

Once in power, Bustamante's position was immediately eroded by the presence of strong APRA affiliations in the pro-FDN camps in both the Senate and Congress, which by constitutional sleight of hand — the overturning of the presidential veto on legislation granted by 1939 legislation — came to dominate the legislative process. Bustamante's initial unwillingness to grant APRA posts in the cabinet at an appropriately senior level also alienated the pro-APRA elements in both houses, thus stimulating further clashes between the president and his nominal supporters. However, economic and political crisis brought down Bustamante's first cabinet in January 1946, and the new team included *aprista* ministers in the Agriculture, Finance, and Public Works portfolios. The inclusion of APRA was politically expedient at this stage. Not only could the party mobilize substantial popular forces; it could also challenge, even ruin, Bustamante's policy initiatives. Despite his misgivings, Bustamante was impelled into a constitutional relationship with APRA. The presence of *aprista* ministers in the cabinet was greeted by commentators in a number

32 823.00 12–3046, No. 8145, Prentice Cooper to Secretary of State Telegram 30 December 1946; 823.00 12–3146, No. 1296, Prentice Cooper to Secretary of State Telegram, 31 December 1946.

33 Carey, *Peru*.

34 823.00 5–945, No. 3254, Edward G. Trueblood to Secretary of State, 9 May 1945.

35 823.00 8–145, No. 54, William D. Pawley to Secretary of State, 1 August 1945.

of ways. Two dominant views were held: first, that APRA ministers simply reflected the true power of APRA in the Bustamante camp, and that eventually the government would be little more than an APRA front; secondly, as the U.S. embassy reported on occasion, that APRA had had a change of heart and had now embarked upon a positive, supportive course of action. Haya was reported as stating that "he and the President had had a complete meeting of minds, and that he [Haya] wanted Bustamante's period in office to be a 'great success.'"[36]

The second phase of the Bustamante government – with *aprista* ministers on board – lasted until January 1947. It has been argued that APRA, in power after so long in the wilderness, lost a great reforming opportunity.[37] Nationalist economic policies, in particular, were watered down; indeed, foreign investment was openly encouraged. No APRA-inspired reforms were enacted and little new resulted from the presence of an *aprista* minister in the Finance portfolio. APRA was even presented by the U.S. embassy as supporting a debt settlement package more favorable to U.S. bond holders than that supported by Bustamante.[38] At the same time, APRA continued to display internal dissension between the populist activists and the wing of the party wedded to formal parliamentary procedures. In April 1946, *aprista* militants attacked opposition presses in various parts of Peru. Compounding the sense of outrage that followed these attacks – an outrage not to be minimized in the context of democratization and the ideology of free speech – accusations were made that the police had failed to act with suitable firmness against APRA militants. U.S. ambassador Pawley reported a conversation with Bustamante in April 1946 in which the president candidly admitted that he should have organized an anti-APRA police force in the early days of his government.[39] This same conversation captured the profound distrust of APRA felt by Bustamante and the pessimism about the future of Peruvian democracy that he displayed as his years in office passed.

APRA–Bustamante relations were not improved by APRA's relative success in the June 1946 elections in which accusations of fraud were made, especially against APRA. The rest of 1946 was marked by uneasy

---

36  823.00 2–646, No. 975, APRA's role in the 1945–8 period is the focus of a heated debate. D. Palmer, *Peru: The Authoritarian Tradition* (New York, 1980), for example, takes the common view that APRA's disruptive tactics should take the major blame for Bustamante's failure. G. Hilliker, *The Politics of Reform in Peru* (Baltimore, MD, 1971) takes the less common view that APRA's behavior was simply in defense of democracy and parliamentary government. Implicitly, he blames Bustamante and the Conservative oligarchy for the failure of the democratization process. The weight of analysis would seem to lie with the former view. For a recent analysis, see Bertram, "Peru 1930–60," *Cambridge History of Latin America*, vol. 8.

37  Bertram, "Peru 1930–60," p. 436.

38  823.00 4–1546, William D. Pawley to Secretary of State Telegram, 15 April 1946.

39  823.00 4–2446, No. 8642, William D. Pawley to Secretary of State Telegram, 24 April 1946.

relations between APRA and Bustamante, and a growing political dispersion signaled by the formation in October of a Partido Social Republicano with an explicitly anti-APRA program, rifts in the FDN on anti-APRA lines in late October and early November, and calls for a "Peruvian Perón" (taken by the U.S. embassy to be Ureta).[40] A rapprochement between APRA and Bustamante in October–November failed to produce any significant stabilization of Peruvian politics, and in any case foundered in the crises of early 1947.[41]

The two events that finally precipitated the ejection of APRA from government were the assassination attempt against the minister of government (December 1946), and the killing of Francisco Grana Garland of *La Prensa* in January 1947. The finger of suspicion was pointed at APRA. On the one hand, APRA appeared to be willing to sponsor terrorism on the streets yet, on the other, to use parliamentary privilege to protect its supporters through, for example, amnesty bills. The combined pressure of these actions led Bustamante to restructure his cabinet in early 1947, at a time when the FDN alliance was finally collapsing. In October 1946, five original alliance members stated their belief that the FDN no longer existed due to APRA's antidemocratic behavior.[42] By early 1947, a number of anti-APRA coalitions appeared to be in formation. A Coalición Nacional Democrática united the Partido Social Republicano, Unión Revolucionaria, Christian Democratic elements, and a few small socialist groups; the PCP, Partido Socialista, and Partido Socialista Popular brought together a leftist opposition; the Unión Nacional included the Right in the form of the Partido Nacionalista, Partido Radical, and Partido Constitucionalista, amongst others. By March 1947, these various coalitions, with little in common but a strong anti-APRA feeling, gave birth to the Alianza Nacional, which, in its criticism of APRA, was destined also to criticize, both directly and indirectly, the Bustamante government.[43] Bustamante made the break with APRA in January 1947. APRA, excluded from Bustamante's cabinet, was now increasingly impotent in parliamentary affairs and forced back to its popular base for action, which led in turn to the various insurrection attempts of 1948.[44]

Given this experience of APRA in these years – disruptive political behavior, links to two major assassination attempts, marginalization from political power, insurrectionary behavior – what explains U.S. embassy ties with Haya and his supporters? Some importance must be given to

---

40 823.00 11–646, No. 660, Prentice Cooper to Secretary of State, 6 November 1946.
41 823.00 11–2246, No. 6937, Prentice Cooper to Secretary of State Telegram, 22 November 1946.
42 823.00 11–446, No. 638, Prentice Cooper to Secretary of State, 4 November 1946.
43 Ibid.; 823.00 3–2847, No. 1385, Prentice Cooper to Secretary of State, 28 March 1947.
44 See Bertram, "Peru 1930–60."

the prodemocracy, pro-United States turnaround that the embassy credited to APRA. However, the most important factor was the explicit anticommunism manifested by Haya during this period, and the ability of APRA to take the anticommunist message into the labor movement.

Haya's anticommunism was not taken for granted in 1945. U.S. Military Attaché Jay R. Reist suggested early in May 1945 that Haya was seeking to bring together the Left in Peru at the expense of the PCP, but "following the dissolution of the Third International, and in the postwar era, it [was] to be expected that world communism [would] seek to work through APRA."[45] However, by the end of May – some eighteen days after his initial report – Reist changed his tune. Reporting on Haya's speech at a huge APRA rally on 20 May 1945, Reist acknowledged Haya's explicit disavowal of communism.[46] In September 1945, a "bitter attack" on communism by APRA was described in another military intelligence report.[47] Further significant reports to Washington on APRA's anticommunism were filed in subsequent years, and the State Department consequently supported this view of Haya and APRA. Haya was considered to be a changed man who was "emphatically opposed to the present international communist line."[48] In a telegram in December 1947, Ambassador Cooper waxed almost lyrical in favor of Haya: "[I] am of the opinion that Haya deserves our moral support in [an] appropriate fight against Communism and I understand at least one American university is contemplating conferring an honorary degree upon Haya which in my opinion would be fortunate at this time."[49]

The labor movement also played an important role in the destabilization of Bustamante's government.[50] Between 1945 and 1947 a further 264 unions were registered formally with the state, with a wide variety of industrial sectors represented in this union expansion. Union action was initially relatively unfettered as Bustamante's reliance on APRA support precluded the use of state repression against unions affiliated to the CTP. The PCP also benefited from this newfound freedom, but generally remained marginal in comparison with the presence of the APRA-dominated CTP. The key issue for unions was the cost of living, which, on a base of 100 in 1944, rose to 112 in 1945, 122 in 1946, 158 in 1947, and

---

45  823.00 5–1145 No. 3263, John Campbell White to Secretary of State, 11 May 1945.
46  823.00 5–2945 No. 3377, Embassy Dispatch to Secretary of State, 29 May 1945.
47  MID R–263–45, J.R. Reist Intelligence Memo, 15 August 1945.
48  823.00 7–2848, Owen to Mills/Tittman Memo (Department of State), 28 July 1948.
49  823.00 12–247, No. 704, Prentice Cooper to Secretary of State Telegram, 2 December 1947.
50  On the role of labor during the period 1945–8, see J. Payne, *Labour and Politics in Peru* (New Haven, CN, 1965); and Sulmont, *Historia*.

204 in 1948. Union wage negotiators were able to parallel, even exceed, this rate of increase between 1945 and 1947, but thereafter, in the face of Bustamante's despairing attempt to salvage his economic strategy, rapidly lost ground. The parallel index for manufacturing sector wages, again on the basis of 100 in 1944, was 117 (1945), 127 (1946), 167 (1947), and 152 (1948). Political concerns intensified economic demands made by unions as APRA's role in government was reduced and the threat from the Right grew. Strikes grew in political intensity in 1947 and 1948, including general strike attempts in Lima in late 1947 and early 1948. One of the outcomes of this militant action was the weakening of the PCP in the organized labor movement, essentially because of its failure to provide clear leadership. It is noteworthy, however, that throughout this period, the PCP played a minor role, offering a degree of support to the Bustamante government, but remaining unable to influence events to any great effect.

The hold of the APRA-led CTP over the growing labor movement was seen to complement Haya's anticommunism. Two issues captured the U.S. embassy's attention above all others in this respect during the 1945–8 period. The first was the intralabor movement struggle between APRA and the PCP. In September 1945, the "bitter campaign" against the PCP waged by APRA was noted to be particularly active in the textile sector as APRA brought the textile workers out of their Confederación de Trabajadores de América Latina (CTAL) affiliation.[51] Also in September 1945, Military Attaché Reist portrayed APRA as making a "preemptive strike" against the PCP presence in the union movement "before soviet funds [could] swamp in to support the [PCP] labor organization."[52] In October 1945, Reist again reported on the labor issue, expressing worries that the PCP "bottom up" mode of organization would have greater long-term success in comparison with the CTP "top-down" approach.[53] Ambassador Pawley expressed similar fears in March 1946, quoting U.S. Consul Hawley in Arequipa: "[The] rank and file of the wage-earning and lower-salaried classes [is] inclined more and more to listen to the appeal of the simple and direct interpretation of Communism whose leaders have virtual control of the Arequipa unions."[54]

The importance of APRA's anticommunism in the union movement grew in the eyes of the U.S. embassy until by August 1948, Bustamante was charged with conniving with Communist unions in his feud with APRA: "The government's anti-APRA labour efforts have even included

51  823.00 5 September memo based on MID R–263–45, J.R. Reist Intelligence Memo, 15 August 1945.

52  823.00 9–1045, No. 241, William D. Pawley to Secretary of State, 10 September 1945.

53  823.00 10–945, No. 375, William D. Pawley to Secretary of State, 9 October 1945.

54  823.00 3–2946, No. 1207, William D. Pawley to Secretary of State, 29 March 1946.

the recognition of known communist labour leaders in preference to *Apris-tas*."[55] The implication of this was clear. Bustamante, not cleared of links to Communist ideas and the PCP, was regarded by the U.S. embassy as driven by his antipathy to APRA and his antidemocratic tendencies into an unholy relationship with communism.

The second issue of concern to the U.S. embassy related to APRA's international involvement with so-called free trade unionism in the Western Hemisphere. APRA and the CTP were closely involved with the formation of an alternative to the CTAL, and this activity was fostered by the U.S. embassy.[56] During a trip to the United States in early 1947, Serafino Romualdi took the opportunity to make concerted overtures to Haya, who visited both the American Federation of Labor (AFL) and the Congress of Industrial Organizations (CIO).[57] Later in 1947, the U.S. embassy commented favorably on APRA–CTP support for the Inter-American Labor Conference to be held in Lima in January 1948, and highlighted PCP attempts to obstruct the conference.[58] The conference, which formalized the split of the moderates from the CTAL, was presented by the embassy as a great APRA–CTP success.[59] Bustamante, therefore, did himself no favor when later in the month he prohibited APRA's international union links.[60]

Bustamante was increasingly isolated. The FDN was in disarray; he was alienated from APRA; he was subjected to criticism from the Center and Right for his failure to deal with APRA; even the U.S. embassy, nominally the supporter of democracy in Peru, was tending to respond more positively to APRA than the president. The constitutional blow that realized the full isolation of the president from civil political forces, and that heralded the fourth phase of his government – July 1947 to October 1948 – was the July Senate boycott by the Right. This, to all intents and purposes, paralyzed the constitutional process and displayed the constitutional muscle of the oligarchy. It is perhaps remarkable that Bustamante continued to hold power for more than a year. His survival has been attributed to the president's obstinacy, and to the support he continued to receive from organized labor, white-collar employees, the professional middle class, and his base, though wavering, in Arequipa.[61]

There was a marked change in tone in U.S. embassy reports in relation

55  823.00 8–2748, No. 694, A. Ogden Pierrot to Secretary of State, 27 August 1948.
56  823.00 10–1546, Embassy Memo to Secretary of State, 15 October 1946.
57  823.00 3–3147, No. 1389, Prentice Cooper to Secretary of State, 31 March 1947.
58  823.00 12–1147, No. 2217, Prentice Cooper to Secretary of State, 11 December 1947.
59  823.00 1–1548, No. 37, R.H. Ackerman to Secretary of State, 15 January 1948.
60  823.00 1–2948, No. 74, R.H. Ackerman to Secretary of State, 29 January 1948.
61  See Bertram, "Peru 1930–60," pp. 425–32.

to Bustamante's policies. The immediate catalyst for this change was the announcement on 12 September 1947 of an indefinite postponement of congressional by-elections and the suspension of civil liberties on 8 December. As an embassy telegram in September put it: "[It is] probable that US interests in Peru will be adversely affected in the long run by [the] present trend of the Bustamante Government away from democratic principles."[62]

The context that gave rise to this reassessment of Bustamante's stewardship was complex. The U.S. embassy traced its origins to the crisis following the Grana Garland assassination in January 1947. The crisis helped to force APRA out of the government, which in turn permitted ultraconservatives to influence the president. However, events around the presidential veto crisis of January 1946 might equally be identified as a starting point in the crisis of the relations between Bustamante, APRA, and the opposition, and the changing attitude of Bustamante himself toward due constitutional process. General Odría, brought into the cabinet in January 1947 as minister of government, was responsible for public order, and implemented the postponement of the election and the suspension of civil liberties, further reinforcing his reputation as "a dangerous counsellor and perhaps his [Bustamante's] master."[63] On the antidemocratic trend of the Bustamante government, the U.S. embassy concluded:

President Bustamante appears to have failed to develop the type of leadership essential to make function constitutional processes and a democratic form of government. . . . [T] this trend could effect American interests adversely, not only by continuing to exalt the Communist unions but also by influencing the government against carrying out its debt settlement plan according to the APRA-backed and Bustamante-sponsored Congressional law passed last February 28th.[64]

By early 1948, the view that Bustamante had veered away from the democratic path was frequently expressed in embassy communications with Washington.

Odría "and his backers" were portrayed as too powerful for Bustamante to oppose, even though they were technically part of his government. And Odría was engaged in overtly provocative acts against APRA at a time when APRA's profound anticommunism, especially in the international labor field, was winning the hearts and minds of the State De-

62 823.00 9–1647, No. 5039, Prentice Cooper to Secretary of State Telegram 16 September 1947.
63 Ibid.
64 Ibid.

partment. Thus, Bustamante's antidemocratic tendencies were coupled with actions directed against a U.S. client in the anticommunist crusade.[65]

Initially, Bustamante had been regarded as weak because he could not deal with the opposition (especially APRA), but he was also initially perceived as a democrat. The hardening of his stance against APRA, particularly after a series of cabinet crises, constitutional confrontations, assassinations, and street clashes, coincided with a reassessment of APRA by the United States in the light of APRA's explicit anticommunism. When Bustamante took tough measures to maintain order, especially in late 1947, APRA became a prime target. Thus, an explicitly anti-Communist, pro-United States, U.S.-linked party faced repression by the democratic government of Bustamante. Hence, the United States came to regard Bustamante as moving rapidly away from democracy at a time of increasing economic and labor instability.

APRA, now marginalized from the formal political process and losing its power in the provinces as Odría moved to replace regional *aprista* authorities by the military, attempted in October 1948 to initiate an insurrection, which was defeated, not least by the failure of APRA to mobilize its own civilian supporters behind the coup. Odría then moved to depose Bustamante, ironically at a time when the president had once again seized the political initiative by attempting constitutional reform.

When Odría seized power in October 1948, U.S. officials briefly speculated on the possibility of the PCP jumping on the coup's bandwagon in view of the recent growth in PCP influence and the "past cooperation between Odría and Communist-line groups."[66] However, these fears were based on Odría's anti-APRA actions in 1947, which in no way supported the view that he was soft on communism. It was not long before the U.S. embassy would declare: "There is no reason to believe . . . that Odría is the least bit sympathetic to communism and communists. In fact he is not unfriendly to the US."[67]

The Odría coup signaled the end of the experiment with liberal democracy at least until 1956, when the *convivencia* once again brought the reforming wing of the oligarchy into power, with APRA support. It also marked a decisive turn away from state interventionism and toward a liberal export-oriented growth model. Bustamante's FDN government was an unsus-

---

65 823.00 2–1948, Memo of Ferreyros/Espy Meeting, 3 March 1948; 823.00 2–1948, No. 6048, Prentice Cooper to Secretary of State Telegram, 19 February 1948; 823.00 1–1548, No. 37, J.H. Ackerman to Secretary of State, 15 January 1948; 823.00 1–2948, No. 74, J.H. Ackerman to Secretary of State, 29 January 1948.

66 823.00 10–2948, No. 9963, Tittman to Secretary of State Telegram, 29 October 1948.

67 823.00 10–2848, Memo, Owen to Mills, Woodward, Daniel (Department of State), 28 October 1948.

tainable, even premature, attempt at democratization during a period in which the political circumstances for such a change were inauspicious. The popular forces mobilized around the FDN were too fragile, and APRA was unable to establish its hegemony. The forces opposed to democratization, though themselves weak as shown by Ureta's failure in 1945, were able to obstruct the democratization process using the threat of APRA as justification. Lastly, the economy remained firmly in traditional hands.

In apportioning blame for the failure of the 1945 experiment – still a live issue in Peru – the supporters of APRA point to its popular power, its progressive agenda, the weakness of Bustamante, and the counterattack from the military and the oligarchy. In this view of the world, APRA represents the option of popular democracy, cut short by Odría. Opponents of APRA point to its disruptive parliamentary behavior, its "goons," assassinations, and insurrections, and its unwillingness to make the compromises necessary for democratization to take root.

Acción Popular, Democracia Cristiana, and the political traditions of the Center gained heart in the mid-1940s as did the individuals, such as Fernando Belaúnde Terry and Héctor Cornejo Chávez, who were to lead the pressure for democracy under Odría. This consequence suggests that the Bustamante experiment played a crucial role in motivating individuals, creating debate, and defining options for the following decade.

The backing for APRA offered by Pawley and Cooper did not protect Haya and his followers under Odría. The United States came to accept Odría as an anti-Communist, pro-foreign investment, pro-United States leader who, though no democrat, kept Peru firmly on the path of U.S.-sponsored rectitude. Moreover, the growth of the Center – Acción Popular and Democracia Cristiana – provided alternatives to APRA for U.S. support. The closeness of the United States and APRA that marked the mid-1940s was not to be revived in later years. For the United States, Peru was once again marginal – until the late 1960s, when the radical, reforming military government of General Juan Velasco Alvarado placed Peru on center stage.

# 7

## Mexico

*Ian Roxborough*

At the end of the presidency of Lázaro Cárdenas (1934–40) – thirty years after the beginning of the Mexican revolution – the Mexican working class was organized as never before into a large and powerful union confederation, the Confederación de Trabajadores de México (CTM). Within this organization, the Communists and other independent leftists controlled a sizeable following. However, in a series of dramatic confrontations and purges in the ranks of organized labor, between 1946 and 1949, the Left and the labor militants were decisively defeated. The culmination of these struggles between union militants and the Left, on the one hand, and the moderate, progovernment leadership on the other, was the so-called *charrazo* of 1948, when the Mexican government intervened in the railway workers' union to impose a conservative leadership. The *charrazo* and similar, related events within the CTM and in other important industrial unions led to organized labor falling under the domination of a small camarilla of trade union leaders, the so-called *cinco lobitos*,[1] who saw their task as that of ensuring labor discipline and providing political support for the ruling party, the Partido Revolucionario Institucional (PRI, formerly the PRM), and its economic project. For most of the postwar period, Mexico's relatively tranquil industrial relations provided an underpinning for the rapid economic growth and political stability that defined the Mexican "miracle."

The formation of the CTM in 1936 was one of the great events of the Cárdenas presidency and of the history of the Mexican working class. Prior to this, the principal Mexican labor organization had been the Confederación Revolucionaria de Obreros de México (CROM), a conservative organization, subservient to the government, and dominated by

---

1 The *cinco lobitos* were Fidel Velázquez, Fernando Amilpa, Jesús Yurén, Adolfo Sánchez Madariaga, and Luis Quintero.

corrupt labor racketeers led by Luís Morones. The formation of the CTM promised to change all this by establishing a militant, authentic union organization. Led by radical ex-CROMist Vicente Lombardo Toledano, a new militant organization, by no means totally subservient to the state, was built out of the ashes of the long since moribund CROM. During the early years of the Cárdenas presidency there was an impressive wave of union organizing under the aegis of the new CTM. Strike activity rose to an unprecedented high; from 11 in 1931, the number of strikes rose to 642 in 1935, and 674 in 1936.[2] During the late thirties and early forties the CTM retained, despite its intimate relations with the state, a substantial measure of autonomy from it.[3]

Perhaps most significantly, one of the major changes on the labor scene in this period was the formation of national industrial unions in railways (1933), in mining and metalworking (1934), and in the petroleum industry (1935). Both railways and oil were state enterprises, and during the Cárdenas period there were experiments with a measure of labor control. These national industrial unions, together with the electricians' union, affiliated with the CTM, forming its core. The rest of the CTM's membership was composed of a large number of quite small unions of an extremely heterogeneous nature.[4] Although the CTM was the most important labor confederation, there were also a number of smaller organizations such as the CROM and the Confederación General de Trabajadores (CGT), which controlled a significant minority of organized labor.

In this panorama of increased mobilization and militancy, the forces of the Left, and in particular of the Partido Comunista Mexicano (PCM) gained positions of considerable strength. Although they were overwhelmingly concerned with maintaining their alliances with the centrist forces in the CTM represented by Fidel Velázquez and, more ambiguously, by Lombardo Toledano himself, the PCM and the militant industrial unions were driven at times into open conflict with the moderates. Both 1936 and 1937 saw serious splits in the CTM. In the 1937 dispute, the Communist-led unions, representing about half of the CTM's membership, left the CTM but were subsequently ordered back into the fold by Earl Browder, general secretary of the Communist Party of the U.S.A.

2 J. Wilkie, *The Mexican Revolution* (Berkeley, 1967), p. 184.

3 There is substantial literature on the CTM and its relation to the Mexican state. See inter alia, V. M. Durand, *La ruptura de la nación* (Mexico City, 1986); S. León and I. Marván, *En el cardenismo (1934–1940)*, vol. 10 of *La clase obrera en la historia de México*, ed. P. González (Mexico City, 1985); J. Ashby, *Organized Labor and the Mexican Revolution under Lázaro Cárdenas* (Chapel Hill, NC, 1963); N. Hamilton, *The Limits of State Autonomy: Post-Revolutionary Mexico* (Princeton, 1982).

4 These were not necessarily craft unions. Basically, they were unions formed on a companywide basis in the industrial and service sectors.

(CPUSA). They returned under the slogan Unity at All Cost – a decision that was to lead to bitter polemics in the future.[5] In November 1939, the Sindicato Mexicano de Electricistas (SME), deeply troubled by the rightward drift of the CTM, disaffiliated, declaring itself "apolitical." The beginning of the 1940s, then, saw the CTM as the hegemonic, left-wing labor organization in Mexico, but one that was deeply divided between three factions: the *cinco lobitos* led by Fidel Velázquez, taking a pragmatic stance on the Right, the Communists and the militants in the industrial unions on the Left, and the *lombardistas* between them.

The Mexican Left was both large and varied. The Mexican revolution and the experience of *cardenismo,* of course, had fostered the growth of a broad nationalist Left, as well as the belief that the Mexican revolution was still, in some sense, alive and that the state could be pressured to take a progressive position. In addition to the left-wing nationalists of various descriptions, a number of purges in the PCM[6] had resulted in the emergence of an ex-Communist Marxist Left in Mexico, which was a force to be reckoned with.

In a context of political polarization and a move to the Left, the Cárdenas presidency was due to end with the 1940 elections. In this situation, there were a number of possible contenders for the candidature of the official ruling party, the Partido de la Revolución Mexicana (PRM). On the Left stood General Francisco Múgica, heir to the *cardenista* legacy. Rather than throw its weight behind Múgica, the CTM decided to support the compromise, conciliationist candidate, Manuel Avila Camacho. This was clearly the choice of Cárdenas himself, worried as he was by growing right-wing mobilization and the specter of a rerun of the Spanish Civil War on Mexican soil. The Left in the CTM could do nothing effective to promote Múgica's candidacy, and had to content itself with verbal protests. On the Right was Juan Andrew Almazán, with substantial support, which included sections of the working class.[7]

The presidential elections of 7 July 1940 were marked by violent clashes and a number of deaths. There was some fear of a possible armed revolt. The incoming administration of Manuel Avila Camacho had to contend with considerable right-wing mobilization. The Unión Nacional Sinarquista (UNS) was formed on 23 May 1937. The UNS was a mass religious movement that had widespread support in rural areas and was seen by

---

5 The relevant document was reprinted with an introduction by G. Pelaez and H. Laborde, *La política de unidad a toda costa* (Mexico City, 1980); See also V. Campa, *Mi testimonio* (Mexico City, 1978).

6 The refusal of Valentín Campa and Hernán Laborde to sanction the assassination of Trotsky, for example, had led to their expulsion from the party.

7 A. J. Contreras, *México 1940* (Mexico City, 197), pp. 77–93; V. M. Durand, *La ruptura,* pp 32–43.

some as a form of Mexican fascism.[8] On the fringe Right, there were groups like the Camisas Doradas modeled after the shock troops of European fascism. More generally, capital, both domestic and foreign, treated the government with, at best, a considerable degree of reserve. In 1938 the entrepreneurs had described the PRM as "a menace to democracy," and in 1939 the prestigious conservative newspaper *Excelsior* had described the second six-year plan being propounded by Lombardo Toledano as "totalitarian."[9] Much of this opposition was brought together with the formation of the probusiness and pro-Catholic Partido de Acción Nacional (PAN) on 14 October 1939.

In the face of this opposition, the government of Avila Camacho adopted a policy of "national unity." In effect, this was a series of moves to distance itself from the Left and to reassure the Right. The new president made a statement that Communists would not participate in the government, and stressed the need to give investors confidence.[10]

In the period between 1938 and 1943, there was a major restructuring of the official party that placated certain sections of the industrialists, brought the middle classes directly into the party, and brought the peasant organization, the Confederación Nacional Campesina (CNC), under direct state control by the selective appointment of professional politicos to key leadership positions.[11] The formation of an employers' association, the Cámara Nacional de la Industria de la Transformación (CANACINTRA), in December 1941 was a key step in creating an organization that could be said to represent "the national bourgeoisie," even though there were serious doubts about its representativeness.[12] It was a key step in breaking private industry's previously monolithic opposition to the government. Another major move was the creation of the Confederación Nacional de Organizaciones Populares (CNOP). This was principally a vehicle for the organization of state functionaries and of middle-class support for the regime, and was run by professional politicians. As the Chilean ambassador to Mexico, Pablo Neruda, said at the time, "If there is a labor sector and a peasant sector, tell me please, what is the popular sector?"[13] Fur-

---

8 On the UNS, see Jean Meyer, *El sinarquismo: Un fascismo mexicano?* (Mexico City, 1979).

9 L. J. Garrido, *El Partido de la Revolución Institucionalizada* (Mexico City, 1982), p. 242.

10 L. Medina, *Del cardenismo al avilacamachismo*, vol. 18, of *Historia de la Revolución Mexicana*, ed. Daniel Cosío Villegas (Mexico City, 1978), pp. 133–62.

11 Garrido, *El Partido.*

12 WNA 812.5042, Letter from Messersmith to Carrigan, State Department, 11 April 1945: "An examination of the list of industrialists shows that there were only three of any importance. . . . The rest of the so-called industrialists there were mostly small people in the drug and pharmaceutical business whom Lavrin got in. . . . Lavrin . . . runs a medium sized drug manufacturing business in Mexico and . . . is essentially extreme left and in my opinion Communistic and . . . was one of the favorite instruments of [Russian ambassador] Oumansky."

13 Garrido, *El Partido* p. 325.

thermore, the institutionalization and professionalization of the military continued.

These moves did not simply add up to a perfecting of the corporatist structure set in place by Cárdenas. They amounted to a virtual silent revolution by the middle sectors and the professional political bureaucracy to reorganize the state apparatus on their own behalf.[14]

In the international sphere, particularly in U.S.–Mexican relations, the Cárdenas period had been one of considerable tension. Shortly after assuming office, Avila Camacho moved to reach an agreement on the still outstanding issues of petroleum expropriation and the foreign debt, and by 1941–2 a rapprochement with the United States had been achieved.

With the Japanese attack on Pearl Harbor in December 1941, the United States mounted pressure on the states of Latin America to demonstrate hemispheric solidarity. The Mexican government, however willing it may have been to join the Allied cause, had to consider potential domestic opposition to entry in the war. However, the sinking of a Mexican tanker, the *Potrero del Llano,* by a German submarine as it was steaming with full lights in the Gulf of Mexico on 13 May 1942, provided the rationale for a Mexican declaration of war on the Axis powers.

From the point of view of the United States, the importance of Mexico in narrowly military terms was as a cover against a possible Japanese attack from the Southwest. The U.S. military wanted radar coverage for the approaches to California (until the end of 1942) and bases for air reconnaissance. There was also concern in the United States that Germany would use Mexico as a base for espionage activities directed against the United States.[15] The Mexican government and ex-President Cárdenas were insistent that there should be no U.S. troops on Mexican soil and that military cooperation should be limited to technicians and the supply of U.S. equipment.[16]

The principal effect of the Second World War on Mexico was that it transformed the economy of that country into an appendage of the U.S. war machine. Mexico supplied strategic goods, mainly minerals, to the United States, and in exchange the United States announced that it would sell essential goods to Mexico. The war therefore saw a substantial reorientation of Mexican trade patterns. In 1937–8 Mexico had one-third of its trade with Europe and 56 percent with the United States. By 1940

---

14  Ibid.
15  L. Rout and J. Bratzel, *The Shadow War* (Frederick, MD, 1986), pp. 55.
16  R. A. Humphreys, *Latin America and the Second World War*, vol. 2 (London, 1982), pp. 54–6
   B. Torres, *México en la Segunda Guerra Mundial*, vol. 19 of *Historia de la Revolución Mexicana* (Mexico City, 1979), pp. 115–21.

the United States accounted for 90 percent of Mexico's foreign trade.[17] In addition, Mexico was also a major supplier of food for the U.S. market, and provided large numbers of *braceros* for North American agriculture. There was an agreement that there would be 4,000 *braceros* by 1942; by 1944 this had grown to 62,000. Some estimates of the number of agricultural workers who went north during the war run as high as 309,000.[18]

The overall effect of the war was a dramatic stimulus to economic, and particularly industrial, growth leading to a 62 percent increase in the industrial labor force, from 568,000 in 1941 to 922,000 in 1945.[19] This growth was accompanied by an acceleration of the inflationary pressures that had begun in 1937 and 1938. Wages consistently lagged behind price rises: by 1946 real wages were half of what they had been in 1939.[20] Like many other Latin American countries, Mexico experienced widespread shortages of consumer goods and of capital and intermediate goods. Supply of these items from the United States was always difficult.

With the declaration of war by the Mexican government, the CTM immediately proposed a suspension of strikes for the duration, and in June 1942, announced that it would form a "workers solidarity pact" with the other major union confederations to settle amicably any inter-union dispute that might arise. These voluntary renunciations of the strike weapon by the unions were accompanied by new legislation restricting the right to strike. Already, before Mexico's entry into the war, President Avila Camacho had modified the labor law so that workers could be fired for participating in illegal strikes. Now with the war, the law of social dissolution was promulgated, giving the government greater power to control public order.

With workers essentially unprotected from the worst effects of the war economy, there was considerable rank-and-file restiveness. Not surprisingly, despite – or possibly because of – the no-strike pledge, the latter part of the war saw an explosion of industrial militancy. From an average of 120 strikes per year in the first two years of the war, the number of strikes in 1943 shot up to 766. With peace in sight, and the feeling that they were in a position to recover some of the purchasing power lost during the war, Mexican workers engaged in an unprecedented number of strikes in 1944. Higher even than during the heady days of the *cardenista* mobilization, strike frequency peaked at 887 in that year.

Although declining real wages were the principal cause of most strikes, there were also a number of inter-union disputes, strikes resulting from

17 Torres, *México*, p. 195.
18 Ibid., pp. 254–71.
19 Ibid., pp. 296–300.
20 J. Bortz, "El salario obrero en el Distrito Federal, 1939–75," *Investigación Económica* 4 (1977): 152–8.

the blockage of the port of Veracruz in 1943 (due to the inability to obtain essential spare parts for machinery), and a number of strikes in the petroleum regions to assert the political power of the union in the selection of candidates for local political posts. In one strike in a mica-producing enterprise in Oaxaca (mica was used in the production of radios), the strikers were accused of being Communists, even though PCM members were amongst the staunchest advocates of the no-strike pledge.[21] In addition to the strikes, 1944 also saw widespread rioting over shortages and inflation. The announcement of new social security legislation in July caused spontaneous rioting in Mexico City as workers protested against compulsory deductions from their pay for a system that was not yet sufficiently developed to offer serious improvements in health care.

A number of strikes at the end of the war caused concern in the U.S. embassy. A strike on the Mexico City tramway raised fears of its possible expropriation by the government, as did strikes on the U.S.-operated Sud Pacífico Railway. An inter-union dispute in the film industry in 1945 also provoked a bout of anxiety in the embassy. The actors had broken with the film industry union, the Sindicato de Trabajadores de la Industria Cinematográfica (STIC), and had set up their own union, the Sindicato de Trabajadores de la Producción Cinematográfica (STPC). As a tactic in its fight with the actors' union, the STIC demanded that distributors of North American films in Mexico each hire two publicity agents provided by the union. The distributors refused and STIC called a strike. In August 1945 Ambassador George Messersmith, repeating previously expressed fears of Soviet subversion, reported:

[There must be] some more basic and hidden reason for this strike [than wages or contract provisions], and there is increasing reason to believe that it is a definite effort on the part of Lombardo Toledano and certain of the more radical labor leaders in Mexico to get rid of the American pictures in Mexico. It is the desire of these people to eliminate any American influence in Mexico and to substitute therefor Soviet influence. . . . The whole life of the motion picture industry in Mexico in many ways is at stake, and what is more fundamental even than that is that there is at stake the question as to whether the Mexican producers will be able to show pictures from any origin they may wish or whether they will be put into the position of showing only Soviet films or such films as may be produced in Mexico under Soviet influence.[22]

Judging the strike to be "inspired by a desire to damage the interests of the United States and by international political considerations," the em-

---

21 Archivo General de la Nación (henceforth (AGN), STPS, boxes 95–6.

22 Washington National Archives (henceforth WNA) 812.5048, 21 August 1945; see also 812.5044, 31 August 1945. See also J. H. Stiller, *George S. Messersmith, Diplomat of Democracy* (Chapel Hill, NC, 1987), p. 213.

bassy "did not hesitate to use its influence."[23] Messersmith said he would "lose [his] personal interest in maintaining the film quota for Mexico" (a wartime U.S. government quota of eleven million feet of rationed raw film per year).[24] The film companies eventually won the strike, and in the opinion of the U.S. embassy:

[The] failure of the STIC and the CTM to attain their objectives constitutes the worst blow that they have received during the entire period of their existence. The situation now is that the prestige of the CTM is virtually nil . . . this means labor trouble.[25]

The rapidly rising cost of living continued into the immediate postwar period and also worried the U.S. embassy. In May 1946 the second secretary ended one of his reports with the following gloomy prognostication:

The most serious practical problem facing the workers today is the high cost of living. The disparity between prices and wages is becoming greater. This raises the question of how long this condition can continue to exist. Statistical studies would lead to the conclusion that the workers cannot possibly make ends meet, and that there must be many cases of real privation; however, the capacity of the Mexican Indian for suffering in silence is difficult to estimate. According to ordinary social theories, the situation would be ripe for revolution. At the most conservative estimate, the situation must be considered unhealthy and nearing a crisis.[26]

He then returned to this issue the following month:

It is hard to say when the breaking point will be reached, but, as the Embassy has reported before, the situation is approaching a crisis, and it is hard to understand how the working classes manage to live under present conditions. The factors are present which could lead to serious trouble and even to a revolution.[27]

In addition to the industrial unrest associated with inflation, the war had also led to a number of serious difficulties in industrial production. Undercapitalization and over-utilization were commonplace, but noticeably so on the railways. In addition, in the state-owned industries there were major problems of labor discipline stemming from the *cardenista* experiments with labor control. By the end of the war, the situation in the railways and in the petroleum industry had become chaotic, with inter-union disputes in the railways adding to already critical operational

23 WNA 812.5048, 11 September 1945.
24 WNA 812.5047, 10 July 1945.
25 WNA 812.5049, 15 September 1945.
26 WNA 812.5045, 21 May 1946.
27 WNA 812.5046, 21 June 1946.

problems. In the petroleum industry, the situation was equally complicated. The Sindicato de Trabajadores Petroleros de la República Mexicana
(STPRM) had been formed by merging a large number of small local
unions. As a result, there were substantial differences in wages and working conditions between the different sections, as well as different histories
of union militancy. The upshot was a union riven by deep divisions and
prone to rapid changes in leadership and policy. The 1940s saw a large
number of strikes in the industry, including a forty-eight-hour stoppage
in April 1946. On that occasion, Fidel Velázquez, general secretary of
the CTM since 1 March 1941 (when Lombardo Toledano stepped down
to devote his energies full-time to the organization of the continent-wide
Confederación de Trabajadores de América Latina [CTAL]),[28] asserted that
the stoppages were unjustified and that two solutions were available: firing
the union leaders or militarizing the industry.[29] Disgusted with the attitude of the CTM, on 10 July the STPRM left that organization. During
the remainder of 1946 the oil industry was the scene of numerous wildcat
strikes. According to the U.S. embassy:

The irresponsible and arbitrary action of the leaders of the various sections of the Petroleum
Workers Syndicate plus the incompetence of the general management clearly shows that
a healthy situation cannot be created in the petroleum industry short of a complete house-
cleaning of both management and labor.[30]

Paradoxically, together with the beginning of a confrontation between
unions and the state, the end of the war also witnessed a renewed effort
at establishing a social pact between management and unions. In April
1945, the CTM and the progovernment CANACINTRA signed the Pacto
Obrero–Industrial. The reasons behind this rather anomalous behavior
must be sought in the vision of the postwar order held by Mexican labor
leaders.

It should be remembered that everything seemed to be in flux. The
Allies had defeated fascism, and were in the process of creating a new
world order. In the closing stages of the war, there was a widespread
belief among certain sectors of the Left that capitalism had transcended
its worst contradictions and that the basis for rapid economic expansion
and genuine democracy existed. With the continuation of the alliance
with the Soviet Union, the role of Communist Parties would need to be

28 On Lombardo's motives in leaving the CTM, see Durand, *La ruptura*, pp. 72–3. The CTAL will
   be discussed in detail later in this chapter.
29 A. Cuello Vásquez, "El movimiento del Sindicato de Trabajadores Petroleros de la República
   Mexicana en 1949" in *Memorias del encuentro sobre historia del movimiento obrero*, ed. J. Woldenberg
   et al. (Puebla, 1981), pp. 390–1.
30 WNA 812.5047, 23 July 1946.

radically transformed. Their experience in the war had indicated how they might reconcile their leftist convictions with real patriotic sentiment, and there was every reason to expect a continuation of this situation.

In the United States, the Communist Party, under the leadership of Earl Browder, adopted this line of analysis and dissolved itself. In Mexico, a country in which a revolution had recently displaced the old oligarchy from the center of political power, and in which the organizations of the working class were an integral part of the ruling party, there existed even more powerful arguments for a perspective of class collaboration. The state itself was committed to the pursuit of industrial growth, and would shelter both the proletariat and the national bourgeoisie under its protectionist umbrella. If the Left in the United States could put economic growth and national unity ahead of class struggle, such arguments were a fortiori applicable in Mexico. Building on the experience of the revolution and the *cardenista* period, first Lombardo Toledano, and then the PCM, took up Browderist positions.[31]

In a number of pamphlets and speeches, Lombardo Toledano set out this perspective. In Lombardo's analysis, CANACINTRA represented the national industrial bourgeoisie, growing up in the shadow of, and under the protection of, the state.[32] The industrialization policy favored by Lombardo was one based on the expansion of the domestic market and, in particular, on the increased purchasing power of the peasantry through an acceleration of the land reform program.[33] The reality, however, was more complex. CANACINTRA was but one among several employers' associations, and by no means the strongest. Moreover, such protectionist policies were seen by many as posing major barriers to an expanded inflow of foreign investment (in turn, seen as a necessary condition for rapid growth). For those who advocated an economic policy based on a reduction in tariffs, a reduced role for the state in the economy, and incentives for private enterprise, Lombardo's policies were unacceptable. However, a no-strike pledge would, in any case, be desirable, and there would be no reason actively to discourage the new capital–labor accord.

The Pacto Obrero–Industrial of 1945 generated a variety of reactions in Mexico. Most of the non-CTM and anti-*lombardista* unions opposed the pact. It was seen by them as a betrayal of union rights, and as a vehicle for Lombardo Toledano's political ambitions. The industrial policy of the pact was widely seen as a protectionist response to the liberal economic program that was pushed by the United States at the Inter-American

31 G. Unzueta, "Crisis en el Partido, crisis en el movimiento" in *Historia del comunismo mexicano*, ed. A. Martínez Verdugo (Mexico City, 1985), pp. 211–12.

32 Lombardo Toledano archive, Congreso Extraordinario de la CTAL, Paris, 10–12 October 1946.

33 V. Lombardo Toledano, "Por la industrialización de México" in *El marxismo en América Latina*, ed. M. Lowy (Mexico City, 1982), pp. 158–60. This is a reprint of a 1944 speech by Lombardo.

Conference on the Problems of War and Peace of February–March 1945, and was embodied in the Treaty of Chapultepec.[34] This protectionism apparently received support from the smaller Mexican industrialists who were concerned about increased U.S. competition in the postwar period.[35] However, the pact was viewed with hostility by the U.S. embassy: "Collaboration between left-wing labor groups and chauvinistic capitalists in Mexico should not deceive anyone; its purpose is to exclude American capital, weaken the Good Neighbor Policy, and, ultimately, bring Mexico into the orbit of direct Soviet influence."[36]

The pact, together with fear of the nationalization of the Mexico City streetcar company (as a result of a strike by the union) and the conflict in the film industry, gave the embassy grounds for concern about future U.S. investment in Mexico. As it happened, the 1945 Pacto Obrero–Industrial turned out to be a dead letter. The success of the pact depended, ultimately, on direct support from the government. Although neither Avila Camacho nor future president Miguel Alemán (who announced his candidacy on 6 June 1945) ever had anything but praise for the pact, the idea was allowed to quietly disappear. On 13 September 1945, Fidel Velázquez announced that there would no longer be restrictions on strike activity.[37] A social pact was not to be the route to the solution of Mexico's labor difficulties.

By the end of the war, the CTM had become heavily dependent on government support and was in many respects an extremely weak and fragile organization. And the selection of Miguel Alemán as the candidate of the official party for the 1946 presidential elections did not bode well for organized labor. Alemán's economic policy would clearly be one of modernizing Mexican industry with the aid of foreign capital. This would require a stabilization of the economy, incentives for private profit, and further restraints on labor. As a result, by 1946 the relations between the CTM and the official party had become very tense. There was substantial opposition within the CTM to Alemán's candidacy. However, Lombardo Toledano had decided to back Alemán to the hilt, and in subsequent years went to great lengths to defend him against his detractors. In part, this behavior of Lombardo's can be explained in the light of the support given in 1946 by the U.S. ambassador in Mexico, George Messersmith, to the presidential campaign of foreign minister Ezequiel Padilla, an economic liberal and political conservative.[38] Alarmed by what

34 G. Kolko, *The Politics of War* (New York, 1968), pp. 458–61.

35 WNA 812.5045, 3 May 1945.

36 WNA 812.5043, 21 March 1946.

37 J. Basurto, *Del avilacamachismo al alemanismo (1940–1952)*, vol 11., *La clase obrera en la historia de México* (Mexico City, 1984), p. 81.

38 On Messersmith, see Stiller, *George S. Messersmith*, pp. 175–222.

he rightly saw as a possible move away from the revolutionary tradition of Mexican politics, Lombardo threw his weight behind a more reliable member of the revolutionary "family." Moreover, faced with a fait accomplit, the CTM, increasingly dominated by the conservative Velázquez clique, sought a rapprochement with the government. Miguel Alemán was designated "obrero número uno de la república" and, in an act of great symbolic importance, in March 1947 the CTM changed its motto from "For a Society without Classes" to "For the Emancipation of Mexico."[39]

By March 1946, observers in the U.S. embassy saw indications that the CTM might be losing its dominant position in Mexican labor.[40] The CTM had begun to lose a number of its constituent unions in 1945, with breakaways in Jalisco and in the state of Mexico. A leading official in the Ministry of Labor told embassy officials in May that "during the last year the CTM has lost a considerable part of its strength." He added that "the present administration would actually prefer to see the CPN [Confederación Proletaria Nacional] the leading labor confederation in Mexico."[41] Peace in the oil industry had been bought temporarily and at a high price. The union in the state-owned *Petróleos Mexicanos* (PEMEX) remained outside the CTM. This was seen by several observers as the death-knell for the CTM.[42]

Other Mexican union confederations attempted to take advantage of the CTM's weakness. On 12 May 1945 the formation of a new labor organization called the Coalición de Centrales Obreros de la República Mexicana (CCO) was announced. This was comprised of the anti-CTM union organizations: the CROM, the Central Nacional de Trabajadores (CNT), the CPN, the Confederación de Obreros y Campesinos de México (COCM) the CGT, a textile union, and an electricians' confederation.[43] And to add fuel to the fire, on 1 June, veteran right-wing union leader

---

39  L. Medina, *Civilismo y modernización del autoritarismo*, vol. 20 of *Historia de la Revolución Mexicana* (Mexico City, 1979), p. 132.

40  WNA 812.5045, 20 March 1946; 812.5045, 27 March 1945. It should be remembered that the embassy continued to see the CTM as a procommunist organization at this time.

41  WNA 812.5045, 3 May 1945.

42  Ambassador Thurston sent an airgram in November 1946 commenting on the oil workers' union's decision to leave the CTM and forecasting the imminent demise of the CTM. "This announcement has caused a sensation in labor and political circles and the conservative press is predicting that it forecasts the dissolution of the CTM. It is significant that this occurred at this time when it is generally being conceded that Fidel Velázquez has been defeated in his race for Federal Senator from the Federal District. . . . If the official returns show that Fidel Velázquez and other CTM leaders have been defeated it is likely that this will effect [*sic*] the standing of the CTM and may even lead to its dissolution." WNA 812.5043, 11 July 1946. As it turned out, Fidel Velázquez was elected.

43  WNA 812.5046, 1 June 1945.

Luís Morones declared that the CCO would conduct an anti-Communist campaign, and accused Lombardo Toledano and the leaders of the CTM of being tools of Moscow.[44]

The situation at the end of the war was an ambiguous one. There was widespread labor unrest, together with considerable political uncertainty. The Mexican one-party system was not as yet fully institutionalized, and in certain circles there were hopes that Mexico might be transformed into something approaching a pluralistic democracy. In 1945 the U.S. ambassador, George Messersmith, for example, strongly backed the candidacy of Foreign Minister Padilla in the hopes that he would bring Mexico fully into the democratic fold.[45] As it turned out, this was an illusion: the forces of continuity within the system were strong, and Miguel Alemán was put forward in June 1945 as the *continuista* candidate, to be duly elected in July 1946 by an overwhelming majority.

Nevertheless, the assumption of the presidency by Alemán on 1 December 1946 took place in an atmosphere of political tension. In addition to labor conflicts, the army was restive and there were continued rumblings of discontent among Catholics. On taking office, Alemán began a program of reform that included a reduction of industrial conflict, reorganization of the economy, continued close ties with the United States, and the extension and consolidation of power in the presidency and the dominant party. The attack on labor began in 1946, but fell far short of Alemán's objectives, and had to be renewed in the following year.

One of Alemán's first moves was to take on the oil workers' union. In his inauguration speech, he warned militant workers in no uncertain terms: "We will maintain the interests of the country above the interests of individuals and groups. . . . Illegal stoppages must not happen."[46] Despite this obvious warning, the STPRM staged a strike on 19 December. Troops were sent immediately to take over oil installations; the strike collapsed within twenty-four hours and the union leadership was fired. Early in January 1947, PEMEX then followed up this decisive action by initiating a legal proceeding known as a "conflict of economic order." The new union leadership, led by Antonio Hernández Abrego, met President Alemán and agreed to an enquiry into the economic situation of PEMEX. The new leadership agreed to seek reaffiliation with the CTM.[47] Com-

---

44  WNA 812.5047, 10 July 1945.

45  Stiller, *George S. Messersmith*, pp. 175–222.

46  M. A. Cuéllar Vásquez, "Golpe al Sindicato de Trabajadores Petroleros de la República Mexicana (STPRM), en 1949" in *Las derrotas obreras 1946–1952*, ed. V. M. Durand Ponte (Mexico City, 1984), p. 106.

47  There is some evidence to suggest that anti-union action by the U.S. government influenced the Mexican government in its resolve to take a tough line with the unions. "There is reason to

menting eighteen months later on this stoppage, the U.S. embassy's labor attaché said:

> The President, in his first labor action, opposed himself to the full power of the Petroleum Syndicate, up until then completely uninhibited in its actions. . . . [It was a] magnificent step . . . which . . . broke the back of labor's arrogance and unruliness in 1946, an action the effect of which lasted for one year.[48]

However, Alemán obviously still felt uneasy about a frontal attack on organized labor as such and preferred a policy of divide and rule.[49] It was hard to imagine how the PRI (as the official party was known after 19 January 1946) might govern without the active support of organized labor, if only in electoral terms.

One major source of uncertainty was the CTM. This was, to judge from its formal ideological position and its affiliation to the CTAL, a leftist confederation. How real this ideological commitment might be, given the well-known cynicism and opportunism of many of its leaders, was something of an unknown quantity.[50] In addition, this once hegemonic organization was suffering severe internal hemorrhaging, and some observers were predicting its imminent demise.

In the complicated maneuvers to redefine the union scene, much depended on the position taken by Vicente Lombardo Toledano. Despite his radical rhetoric, he had come out as an unconditional supporter of Alemán and had thrown his weight onto the scales against the oil workers.[51] Was there a possibility that a head-on collision with the entire

believe (and the Director General of PEMEX is alleged to have made a statement to that effect) that the firm attitude recently taken in the United States toward John L. Lewis made a deep and favorable impression in Mexico, and that the trend in this country and in the new Government toward more conservative practices and greater discipline received needed encouragement therefrom." WNA 812.5045, 24 December 1946.

48 WNA 850.4, 14 July 1948.
49 WNA 850.4, 20 July 1948.
50 A U.S. embassy report described the secretary general of the CTM, Fernando Amilpa, as "both personally and physically unattractive. His reputation, even in Mexico, is particularly unsavoury. . . . His corruption and opportunism are probably among the greatest to be found in a notoriously corrupt and opportunistic labor movement." WNA 812.5043, 25 May 1948.
51 A memorandum from FBI director J. Edgar Hoover to the State Department commented on the situation in Mexico in 1947. "Source E states that during November, 1946, Lombardo met privately with President Miguel Alemán in order to discuss insistent demands being made against the government by the petroleum workers. . . . Lombardo admitted his inability to deal with the recalcitrant representatives of the petroleum workers, and it was suggested by Lombardo that President Alemán would have to employ direct measures on behalf of the Mexican Government in order to bring peace into the relationship between the government and the petroleum workers. . . . Having assumed the role of a defender of the Alemán administration, Lombardo Toledano has alienated a number of leaders with the Petroleum Workers' Syndicate, thus producing further discord within the CTM, where a division has been created by reason of Lombardo's known

union movement might be avoided? Much would depend on the outcome
of a complicated set of conflicts that came to a head in 1947 and 1948.
There were three central elements: the internal struggle within the CTM
between the Leftists, Fidel Velázquez, and Vicente Lombardo Toledano;
the efforts of the militant national industrial unions to displace the CTM
from center stage; and the effort of Lombardo Toledano, with the support
of the Mexican Left, to form the Partido Popular as a counterweight to
the PRI. Each of these three areas of conflict was linked to the other two.
Their resolution required a major act of political will by the Alemán
administration.

The CTM was in deep trouble: it had lost much support among the
rank-and-file through its no-strike pledges; some of the major industrial
unions were restive and ready to go on the offensive, but were held back
by the CTM leadership; and the organization as a whole was riven by the
same internal disputes that had accompanied it since its foundation. In
March 1947 elections were held for a new general secretary of the CTM.
The Left put forward the leader of the railway workers' union, Luis Gómez
Z., against the candidate of the *cinco lobitos,* Fernando Amilpa. In one of
those moves that often baffled the Mexican Left, Lombardo supported
Amilpa's candidacy. When the result was declared in favor of Amilpa,
Gómez Z. and the railway union withdrew from the CTM in protest. On
20 March, Gómez Z. formed the Confederación Unica de Trabajadores
(CUT) as a rival to the CTM.[52] The CUT was formed by the telephone,
streetcar, and railway unions, though the railway workers' union continued
to be its principal support, both numerically and financially.

Despite Alemán's earlier efforts, conflict in the big industrial unions
continued and appeared to be about to pose a more serious threat to the
government's plans for economic growth. In February 1947, the *oficial
mayor* of the Ministry of Labor told the American embassy that strikes
and work stoppages "constitute just about the greatest impediment to
the progress of Mexico that has existed during recent years."[53] In many
ways the situation on the railways was seen as a test case. Discussing
labor problems on the Sud Pacífico Railway with an embassy official, the

---

preference of Fernando Amilpa as future General Secretary of the CTM. As of the close of
December, 1946, according to source E, Lombardo is not only held in low esteem by a number
of political leaders surrounding Miguel Alemán, but also Lombardo's position is weakened by
the fact that he is opposed strongly by dissident elements within the CTM.... According to
source C, if Amilpa obtains the leadership of the CTM, that labor organization will follow a
policy of unconditional support to the Alemán administration . . . and can be expected to support
the United States in case of a new war." WNA 812.5043, 2 July 1947.

52  "[T]he archetype of [the] Mexican labor leader . . . [Gómez Z. was] dominated by a lust for power
and wealth." WNA 812.5043, 25 May 1948.

53  WNA 812.5043, 18 February 1947.

vice-president and general manager, Mr. Vandercook, is reported to have said:

This situation can't continue. We've got to have discipline among labor and get better efficiency or we can't stay on a paying basis and had better quit now. . . . This strike is the big test. If the Government takes a firm stand and disciplines labor, then I think American capital will be encouraged to enter Mexico. If the line is nationalized, I think it will mean the end to further investments by American capital in Mexico.[54]

The president of the line, Mr. Small, blamed the troubles on "radical, Communistic leaders." He thought the government would do something about getting rid of them when the "right time" came, and went on to explain:

Now isn't the time. The Government is aware of the situation. A lot depends on what happens in the United States. If labor is kept in line there, then the Government here will keep Mexican labor in line.[55]

It was clear that the other big industrial unions would join in opposition to the CTM. On 10 January 1948, the railway, mining, and petroleum workers' unions signed a solidarity pact, declaring that they would come to each other's aid in the event of a strike. There was intense speculation as to whether the electricians, led by the popular Juan José Rivera Rojas, "the Dapper Dan of the Mexican labor movement,"[56] would join the solidarity pact. They were generally believed to be highly supportive of it,[57] though in fact they tended to remain somewhat aloof.

Commenting on the formation of the solidarity pact, the U.S. embassy noted:

The Government . . . has been strongly supported by the CTM; but it is clear that the value of this support is decreasing daily, and that at the present moment the CTM is faced with reduction to the status of a second-rate organization. . . . Of one thing, however, there can be no doubt: that a major upheaval is taking place in the Mexican labor scene.[58]

At the same time as labor unrest was mounting and the impending disintegration of the CTM appeared to augur a shift in the contours of Mexican industrial politics, a project to start a new "Popular Party" threatened to alter the bases of the revolutionary party's domination of the political system. Beginning in 1946, and continuing through 1947,

---

54 WNA 812.5045, 9 July 1947.
55 Ibid.
56 WNA 850.4, 17 February 1948.
57 WNA 812.5043, 7 January 1948.
58 WNA 812.5043, 8 March 1948.

large sections of the Mexican Left engaged in a series of discussions tending toward the formation of a Partido Popular. These discussions were particularly difficult because of the tensions and suspicions between the Communists and Lombardo Toledano on the one hand, and the Communist dissidents and independent leftists, such as railway union leaders Valentín Campa and Luis Gómez Z., on the other. Nevertheless, progress was made and the Partido Popular was officially launched in June 1948.

The role the Partido Popular might play in Mexican politics remained as yet undefined. It might undermine the PRI's effective monopoly of power and emerge as a serious oppositional force on the Left, or it might be coopted by the government through a variety of pressures and inducements. Speculating on why the Mexican government should subsidize Lombardo's attempt to form a new political party, the third secretary of the American embassy said that Lombardo's

policy of National Unity offers the Government the prospect of coordinated and canalized cooperation from an important sector of organized labor with a consequent assurance of a decrease in disrupting labor difficulties. This is of added importance at this time because the prospects are not bright that the new Campa–Gomez Z. labor central will be so cooperative and sympathetic with the Government as Lombardo and his followers promise to be. . . . It therefore appears in the Government's interest to cancel the influence of the Campa–Gomez Z. labor central, and possibly it can best do this by strengthening Lombardo and the CTM forces. Lombardo being an old hand at working to mutual advantage with the Government, and labor in Mexico having derived so much of its present strength through Government support, the dangers to the vested political interests of the country from the formation by Lombardo of a working-class party are less than might naturally be imagined.[59]

The Partido Popular seemed to have all the potential of becoming a mass party.[60] The initial idea was that dual membership in the Partido Popular and the PRI would be permitted. Rather than be a direct rival to the PRI, the Partido Popular would act as a sort of ginger group to keep the PRI on the revolutionary road.[61]

Had the Partido Popular and the national industrial unions been able to come together, they would probably have constituted a force that was sufficiently powerful to displace the CTM from its once hegemonic position, with untold consequences for the nature of the Mexican political system as a whole. However, this fusion of the new party with the economic muscle of the big unions did not come about. This was due to the resolution of the internal conflicts in the CTM and to government intervention in the national industrial unions, the *charrazo*.

59 WNA 812.5043, 11 March 1947.
60 F. Barbosa Cano, "El charrazo contra el STPRM," vol. 2 of *Memorias del encuentro*, p. 361.
61 V. Lombardo Toledano, "El Partido Popular" in *El marxismo*, pp. 161–2.

At the Fourth Congress of the CTM in March 1947, the CTM had passed a resolution calling for the formation of the Partido Popular and pledging CTM support for the initiative. At the same time, the conference was addressed by Miguel Alemán, who stressed the need for a "política de órden y progreso." At the Thirty-Second National Council of the CTM, in October 1947, Amilpa declared himself against allowing members of the CTM to join the Partido Popular. Amid a mounting anti-Communist campaign, some of the *lombardistas* in the CTM were expelled at this meeting.[62] In December Amilpa broke relations with the CTAL, and Lombardo Toledano himself was expelled on 7 January 1948. In less than a year the CTM had completely reversed its position on the Partido Popular, and Vicente Lombardo Toledano, once the unquestioned leader of Mexican unionism, had been ignominiously pushed aside by a clique of conservative union bosses.

To some extent this outcome was the result of the internal factional disputes that had been simmering in the Mexican union movement since the mid-1930s. However, there was also a significant international dimension. The perennial efforts to create international labor confederations of varying ideological hues were accelerated with the global struggle of the Second World War and its aftermath. Despite a widespread indifference to international labor issues by the bulk of Mexico's labor leaders, Mexico played an important role in this ideological struggle. This was primarily due to the fact that the CTAL had both its organizational headquarters and its leadership in Mexico. The CTAL had been formed in 1938 and grew rapidly under the leadership of Lombardo Toledano. By 1944 it claimed an affiliated membership of 3.3 million in sixteen countries.[63] It is probable that much of its funding came from the CTM. As part of this general policy of support for the CTAL, Lombardo Toledano withdrew from active involvement in the CTM after 1941 in order to work full-time for the CTAL. In the intense ideological struggle over international unionism in the 1940s,[64] the CTAL was viewed with hostility by Washington for its pro-Communist leanings, and various efforts were made by both the State Department and the AFL to provide a viable alternative to this confederation. These efforts had an impact on the domestic politics of Mexican unions, and were a contributory factor in the struggle of the *cinco lobitos* to free themselves from Lombardo's tutelage.[65]

---

62 Medina, *Civilismo*, vol. 20 of *Historia de la Revolución*, pp. 139–40.

63 H. Spalding, *Organized Labor in Latin America* (New York, 1977), p. 255.

64 A useful account of international union politics in this period is G. K. Busch, *The Political Role of International Trades Unions* (London, 1983).

65 However, despite considerable U.S. interest in an anti-Communist campaign in Mexican unions,

The principal factor, however, seems to have been Lombardo's inability to develop a solid base among Mexican unions after he turned his attention to international affairs. Despite the similarity of his position and that of the Communists,[66] there were tensions between Lombardo and the PCM, as well as distrust between Lombardo and the leaders of the national industrial unions. Trying to maintain a position of equilibrium between the two factions proved too much, and in the process Lombardo was expelled from the CTM. The expelled *lombardista* unions formed the Alianza de Obreros y Campesinos de México (AOCM) in March of 1948. As the U.S. embassy commented:

with the exception of Lombardo Toledano and the PCM, there seems to have been little interest in international union politics amongst Mexican labor leaders. "Mexican organizations are . . . so involved with their own petty rivalries that they find little time for international organizations." WNA 850.4, 29 July 1948. Despite constant nagging from the U.S. embassy, the CTM was in no great hurry to withdraw from the World Federation of Trade Unions (WFTU), and there was little interest – apart from Luís Morones – in links with North American unions. In 1949, the first officer of the U.S. embassy had a conversation with Fernando Amilpa and reported that he (Amilpa) still thought the Congress of Industrial Organizations (CIO) was under Communist influence and that the American Federation of Labor (AFL) had "no serious interest in Latin America, does not understand Latin American mentality and has little to offer Latin American labor."

Moreover, the roving ambassador sent by the State Department to Latin America at the end of the war, Serafino Romualdi, antagonized Luís Morones of the CROM with his rather high-handed manner. WNA 812.5043, 8 July 1947.

After the fall of Morones from his preeminent position in 1928, most Mexican union contacts were with the CIO, particularly with the more left-wing leaders. This caused concern in the U.S. embassy, which recommended action by the State Department to wean them away from Lombardo Toledano's influence. Attempts to restart the Pan-American Federation of Labor as a rival to the CTAL were seen by the embassy as counterproductive. With the expulsion of the *lombardistas* from the CTM, links between that organization and the CIO were effectively broken.

66 The relationship between Lombardo Toledano and the PCM greatly exercised the U.S. embassy. Was Lombardo merely a leftist with a position that was in many respects similar to that of the Communists, or was he a secret member? Whatever the case, U.S. officials were in no doubt as to where Lombardo stood.

Ambassador Messersmith believed that the "keynote to Lombardo's character is his love of publicity, his desire for power and for some reason which I cannot explain a deep seated hatred for the United States. . . . [He] is one of the most dangerous men whom we have to deal with." Messersmith went on to note that Lombardo Toledano was attempting to establish contact with American labor leaders and recommended that the State Department should dissuade American unionists from having dealings with Lombardo Toledano. "It would, I believe, be a very fatal thing for us in the whole American picture to aid these ambitions of Lombardo. . . . We would be creating a Frankenstein of no mean dimensions." WNA 812.5042, 11 April 1945. Since it is not easy to imagine Lombardo Toledano as a Central European scientist, one must assume that Messersmith intended to refer to Frankenstein's creation, rather than to the man himself.

In a report on Lombardo Toledano in May 1947, the embassy's reporting officer said, "Lombardo is our country's most dangerous enemy in Mexico. . . . With Russia's interests coming into conflict with those of the United States after the end of hostilities, Lombardo has reverted to the role of a bitter and dangerous enemy of our country." WNA 812.5043, 16 May 1947.

Just what Lombardo's purpose is in forming this new organization at this time is hard to say with assurance. As it stands it is an organization small in numbers and weak in influence ... it is hard to believe that it will be joined in anything like its present form by the great industrial syndicates.[67]

However, at this time the correlation of forces hardly appeared to favor the CTM. Although the *fidelistas* now had exclusive control of the CTM without the necessity of having to deal with a substantial left-wing minority, they had suffered a considerable loss of membership, and in the eyes of many observers appeared also to be in a weak political position. It is estimated that the CTM had about 100,000 members at this time, compared to the 200,000 members of the three industrial unions that had signed the solidarity pact of 10 January 1948 (railway, mining, and oil), and compared to the estimated 130,000 members of the AOCM. In addition, other labor confederations and the nonaffiliated textile workers comprised another 400,000 workers.[68]

The big battalions of organized labor were now arrayed against the government and the rump of the CTM. If they could ally with the *lombardistas,* the Mexican state would face a formidable opponent and the PRI's monopoly of power might be broken. The CTM would become a minor part of the union scene and labor support for the government would no longer be taken for granted. This was not to be.

The announcement of a devaluation of the peso in July 1948 prompted an immediate response by the industrial unions, who demanded an immediate wage increase for all Mexican workers and the resignation of those cabinet members it held responsible for the situation. It was clear that the government had to stand firm on its stabilization policy.

Meanwhile, in order to dedicate himself to full-time organizing of the CUT and the solidarity pact, Gómez Z. had stepped down on 1 February 1948 as general secretary of the railway workers' union, the Sindicato de Trabajadores Ferrocarrileros de la República Mexicana (STFRM). In his place was elected a colorless individual by the name of Jesús Díaz de León, nicknamed "el Charro" for his proclivity for dressing in the traditional Mexican cowboy style. In the words of a U.S. embassy report:

Díaz de León does not appear to be a particularly strong or forceful character ... there is little doubt that in Díaz de León he [Gómez Z.] has a weak and faithful agent through whom to control the railroad workers. Díaz de León is personally very unprepossessing. He is small and washed-out looking. ... His ideological beliefs are not known, but it is very questionable whether they can run very deep.[69]

67 WNA 812.5043, 10 March 1948.
68 Medina, *Civilismo,* vol. 20 of *Historia de la Revolución,* p. 146.
69 WNA 812.5043, 25 May 1948.

On September 28, Díaz de León produced a surprise: he accused Gómez Z. of financial irregularities. Apparently, Gómez Z. had been shifting union funds to the CUT with the full knowledge of the leadership, but without explicit authorization. Instead of taking the matter to the union's Comité de Vigilancia, as was normal practice, Díaz de León chose to take the case to the Procurador General de Justicia. Warrants were issued for the arrest of the accused. Gómez Z.'s supporters in the union reacted: the Comité de Vigilancia removed Díaz de León from his post and re-instated Gómez Z. as general secretary. A confused situation reigned in the union for several days, with supporters of Díaz de León (and, it was rumored, the police) seizing the union offices, and with both sides appealing to the Ministry of Labor for official recognition. On 27 October the Ministry of Labor pronounced in favor of Díaz de León.

Most commentators accept that Díaz de León acted at the direct instigation of the government. This was certainly the view of the U.S. embassy.[70] Whatever his motives, the effect was dramatic. He carried through a major purge of the militants and delivered a now tame union back to the CTM. The solidarity pact had received a devastating blow. Supporting Díaz de León's *putsch* was a risky move by Alemán,[71] taken in the midst of a growing political crisis. It had taken him nearly two years to make the decision to confront union militancy.

The *charrazo* in the railway union was a strategic defeat for the militant unions, but the war was not yet won. The government had now to pursue its advantage in the railways, and to extend its sphere of operations to the other unions. Shortly after the *charrazo* in the railway union, the Mexican government moved to reaffirm managerial authority on the railways. It presented a "conflict of economic order" to the Federal Labor Court, which approved it within a matter of hours. As an observer at the U.S. embassy noted, "In a sense the Federal Board of Conciliation and Arbitration has reversed, in a few hours, the trend of more than a decade."[72]

Meanwhile, the oil workers' union and the miners moved ahead with plans to form a new union confederation, and the gap between the industrial unions and the *lombardistas* was papered over.

---

70  WNA 812.5043, 29 October 1948.

71  The gravity of the situation may be judged by the content of a conversation between Ambassador Thurston and Messersmith in which Messersmith said "he [Messersmith] did not attach much significance to the recent reshuffling of zone commanders but that it could be anticipated that the Army might support a movement against the government if it had first started among the four major unions. . . . Nevertheless, he [Messersmith] said, President Alemán is still strong enough to stop any subversive movement if he takes early and decisive action." WNA 850.4, 12 March 1948.

72  WNA 812.5043, 18 November 1948.

The formation of the Unión General de Obreros y Campesinos de México (UGOCM) on 22 June 1949 was a last-ditch effort by the union militants to bolster their position. As the U.S. embassy commented:

> They may feel that they must use what authority still remains to them over the Mine and Petroleum Workers' Syndicates to commit these two organizations to the Central before it is too late to accomplish even that. Even now their success is far from sure. They represent only one of two considerable currents in the leadership of each of the two syndicates, and face, if not total failure, at least the disapproval and secession of a number of sections in each organization. This danger is perhaps strongest in the Petroleum Workers', where a number of the sections have already returned to the CTM. The antagonism between Ibáñez, Secretary General of the Syndicate, and Chiñas, is, of course, well known, and it is significant that the former was not present at this meeting.[73]

The government-controlled labor courts systematically voted against strike action taken by the UGOCM,[74] and the organization soon collapsed.

Alemán, meanwhile, continued a two-pronged strategy of offering a number of concessions to organized labor and supporting the CTM, on the one hand, and preparing an attack on the other industrial unions, on the other hand. Immediately upon reorganizing the contracts on the railways, the government took action to demonstrate its backing of the CTM. It supported Amilpa's presentation in the Chamber of Deputies of a constitutional amendment that would strengthen "labor immobility."[75]

Alemán also came out against the so-called Corona thesis, which had been the subject of intense agitation by the unions. In early 1948, a Mexican judge by the name of Luis G. Corona had ruled that strikes were illegal during the two-year period covered by a collective contract. Only at the expiration of the contract could workers strike. This ruling had generated considerable opposition among the unions, and pressure put on the Supreme Court to reverse the ruling was yet another way in which the government could offer something to its supporters in the labor movement.

After the *charrazo,* the CTM set about rapidly reestablishing its erstwhile position as the principal union confederation in Mexico. Obvious government support was the main resource it possessed, though a certain amount of "brisk gunplay" was also involved.[76] With the militants in the railway union defeated, the government now moved ahead to deal with labor indiscipline in the other unions.

The conflict in 1946 between President Alemán and the oil workers'

---

73 WNA 812.5043, 4 May 1949.
74 Medina, *Civilismo,* vol. 20 of *Historia de la Revolución,* p. 173.
75 WNA 850.4, 15 December 1948; 812.5042, 23 February 1949.
76 WNA 812.504, 3 November 1949.

union, the STPRM, has already been discussed. Alemán's decisive action brought a measure of peace to the industry, but by 1948 the militants were once more in control of the union and threatening strike action. At the union's Fifth Convention in December 1947, the Hernández Abrego leadership was expelled from the union and the PCM member, Eulalio Ibáñez, was elected general secretary. It was agreed that the union would remain independent of the CTM. The Ibáñez leadership returned to a confrontationist policy, and was soon involved in bitter polemics with the Minister of Labor, who it accused (probably correctly) of intervening in internal union affairs to support opponents of the union leadership. Exacerbating the situation were moves in mid-1948 to bring American companies back into the industry.[77]

In January 1949 the union called a strike, but before the strike broke out, it settled on a pay rise with the company. Although this was the highest pay increase in the postwar period, there was substantial dissatisfaction among the rank-and-file, and Ibáñez was temporarily voted out of office. (He was shortly thereafter reinstated, with 57 percent of the membership in favor, and 43 percent against.)[78] Finally, in December 1949 during the Sixth Convention, the sectional leaders who had recently been voted out of office called a rival convention that was recognized as the authentic convention by the Ministry of Labor. The Ibáñez convention was broken up by police. A deeply divided union had finally succumbed to another *charrazo*.[79] In January 1950, the STPRM returned to the CTM.

The miners' union, the Sindicato Industrial de Trabajadores Mineros, Metalúrgicos, y Similares de la República Mexicana (SITMMSRM), was the last to undergo a *charrazo*. The strength and autonomy of the locals in the miners' union offered a base for resistance.[80] In May 1950, the Sixth National Convention of the miners' union was held. Strikes were pending at the Nueva Rosita, Palau, and Cloete mines, which were crucial for the supply of inputs for the Monterey steel industry. Delegations representing 39,000 members (out of the 52,000 total) were denied entry and decided to hold a parallel convention. The militants elected Antonio García Moreno as general secretary, and the progovernment convention elected Jesús Carrasco. The progovernment leadership then used the *cláusula de exclusión*[81] to expel the militant leadership from the union and to

---

77 Cuéllar Vásquez, "Golpe al Sindicato" in *Las derrotas*, p. 116.

78 Cuello Vásquez, "El movimiento" in *Memorias*, p. 399.

79 The leader of the rival convention, Gustavo Roldán Vargas, curiously, was also nicknamed "el Charro." Cuéllar Vásquez, "Golpe al Sindicato" in *Las derrotas*, pp. 121–2.

80 Unzueta, "Crisis en el Partido" in *Historia del Comunismo*, p. 206.

81 The *cláusula de exclusión* was a standard clause in Mexican union contracts that provided for a closed shop. Consequently, if a worker was removed from the union, the employer would have no option but to terminate his or her employment.

suspend the militant sections, including Nueva Rosita, Palau, and Cloete. In September and October of 1950, these mines went on strike despite rulings by the government that the strikes would not be legal. With the onset of the Korean War, mineral prices had risen by something like 60 percent. The army was sent into Nueva Rosita, and the town took on the appearance of an armed camp. A deliberate attempt was made to starve the miners into submission: union funds were seized; electricity and water were cut off; hospitals, schools, and shops refused to deal with the strikers or their families. The government-controlled press began a campaign to demonstrate that the leadership was intent on sabotage. By December 1950, 3,600 of the work force of 5,800 had returned to work and had been joined by 1,500 strikebreakers supplied by the progovernmental union. Finally, on 20 January 1951, the striking miners decided to form a "caravan of hunger" and march on Mexico City. Some 4,000 men set off on the *caravana del hambre* and arrived in Mexico City fifty days later. The government continued to maintain a firm position, despite pleas from the state governors of Coahuila, Nuevo León, and Tamaulipas. After camping out a month in Mexico City, the marchers agreed to return to Nueva Rosita in return for a promise to immediately reemploy 1,000 of them, and to give the others preference in new hirings. As it transpired, only 600 were readmitted to the mine. A thorough defeat had been inflicted on the militant section of the miners' union.[82]

The strike at Nueva Rosita and the subsequent *caravana del hambre* were the last gasp of the militant unionism of the 1940s. By 1950 the situation was completely under control. The oil workers' and miners' unions had returned to the CTM, the projected new labor confederation, the UGOCM, had collapsed, and the Partido Popular had been reduced to impotence.

The servility of the new union leadership and the continuing dissatisfaction of the rank-and-file are well illustrated in the following letter, written by Díaz de León to Miguel Alemán in March 1950, complaining about continuing restiveness (which he attributed to Communist agitation and propaganda) in the railway workers' union:

This disorientation has as its goal the preparation, perhaps as part of a vast plan of national agitation, the feelings of the railway workers against the government and the attempt in the coming union elections of the demagogues of the group captained by Luis Gómez Z. and Valentín Campa to take over once again the organization. For my part . . . up to now I have tried to control the union; but in order to stop the disorientation campaign which with the pretext of a wage rise is being taken advantage of by the agitators, I beg you dearly [ruego a Ud. encariciadamente] to have the goodness to authorize me – if you think

82 Basurto, *Del avilacamachismo*, vol. II of *La clase obrera*, pp. 226–7.

it prudent – to inform my fellow-workers that the rise . . . will be granted shortly in the form and amount which you will decide [que Ud. se dignará determinar].[83]

By 1948 a serious challenge to the Mexican political establishment had been beaten off. The next two years were devoted to mopping up, and by the early fifties the Mexican economy was in a position to embark on a sustained period of rapid growth. The political underpinnings of this growth-model were, on the one hand, the political stability enshrined in the unchallenged rule of the revolutionary party and, on the other hand, the smooth functioning of Mexico's brand of corporatist industrial relations, which came to be known as *charrismo.*

Many of the processes leading up to the *charrazo* of 1948 owed little to the emerging Cold War climate. The immediate origins of the *charrazo* must be sought in the coming together of the "rectification" of *cardenista* mobilization, the impact of the Second World War on union mobilization, and the perception by the Alemán administration at the end of the war that Mexico's economic destiny required solid foundations. It was a fear of wage inflation, rather than a concern to combat communism, that motivated President Alemán in his struggle with the unions.[84]

There were, of course, many sincere and genuine anti-Communists in Mexico, and the ending of the wartime alliance with the Soviet Union provided them with an appropriate climate in which to propagate their ideas. Luís Morones's CROM was in the forefront of much of the anti-Communist agitation. The U.S. embassy clearly wished to promote further anti-Communist activity, and the U.S. ambassador raised the matter directly with Miguel Alemán.

Given Alemán's refusal to make an issue of anticommunism, there is not a great deal of evidence to suggest that Mexico was swept as fully into an anti-Communist campaign as the United States might have wished. Instead, it is reasonable to suppose that much of the Mexican government's anticommunism was largely an exercise in symbolic behavior aimed at appeasing the United States.

Where the United States did exercise influence in this area, however, it was largely through force of example. It is clear that the Mexican government looked to the United States to give a lead on how to deal with labor. The miners' strike in the United States, the passage of the Taft–Hartley legislation, and the 1948 presidential campaign were all closely followed in Mexico.

---

83 AGN, Ramo Presidentes, Miguel Alemán, 432–3, letter from Díaz de León to the President, 3 March 1950.

84 In a interview with the U.S. ambassador, President Alemán told him at great length that communism in Mexico was "a matter of relative insignificance" and that the government was in complete control of the situation. WNA 812.00B, 2 December 1948.

The Mexican government was increasingly preoccupied with organized labor from the last part of the war onward for basically domestic reasons. The continuing economic problems and the perceived problem of labor indiscipline in the railways and the oil industry clearly were a source of mounting concern for the Mexican government. The increasing industrial unrest, the crisis and apparent death agony of the CTM, and the emergence of a powerful and militant union bloc, potentially opposed to government economic policy, were the central events on the industrial relations scene at the end of the war. These must have been viewed with concern by the Mexican government. Underlying this was the determination of the Miguel Alemán administration to pursue an industrialization policy. This meant support for foreign investment, a devaluation of the peso, and a determination to hold wage increases in check. Growing union militancy was clearly seen by the Alemán government as a major threat to the success of its economic program. The moves made by the Truman administration in the United States to check union power in that country were followed with close interest in Mexico and doubtless served to stiffen the resolve of the Alemán government.

Prior to 1946 the situation was unclear. There was considerable uncertainty about the shape of the postwar world. There also existed a strong current within Mexico of support for a nationalist economic development program. As expressed in 1945 in the Pacto Obrero–Industrial, this economic nationalism was viewed with hostility by the United States. Within Mexico, however, there was a certain logic to the nationalist economic program. It represented a return to *cardenismo,* and fitted naturally with the prevailing interpretation by the Communist Party of the need to form an alliance with the progressive national bourgeoisie around an industrialization program. A couple of years were to elapse before the reality of the Cold War became so enduringly defined that it became the primary determinant of world politics. In that interval, as the episode of Browderism demonstrates, the international Communist movement seems to have thought that an extension of the wartime alliance might have been possible. That such hopes were rudely dashed within a few years should not blind us to the fact that, at least in the eyes of the people living through this period, not all was as yet defined and a "window of opportunity" existed. It was slammed shut in part by the international campaign of the United States against communism, but also in part as a result of a series of domestic struggles. Such struggles were neither doomed to failure nor overdetermined by the international conjuncture.

The struggle in Mexico was not over the establishment of democracy. What was at stake was union independence and the nature of the Mexican growth model. However, controlling the unions went hand-in-hand with reorganizing the official party to secure its monopoly of power. The two

# 8

## Cuba

### Harold Sims

The Second World War had a profound impact on economy, society, and politics, and not least on organized labor, in Cuba as in the rest of Latin America. Cuba, however, differed somewhat from the other Latin American countries in that by the early 1940s as much as half of the work force was already unionized, and at least half these workers were in the agricultural sector. Both "revolutionary" and "populist" governments in the 1930s had granted workers new rights and a new status, and sought to incorporate them into the political system – and to control them. During the war, the Cuban government demanded and secured support from the unions and sacrifice from their members, including no-strike pledges. The last year of the war (1944–5) and victories for the Allies brought democratic elections, but it also unleashed pent-up demands from workers for wage increases and raised political expectations on the Left, both Communist and non-Communist. In the postwar struggle for the control of organized labor, which was intense and violent, the United States to a degree supported the non-Communist elements. In Cuba, unlike the rest of Latin America, labor militancy persisted after the purges of 1947–8 and the virtual elimination of Communist leaders, especially in the urban sector. But there was no union resistance to the return to dictatorship in 1952.

Cuban labor first began to organize itself at the end of the nineteenth century. Anarcho-syndicalists launched the effort, but they were eventually driven underground by the brutal dictatorship of Gerardo Machado during the late 1920s. The destruction of the anarchists, and the onset of the World Depression, facilitated the rise of a Communist leadership that, by 1931, had gained control of the labor movement.[1] During the

The author wishes to thank George Reid Andrews, Samuel Farber, and James Lewis for their criticism of earlier drafts.

1 Samuel Farber, *Revolution and Reaction in Cuba, 1933–1960: A Political Sociology from Machado to*

Depression, which hit Cuban exports (mainly sugar) hard, Cuban workers were without trade union rights and strikes were rare. But in 1933, workers belonging to the Confederación Nacional de Obreros Cubanos (CNOC) launched sporadic work stoppages, culminating in a general strike. Machado called in the CNOC leadership (by this time Communist) and persuaded them to call it off,[2] but the leaders found that they no longer controlled the workers. When the entire transport sector went out in early August, commerce and industry joined forces with labor, and the regime collapsed.[3]

A revolutionary nationalist government (September 1933–January 1934) sought to instill "nationalism" in labor's ranks while granting workers' demands.[4] The list of significant measures decreed for the benefit of labor was a long one: the eight-hour day; compulsory organization of professionals; the creation of a Ministry of Labor; repatriation of foreign agricultural workers; compulsory arbitration of labor disputes; a weekly indemnified rest period; the requirements that 50 percent of all workers in a given category be Cuban, and that all union officials be native-born; improvements in the industrial accident law; a reaffirmation that all wages must be paid in legal tender; declaration of the nonattachability of all salaries of workers and employees; and the establishment of a minimum wage. The government also took up the issues of agrarian reform and rural housing, but its tenure was too brief to launch effective programs in these areas.[5] Of particular importance to workers were the commitment to repatriate foreign laborers and the 50 percent law. The former was needed to maintain (or restore) access to jobs, in view of the migration to Cuba of an estimated 150,000 Haitians and Jamaicans from 1921 to 1933. The latter was aimed at Spaniards and, to a lesser extent, U.S. workers. The positive response of labor to the revolutionary regime can be gauged by the mood of the CNOC's Fourth Congress, which met in early January 1934 – the largest assembly of its kind, attracting 10,000 delegates.[6]

The government of Dr. Ramón Grau San Martín – reformist and pro-labor – created a paternalistic Ministry of Labor in order to reduce the influence of its opponents (principally the Communists) on the Left. And

---

*Castro* (Middletown, CN, 1976), p. 65; Hugh Thomas, *Cuba: The Pursuit of Freedom* (London, 1971), p. 596.

2 Farber, *Revolution,* pp. 64–5, 68; Thomas, *Cuba,* pp. 615–16, 618.

3 Charles E. Thomson, "The Cuban Revolution: Fall of Machado," *Foreign Policy Reports* 11(18 December 1935):254.

4 Charles A. Page, The development of organized labor in Cuba, (Ph.D. diss. University of California, Berkeley, 1952), pp. 76–7.

5 Ibid., p. 77; Farber, *Revolution,* p. 43.

6 Thomas, *Cuba,* p. 647.

to consolidate worker support, it used compulsory arbitration (a policy seized on to advantage by the Communists after 1938).[7] There was a second negative aspect to Grau's labor legislation, which would prove useful to the counterrevolutionary government that followed. Strikes could legally be called only after a compulsory waiting period, and at least eight days' notice had been given to the Ministry of Labor. Disputes were submitted to "commissions of social cooperation" followed by a prolonged period of negotiation and appeal, after which, if workers remained discontented, they could strike, "except in cases where the demands had been satisfied, or had been declared illegitimate by the Commission."[8] These and other provisions practically eliminated the "legal" right to strike. Labor was legitimately organized, with state approval, but had lost its autonomy to the Ministry of Labor.

When in January 1934 ex-Sergeant Fulgencio Batista removed the revolutionary government weakened by U.S. nonrecognition, organized labor responded with a concerted effort to bring down the new dictatorship through the general strike, a weapon that had proven effective against Machado. Initially, in January, the new regime sought to pacify labor through concessions; a minimum wage was authorized for the first time, setting pay at $1.00 per day in the cities and sugar mills, and $.80 per day for rural labor, although this new standard was only gradually (and never completely) implemented. Secondly, a new measure made it illegal to dismiss a worker without cause – a provision that would have profound implications for the future. Of course, this, too, was not immediately, or evenly, enforced.[9] But labor could not be cowed so easily, nor was it willing to accept the loss of the right to strike. In February the tobacco workers (30,000 strong) went on strike. When violence flared up, President Carlos Mendieta suspended constitutional guarantees, and decreed that all unions refusing to accept the regulations concerning strikes were dissolved.[10] Under this Law of National Defense, no new demands could be made on employers for six months following a strike.[11]

The struggle between the dictatorship and labor culminated in March 1935 in the greatest strike of Cuban history. The effort commenced with cigar workers and spread to the docks, to electricians, printers, truck, bus, and other drivers, chemical and hospital workers, and ice distributors. The action was much larger than any Machado had faced – more than 200,000 workers went on strike. But the strikers were met by the com-

---

7 Farber, *Revolution*, pp. 43–4.
8 Raymond L. Buell et al., *Problems of the New Cuba* (New York, 1935), p. 202, cited in ibid., pp. 45–6.
9 Thomas, *Cuba*, p. 698.
10 Ibid., pp. 691–2.
11 Buell et al., *New Cuba*, pp. 203–4, cited in Farber, *Revolution*, p. 46.

bined military and police forces of the regime. At least 100 participants
were killed, and hundreds more wounded or arrested. Batista broke the
strike, drowning in blood the final act of resistance to the regime. In the
repression that followed, most labor unions were dissolved, their headquarters raided, and funds seized.[12] The Communists' links with organized
workers were particularly damaged.[13] In October 1935, the sixth Plenum
of the Central Committee, adopting the Comintern line, formally introduced an antiimperialist Popular Front strategy that would include syndicalist unity.[14]

By late 1935, the tide of repression had turned, and governmental paternalism was resumed. Batista's Ministry of Labor was built on the
foundation erected by the revolutionary government. Workers' organizations would therefore function more like pressure groups than labor
unions, becoming reformist, not revolutionary, in nature.[15] Puppet governments of the late 1930s, backed by Batista, added to labor's gains:
the eight-hour day and forty-four-hour week (with pay for forty-eight
hours); thirty days of paid vacation; nine days sick leave with pay; four
added paid holidays; and six weeks of leave during childbirth for women
workers. In some cases, wages were tied to the cost of living, and factories
could not relocate, nor dismiss employees without cause. In addition, a
decree inspired by the U.S. Wagner Act guaranteed the right to collective
bargaining.

Like other populists, Batista sought to strengthen his government by
attempting to bring organized labor under state control, a task that proved
difficult until 1937 when he turned to the Cuban Communist Party.
Apart from their divisive role in creating "Soviets" in some sugar mills,
the Communists had "missed" the revolution of 1933–4. Batista now
allowed the party a free hand in organizing labor. The Communists'
Partido Unificado Revolucionario (PUR) began to reconstruct the labor
movement with loyal party members at its head. Batista, labor, and the
Communists all benefited from the new Popular Front atmosphere.[16] In
return for unaccustomed tolerance, the Communists demonstrated marked
moderation, a stance their own leaders would later criticize for its lack

---

12 Jean Stubbs, *Tobacco on the Periphery: A Case Study in Cuban Labour History, 1860–1958* (Cambridge,
    1985), pp. 137–8; Thomson, *Cuba*, pp. 273–4; Farber, *Revolution*, pp. 48–9; Thomas, *Cuba*,
    p. 699.
13 Adam Anderle, "Algunas problemas de la evolución del pensamiento antiimperialista en Cuba
    entre las dos guerras mundiales: Comunistas y apristas," *Acta universitatis Szegediensis, Acta Historica*
    2(1975):46; Farber, *Revolution*, pp. 48–9, 68–9.
14 Anderle, "Comunistas y apristas," pp. 56–8.
15 Farber, *Revolution*, pp. 136–7.
16 Ibid., pp. 85–7.

of anticapitalist zeal.[17] In 1938, the Communists consolidated their hold on both the labor movement and the Ministry of Labor.[18] This action led many young, ambitious politicians to become "Communist" labor leaders, though they were barred from top positions, which were reserved for the genuine Communists.[19] Often, these same individuals later joined labor organizations in competition with the Communists.

The formation of a new national labor confederation followed the creation in 1936 of the Federación Tabacalera Nacional (FTN), the first of the new industrial unions, and the meeting of the first National Congress of Tobacco Workers occurred in 1938.[20] Early in January 1939, elections were held in local and provincial labor organizations to select around 1,500 representatives from 576 unions to attend a labor congress to be held on 23–8 January. The result was the creation of the Confederación de Trabajadores de Cuba (CTC). Lázaro Peña, the black tobacco workers' leader and a member of the PUR, was elected secretary general. Resolutions were passed urging changes in existing labor legislation,[21] and the CTC affiliated with the Mexican Lombardo Toledano's Confederación de Trabajadores de América Latina (CTAL). Demands included a minimum wage of 1 peso 20 centavos per day in agriculture and 1 peso 50 centavos daily for unskilled industrial workers; compliance with the law requiring payment in currency; the legal requirement of the closed shop; the establishment of retirement funds; modification of the industrial accidents law; repeal of restrictions on the right to strike; and the creation of a Syndicate of the Unemployed. Opposition was expressed to racial discrimination and to fascism, and support was sought for making the Communist periodical *Hoy* the official organ of the CTC.[22] By 1939 there existed a so-called Batista Pact, not directly with the Communist Party, but with the CTC and organized labor.[23]

The revitalization of organized labor resulted in rapid gains in strength and numbers. There had been some 200,000 enrolled in unions in 1938, 80,000 of whom were tobacco workers. By 1940, the total had risen to nearly 350,000. In October 1939 delegates from 78 sugar workers' unions had convened to form the Federación Nacional de Obreros Azucareros

17 Ibid., pp. 140–1.
18 Ibid., pp. 43–4.
19 Page, Organized labor, p. 217.
20 Stubbs, *Tobacco*, p. 142.
21 Page, Organized labor, pp. 102–4, note 52. The first congress of the CTC was followed by others – a second in 1940 with 592 unions and 218,000 members represented, and a third in 1942 with 973 unions and 407,000 members represented. Stubbs, *Tobacco*, pp. 143–4. The fourth convened in 1944 and the fifth in 1947. A first National Peasant Congress was held in 1945.
22 Page, Organized labor, pp. 103–4.
23 Ibid., p. 91.

(FNOA), strengthening organization in the fields and sugar centrals.[24] For the 1940 *zafra* (harvest), the FNOA demanded recognition, a 25 percent wage increase, regulated hours, and overtime pay. In 1941, the FNOA alone could claim more than 100,000 members. Thus, at the onset of the Second World War, between one-third and one-half of Cuba's workers were organized. Industries with the highest levels of organization included sugar, tobacco, transport, and manufacturing, especially textiles. The most important sector to remain outside was coffee. Roughly three-quarters of the unionized belonged to unions affiliated with the CTC. The confederation was organized along industrial lines, and many local and provincial federations were to be found in its ranks. Despite growth and organization, the CTC never became wealthy. Only 19 percent of the membership regularly paid dues to the central organization, and only 47 percent subscribed to their local unions. Cuba's slow recovery from the Depression possibly explains the lack of financial commitment by the majority.[25]

Political opposition to Batista centered on the Partido Revolucionario Cubano–Auténtico (PRC–A), whose members saw themselves as the civilian heirs of the Revolution of 1933. They too were interested in organizing labor. The Auténtico party established the Comisión Obrera Nacional (Auténtica) (CONA), which was directed by an ex-Communist who had never been a worker, Eusebio Mujal Barniol. Federations and unions would now be Communist, Auténtico, or independent, depending on the identity of their organizers. Benefiting from government support, by 1940 the Communists controlled the sugar, tobacco, and transport workers – who collectively constituted the most important unions and federations. PUR members also led two of the six provincial federations, those of Oriente and Las Villas. Auténticos dominated the restaurant workers' federations, and maintained minority representation within the sugar and maritime unions. Independents controlled the unions of maritime workers, public employees, and electricians. Four of the six provincial federations, including Havana, had representatives from all three factions within their leaderships.[26]

Nearly 50 percent of the total labor force (500,000 of 1,086,000 workers) was engaged in seasonal employment. Sugar workers (45 percent) had regular employment only 90–100 days yearly. And this also affected

24 Evelio Tellería Toca, *Los congresos obreros en Cuba* (Havana, 1973), pp. 277–318; Page, Organized labor, pp. 87–9; Grupo Cubano de Investigaciones Económicas, *A Study on Cuba* (Coral Gables, FL, 1965), p. 727.

25 Thomas, *Cuba*, pp. 91, 95, 97, 100; Grupo Cubano, *Study on Cuba*, p. 726.

26 Tellería, *Congresos obreros*, pp. 331–3; U.S. Office of Strategic Services (OSS), *The Political Significance and Influence of the Labor Movement in Latin America: A Preliminary Survey: Cuba* (Washington, D.C., 18 Sept. 1945), R&A No. 3, 076.1.

railway and dock workers, since transporting Cuba's major export was a principal activity in these sectors. The seasonal nature of so much employment made it difficult to maintain coherent labor organization.[27] Whereas labor leaders in Havana, where one-third of the employed were to be found, had clout and could solve problems, provincial leadership was often powerless. Top-level labor leaders were usually drawn from the ranks of the workers; only rarely were they lawyers, doctors, or professors.[28] But the gap between the national chiefs and the rank-and-file widened.[29] The leadership chose not to create a labor party, preferring the role of loyal political opposition.[30] Finally, there was only minimal interaction with the American Federation of Labor (AFL), even though the bloodiest strikes tended to be against U.S. firms – in sugar, shipping, railways, textiles, and tobacco.[31]

Batista had attempted to legitimize his de facto authority in 1939 by calling a constitutional convention in which the Communists played a major role, particularly in drafting articles that affected labor. The resulting fundamental document was sufficiently progressive for even the revolutionaries of the late 1950s to claim as their credo. The articles touching on labor matters (twenty-seven in all) reinforced government's role, promoted wage increases in urban trades, and granted social security benefits to a portion of the working class. The Constitution held that the "right of organization is recognized for employers, private employees, and workers, for the exclusive purpose of their economic-social activity"; that union officials "shall be exclusively Cubans by birth"; that twenty people were sufficient to establish a union; and that the Ministry of Labor should have "the responsibility for the financial liquidation of the association," should a union decide to dissolve itself.[32] The Communist delegates obtained a rule granting the right of "tenure" to employees after six months in the job, effectively penalizing capitalist growth and inhibiting new investments in the future.[33] In practice, constitutional provisions would "be held in reserve to be used to force concessions for Cuban workers and to insure more Cuban participation in management," according to *Business Week*.[34] Constitutional and labor laws were more likely to be implemented in large plants where unions

27 Page, Organized labor, pp. 168–9.
28 Farber, *Revolution*, p. 113.
29 Page, Organized labor, p. 170.
30 Ibid., p. 299.
31 Ibid., pp. 167–8. See also Stubbs, *Tobacco*, for discussions of strikes against U.S. firms.
32 Ben G. Burnett and Moisés Poblete Troncoso, *The Rise of the Latin American Labor Movement* (New York, 1960), pp. 313, 316, 319.
33 Farber, *Revolution*, pp. 95–6.
34 12 October 1940, p. 64, cited in ibid., pp. 96–7.

were strong, of course, and much less likely to be enforced in smaller businesses in which unions were weak, or where bribery of government officials precluded enforcement.[35]

Following promulgation of the new Constitution, elections were held in an open atmosphere. Batista easily defeated his Auténtico rival, receiving enthusiastic support from the PUR. Labor support for an elected President Batista depended on his continuing responsiveness to union demands. A case in point would be the FNOA, which, by 1940, had over 100,000 members.[36] Wages in sugar were greatly influenced by the size of the U.S. quota and sugar prices. In 1941 the quota was 2,399,004 tons and the price 1.69 cents per pound; in 1942 the quota rose to 3,950,000 tons and the price to 2.65 cents. As a result, in 1942 the FNOA demanded a 30 percent wage rise; Batista initially suggested between 15 and 25 percent, then authorized 50 percent! In 1944 when the FNOA requested 20 percent, Batista gave just 10 percent. But in 1945, when the sugar price rose to 3 cents, the president permitted a wage increase of 32 percent.[37] Clearly, FNOA officials were usually quite successful in their representations to the state.[38]

In 1942 Cuba's entry into the Second World War as an ally of the United States was welcomed by labor leaders. Even the Communists, who after the collapse of the Hitler–Stalin Pact had become enthusiastic supporters of the Allies, moderated their earlier radicalism; by 1944 Blas Roca asserted that the nationalization of public services would be sufficient "socialism."[39] Labor's cooperative attitude can be seen in a resolution at the second Congress of the CTC in 1942:

While war conditions last, the Cuban workers wish to avoid all strikes and conflicts capable of paralyzing production; but at the same time, they insist that their suggestions for the creation of machinery for conciliation and arbitration shall be given due consideration, as well as the suggestion for direct negotiation between the syndicate and management.[40]

35  Ibid.
36  Page, Organized labor, pp. 95–6.
37  Ibid., pp. 96–9.
38  Charles Page provides a revealing insight into the lives of these leaders who, during the dread *tiempo muerto*, were as affected as the workers: "[in the] Rosario syndicate, the vice-secretary general returned to the barber trade; the secretary of finance took up his former skill of cabinet maker, while yet another member of the executive committee became a cook on a railroad." Ibid., p. 203, note 63.
39  Carlos Rafael Rodríguez, interviewed by Thomas (*Cuba*, p. 734).
40  Burnett and Poblete Troncoso, *Latin American Labor Movement*, p. 199, cited in Page, Organized labor, p. 105.

In April 1942, Batista finally gave official status to the CTC.[41] Under its Communist leadership, the CTC had direct access to the Ministry of Labor.

Hostility to the no-strike pledge soon produced a schism in both the PUR and labor. A faction broke away from the Communists, the Auténticos, and Joven Cuba to form Acción Revolucionaria Guiteras (ARG). Its leaders were ex-Communists who had been anarcho-syndicalists prior to joining the PUR. The ARG was secret and addicted to the teachings of Georges Sorel. It founded a leadership school to train a new revolutionary elite. The ARG preferred direct action and attempted to frustrate the collaborationist policy dictated by the CTC. Eventually, in order to oppose the Communists, the ARG established an alliance of convenience with the Auténtico labor leadership.[42] Ideological militancy was not a characteristic of labor's rank and file, however; in the 1942 by-elections, for example, the majority of labor voted for nationalist parties.[43]

The CTC suffered an ideological split in 1943 as the Auténticos developed aspirations to compete with their enemies from 1934, Batista and the Communists, for influence over the workers. Lázaro Peña was sufficiently concerned to denounce the Auténticos as

a group of adventurers, agents of management, and petty politicians, who would call themselves the PRC without any true responsibility to that party, in order to accomplish the purposes of the diversionists, of the obstructionists, and of the traitors, Mujal and Company, who desire complete control in order to impose on the PRC their reactionary policy of open service to fifth-columnism. In their hands the CTC would be an instrument of persecution and political pressure, of corruption and degeneration of the labor movement.[44]

Auténtico propaganda denigrated the Batista regime because of its alliance with the Communists. Mujal, an ex-Communist and the president of the PRC–A's National Commission of Social Affairs, declared in a political pamphlet of June 1944:

The Ministry of Labor [under Batista] . . . has been converted, as the people of Cuba know, into a branch of the Communist Party. In the [future] government of Dr. Grau San Martín . . . [it] will be a Ministry of Labor, and not as it is now, a Ministry of Lázaro Peña or any other Communist leader.[45]

41 Thomas, *Cuba*, p. 733.
42 The ARG claimed a membership of 8,000 by the 1950s. Page, Organized labor, pp. 173–4, note 58.
43 Farber, *Revolution*, p. 141.
44 Quoted in Page, Organized labor, pp. 104–5.
45 Quoted in ibid., p. 104.

The *mujalistas* were ambitious and needed a party to support them. Since there were no possibilities in the Batista camp in 1943, they chose the PRC–A, and formed the CONA. The principal figures were Mujal, Francisco Aguirre, secretary general of the restaurant workers' federation, Emilio Surí Castillo, future secretary general of the Federación de Trabajadores Azucareros (FNTA), and two lesser known individuals.[46] The Communists weakened their cause at this time by carrying out controversial purges within their own ranks – expelling such popular figures as the bus driver's leader, Arsenio González, and the student intellectual Rolando Masferrer. The latter soon founded a newspaper dedicated to demonstrating that Communist leaders (including those in labor) were not above reproach, financially or morally.[47] Partly to symbolize their cooperative attitude and continuing "moderation" during the war and also under the influence of Browderism, the PUR changed its name in 1943 to Partido Socialista Popular (PSP).

With national elections approaching, the Batista government decreed on 1 April 1943 a new code of social legislation that, had it been implemented, would have expanded the rights of labor well beyond those contained in the Constitution of 1940,[48] or those to be found anywhere in the hemisphere. In all, nine new rights – many anticipatory of socialist programs attempted in the Castro era – were acknowledged. To promote these goals, a Cuban Institute of Social Security was contemplated, and pensions of from 300 to 1,100 pesos per annum were discussed.[49] This ambitious program was intended to cement relations between Batista's Democratic Socialist Coalition and Cuban workers in the months preceding the 1944 election. But unemployment was high in 1944, especially in Havana, and this might be expected to have a greater impact than public pronouncements.

The elections of 1 June 1944 proved once again to be free. This time, however, Batista confronted a new democratic spirit among the electorate. Carlos Saladrigas, the candidate of the Democratic Socialist Coalition, was rejected in favor of an alternative civilian leadership, the men of the revolution of 1933–4, whom Batista had betrayed. The Auténtico leader, Ramón Grau San Martín, won handsomely – an outcome that shocked the Communists who petulantly called on the "chief" to disavow the election result and retain authority. They sensed what the verdict of the electorate could ultimately mean for the PSP's position in organized labor.

---

46  Ibid., pp. 113–14.

47  Jorge García Montes and Antonio Alonso Avila, *Historia del Partido Comunista de Cuba* (Miami, 1970), pp. 315–16.

48  The code (Decree No. 1900) was drafted by Dr. Carlos M. Raggi Ageo. Page, *Organized labor*, p. 246.

49  Ibid.

Thus, Batista's eventual departure on 9 October 1944 was greatly lamented by his old allies on the Left.[50]

The election in 1944 had indeed serious implications for organized labor. Competition between Auténticos and Communists had been intensifying since the 1940 elections. In 1942, when the Communists were victorious in a majority of contests for CTC offices, Mujal and the Auténticos had split the confederation rather than give way to their ideological rivals. But the Second World War and U.S. pressure on Cuba soon forced the Auténticos to recognize that the exigencies of the day required a united front against fascism, and the unity of the CTC was tenuously restored. Batista's government supported the mainstream CTC and its Communist leaders. With Grau in office, however, the alliance of the PSP with the state would survive for just two more years. Auténticos could now launch an assault on the strongholds of the Communists with benign support from official sources; Mujal could confront Peña with greater confidence and increased funding. In preparation for its conflict with Mujal's CONA, and in defense of its support for Batista, the PSP drew up a document in June 1944 that appeared to threaten a general strike. In the end, however, the Communists decided to approach the Auténticos, offering cooperation and demanding only guarantees for the CTC's Communist leadership. Formal talks began with Grau himself, and the United States even intervened, with wartime unity in mind, requesting that Peña be retained as head of the CTC. Grau relented, providing the requested guarantees.[51]

Initially, Grau's inauguration brought little apparent change. The Communists and organized labor were too strong to be taken on frontally. Grau feared the Communists, and sought to maintain labor harmony. The subsequent campaign to undermine the PSP leaders by vilification (or worse) was undertaken by Mujal's CONA, operating at the union level. The Communists responded by accusing CONA of receiving U.S. funds for the mission. This the Auténticos denied; it was, their spokesman claimed, "a fabricated calumny, like so many claims put forward by the Communists."[52]

The atmosphere at the CTC's Fourth Congress in December 1944 could best be described as repressed hostility. The solution contrived at the congress was to allot an equal number of Executive Committee posts to each principal contender and the remainder to the independents, providing

50 Roca praised Batista as a "magnificent reserve of Cuban democracy." Quoted in Thomas, *Cuba*, p. 736.

51 García Montes and Alonso Avila, *Partido Comunista de Cuba*, pp. 325–6.

52 Page, Organized labor, p. 114. No support for the Communist claim is present in the U.S. State Department's confidential post records for these years.

the latter with the determining votes. Under this compromise agreement, Peña was allowed to remain as secretary general.[53] Peña's keynote speech was cautious, eulogizing "proletarian unity" as well as President Grau. The resolutions were conciliatory: support for the Good Neighbor Policy and for "government efforts" on behalf of workers. Grau and Dr. Carlos Azcárate, his labor minister, attended the closing session and were warmly received; a temporary pact was sealed,[54] which would last into 1946, at which time an Auténtico electoral victory, plus the onset of the Cold War, would make a break feasible in the eyes of the PRC–A.[55]

Grau favored compromise, for the moment, since the Communists controlled between 25 and 33 percent of organized labor and dominated the crucial sugar and tobacco workers' unions. Strikes would have damaged the new democratic government, providing Batista with a pretext for a coup d'état. Peña compromised as well. In February 1945 the Executive Committee of the CTC attended a joint luncheon with their counterparts of the Asociación Nacional de Industrialistas Cubanos (ANIC). Peña, the honored guest, spoke on "Collaboration between Workers and Employers."[56] Thus the PSP succeeded in retaining control of labor after the war and, in order to please Auténtico politicians, the wartime no-strike policy was retained in the postwar era. The conciliatory CTC leadership advocated, in practice, a policy of wage freezes that led their members to lose some ground.[57]

If we are to believe the estimates of the Office of Strategic Services (OSS), despite the conflictive situation in the CTC, its membership burgeoned during the final years of the war.[58] According to official statistics, union membership rose from 269,000 in 1944 to 341,000 in 1945. Since the Ministry of Labor itself, however, did not maintain statistics on union membership,[59] "official" figures are highly suspect. Moreover, in several occupational categories, the 1945 "official" figure is in fact lower (and considerably so) than that of 1944. Only in the case of sugar workers are the numbers significantly higher. Can we speculate then that, in fact, union membership was declining in the midst of the evolving split in

53 García Montes and Alonso Avila, *Partido Comunista de Cuba*, pp. 324–6; Mario Riera Hernández, *Historial obrero cubano, 1574–1965* (Miami, 1965), p. 130; James O'Connor, *The Origins of Socialism in Cuba* (Ithaca, NY, 1970), pp. 180–1; Page, Organized labor, p. 179.

54 García Montes and Alonso Avila, *Partido Comunista de Cuba*, pp. 332–3.

55 Farber, *Revolution*, p. 138.

56 Ibid., pp. 137–8. For a list of the members of the CTC Executive Committee, 1944–5, and their political affiliations, see OSS, *Preliminary Survey*, appendix.

57 Farber, *Revolution*, p. 106.

58 For a detailed analysis of the CTC in 1945, see OSS, *Preliminary Survey*, pp. 22–30.

59 Page, Organized labor, p. 100, note 46; Stubbs, *Tobacco*, p. 172.

CTC leadership? Perhaps, but the shaky nature of the data should make us skeptical of any conclusion.

Inflation surged at the end of the war, but in contrast to the period after the First World War, the price of sugar in the world market also continued to rise (from 2.99 cents per pound in 1944, to 5.05 cents in 1948).[60] This meant that Grau could allay discontent by raising wages in the sugar sector. In any case, since sugar workers' wages were tied by law to the world price of sugar, Grau had little choice.[61] This legal provision, like the labor regulations restricting mechanization, the prohibition on cane cutting machines, and the persistence of hand loading, actually obstructed modernization in the sugar industry.[62] As a result, roughly 500,000 workers were required at harvest time, nearly 400,000 as cane cutters, and 100,000 in the mills. This accounted for more than one-third of the Cuban work force in the winter season.[63] We should not mistake these workers for active union members, of course, due to their geographical mobility, and the fact that in 1946 only 12.7 percent of agricultural workers were "permanently" employed.[64]

Armed violence multiplied in 1944 and 1945, as the PRC–A employed thugs from the "revolutionary organizations" that proliferated during the Grau era – some of them subsidized by the Ministry of Education – in attacks on Communist trade union leaders.[65] The PSP was, by now, in the throes of the Duclos–Browder affair, attempting to purge itself of Browderism, a process that was completed in January 1946 at the party's Third National Assembly when Roca led the final recantation.[66] Communist periodicals began to break from the "tolerant" mode of the Popular Front, detecting renewed imperialist trends at work to the North.[67] Stalinism dictated a new line in the late 1940s. In foreign affairs, U.S. imperialism was to be denounced, but in domestic politics, few if any changes were required.[68] In February 1946, the Eleventh Congress of the CTC passed without serious incident, though the Cuban Educational Association condemned Communist control of teachers' organizations. A more portentous event was occurring at this time in Miami. Mujal,

60 Page, Organized labor, p. 108. Page erroneously calculates this as 200%.
61 Ibid., p. 234.
62 Thomas, *Cuba*, p. 1144.
63 Hugo Vivo, *El empleo y la población activa en Cuba* (Havana, 1950), passim, cited in ibid., pp. 1151–2.
64 Lowry Nelson, *Rural Cuba* (Minneapolis, 1950), p. 135.
65 Thomas, *Cuba*, p. 744.
66 García Montes and Alonso Avila, *Partido Comunista de Cuba*, p. 365.
67 Stewart Cole Blasier, The Cuban and Chilean Communist Parties, instruments of Soviet policy, 1935–48 (Ph.D. diss., Columbia University, 1956), p. 192, cited in Thomas, *Cuba*, p. 745.
68 Farber, *Revolution*, p. 138.

Aguirre, and Juan Arévalo (CTC foreign secretary and maritime workers'
union leader) were engaged in talks concerning how best to purge the
Cuban labor movement of Communist leadership.[69] Clearly, independent,
socialist (Arévalo), and Auténtico leaders sought U.S. government and
AFL support for their endeavor.

The elections of 1946, in which the PSP and CTC leaders backed PRC–
A candidates, represented the high-water mark of Communist membership (prior to the 1960s) and vote-garnering potential: party members
only amounted to some 37,000, but roughly 197,000 voters cast ballots
for the party's candidates (compared with 130,000 in 1944).[70] It was, of
course, the lull before the storm. In 1947 the PSP and its CTC leaders
would confront disaster. For a variety of reasons, the PSP labor leadership
was vulnerable. Their role in the bureaucratization of the unions, failure
to act "democratically," occasional lapses into violent or threatening tactics, and excessive reliance on government favors, all left them open to
criticism.[71] Pursuing and strengthening the "bread-and-butter" approach
to labor union activity had led, logically, to the growth of a nonideological
workers' movement that, as revealed by its voting in national elections,
did not need the Communists to continue its special relationship with
the Cuban state. But more importantly, by following the Stalinist line,
Peña and his colleagues provided a convenient rationale for the actions of
the ambitious Auténticos and independents.

As the Cold War arrived in Cuba, the Auténticos dropped all pretense
of compromise. The North Americans did nothing publicly to oppose the
continuation of Communists on the Executive Committee of the CTC,
but the U.S. ambassador made his government's anti-Communist position
clear to President Grau. The United States was not in agreement, he
declared, with the policy pursued by the Cuban state "by which the
Communist Party was permitted to expand with the use of funds belonging
to the Cuban people."[72] A number of independents joined the Auténticos
in the offensive against the Communists. Some major federations that had
traditionally been Communist preserves had fallen into Auténtico hands
by the Spring of 1947. Surí Castillo had gained control of the sugar
workers, while Gilberto Goliat now led port workers, to cite two important examples. And major Communist leaders, such as León Rentería
and Vicente Rubiera, were defecting to the Auténticos. In addition,
tobacco manufacturers desperately needed to undercut the CTC position
on the introduction of machines. By April 1947 Grau agreed that the

---

69 Thomas, *Cuba*, p. 748; Stubbs, *Tobacco*, p. 149.
70 Farber, *Revolution*, p. 138, note 38.
71 Ibid., p. 140.
72 *El Siglo* (Havana), 30 April 1947, quoted in Page, Organized labor, p. 114.

time was right for the Auténticos' open attempt to unseat the CTC's Communist leadership.[73]

Battle was finally joined at the Fifth Congress of the CTC in April 1947. The issue that touched off the confrontation was an opposition charge that the Communists had manipulated union elections in an attempt to pack the delegate list. A roundtable convoked by Grau himself failed to resolve differences since it was clear that the post of secretary general was not negotiable.[74] Peña believed a Communist majority could only be assured by having the Credentials Committee limit the issuance of documents, but both Auténticos and independents were alert to the strategy.[75] On 2 April, an Auténtico, Aguirre, secretary of the Credentials Committee, refused certificates "to delegates the legality of whose election was in dispute," in each case a Communist. That evening, a PRC–A council member and sugar leader from the Central Baltony, Félix Palú, was beaten and fell to his death after leading a march to the offices of the railway switchmen's union to seize credentials.[76] In the ensuing turmoil, the PSP offices were fired on and a Communist, Pelayo de la Rosa, was wounded. Confronted with escalating violence, the labor minister, Dr. Carlos Prío Socarrás, ordered the Congress suspended that same evening, and authorized the naming of a Cleansing Credentials Commission, which was convened with all three tendencies represented.[77] Two days later, the Havana police raided the CTC's temporary headquarters in the Cigar Makers' Hall, resulting in six arrests for weapons possession.[78]

By May Day, the division within the CTC was irreconcilable. Auténticos marched in the parade carrying portraits of the martyrs killed by the Communists (Sandalio Junco, José María Martín, Pedro and Fermín Escrich, Antonio Barreras, and Félix Palú).[79] Then Peña made a fateful decision. He decided not to await the report of the "cleansing committee." Instead, he authorized the holding of a CTC congress on 4–9 May, without official approval. The 1,403 delegates who attended were expected to elect the single slate of candidates proposed by the Peña camp.[80] Dissident

---

73 Thomas, *Cuba*, pp. 752–3. On the issue of machines, see Stubbs, *Tobacco*, pp. 147–57.

74 On these preliminary maneuvers, see García Montes and Alonso Avila, *Partido Comunista de Cuba*, pp. 382–3.

75 Ibid. For a brief pro-Peña, pro-CTC(c) version of these events, see Stubbs, *Tobacco*, p. 149.

76 Three different detailed accounts have appeared: Page, Organized Labor, pp. 115–17; Thomas, *Cuba*, p. 752; and García Montes and Alonso Avila, *Partido Comunista de Cuba*, pp. 382–3. I found the latter most convincing.

77 García Montes and Alonso Avila, *Partido Comunista de Cuba*, pp. 382–3; Thomas, *Cuba*, p. 753.

78 Two of those arrested were Peña and Joaquín Ordoquí, both Communist leaders and congressional deputies. Page, Organized labor, pp. 117–18.

79 Ibid., p. 115, note 75.

80 García Montes and Alonso Avila, *Partido Comunista de Cuba*, p. 383.

officials in a number of unions now openly joined the Auténticos; only unions with a large rank-and-file Communist membership remained loyal to Peña's CTC. As a result, the Auténticos broke with Peña, permanently splitting the union movement, bolstered as they were by the addition of seven new federations to their ranks. The "new converts" included unions in the power plants, salesmen, workers in the confectionary, cinema, and telephone industries, and cobblers.[81]

The anti-Communist CTC leadership took three steps to protest against Peña's congress and to penalize the PSP leaders who were still in charge of CTC headquarters: first, nationwide demonstrations were staged against Peña's Executive Committee; second, union leaders at the Nicaro Nickel Company, the telephone company, and the dime stores were expelled for having attended Peña's congress; and third, union dues were withheld from the CTC. Key federations, whose contributions had been crucial to the financial well-being of the CTC – particularly the electrical and telephone workers' unions – now abstained, placing the CTC in dire financial straits. The new anti-Communist alliance included most white-collar employees, as well as skilled workers.[82]

On 6 July 1947, the split was formalized when dissidents called an independent congress with the intention of forming an alternative CTC. Some 1,382 delegates attended, representing 290 unions. Absent were delegates from 301 *sindicatos fantasmas,* or *de bolsillo,* which had belonged to the Communist leadership bloc. The delegates were either Auténticos or independents; both joined in the creation of a CTC(A). Henceforth, their PSP-led counterpart would be dubbed the CTC(C).[83] Angel Cofiño, an ex-Communist who was now a nominally independent socialist, was elected secretary general of the CTC(A). Cofiño was also secretary general of the Federación Sindical de Plantas Eléctricas, Gas, y Agua (FSPEGA), and a leader of the Comisión Obrera Nacional Independiente (CONI).[84] The Grau government clearly approved of the anti-Communist moves in the context of the Cold War and in light of the outcome of the 1946 elections. It first ordered state intervention in the Communist CTC radio station, Mil Diez, whose accounts revealed a *desfalco* (extortion) of over 100,000 pesos. In return, the Communists dubbed the new confederation of labor the "CTCK," contending that it was subsidized by "part K" of the national education budget. (The PSP called its organization the "CTC *unitaria,*" implying that it was they who sought unity.)[85] On 17 July the government sent troops to the docks to confront the Communist-led

81  Page, Organized labor, pp. 119–21.
82  Ibid., p. 122.
83  Ibid., pp. 123, 125.
84  Ibid., pp. 123–5; García Montes and Alonso Avila, *Partido Comunista de Cuba,* p. 383.
85  García Montes and Alonso Avila, *Partido Comunista de Cuba,* p. 383.

striking port workers. Then on 29 July, the labor minister, Prío, evicted the CTC(C) from the Palace of Labor.[86] The Communists responded with protest strikes by the unions they controlled – in the textile industry, slaughter houses, the cattle and tobacco industries, and the music business. The government met these challenges on 9 October by issuing decrees through the Ministry of Labor declaring the CTC(C)'s May congress illegal, and recognizing the legitimacy of the CTC(A).[87]

The Communists responded to the legalization of the CTC(A) by attempting a general strike. Their only success was among the Havana port workers and streetcar operators, plus some tobacco workers.[88] The state reacted by arresting 600 strikers and 115 labor leaders, including Peña. On orders of the Emergency Court of Havana, 71 Communist labor leaders were held without bail. This freed the membership to elect new leaders, and, generally, individuals favorable to Cofiño and the CTC(A) were installed. Management seemed encouraged by this outcome, particularly in the bus companies, where some 500 striking workers were fired. When those affected protested before the Ministry of Labor, police fired into the crowd, wounding three.[89] In the autumn, most of the larger unions came over to Cofiño's CTC(A), leaving pro-Peña minorities behind. The desperate Communists then attempted to frustrate the start of the winter *zafra*, but the effort failed.[90] Suddenly, the Communists found themselves banished to the opposition, a status they had not suffered since the 1930s.[91] And the violence continued. Jesús Menéndez, the leader of the CTC(C) sugar workers, and Aracelio Iglesias, the CTC(C) dock workers' leader, both Communists, were murdered in 1947 and 1948, respectively.[92] While Menéndez was killed by an Army officer, much of the CTC(A)-promoted violence was carried out by members of the anti-Communist ARG, whose alliance with the Auténticos brought them $100 per month for each of the twelve "activists," two in each of the six Cuban provinces. Once the CTC(A) was formally constituted, the ARG was rewarded with 9 members on the Secretariate and 23 on the Executive Committee.[93]

Political differences between the two confederations were clear from the outset. Their constitutions were markedly different, especially with respect to attitudes toward democracy and dictatorship. The CTC(A)'s fundamental charter promised "to combat all systems of dictatorship of

86 Thomas, *Cuba*, p. 754.
87 Page, Organized labor, pp. 125–6.
88 García Montes and Alonso Avila, *Partido Comunista de Cuba*, p. 384.
89 Page, Organized labor, pp. 127–8.
90 García Montes and Alonso Avila, *Partido Comunista de Cuba*, p. 384.
91 Thomas, *Cuba*, p. 756.
92 Ibid., pp. 761, 1122. See especially, Juan Portilla, *Jesús Menéndez y su tiempo* (Havana, 1987).
93 Page, Organized labor, pp. 173–4, note 58; Farber, *Revolution*, pp. 120–1.

whatever class anywhere in the world." The CTC(C)'s simply pledged "to combat all systems of reaction or of Fascism which attempt to overthrow the democratic order." Future international affiliations of the two organizations also revealed their orientations. The CTC(A) affiliated with the anti-Communist Confederación Interamericana de Trabajadores (CIT), whereas the CTC(C) retained its links to Lombardo Toledano's CTAL, which, for the moment, still enjoyed Communist support.[94]

A third position in the Cuban labor conflict was that of Eduardo Chibás and his Partido del Pueblo Cubano (Ortodoxo) (PPC–O), founded on 15 May 1947. Chibás, among whose disciples would be the young Fidel Castro Ruz, was anti-Communist, but he opposed the violent Auténtico method of removing Communist leaders from the CTC, which he knew would split the labor movement.[95] But the Ortodoxos arrived on the scene too late, missing the recruitment opportunity offered by the burgeoning conflict in the ranks of labor. They favored social welfare and lent support to a number of strikes, but the Ortodoxos were never radical. In the final analysis, the party favored a harmonious atmosphere between all the "factors of production," as Chibás once said.[96]

Grau could recognize the Auténtico-independent CTC(A) without fear of an overwhelming labor reaction. The result was the collapse of Peña's CTC(C); the new, official entity was the only confederation with clout.[97] But there was a second and unexpected result: an increase in militancy on the part of unions in all camps. Competition between rival unions became heated. Leaders loyal to the PSP had to be more militant than in the past in order to produce results that would assure their retention of union posts. Auténtico leaders, often viewed as politicians rather than labor bosses, had to use their political connections for the benefit of the membership.[98] As a result, Cuba experienced prolonged labor conflict, forcing the government to intervene repeatedly. This meant temporary state management of enterprises, which often led to stagnation. Interventions of this nature were opposed by management, of course, except where they relieved owners of the responsibility of choosing which of the competing federations should be recognized.[99] Another and equally important result of the decline of the Communist CTC was the increased tendency of workers, having escaped the ideological atmosphere promoted by PSP leaders, to respond to reformist, populist political overtures. However, cigar and cigarette manufacturing unions, for example, offered

94 Page, Organized labor, p. 300.
95 Farber, *Revolution*, pp. 123–4.
96 Ibid., p. 128.
97 O'Connor, *Socialism in Cuba*, p. 180; Page, Organized Labor, p. 128.
98 Farber, *Revolution*, p. 130.
99 Ibid., pp. 130–1; Stubbs, *Tobacco*, p. 151.

stiff resistance; 73 percent of their members continued to support their Communist leaders as late as November 1948 when the Ministry of Labor handed over their headquarters to the CTC(A), after which mechanization of several factories proceeded against the workers' wishes.[100]

In the elections of 1948, the Auténticos put forward Dr. Carlos Prío, the former labor minister, as their candidate, revealing the importance ascribed to the labor post in Cuba at that time. The Communists, who in March had attempted to forge an electoral alliance with the Ortodoxos but had been rebuffed, were now excluded from the system. Securing only 7.22 percent of the vote, they lost their three Senate seats (though they retained nine deputies).[101] Prío aspired to turn the PRC–A into an *aprista*-style party (modeled after Haya de la Torre's movement in Peru), leftist but anti-Communist, with a significant base in labor. Peña and his colleagues faced mounting difficulties: only unions affiliated with the CTC(A) could legally sign collective contracts. Communist officials of unions found themselves under pressure to resign to facilitate recognition of their syndicate by the state. If a union lacked legality, employers were not required to bargain. As a consequence, a number of unions, including many in which Communists had considerable influence, soon reentered the official CTC in order to regain legal status and retain collective agreements. Apparently, Communist leaders generally did not fight this tendency – it would have been pointless in any case.

In addition to Auténticos and Communists, other factions and leaders were engaged in coalition building in order to strengthen their positions within the labor movement. A variety of terrorist groups were also at work, the most visible being the ARG, which continued to advocate direct action. There were also Peronists with ties to the movement led by the new populist leader of Argentina, Juan Domingo Perón. To promote street actions, Peronists supported the ARG, led by Jesús González Cartas ("El Extraño"), providing new automobiles in exchange for promotion by the ARG of Justicialist ideas.[102] Peronism gained strength among workers with the founding of the Agrupación de Trabajadores Latinoamericanos (ATLAS), which aspired to replace Vicente Lombardo Toledano's CTAL by advocating a "third position" in the antiimperialist struggle. Most notable among Cuban adherents to the Peronist cause were Marcos Antonio Hirigoyen of the transport sector, a member of ARG, and Vicente Rubiera, secretary general of the Federación de Trabajadores

100 Farber, *Revolution*, pp. 142–3. Farber argues vigorously, however, that most workers were unaffected by Communist political training. On the tobacco manufacturing case, see Stubbs, *Tobacco*, pp. 150–4.

101 Thomas, *Cuba*, pp. 756–7.

102 García Montes and Alonso Avila, *Partido Comunista de Cuba*, p. 399.

de Teléfonos (FTT). As Peronism gained strength, Cofiño was drawn into a pact with ATLAS that he thought might fortify his position as secretary general of the CTC(A). This agreement soon placed Cofiño in an awkward position, however. An effort was underway to found an Organización Interamericana de Trabajadores (OIT) that would be in direct competition with the Peronist body. Cuban participation in the OIT was advocated by the Auténtico leadership and the independent Cofiño's compromise with the Peronists soon undermined his position.[103]

In November 1945, the PSP's Executive Committee met to evaluate the critical situation of the party and the CTC(C). The major topic of debate was the situation on the sindical front. The Communists accused the regime of resorting to violence, noting the deaths of four militants, and denounced the CTCK, as they called it, for serving as "an instrument of the bourgeoisie and the government." The committee called for new stress on syndicalization in the agricultural sector, and especially for the formation of "struggle committees" on coffee farms, and renewed efforts in the sugar sector.[104]

The Sixth Congress of the official CTC met in late 1948 with tensions high among members of its Executive Committee. The Auténtico majority had forced the resignation of Cofiño as a result of his agreement with the Peronists. Vice-Secretary General Aguirre, an Auténtico, had assumed the post. But relations between two major clusters within the CTC(A), the CONI (loyal to Cofiño) and the CONA (pro-Auténtico), had worsened when the ousted Cofiño set about creating an alternative independent confederation, the Confederación General de Trabajadores (CGT), which would be anarcho-syndicalist in orientation. Cofiño apparently had some hope of gaining official recognition because his brother-in-law, Orlando Puentes, was minister of the presidency. But this was not to be; Prío liked anarchists no better than had Machado.[105] Sensing the opportunity presented by these new divisions within the official CTC, the Communists attempted to take advantage. They created committees for the defense of workers' demands, which resorted, once again, to what in other times they themselves would have called "economism." The tactic seems to have failed to strengthen their position, but their options were few; they chose not to resort to extralegal tactics.[106]

The outcome of the CTC(A)'s Sixth Congress was a series of compromises aimed at building unity within the non-Communist sector of the labor leadership. Mujal was elected secretary general and plans were laid

103 Ibid., p. 400.
104 Ibid., p. 401.
105 Harold D. Sims, "Cuban Labor and the Communist Party 1937–1958: An Interpretation," *Cuban Studies/Estudios Cubanos* 15(Winter 1985):49.
106 García Montes and Alonso Avila, *Partido Comunista de Cuba*, pp. 403, 406–7.

for new demands for benefits. The principle of *equidistancia* in politics was established – the PRC–A could not count on uncritical support from labor. The CTC(A) reiterated its anti-Communist militancy and affiliated with the Confederación Internacional de Organizaciones Sindicales Libres (CIOSL), whose Latin American branch was the Organización Regional Interamericana de Trabajadores (ORIT). The appearance of unity emerged from the CTC(A) congress, while the PSP found itself more marginalized than ever.[107]

By 1950, the CTC(C) controlled no national confederations and fewer than 10 percent of the unions, although these may have contained roughly 25 percent of organized labor (mainly rural). Its strength in the sugar sector seems greater than the CTC(A) was willing to admit.[108] As late as 1952, the Communists still controlled perhaps 40 of 120 sugar mill locals,[109] but there were few other sectors in which they retained importance. One such sector was the barbers, who refused to abandon their Communist leadership; in 1950, of 16,000 organized barbers, only 7, all officers of a pocket syndicate, were Auténticos.[110] The Havana port workers, the best paid laborers in Cuba, were divided, with one cluster represented by the CTC(C) despite the union's corruption and generally unsavory reputation.[111] On the other hand, the construction workers, one of the oldest guilds, had accepted Auténtico leadership in 1947.[112] But the Communists' old image was not easily dispelled. In an April 1950 interview, Jorge Martí, the information chief at *El Mundo*, asserted that the "Communist labor leaders still have great prestige because of their intelligence and scrupulous honesty and fighting spirit."[113]

Continuing loyalty to the CTC(C) could be costly: despite Auténtico opposition, a tram strike was called on 6 March 1950, resulting in the arrest of seventy conductors, and a police takeover of the trollies.[114] A switch of confederations could be bought: Mujal had promised the bank employees a pay rise in 1949; the government delivered it in September; in the spring of 1950, their union affiliated with the CTC(A).[115] And there was no letup in government actions against the Communists. Persecution of PSP members heightened between August and November 1950. On 24 August police closed the two most important party peri-

---

107 Ibid., p. 403.
108 Page, Organized Labor, p. 160, note 39. Page's interviews produce conflicting estimates.
109 Sims, "Cuban Labor," p. 51.
110 Page, Organized labor, p. 186.
111 Thomas, *Cuba*, p. 1179.
112 Quoted in Page, Organized labor, p. 112, note 70.
113 Ibid., pp. 335–6. Page witnessed these events.
114 Ibid., p. 187.
115 Ibid., p. 197.

odicals, banned broadcasting over Mil Diez, and carried out searches of PSP headquarters throughout the island.[116]

The CTC(A) was willing occasionally to collaborate with the government when the outcome clearly compromised workers' interests. Cuban labor had traditionally resisted mechanization, particularly in textile and cigar manufacture.[117] On 11 March 1950, the administration decreed the mechanization of the sector of cigar manufacturing that served the export market, plus 20 percent of the "noncompetitive" home market. Thousands of small provincial manufacturers and their workers were threatened, a matter that did not affect the CTC(A) since these sites were seldom organized. A strike resulted on 27 March, and the leaders were arrested. This provided the CTC(C) with an opportunity to champion provincial labor and small business, but to no avail.[118]

By March 1951, differences between Auténticos and independents in the leadership of the CTC(A) had been overcome – in time for the confederation's Seventh Congress. Only the Communists continued to be marginalized. The gathering demonstrated the coerced unity achieved by the federations: without exception they were all represented. Mujal was ratified as secretary general, and speeches reflected economic gains achieved since the last meeting: higher salaries, reductions in the workday, new retirement funds, and improved collective agreements. More controversial was the leadership's proposal that the congress recommend an obligatory dues checkoff. Both the employers and the Communists objected to it, but the delegates eventually approved the measure, convinced, they said, that it would guarantee the financial and political independence of the CTC(A). Understandably, Peña chose to spend those days in Mexico, attending a Latin American agricultural conference, a purely symbolic event sponsored by the Federación Sindical Mundial (FSM).[119]

As a result of this new labor unity, Prío faced serious worker discontent toward the end of 1950. Disputes on the docks concerning containerization grew more serious and, soon, the CTC(A) threatened a general strike over the formation of an employers' union, the Confederación Patronal. Bus drivers also threatened to strike to save their seven hours of pay for six hours of work arrangement. The unions were equally militant in 1951. President Prío could only end strikes by railway workers and dock workers by increasing their pay through subsidies derived from state funds.[120] On

116 Thomas, *Cuba*, p. 765.
117 The problem is explored at length in International Bank for Reconstruction and Development, *Report on Cuba* (Washington, D.C., 1951), pp. 134, passim. See also Stubbs, *Tobacco*, pp. 147–57; Thomas, *Cuba*, pp. 1164–6.
118 Page, Organized labor, pp. 330–2.
119 García Montes and Alonso Avila, *Partido Comunista de Cuba*, p. 422.
120 Thomas, *Cuba*, p. 766.

20 September Prío lashed out at both the CTC(A) and the PSP for the plethora of strikes. The press also came under attack, a condition that ended only when the newspapers themselves went on strike in protest.[121] A report published in October revealed that during the previous ten months, there had been "120 strikes and 151 demands for salary increases, an all-time record."[122]

Close collaboration with the state was the ideal pursued by the leadership of the CTC(A) – a goal that would not change completely when Batista, the Auténticos' old enemy, seized authority once again by a coup d'état in March 1952. Writing in that year, Charles Page commented that "the present CTC[A] leaders draw their strength from the Government. They are the government's lobby with the labor movement, rather than the workers' representatives before the government."[123] The second *batistato* that followed would be characterized by a new deal arranged between the dictator and the leadership of organized labor. The CTC(A) leaders had developed a new and enthusiastic interest in "transactions," an essential and corrupting part of twentieth-century Cuban political culture. Mujal and his fellow Auténticos and independents, although not pleased by Batista's seizure of power, were, nonetheless, unwilling to risk their privileged positions, and that of the CTC(A), by resisting the overthrow of the Auténtico government. As CTC boss and a national senator, Mujal received an annual income of some $280,000.[124] The wealth of the labor leadership had become a source of scandal by the early 1950s. Batista moved to exploit this tendency to greed by decreeing a mandatory dues checkoff of 1 percent, favored by the CTC(A) leadership; this was just one of the deals he made with the *mujalistas*. The result was a new "special relationship" between the dictator and organized labor, in exchange for "a vast number of restrictive practices, . . . [some] limitations on mechanization and . . . bans on dismissals."[125]

In an export-led economy like Cuba's the export sector, in both its rural and urban dimensions, had the most highly organized labor force. It was therefore inevitable that there be a battle between Communist and non-Communist cadres for control of workers in these most important sectors of the economy. During the Depression and the Second World War, the state compromised with Communist labor leadership, which in turn was induced to make "economist" demands, sacrificing its doctrinaire revolutionary program. But with the advent of the Cold War, the state found

121 Ibid., pp. 765, 770–1.
122 *Hispanic American Report* (Sept. 1951), p. 16, cited in Farber, *Revolution*, p. 130.
123 Page, Organized labor, p. 223.
124 Ibid.
125 Thomas, *Cuba*, p. 1173.

it convenient to collaborate in efforts by anti-Communist labor leaders to seize control of unions and federations. The growth of labor militancy after the purges of 1947–8 became a problem for the Auténticos and may have contributed to Batista's reemergence. Strikes multiplied, workers made significant gains, and laws were passed restricting the freedom of action of foreign owners. Ironically, this occurred after the Communists lost control of organized labor, and at a time when the price of sugar, the dominant export, was steadily increasing. Prío was in a difficult position throughout 1948–52, faced as he was with worker militancy and a labor leadership that was often independent. Sensing the misplaced priorities of the CTC(A)'s Havana leadership, unions took the initiative in pursuit of their own welfare.[126] But there was a negative side to labor militancy. Hugh Thomas was not exaggerating when he commented that "[d]ifferent groups of workers developed into rigid, jealous, exclusive, essentially conservative castes of privilege, jobs passing from father to son."[127] Nowhere was this more evident than in the electrical workers' union, which had little gangsterism and considerable union democracy, but suffered from nepotism and racism in, essentially, a closed-shop atmosphere.

A basically urban nation in the 1950s, Cuba provided workers with unusual opportunities to exert political influence.[128] Compared to other Latin American countries, unions were relatively strong. More than half the Cuban work force, over a million people, were organized in more than 1,600 trade unions. The strongest syndicalized sectors included sugar (with roughly 45 percent of the organized), manufacturing, transport, communications, utilities (electricity, gas, water), hotels and restaurants, banks, and large retail stores. Weak or unorganized sectors were limited to petty commerce, cattle raising, coffee, and small farming outside of sugar.[129] Yet, approximately half of organized labor was located in the countryside – a unique case in Latin America. It was in rural unions that the Communists remained entrenched.

Cuban workers were "North Americanized," as Samuel Farber has observed, especially in their desires and expectations.[130] This may help to explain their "bread-and-butter" orientation and their lack of ideological commitment, despite more than a decade of Communist tutelage. There was fundamentally, contrary to the sociologist Maurice Zeitlin's conten-

126 Farber, *Revolution*, p. 131.
127 Thomas, *Cuba*, p. 1174.
128 Farber, *Revolution*, pp. 131–2.
129 U.S. Department of Labor, Bureau of Labor Statistics, Foreign Labor Information, *Labor in Cuba* (Washington, D.C., 1957), p. 3, cited in ibid., p. 133.
130 U.S. Department of Commerce, *Investment in Cuba* (Washington, D.C., 1956), p. 24, cited in Farber, *Revolution*, pp. 133–4.

tions, a lack of ideology in organized labor's rank and file. Only during the World Depression was there class solidarity. Farber characterizes the mood as "militant-reformism," an absence of revolutionary sentiment. The prevailing outlook was pragmatic or economist and, as a result, politically active only in the mainstream. As Charles A. Page saw it, based on his extensive interviews in the early 1950s, the attitude was "above ideology." The ARG, for example, professed anarcho-syndicalism, but its leaders were prone to behave like gangsters. Many union leaders who had been Communist in 1939, readily became Auténtico in 1947. Workers often voted differently in national elections than in union elections, favoring nationalist populist parties over those that appealed to class interests alone. At the local syndicate level, the rank and file tended to support whomever "delivered the goods."[131] In this atmosphere, gangsterism was tolerated and, indeed, utilized in the process of purging Communist control. The greater the number of Communist union members, the more likely the use of gangsterism in syndicate takeovers.

By the 1950s, the issue of job security had become all-important. This resulted from the specter of chronic or seasonal unemployment, which was due to the experience of the sugar industry. The quest for job tenure fed into the battle against mechanization (cutting machines would not be introduced into Cuban sugar fields until Fidel Castro cowed the unions). Cuban cigar makers could not compete with the highly mechanized North American producers, yet they fought off machines until the early 1950s. Entrepreneurs were hesitant to risk further investment. The result, according to Farber, was a stalemate between workers and employers,[132] which encouraged opportunism on all sides. Genuine bargaining between labor and management could not be risked under such circumstances; the Ministry of Labor would decide the outcome of all conflicts.

State intervention also contributed to the expansion of union bureaucracy. Intervention occurred, both officially and unofficially, and sought to prevent genuine independence of labor. Following the Depression, unions were not wholly free to control their own affairs. Farber, giving perhaps too little attention to the anarchist period (1880s–1920s) during which labor was certainly repressed by the state, has contended that Cuban organized labor lacked a period of independent development, making cooptation by the state easier.[133] In truth, it might be argued that the birth of populist governments made cooptation necessary and the onset of the Cold War made ideological "correctness" a priority. The Communists, who, like the Auténticos, sought to exploit that state interven-

---

131 Page, Organized labor, pp. 172–4; Farber, *Revolution*, pp. 134–5.
132 International Bank, p. 528, cited in Farber, *Revolution*, pp. 135–6.
133 Farber, *Revolution*, p. 136.

tion, found it difficult to survive as a force in the labor movement without the exercise of such interventionism on its behalf. Outside the government coalition, the PSP found it impossible to maintain the CTC(C) as a rival confederation. By 1951 the Communists, desperate, were unsuccessfully attempting to reenter the CTC(A). As a result, the decline of the PSP proceeded apace throughout the 1950s,[134] and its reintegration would not be attained until Fidel Castro intervened on its behalf in 1959. During the Batista dictatorship (1952–8), workers lost some ground. As Batista came increasingly to rely on foreign capital, he continued the trend begun under the Auténticos of allowing limited technological change, which inevitably reduced the demand for labor. Eventually, he even permitted compensated layoffs, though his legislation fell short of the system of dismissal wages recommended by IBRD in 1951, which was in use in other Latin American countries. He would not, however, alienate organized labor to the point where the *mujalistas* would be forced to work against him. As a consequence, the revolutionaries of the late 1950s found it difficult to mobilize organized labor for the anti-Batista cause.

134 Ibid., pp. 138–9.

# 9

## Nicaragua

*Jeffrey Gould*

The durability of the Somoza regime distinguishes the political experience of Nicaragua from that of other Latin American countries in the middle decades of the twentieth century. But the unusual dynastic quality of the regime should not obscure the similarities between Nicaraguan politics and those of the rest of the continent at certain points. During the period 1944–8, in particular, the relationships between the regime, the opposition, and the labor movement paralleled those of other countries.

Early in 1944 the labor movement in Nicaragua emerged to become, albeit briefly, an important social and political force. And, inspired by the Allied cause, a democratic opposition movement rapidly gathered momentum during the same years as labor's ascent. University students led major protest strikes against the regime in 1944 and 1946. The opposition twice forced Anastasio Somoza García to renounce his candidacy for reelection. Moreover, the opposition and the labor movement succeeded in forcing a measure of democratization in 1946. In November of that year, however, regime repression and growing anticommunism among the political elites pushed the Left and the leftist labor movement into a downward trajectory. The elections of February 1947 were won – fraudulently – by Somoza's presidential candidate, Leonardo Argüello. And in June Somoza closed off the democratic opening after he engineered a *golpe* against Argüello, who had asserted his independence of Somoza and had chosen to work with the opposition and the unions to democratize Nicaragua. In January 1948, the regime jailed most of the leaders of the labor movement.

The United States, as in the rest of Latin America, promoted first

I would like to thank the Fulbright–Hays Foundation Social Science Research Council for financing my research in Nicaragua. Lowell Gudmundson made critical remarks on an article that I published several years ago that I have tried to address in this work. I would also like to thank David Brooks, Matt Karash, and Maria Elidieth Porras for their assistance in preparing this work.

243

democratization and then anticommunism in Nicaragua. From 1944 until 1946, in addition to stimulating the growth of the democratic opposition, the State Department prodded Somoza to step aside and hold free elections. By late 1946, anticommunism, at least to some extent an import from the United States, contributed to the breakup of the alliance between labor and the democratic opposition. Moreover, the U.S. commitment to democracy did not go so far as to ensure free elections in February 1947. Nevertheless, for nearly one year (until May 1948), the United States refused to recognize the de facto governments that followed the overthrow of Argüello. The nonrecognition policy provided significant, but tardy, backing for the repressed and divided opposition. Somoza's commitment to anticommunism, however, helped him to regain U.S. recognition and support for his regime. In Nicaragua, as in Latin America as a whole, democratic reformism had been defeated.

On 11 February 1936, a largely spontaneous general strike of between 5,000 and 8,000 workers, including taxi drivers, construction workers, railway employees, artisans, and domestic servants, marked the beginning of Anastasio Somoza's four-month struggle for power. Somoza, the National Guard commander-in-chief, intervened on behalf of the strikers, focused their anger against President Juan B. Sacasa, and repressed the small leftist group, the Partido Trabajador Nicaragüense (PTN), which attempted to prolong the strike. During the next two months, Somoza mediated dock and railway strikes, earning the support of urban workers. After taking power in late May 1936, Somoza restricted the incipient labor movement that he had helped to inspire. Thus, without losing significant worker support, Somoza established himself in the eyes of the ruling elite as the only person capable of communicating with the masses and thus eliminating the "communist threat."[1]

Somoza's coup had the aura of a popularly supported insurrection, and encountered relatively little opposition from any sector of society. The enforced silence of the Sandinista subculture – among the northern peasantry and in the universities – permitted Somoza to portray himself not only as the peacemaker and defender of the working class, but also as a nationalist.

Somoza could project such a populist image, in particular in western Nicaragua, because he was able to forge political ties with the *obrerista* faction of the Partido Liberal Nacionalista (PLN). Independent artisans,

---

1 *La Prensa*, 10–20 February 1936; U.S. State Department, RG 59, 817.00/8380 (February 1936). For a view of the effect of Somoza's movement on workers in the San Antonio sugar mill, the largest manufacturing establishment in Nicaragua, see Jeffrey L. Gould, *To Lead as Equals: Rural Protest and Political Consciousness in Chinandega, Nicaragua 1912–1979* (Chapel Hill, NC, 1990), pp. 38–45.

many of whom owned small workshops employing several workers, formed the leadership of this faction. From 1912 to 1926, these artisans formed the backbone of the Liberal antiinterventionist movement. A group of *obreristas* broke with leadership of the Partido Liberal to support Sandino. Throughout the 1920s and early 1930s, they often ran successful candidates for municipal office on prolabor platforms, stressing the rights of workers and owner-artisans against the agrarian elite. One *obrerista* leader recalls:

> There was no social distance between the small entrepreneur and the worker. In those years the small entrepreneur was himself a worker, who made economic sacrifices to start his little workshop. Therefore he was considered a *compañero* in the struggle.[2]

*Obrerismo* was more a language of worker affirmation and antielitism than a class-specific ideology. Even before 1936 Somoza was able to penetrate this realm of artisans and workers who were anxious to claim full rights as citizens in a society still dominated by an agrarian-based elite. Thus, from 1936 until the early 1940s, the majority of the *obrerista* leadership offered Somoza support, on the condition that he fulfill his prolabor promises.[3]

During his first decade in power (1936–46), Somoza made little effort to alter the agro-export nature of the Nicaraguan economy. Nevertheless, the virtual collapse of the coffee trade in the 1930s and the prohibitively high costs of U.S. imports during the Second World War compelled Somoza to aid the development of alternative industries. In particular, he offered important tax incentives to domestic sugar and textile producers, as well as to foreign mining and rubber interests. In the early 1940s, Somoza, as a private entrepreneur, participated in the establishment of three import-substitution industries: textiles, cement, and matches.[4] At the same time that Somoza accumulated capital, however, he helped to foster the incipient growth of a working class. Five manufacturing industries founded during the Second World War employed approximately 1,000 workers. At the same time, new urban population

---

2 Domingo Ramírez, "Apuntes sobre el movimiento obrero chinandegano," personal communication, Chinandega, 1984.

3 I examine the Chinandegan *obreristas* in detail in *To Lead as Equals*, pp. 65–84.

4 It is worth enumerating Somoza's direct contribution to the concentration of, if not the development of, capital. According to Jaime Wheelock, in *Imperialismo y Dictadura*, (Mexico City, 1975) by 1945 Somoza owned fifty-one cattle ranches, forty-six coffee plantations (mostly expropriated from Germans), two sugar mills, an airline (with flights to the mines), a gold mine, a milk plant, the daily newspaper *Novedades*, as well as three factories. He also grossed $175,000 annually in U.S. mining kickbacks. On Somoza's growing empire, also see Knut Walter's fine study, The regime of Anastasio Somoza García and state formation in Nicaragua, 1936–1956 (Ph.D. diss., University of North Carolina, 1987).

demands for food and clothing, and wartime restrictions on imports put pressure on artisanal workshop-owners, leading to the growth of small manufacturing establishments and the proletarianization of many artisans. Thus, by 1945, approximately 8,000 of 23,000 workers employed in manufacturing establishments labored in shops that employed more than five people.[5]

The number of transportation and mine workers also grew significantly during Somoza's first decade. In 1940–5, the transport sector expanded by 250 percent. The mining of gold and silver, Nicaragua's principal exports during the Second World War, employed five times more workers in 1945 than a decade earlier. The Somoza regime undertook major public works projects – building railways, the Pan-American Highway, and other roads. Indeed, from 1943 to 1945, public works accounted for over 40 percent of the national budget.[6] As a result, the building construction trades employed nearly 5,000 workers in 1944–5, and road construction employed 3,000 workers. Thus in 1945, the mining, construction, and transportation industries combined provided jobs for over 18,000 workers.[7] Although the growth of the urban working class was substantial and politically significant, the workers were still dwarfed by the over 200,000 rural laborers and peasants.

Public employment as a whole rose from some 6,000 in 1936 to 15,000 in 1941, promoting the growth of a middle class. By 1950, professionals, office workers, and managers (including petty entrepreneurs) would make up 7 percent of the economically active population and over 18 percent of the urban work force.[8] This new middle class, like the working class, would make increasing demands on the regime in the 1940s.

Inflation, currency devaluations, and import restrictions gnawed away at Somoza's support among all social classes between 1937 and 1944.[9] In response to his declining popularity and to the development of an elite-led opposition movement, Somoza ended the repression of the extremely weak labor movement late in 1943, and sought to regain popularity through the sponsorship of labor unions.

5 The 1950 census classified people in establishments of more than five salaried employees as workers, and those in smaller shops as artisans. This is based on the 1940 census as reported in "Economic Situation of Central America," September 1945, U.S. Department of Commerce, and *Boletín de Estadística,* 1945, Dirección General de Estadistica (DGE).
6 See Walter, The regime of Anastasio Somoza García, pp. 156–8.
7 Ibid.
8 *Censo General de Población de la República de Nicaragua,* 1950, (Managua, 1951). If the ample category of *gerente* in commerce is eliminated, the national figure for the middle class drops to under 5 percent. In addition, an estimated 16,000 wealthy farmers formed approximately 5 percent of the economically active population.
9 For more details about the 1937–43 period, see my article "Amigos peligrosos, enemigos mortales: Somoza y el movimiento obrero, 1944–1946," *Revista de Historia* (November 1986).

International as well as domestic considerations influenced Somoza's actions. Nicaragua was allied to the United States and thus, during the war, with the USSR. After the triumph at Stalingrad, the prestige of the Soviet Union grew significantly, even beyond the Left. The *somocista* labor paper *Tribuna Obrera* exclaimed, in late 1943, that the USSR "was going to lead humanity's way." Somoza himself invited Vicente Lombardo Toledano, the leftist Mexican labor leader, to a rally in Nicaragua at the end of 1942. According to one U.S. observer, Lombardo made a much-applauded "masterpiece speech."[10] It would be reasonable to assume that Lombardo's reception impressed Somoza. The dictator's subsequent tolerance of the labor movement reflected his fear of a small, but dynamic opposition movement of students, professionals, businessmen, and Conservative oligarchs, as well as of students' efforts to attract labor support. In this new situation, a small group of Marxist workers, the future Partido Socialista Nicaragüense (PSN), emerged out of clandestinity to agitate for the long-promised Labor Code and to organize unions, notably in the new tobacco and textile factories.[11]

In April 1944, Somoza gained much support in the labor movement by calling for legislative approval of the Labor Code, incorporating many of the labor movement's long-standing demands: the legalization of unions and strikes, compensation for on-the-job accidents, one month's paid vacation, and minimum-wage guarantees. Congress discussed and approved the Labor Code in November 1944.

Somoza also strove to unify the labor movement so that its support could be more effectively used against the opposition. In April 1944 he encouraged labor unity by urging the creation of a *central sindical única* to terminate the rivalry between the Left and the "officialists." Generational experience and social background differentiated the two groups. The pro-Somoza group, led by Jesús Maravilla, Roberto González, Alejandro del Palacio, Absalón González, and Emilio Quintana, represented the old guard of the movement, who had spent much of the 1930s in prison. The overwhelming majority were artisan shopowners. In Chinandega, the *somocista* labor leaders of the 1940s were the well-known *obreristas*, artisans who had been popular political leaders for two decades. In contrast, younger, less experienced wage laborers predominated in the leadership of the PSN, particularly in Managua, León, and Chinandega.[12]

10 James Stewart to the Secretary of State, 4 December 1942, U.S. State Department, 817.00/8954.

11 Carlos Pérez and Onofre Guevara, *El movimiento obrero in Nicaragua* (Managua, 1985), pp 53–5.; *La Flecha*, 28 September 1944.

12 There are clear regional distinctions in the PSN. The Masaya branch was composed primarily of artisans, shop owners, and intellectuals. See U.S. State Department 817.00B–8 to 51, 1944, for FBI reports on PSN activists.

Although the PSN was a Marxist party and the pro-Somoza faction was predominately non-Marxist, the key practical issue separating the two groups was the Left's antagonism to Somoza.

Somoza took a major step toward assuaging Socialist political antagonism in May 1944 by publicly apologizing to PSN leaders for having jailed them. "I made a mistake," Somoza said. He had not realized that the leftists were "Nicaragua's best sons."[13] He also presided over a workers' and peasants' congress, which aimed to bring together these two factions of the labor movement. In his opening address on 26 May 1944, expressing his unequivocal support for the labor movement, Somoza recognized workers as semi-autonomous subjects with whom he had an especially benevolent relationship: he performed positive acts for them, but they also made "conquests." Somoza expected labor endorsement for his reelection plans; he needed the tactical support of an organized labor movement to balance against his opposition: the oligarchic Right and middle-class dissidents. Moreover, only "an organized Nicaragua" would legitimize Somoza's variant of populism, whose goal was to enshrine his own economic group as the dominant fraction of the bourgeoisie. The Labor Congress, however, would not commit itself to an electoral endorsement of Somoza. PSN sympathizers formed a decisive majority among the over 200 delegates. Their insistence on autonomy from the state provoked verbal and physical violence and threatened to abort the labor unity process. In the end, however, leftists maintained unity by electing the *somocista,* Absalón González, as president of the Comité Organizador de la Confederación de Trabajadores Nicaragüenses (COCTN), and by "conceding a qualified vote of confidence" to Somoza.[14]

Why did the Left respond favorably to Somoza? The Left's offer of "a qualified vote of confidence" for Somoza can only be understood in the context of a young, potentially expansive labor movement, weakened by internal division, constantly harassed by management, and seriously threatened by the possibility of a right-wing takeover. Leftist labor militants, in April 1944, recognized that Somoza "offered rights to the workers," and the Conservative-led opposition seemed to offer a return to the dark ages.

The anti-*somocista* opposition, however, was a much more complex phenomenon than can be subsumed under the category "reactionary."

13  *La Nueva Prensa,* 23 May 1944; There is another interpretation of the expression *me equivoqué.* In May 1944 after the postponement of the congress, a group of union leaders went to "La Fundadora" to negotiate with Somoza, who was initially quite cold to the delegation and called them "Communists." The unionists did not respond at first. Only the Socialist Augusto Lorío and Ramírez had the *valor* to correct Somoza's false impression. Then Somoza made his "I made a mistake" statement (Interview with D. Ramírez, Chinandega, March 1984).

14  U.S. State Department, 817.00B/51; *La Nueva Prensa,* 28 May 1944.

Indeed, students who claimed Augusto Sandino as their inspiration formed the nucleus of the most dynamic sector of the opposition movement. They could mobilize nearly all of Nicaragua's 600 university students, most high school students, as well as popular sectors in León and Managua. During June 1944, student-led demonstrations, in solidarity with the democratic revolutionary movements of El Salvador and Guatemala, represented the first phase of a cycle of protests and repression that nearly toppled the Somoza regime.[15]

The student movement did not, however, form a homogeneous ideological block within the opposition. Student radicals identified with the *sandinista* tradition considered it necessary to build a broad alliance in order to overthrow Somoza, even at the expense of ceding a leadership role to the Conservatives. The student radicals, however, sympathized with the labor movement, and worked closely with pro-Socialist student activists.[16] The small group of pro-Socialist students actively participated in the June and July demonstrations and suffered the same repression as the other oppositionists (the police arrested 62 students). Moreover, they helped persuade over 200 workers to join anti-*somocista* protests.[17] The pro-Socialists, however, disagreed with the student radicals about the presence of anti-Communist Conservatives in the leadership of the opposition. The Socialist students considered it necessary to infuse the anti-Somoza movement with prolabor ideals, whereas the radicals, while ardently espousing the same goals, tolerated a tactical alliance with the Right.

Representing different political traditions and constituencies, the Partido Conservador Tradicionalista (PCT) and the Partido Liberal Independiente (PLI) joined forces in 1944 in order to oust Somoza. The Conservatives, representing primarily sugar, commercial, and cattle interests, under the leadership of rightist intellectuals, had specific economic and political grievances against the regime. Somoza, since 1940, had harassed the Conservatives by declaring the majority party faction illegal, by arresting its leaders, and by closing its social clubs.[18] From the Conservative perspective, Somoza's politics and economics formed a unified threat. Thus, Somoza's acquisition of two sugar plantations and the eco-

---

15 See *La Flecha* and *La Nueva Prensa*, 26 July 1944, 4 July 1944.

16 Miguel Blandón, *Entre Sandino y Fonseca Amador* (Managua, 1980), pp. 19–21. Blandón suggests that a group of university students formed a Socialist party cell. One of the activists that he cites, Dr. Mario Flores Ortiz, however, claims that although they worked closely with the PSN, the students only became members later on (in his case in 1945) (Interview with Flores Ortiz, Managua 1990).

17 U.S. State Department, 817.00, 3 July 1944; Blandón, *Entre Sandino y Fonseca Amador*.

18 U.S. State Department, 817.00/836; Carlos Pasos and Manuel Cordero, *Nicaragua bajo el régimen de Somoza* (San Salvador, 1944), p. 5; U.S. State Department, 817.00/8757, 6 March 1940.

nomic coercion he used against the Conservative-owned San Antonio sugar mill was threatening to undermine another oligarchic pillar – the sugar monopoly.[19] Conservative opposition increased as Somoza made concessions to the labor movement. Not only were many Conservatives opposed to the labor movement on principle, but they feared that Somoza would use an agrarian reform and labor strikes against their own debilitated economic interests.

The PLI had been founded in March 1944 by urban professionals, businessmen, students, and ex-Somoza regime officials.[20] Members shared a profound rejection of the regime, but the roots of the antagonism were quite diverse. Different Liberal Independents resented official corruption, unfair business practices, the betrayal of Liberal principles, and/or the lack of professional opportunities in a backward society. The Chinandegan PLI, for example, had difficulty developing a common program because one leader, a tannery owner, engaged in anti-union repression despite the union activities of other party militants.[21] On a national level, the very diversity of interests of PLI members, ranging from pro-*sandinista* students to businessmen upset at price controls and government extortion, allowed the professional politicians to assume party leadership. Although PLI leaders actively courted Socialist support in 1944, they refused to jeopardize their alliance with the Conservatives or the business interests of key members by accepting the PSN conditions for joining the opposition movement – the immediate promulgation of the Labor Code and party legality.

The failure of the opposition to offer those guarantees to the PSN strongly conditioned the party's decision not to support a general strike against the regime in July 1944, thereby weakening the opposition movement. According to a State Department report, "In fact it was the failure of labor to join in the general strike which probably saved the day for the Administration."[22] At the PSN inaugural meeting on 3 July, attended by *somocista* labor leaders, a PSN leader urged Somoza to withdraw the National Guard from the streets so as not to "soil their hands with the blood of reactionaries," and to let the organized labor movement defend the regime.[23] The political value of such statements allowed Somoza to use National Guard repression against an opposition movement that he could successfully portray as dominated by nazi-fascists.

---

19  U.S. State Department, 8/7/836, pp. 8–9; 817.00/8753.1, 12 June 1947. In 1940 Somoza tried to force the Ingenio San Antonio to sell the plantation for 7 million córdobas (less than $2 million). The stockholders wanted at least $3 million.

20  Walter, The regime of Anastasio Somoza García, p. 262, found that twelve of the fourteen founding members of the PLI were lawyers.

21  For more details, see Gould, *To Lead as Equals*.

22  U.S. State Department, 817.504/7–1344.

23  Guevara and Bermudez, "Historia del movimiento obrero."

PSN support for Somoza, however, was neither unconditional nor unanimous. Thus, that same inaugural manifesto called for unconditional freedom for all political prisoners and attacked all monopolies as the main cause of the high rate of inflation. Given that the existence of Somoza's milk, match, and cement monopolies was well known in urban Nicaragua, the PSN thus implicitly criticized the regime that they politically supported. Finally, the party refused to endorse Somoza's reelection, the focus of opposition anger.[24]

Many members of the party did not agree with the PSN's 3 July manifesto. Socialist student and worker participation in opposition demonstrations showed the degree of Somoza's unpopularity with PSN rank-and-file militants. While all party members favored an anti-*somocista* alliance, with prolabor guarantees, one faction considered the overthrow of Somoza a priority. For this leftist faction, the growth of the labor movement would only be guaranteed by an alliance with the *sandinistas* and other progressive elements of the PLI. During the height of the turmoil, Somoza encouraged the antiopposition faction of the PSN by promising union rights for agricultural workers and miners. This group then apparently acted unilaterally without consulting those who sympathized with the opposition.[25]

On 6 July 1944, Somoza nevertheless announced that he would not run for reelection. He thereby acceded to the principal opposition demand and effectively defused the movement, ending the worst political crisis of his career. By September, Somoza considered that his position was strong enough to free hundreds of political prisoners seized during the crisis; at the same time, he realized that he could not repress a labor movement that had become such an important base of support.[26]

The rapid development and expansion of labor unions and the first industrial working-class actions in 1944 were a direct consequence of the

24 *Nueva Prensa,* 4 July 1944.
25 On Somoza's offer, see U.S. State Department, 817.00B/51. On the participation of Socialists in the demonstration, see Blandón, *Entre Sandino and Fonseca Amador,* pp. 21–4, and Armando Amador, *La depresión en un sistema dictatorial* (Guatemala City, 1949), p. 13; on PSN–PLI talks, see Juan Lorío, *Unión nacional en Nicaragua* (Guatemala City, 1946); Pedro Turcios and Antonio Hernández Torres, in interviews in October 1983, and Mario Flores Ortiz, in an interview in 1990, emphasized the participation of pro-Socialist workers and students in the June–July anti-Somoza demonstrations. Flores Ortiz suggests that many of the most intransigent anti-*somocistas* within the party were of Conservative background. In *El movimiento obrero,* Guevara and Pérez argue convincingly that Juan Lorío and Hernández Seguía took the decision to promulgate the pro-Somoza founding party manifesto, without consulting the rest of the Central Committee or the party rank-and-file (pp. 109–12). Two weeks later, other party leaders formally condemned that decision. For further discussion of the division, see Jeffrey L. Gould, "For an Organized Nicaragua: Somoza and the Labour Movement, 1944–8," *Journal of Latin American Studies* 19(November 1987):363–4.
26 *La Flecha,* 26 August 1944.

tactical alliance with the Somoza regime. From June 1945 and throughout the following year, the labor movement consistently maintained some 15,000 members and sympathizers organized in over 100 unions. At their peak, unions represented more than 50 percent of all mine, transport, and factory workers.[27] August 1944 to June 1946 represented the period of greatest union expansion in prerevolutionary Nicaraguan history.

The wartime employment situation was also generally favorable during the initial stages of labor organization. Due to relatively high wages, Somoza's U.S.-financed public works programs absorbed so much urban skilled and rural unskilled labor that rural employers complained constantly of a labor shortage. The tight labor market tended to increase the degree of union autonomy with respect to the regime. Thus, for example, the construction union directly attacked Somoza for breaking the Labor Code as well as contributing to the unemployment problem when the government fired, without the required one month's notice, 200 construction workers at the Casa Presidencial site.[28]

Wartime inflation, driving down real wages, also contributed to the growth of the Nicaraguan labor movement. In early 1948, even the highest paid Nicaraguan workers earned less than the minimum income necessary to feed, clothe, and house a family of five members. The situation of the average worker had become desperate, although it was probably somewhat cushioned by extended families with monthly income. The workers' struggle to organize unions had become a fight for survival, as can be seen from the following table that shows wartime price increases.

The enactment in April 1945 of the Labor Code, the state's guarantee of the union militants' right to organize, was undoubtedly the single greatest spur to the development of the labor movement. However, despite Somoza's promise to PSN leaders in June 1944, the code forbade agricultural strikes during planting and harvest, thus impeding labor union

---

27 See Gould, "For an Organized Nicaragua," pp. 353–87. Appendix B on page 386 lists the unions and their estimated membership at their highest point, regardless of whether the unions were recognized by the Ministry of Labor. Thus, for example, I estimate that 2,600 of the some 5,000 miners belonged to unions. Nevertheless, a highly efficient repression against the miners began as soon as the unions were organized, and by late 1946, the unions held at most one quarter of the membership; however, other unions were organized during 1945–6. Clearly, the preexisting image in Nicaraguan historiography of a "weak mutualist movement" led by artisan-socialists must be drastically revised. Proportionately, the percentage of union members in the active work force during 1945–6 would only be surpassed after the 1979 revolution.

28 *Voz Obrera*, 28 July 1945. Similarly, in 1945 the Federación de Trabajadores de Managua (FTM) challenged Somoza to resolve the unemployment problem. Uniting some 45 unions under the political hegemony of the Socialists, they issued a program that called for state construction of schools, hospitals, and six thousand houses, as well as public financing of shoes for all barefoot children and of books to teach reading.

Table 9.1. *Price index of selected products in córdobas (1942–1945)*

|  | Quantity | 1942 | 1943 | 1944 | 1945 |
|---|---|---|---|---|---|
| Rice | 1 lb. | 0.184 | 0.261 | 0.261 | 0.546 |
| Meat, popular cut | 1 lb. | 0.233 | 0.310 | 0.313 | 0.761 |
| Beans | 1 lb. | 0.150 | 0.214 | 0.220 | 0.514 |
| Milk, raw | 1 qt. | 0.218 | 0.288 | 0.290 | 0.654 |
| Cheese (*cuajada*) | 1 lb. | — | 0.687 | 0.660 | 1.448 |
| Sugar | 1 lb. | — | 0.307 | 0.310 | 0.533 |
| Work trousers | 1 pair | — | 6.32 | 7.65 | 10.30 |
| Shirts | 1 | — | 4.32 | 4.89 | 5.60 |

*Source: Anuario Estadístico*, 1942, 1943, 1944, 1945, Ministerio de Hacienda, Managua.

efforts to organize the more than 100,000 farm laborers.[29] One crucial limit of Somoza's "populism" was thus synthesized in the Labor Code: labor organization in the agro-export economy – represented in the 1940s primarily by coffee and sesame industries – would not be permitted to challenge the prerogatives of private capital. Nevertheless, given the level of Nicaraguan development, its subordination to the United States and to the dictator's own economic power, Somoza's brand of populism in 1944–5 was potentially quite explosive.

Following Somoza's momentary pacification of the opposition, militants of both wings of the labor movement maintained pressure on Somoza to push the Labor Code through Congress, and, in the workplace, struggled to make the law an immediate reality. From August to December 1944, Nicaraguan workers struck in several sectors of the economy. On 27 August 1944, for example, 100 out of 200 workers in the Cervecería Nacional struck without success, demanding wage increases and the re-hiring of fired militants.[30] Similarly, shoemakers, printers, and railway and communications workers struck to defend union organization.[31] These strikes derived in large part from management's counteroffensive to the imminent threat posed by the Labor Code. At the same time, the strikes were a clear demonstration that militants would act autonomously to make the code a reality.

The Somoza regime's response to the strikes was quite ambiguous. The

---

29 See Labor Code, *Gaceta Nacional*, 2 February 1945, title 6, chap. 3, where planting and harvesting are defined as in the "collective interest." Labor opposed this clause, which did involve the betrayal of June 1944's promise. Later amendments further obstructed labor organizing in the field by requiring 60 percent literates in any peasant union.
30 *La Flecha*, 25 August 1944.
31 *La Nueva Prensa*, 21 November 1944; *Unidad*, 19 November 1944; *Carreteras*, 29 October 1944.

Minister of Agriculture and Labor, José Zelaya, stated that solidarity strikes (as well as several eight-hour strikes) would be illegal once the code was promulgated, since the firing of union militants would also be illegal. The state thus would ensure that neither anti-union repression nor strike action would occur.[32]

Somoza's newly adopted neutrality in labor–management conflicts can be seen in a strike in September 1944 against the Pasos, Arellano y Compañía (PAYCO) textile mill. The fact that the co-owner, General Carlos Pasos, played a leading role in the opposition PLI undoubtedly heightened this neutrality. When the government limited imports, PAYCO hoped to meet the sudden increased demand for textiles by establishing longer work weeks. Between July and September, management accelerated production by 20 percent (28,000–35,000 yards).[33] Textile workers in PAYCO had begun to organize themselves in October 1943. By September 1944, 132 out 232 workers had joined the union. During that month management fired the union militant and PSN leader Manuel Pérez Estrada. On 28 September union leaders called a meeting attended by approximately 190 workers. The assembly discussed and approved the following demands: 1) the immediate rehiring of Pérez Estrada; 2) a salary raise of 40 percent; 3) an eight-hour day for skilled workers; 4) two bathrooms; 5) reform of the penalty system for mistakes; 6) no reprisals.[34] PAYCO responded by offering 10 to 25 percent wage increases to any worker willing to break the strike, as well as by denouncing "Communist agitation" in the press. Thirty-six union members accepted the management offer. However, the majority of workers remained on strike, receiving strike benefits from other unions during the five-day strike. After two days, Minister Zelaya called both parties to negotiate, and PAYCO ceded ground. They agreed to 20 and 25 percent wage increases as well as to the other demands, except for the rehiring of Pérez Estrada. The PSN leader convinced the other strikers to accept the contract.[35] The strike, although only partially successful, demonstrated the potential of the labor movement to exact concessions from capital. Carlos Pasos's role in the opposition undoubtedly conditioned the

---

32 *Memorias del Ministerio de Agricultura y Trabajo*, 1944, (Managua, 1944), p. 134.

33 *Unidad*, 3 September 1944; *Unidad*, 3 and 10 September 1944; *La Nueva Prensa*, 1 October 1944.

34 *La Flecha*, 28 September 1944; *La Nueva Prensa*, 1 October 1944; *Memorias*, 1944, p. 133. Apparently the regime had already passed an eight-hour law before the Labor Code went into effect. Curiously, the union demanded the eight-hour day only for skilled workers. Operatives were not included because they "voluntarily" worked two shifts and presumably earned C\$3.40–C\$5.0 daily. A 40 percent salary increase might then permit them to work the single shift. Male workers earned C\$4 daily.

35 *La Nueva Prensa*, 1 October 1944.

relatively neutral role of the state during the conflict. The regime wanted to end the strike, but it did not resort to repression.

Although the PSN led the majority of strikes, the pro-*somocista* tendency also organized and participated in strike movements during this period. The Liga Nacional de Motoristas, founded in the mid-1930s, had grown to be the largest *somocista* union. In September and October of 1944, the Liga organized the drivers, helpers, mechanics, and machinists of the newly founded national cement factory in San Rafael de Sur (1942). In October 1944, the Liga declared a strike and after two days won salary increases for its members.[36] In addition, the union organization spurred the development of the Sindicato Nacional de los Trabajadores in 1945, which included the approximately 200 workers in the factory. The Liga strike and the subsequent union organization were significant for one reason: Somoza was coproprietor of the factory.[37] The following year, the Somoza regime's policy was much less magnanimous toward the cement workers' union.

In September 1944, Liga members who worked on the Pan-American Highway petitioned the government for wage increases, alleging that their salary barely covered their personal expenses and left them nothing to support their urban-based families.[38] In September, the government authorized a 4-cent wage increase. The Liga continued to agitate over the next three months for a substantial raise. It apparently organized 400 drivers out of the over 2,000 highway project–related workers. On 11 December over 2,000 highway workers put down their tools in demand of a 100 percent wage increase.[39] Somoza reacted rapidly to the first strike in the public sector. He flew to various construction sites to talk to the workers. He then called a meeting of the Liga leaders, with the exception of their president.[40] Somoza refused to include the union president in the negotiations, accusing him of being "an outsider to the movement."[41] Acting on cue from the dictator, the pro-*somocista* Comité Organizador de la Confederación de Trabajadores Nicaragüenses (COCTN) denounced the strike movement. However, the PSN-led carpenters and coachmens' union threatened a sympathy strike. After two days, Somoza offered a 65

---

36 *La Nueva Prensa*, 20–23 October 1944; *Unidad*, 26 October 1944.

37 The president's reaction to the Liga strike is unknown, but given the urgency of cement production for the highway to Puerto Somoza (today Puerto Sandino) and the fact that the Liga represented a minority of the cement workers, he probably accepted the minimal loss of profit.

38 *La Flecha*, 26 August 1944, 19 September 1944.

39 Ibid., 10–13 December 1944; See also U.S. State Department, National Archives, 817.504/12–1944, 19 December 1944. Ambassador Stewart claimed that 4,000 workers took part in the strike and that the threat of a solidarity general strike forced Somoza's hand.

40 *La Nueva Prensa*, 12–13 December 1944; *La Flecha*, 12–13 December 1944.

41 Ibid.

percent wage increase. The leadership, with the exception of the union president, immediately accepted the proposal.[42]

Within a month, the Liga Nacional de Motoristas ceased to exist. On 23 February 1945, security agents arrested the union president.[43] The experience of the union leader provided a very clear lesson as to the limits of *somocista* unionism. The union leadership of the Liga had, in effect, rebelled against the regime. The COCTN isolated the union leader and then, together with Somoza, reincorporated the workers into a new *somocista* organization. Thus, by late 1944, Somoza emerged victorious from his first serious confrontation with organized labor; he had seriously weakened the autonomy of an important sector of the labor movement, yet had enhanced his image as *el jefe obrero*.

In 1945 the PSN wing of labor continued not only to maintain a leadership position in the movement (particularly in Managua, Masaya, León, and Chinandega) but, moreover, exerted increasing autonomy with respect to Somoza. On the other hand, the *somocista* wing penetrated into the nascent industrial sector in which Somoza was acquiring definite economic interests in, for example, matches, cement, textiles, and liquor in order to combat the spread of PSN influence. Nevertheless, the *somocista* unions had to respond to the aspirations of the rank and file. The ensuing conflicts between the Somoza regime and the distinct sectors of the labor movement, and the increasing divisions within the latter, decisively conditioned the events of 1945 and 1946, the high-water mark of Nicaraguan unionism.

PSN support for Somoza in November 1944 depended on essentially the same variables as in July: Somoza's support for the Labor Code; rightist Conservative opposition to both Somoza and labor; and the PLI refusal to break with the Conservatives. In no way did the PSN declare unconditional allegiance to Somoza in 1944. Rather, PSN declarations showed a consistently critical posture toward Somoza's political and economic policies. The party and the unions during the period July–December called for freedom of political prisoners; freedom of political parties and the press; the breaking up of monopolies; rigid price controls; renegotiation of mining contracts; agrarian reforms; and rapid promulgation of the Labor Code. Moreover, the PSN set strict conditions on its support. If Somoza did not fulfill his democratic and social promises, a party statement

---

42 *La Nueva Prensa*, 13 December 1944; *La Flecha*, 13 December 1944; *La Nueva Prensa, La Flecha*, 14 December 1944; *La Flecha, La Nueva Prensa*, 14 December 1944; U.S. State Department, 817.5045, 14 December 1944.

43 Letter, Liga Motorista to Somoza G., 22 January 1945, in the presidential archive in Archivo General de Nicaragua, file 47; *La Flecha*, 23 February 1945.

warned, it would have to "consider the convenience of changing tactics and even resorting to armed conflict."[44]

Following the October–November strikes and this declaration, Somoza's position toward the PSN hardened significantly. On 19 November the *somocista* majority in the COCTN expelled two PSN militants for the sin of "political affiliation."[45] On 21 November the Ministro de Gobernación denied legal status to the PSN. The regime's justification of this repressive measure is quite revealing: "Socialism . . . has nothing new to offer the Nicaraguan proletariat, since the Liberal Party has incorporated these principles into its program and is putting them into practice."[46]

The regime attempted to portray the Left as a foreign-dominated version of what the national labor movement could do more efficiently and authentically under the guidance of *el jefe obrero*. Somoza, during this period, attempted to dynamize the ideology and practice of *obrerismo*, aiming in particular to strengthen the dike separating the popular classes from the rising tide of middle-class and elite opposition. Both the *somocistas* and the PSN leadership emerged from the same *obrerista* tradition. They spoke the same anti-elitist language of social justice and workers' pride. Although many *somocista* labor leaders were speaking from a more distant podium – as politicians or shopowners – in the 1940s and beyond, the language of *obrerismo* still provided a means of internal communication, with resonance and meaning. The Socialist labor militants, however, spoke from the workshop floor, concerned not with politics but with immediate workers' rights. They struggled, often successfully (for example, in Chinandega where they dominated the labor movement), to enforce the Labor Code, which they portrayed as a union conquest rather than a gift from Somoza. By mid-1946, it was clear that the *somocistas* could only reappropriate *obrerismo* and gain control of the labor movement through the repression of the Left.

The close working relationship between the COCTN and Somoza provided very obvious advantages for *somocista* union organization. Aside from the provision of material aid, such as transportation and publicity, the COCTN–state relationship allowed the labor leaders to act as concrete expressions of the moral and political authority that Somoza, to varying degrees, still possessed, especially among non-Managua workers. Al-

---

44  *Unidad*, 7 November 1944.
45  *La Nueva Prensa*, 20 November 1944; *La Flecha*, 2 January 1945, 9 January 1945. Whatever the merits of their argument, the *somocista* attack against them strengthened, as it were, the "syndicalist deviation" of the PSN militants. In response, the Socialists could plausibly and somewhat successfully counterattack against the *somocista* unionists, charging them with injecting politics into the unions.
46  *La Nueva Prensa*, 22 November 1944.

though Somoza's direct access to the labor movement allowed him personally to intervene in conflicts at any given moment, the phenomenon
of *somocista* unionism as a whole is not, however, reducible to a hierarchical
relation in which *somocista* unions responded to state orders. Rather, the
exigencies of maintaining worker support, often in the face of PSN competition, impelled *somocista* union leaders to act with a degree of autonomy
from the state.

*Somocista* unionism was an integral component of Somoza's strategy to
foment labor–capital harmony, politically debilitate the landed oligarchy,
and establish *somocista* hegemony over the Nicaraguan bourgeoisie.[47] This
strategy, however, faced an important obstacle. Union wage demands
encountered substantial resistance from employers, including Somoza.
This contradiction sullied the *obrerista* image of the *somocistas,* weakened
the COCTN, and benefited the Left, as can be seen in the labor conflicts
at, for example, the Momotombo match factory in León, on the Pacific
coast, in March 1945, and the gold mine at La Siuna, in the Atlantic
coast department of Zelaya, in April. Repeatedly, *somocistas* would organize
factories, mills, and mines, only to have the unions crushed in strikes
and lockouts or won over by more militant Socialists.

The May Day rally of 1945 revealed both the weakness of *somocista*
unionism, and the increasingly antagonistic relationship between the *jefe
obrero* and the Left-dominated labor movement. During the several weeks
preceding May Day, Managua union organizers worked continually to
bring out the entire union membership of the city. Somoza's presence at
the rally undoubtedly attracted many additional demonstrators. Yet the
overwhelming majority of the over 30,000 people who attended the May
Day demonstration were union members or sympathizers almost entirely
from the Managua region.[48] From the rostrum, the president could read
the signs and banners of the workers – "Queremos tierras" – "Que bajen
los precios del consumo popular" – "Prisión para los especuladores" –
"Que se abra la Central Sindical de Masaya." This was not a day of homage
to *el jefe obrero.* The speeches of the union leaders echoed the slogans, but
also specifically outlined a program of agrarian reform, enforcement of
the Labor Code, abolition of distribution monopolies, state production
planning, and a political program of democratic "national unity." The
emotional response of the crowd revealed strong support for the program.

47  On Somoza's struggle for hegemony over the bourgeoisie, see Amaru Barahona, "La era dinástica
    hasta el pacto Somoza–Augero (1937–1971)" in *Economía y sociedad en la construcción del estado en
    Nicaragua,* ed. Alberto Lanuza et al. (San José, 1983), pp. 225–38. For an important example
    of the limits of *somocista* unionism on the Atlantic coast, see Gould, "For an Organized Nicaragua,"
    pp. 372, note 51.
48  *La Flecha,* 2 May 1945; *Novedades,* 2 May 1945; *La Nueva Prensa,* 2 May 1945; *Voz Obrera,* 4
    May 1945.

Perhaps inspired by the massive presence of an independent workers' movement, Juan Lorío stepped to the podium and stated:

My people cannot eat bread, they cannot drink milk. Those of us who yesterday refused to take part in an old-style revolution, today we are realizing a civic revolution, in order to make simple, but honest suggestions, which come from the bottom of our hearts.[49]

Arguing that the working class would live better in an atmosphere of democracy, Lorío proceeded to enumerate Nicaragua's economic ills and particularly attacked the U.S. mining companies. Lorío ended his speech with an outline for an alternative economic strategy of autonomous development, and suggested that the inordinate expenditures on the National Guard could be used to foster productive enterprises. Thousands of workers showed their approval of Lorío's speech with tumultuous applause.[50] Clearly perturbed by the biting critique, Somoza composed himself, then walked to the podium and declared that he did not need "lessons in democracy."

I am stepping down from the Presidential Palace to immerse myself in this multitude. I am now just another worker. . . . The . . . dawn is arriving. A world is being born without exploiters or exploited, without oppressed or oppressors, with no more conquests than those of science and work, a world with trees whose branches can be reached by the children.[51]

The ovation for *el jefe obrero* healed the wounds inflicted by Lorío. Somoza had successfully presented himself as but another member of a fighting working class, the subject of Nicaragua's destiny. However, he must have recognized that the monster he had helped to create – the labor movement – was already massive and could indeed threaten to make him "just another worker."

Somoza wanted the support of a united labor movement to withstand the opposition attacks in 1944 and 1945. Despite his fluency in the language of *obrerismo,* and his cultivation of the *somocista* union leaders, the movement as a whole continued to escape his control and continually threatened his conjunctural economic interests. On 18 August 1945, a week after the PSN reiterated its opposition to Somoza's new reelection plans, the government ordered the arrest and deportation of the leadership group of the PSN.[52] When he repressed the PSN leadership (leaving PSN

49 *La Flecha,* 2 May 1945.
50 Interview with Pedro Turcios (Managua) and Antonio Hernández Torres (Chinandega), 1983.
51 *La Flecha, Novedades,* 2 May 1945.
52 *Voz Obrera,* 18 August 1945; *La Nueva Prensa,* 18–25 August 1945; *Novedades,* interview with Antonio Hernández, Chinandega, 1983. The arrests came one week before the scheduled founding convention of the Confederación de Trabajadores Nicaragüenses (CTN). The government also cancelled the convention, in which the *somocistas* would have found themselves marginalized.

sympathizers in the unions unharmed), Somoza was careful to attack them as Communists and not as labor leaders. The jailing and deportation of the PSN leadership, however, pushed labor activists closer to the opposition, in particular its radical student wing. Nevertheless, the political and cultural divide between workers and middle-class dissidents proved to be a difficult obstacle to unity.

The anti-Somoza opposition and the labor movement each reached their apogee during 1946. If they had created a stable alliance during that year, they might have ousted Somoza, particularly during the twenty-six-day administration of Leonardo Argüello in May 1947. Twice, the PSN and the opposition came close to making such an alliance. Yet though the PSN had broken with Somoza and many opposition leaders sympathized with the party's social program, all unity efforts ultimately failed. The inability of the two movements to unite against the regime derived from a gulf in Nicaraguan political culture that Somoza strove to perpetuate. This class-rooted division between labor activists and the middle-class oppositionists would continue to benefit the regime well into the 1960s. Reflecting on the origins of this gulf in the 1940s, I wrote elsewhere:

> The obrerista version of populism, heavily accented with artisanal social pride, became the dominant political idiom throughout western Nicaragua. . . . From its beginnings obrerismo had been with a few exceptions largely incomprehensible to middle-and upper-class anti-Somocistas. . . . Somoza's ability to address urban workers did not necessarily earn him their unequivocal political support. Yet many workers tolerated Somoza to a degree the middle class and elite opposition found, at best, distasteful.[53]

Mutual suspicion rooted in the PSN's support for the regime in 1944, the growth of an anti-Communist wing of the opposition, and the constant visits of opposition leaders to the U.S. embassy tended to exacerbate this fundamental division between the two movements despite their shared goals of democratizing Nicaragua and their brief moments of alliance.[54]

The year 1946 started off on a dramatic note of unity, as the labor movement actively supported an anti-Somoza rally in Managua that drew over 50,000 participants (Managua's population was barely 100,000).

---

53 Gould, *To Lead as Equals*, pp. 188–9.

54 Throughout 1946, the PSN criticized the embassy in somewhat muted terms and indeed praised its nonintervention policy, although they did lambast "the reactionary circles of U.S. imperialism." However, they constantly criticized the opposition's strategy of depending on the United States. For example, the PSN paper *Ahora*, on 24 August 1946, wrote: "The opposition leaders have the weakness of looking for protection from the U.S." Later in the year, the PSN's nationalistic reaction to the opposition's trips to the embassy would be combined with a growing "anti-yanquismo," a direct product of the Cold War. However, it is important to stress that the student wing of the opposition also opposed the pro-U.S. strategy of their elders.

Somoza quickly moved to counter that impressive display of unity by making concessions to the labor movement, negotiating with the PLI, and by mobilizing his own display of popular support.

In February 1946, Somoza permitted the founding convention of the Socialist-dominated Confederación de Trabajadores Nicaragüenses (CTN). The CTN brought together 67 unions and 5 departmental federations, representing over 15,000 members. By the end of that year, the CTN had organized 140 trade unions, 2 additional departmental federations, 4 industrial federations (railway, port, sugar, and mine workers), and numerous peasant unions.[55] The PSN now guided the labor movement in all phases of its activity, from shop-floor struggles to implement the Labor Code, to national political battles.[56] Somoza apparently engaged in some negotiations with the PSN, courting its electoral support. Although the Socialists probably numbered no more than 1,200 members in 1946, the party, through its control over the CTN, was capable of delivering at least 10 percent of the vote, thus potentially influencing the outcome of the elections.[57] The PSN, however, having felt Somoza's repressive hand once too often, rejected the exchange of electoral support for the regime's candidate in return for the legalization of party activities and the concession of four Socialist deputies.[58] Although the leftists wanted legal status and congressional representation, they wished to obtain them through an alliance with the democratic opposition.

Despite the fact that the opposition had forced him to renounce his own candidacy, Somoza's position during the first months of 1946 was still quite strong. His negotiations with the PLI for a single Liberal

---

55 *La Nueva Prensa*, 3 and 12 February 1946; U.S. State Department, 817.00/31–1046. Approximately 50 percent of the union membership belonged to the Federación de Trabajadores de Managua (FTM).

56 In 1946 one State Department analyst wrote on the PSN: "The political strength of this relatively small group of leaders therefore rests largely on its concededly effective organization and the corresponding realization that they may be in a position to command the political support of organized labor." Report on Labor, Barry T. Benson, Chargé d'Affaires, 30 July 1946, U.S. State Department, 817.00/10–3146, p. 2.

57 Somoza's National Defense chief gave the 1,200 member estimate (U.S. State Department, 817.00/10–3146). The PSN, in 1946, attracted 5,000 people to its rallies in Managua and 500 in the departments (*Voz Popular*, 26 August 1946). The PSN weekly paper *Ahora* had a circulation of 3,000 copies, before a campaign that probably elevated it to over 4,000 (U.S. State Department, 817.00B/12–446; on the circulation campaign and its weekly results, see *Ahora*, December 1946–February 1947). In comparison, in 1952 at the height of the Left's advance in Guatemala, the weekly *Octubre* had a circulation of 3,000. See Victor Bulmer-Thomas, *The Political Economy of Central America since 1920* (Cambridge, 1987), p. 140.

58 U.S. State Department, 817.00/10–3–46, makes reference to the Somoza–PSN negotiations earlier in the year. Assuming the report was correct, the negotiations must have taken place between the late January 1946 opposition demonstration, supported by the Left, and May Day, when the relations between the labor leaders and Somoza were quite cool.

candidate (April–July) weakened the opposition by stalling Conservative–PLI unity talks. Moreover, Somoza's own potential electoral strength was still considerable as evidenced by a proregime rally in Managua attended by 40,000–50,000 peasants. The student newspaper *El Universitario* described the rally as the "largest demonstration in history."[59]

The different reactions of the students and the PSN to this and other *somocista* demonstrations reveals something of the perceptual divide between them. The students had no contact with the peasants whom they felt they had to educate and care for following the fall of Somoza. They could not conceive of them as potential *somocista* voters: either Somoza controlled them by terror or by demagoguery. However, to the Socialists the peasant demonstration in Managua showed that Somoza could win the votes of the "peasants that vegetate in the latifundios" in a "free" election by resorting to a variety of tactics that included, but were not limited to, liquor and intimidation.[60] *Somocista* appeals to Liberal party loyalty in the northern departments where the PLI had yet to make an impact would, for example, account for 15 percent of the vote. In a countryside devastated by the Liberal–Conservative civil war only twenty years earlier, the appearance of the *caudillo* Emiliano Chamorro as a leader of the opposition influenced many Liberal peasants to support the regime. In addition to the Liberal peasants (the rural sector represented 65 percent of Nicaragua's population), the regime, in the view of the PSN, would also pick up votes from *somocistas* and *obreristas* in León and Chinandega, several thousand government workers, and some rightist Conservative landowners and their peons. Somoza's political base of "tens of thousands of peasants and agricultural laborers that he [could] call for this or that,"[61] however illegitimately maintained, could well provide the regime candidate with the margin of victory.

The PSN's recognition that Somoza might win a free election sharply distinguished it from the rest of the antiregime forces. Whereas the PLI and the Conservatives incessantly emphasized the necessity for U.S. supervision of the elections, the Left argued that Somoza had to be defeated politically (whether in free elections or after a fraud). The Left recognized that Somoza legitimated his populist-style rhetoric with actions: the prevention of civil wars that had decimated the rural population during the previous forty years, land titles to rural squatters, roads and railways that at least initially benefited peasants, and, of course, the Labor Code. The opposition in alliance with the PSN would have to offer an alternative to

59 *El Universitario*, March 1946.
60 *Ahora*, 4 August 1946.
61 *Ahora*, 10 November 1946, declaration of PSN leader Juan Lorío.

the *somocista* rhetoric and record in the countryside in order to win the elections and enforce their outcome.

The Socialists understood the situation in the countryside far better than the middle-class democrats for they were making serious efforts to organize rural workers. In Chinandega in 1946, Socialist labor activists organized five peasant unions as well as rural workers at the San Antonio sugar mill. Leftist labor militants also successfully organized unions in the rural areas of Managua and Masaya. This organizing experience showed them that they could, in fact, loosen the grasp of Somoza and his *terrateniente* allies. But to defeat Somoza both at the polls and beyond, the Socialist labor program – with its call for agrarian reform, peasant unionism, and rural electrification – would have to be included in the opposition platform. Throughout the year, the PSN consistently stressed the necessity of organizing the opposition around a social program that would chip away at Somoza's control over the rural masses and drain the remnants of his *obrerista* support in the cities. As late as December 1946, the PSN still believed that regime candidate Leonardo Argüello could beat the Liberal–Conservative opposition candidate Enoc Aguado because he could "make guarantees to the working people" and to the Liberal peasantry.[62]

Some groups within the opposition did offer the labor movement guarantees and support for the Labor Code. The PLI's program, in particular, called for "social justice," a minimum wage, and protection for small and medium property threatened during the 1940s (and later) by the latifundistas. The PLI also courted the support of the Socialist-dominated labor movement. The *Liberal Independiente*, the party organ, referred enthusiastically to the "successful" rally of the Confederación de Trabajadores Nicaragüenses, attended by 6,000 workers in Managua; the paper also lauded a PSN leader for his "brilliant" speech. In general, however, the political-cultural divide between the PSN and the PLI as well as the rest of the anti-Somoza movement was perpetuated: whereas the Socialists assessed the middle and upper classes in terms of their attitude and behavior toward labor, the opposition could only conceive the political world in terms of the *somocista*/anti-*somocista* antinomy.

In June 1946 the PSN signed a tentative accord with the small Partido de Unificación Centroamericano (PUCA) and the Federación Universitaria Nicaragüense (FUN), forming the Bloque de Liberación Nacional (BLN). The agreement pledged mutual support in the struggle against the Somoza dictatorship and outlined a progressive social program, bearing the imprint of the PSN. The Socialists took the first step toward concretizing the agreement by urging workers to support a student-called demonstration to commemorate the events of 27 June 1944: "The students have earned [their prestige] fighting valiantly for the people. The workers will join the students on that day."[63] The PSN, by commemorating the student movement that they had opposed in 1944, tacitly admitted an error, or at the very least offered a symbolic apology to the students. Nonetheless, the students had no time to reciprocate the gesture before a new rift between the incipient allies developed.

The National Guard repressed the 27 June demonstration, injuring and arresting many demonstrators; Somoza then closed the Central University in Managua. In response perhaps 3,000 university and high school students in the principal cities of Nicaragua launched a protest strike. The student leaders "demanded" that the PSN (and other parties) organize a nationwide general strike to protest the repression and "to liberate Nicaragua." Nonetheless, in the words of the *sandinista* student leader, Reynaldo Antonio Tefel, "Due to party interests and ideological differences, and worse, mutual suspicion, the general strike, almost a reality . . . did not come off . . . to the detriment of Nicaragua."[64] Another student leader was more blunt, citing as the cause of the strike's failure "insurmountable obstacles like the intransigence of some Socialist leaders of Managua."[65] Both opposition leaders shared the view that the strike might have toppled the regime and that the Socialists bore a major responsibility for its failure. The students then withdrew from the Bloque de Liberación Nacional.[66]

Tefel was surely correct to underscore "mutual suspicion" as the root of the general strike's failure. That suspicion, rooted in the radically distinct lived experiences of the two movements, was only deepened by the failure of the strike. For the students and other anti-*somocistas*, the PSN's intransigence indicated that it had not severed its roots in *somocismo* and therefore could not be fully trusted. The Socialists, although not giving up their hopes for an alliance with the PLI, could not tolerate anti-Communist Conservatives within the coalition. The democratic and labor movements, both at the peak of organizational strength, had combined to create the conditions necessary to wrench major concessions from the regime – yet in a few days that opportunity had slipped away.

In October 1946, despite a rising crescendo of anticommunism from Conservatives and some Liberal Independents (and the Somoza regime), a PSN–opposition alliance, once again, came close to fruition. The op-

63 *Ahora*, 23 June 1946.
64 *La Flecha*, 6 July 1946.
65 *El Liberal Independiente*, 4 July 1946.
66 That the student organization did not ratify the pact at a meeting was reported in *La Prensa* on 5 July 1946. *Ahora*, on 14 July 1946, referred to the students' failure to ratify the pact.

position's presidential nomination of Enoc Aguado, in particular, spurred the reconciliation process between the Socialists and democrats. The PSN had pushed strongly for Aguado's nomination, protesting vigorously against "the sabotage of the reactionary sectors of the Conservative party, systematically attacking Aguado."[67] Gratified that Aguado won the nomination, the Socialists proposed an electoral alliance with the PLI. In return for their support, the Socialists asked for four congressional nominations and a guarantee of legal status for the party. Aguado, in turn, despite some dissension in the PLI leadership, responded positively to the PSN offer of electoral support, accepted their minimum program, and recognized their right to legal status. But he claimed that he could not offer the party four deputies since the nomination process had already taken place. While Aguado was offering this tentative endorsement of an alliance with the PSN, provincial PLI leaders were taking even stronger positions in favor of the Socialists. Julio Selva, the Liberal Independent leader in Masaya, in response to rumors that some PLI leaders opposed an alliance with the PSN on the grounds that the Socialists were *somocista* agents bent on sabotaging the opposition, issued the following declaration: " . . . it is precisely the PSN who can really maintain . . . militant, mass support for a progressive and democratic government . . . in Masaya we have observed the large, mass following of the Socialist Party."[68] Finally, in late October, student and PLI leaders were guests at a PSN rally attended by over 5,000 party sympathizers in Managua.

Nevertheless, the same class contradictions that undermined the anti-Somoza movement of 1944 contributed to the stillbirth of the popular democratic alliance of 1946. Another strike movement – this time of textile workers – put the incipient labor–democratic alliance to a test that it could not pass. It is unclear whether General Carlos Pasos, owner of the nation's largest textile factory and a leader of the PLI, acted out of a desire to break the incipient PSN–opposition alliance. However, he probably did provoke a strike in his mill in order to eliminate the textile workers' union and facilitate a process of rationalization. On 2 November, Pasos obliged his 350 workers to sign thirty-day individual contracts that would deny them protection under the Labor Code. On 9 November, the CTN warned that Pasos was provoking a strike, confident that he would win and thus crush the union.[69] Three days later Pasos confirmed these fears by firing twenty-three union militants. On 13 November, some 250 PAYCO textile workers struck in protest against the firings and the individual contracts. Fifty

---

67 *Ahora*, 24 August 1946.

68 *La Nueva Prensa*, 2 November 1946.

69 *Voz Popular*, 9 November 1946. One month earlier, Pasos had challenged the union to go on strike for holiday pay: "Go on strike and leave and don't come back because I'm not going to give you a penny," the general was quoted as saying (*Ahora*, 6 October 1946).

workers remained on the job. For two weeks, the strikers, sustained by CTN contributions, surrounded the factory around the clock, attempting to block the entrance of food and materials as well as the exit of strikebreakers. Whereas Somoza hinted that the workers had justice on their side, his National Guard acted erratically, at times permitting picket lines, and at times protecting the strikebreakers. The National Guard also banned CTN solidarity demonstrations in Managua.

The strikers were at a serious disadvantage without Somoza's support, or at least the sort of neutrality that they had often enjoyed from the regime in 1944. Although the majority of the textile workers supported the strike to the end, an increasing minority accepted Pasos's offers of guaranteed employment (despite his threat to fire over 80 strikers) and the withdrawal of the thirty-day contracts. The textile union leaders had tried hard to avoid a strike precisely because they had foreseen its potential weakness. Without closed shops to back them, Nicaraguan unions needed near-unanimous worker support (which they rarely attained after 1944) to avoid turning the strikebreakers' "right to work" into the main issue of the strike. Similarly, the presence of at least 50 strikebreakers inside the plant led to several violent incidents. Despite the fact that Pasos and a relative of a strikebreaker fired the only shots, most newspapers depicted the strikers as the violent force. Moreover, the textile union, provoked into rapid action, did not follow the time-consuming prescriptions of the Labor Code for legal strike action. The Junta de Conciliación, undoubtedly prodded by Somoza, thus found it simple to rule against the legality of the strike, while at the same time recognizing the "justice" of the strikers' stand against the individual contracts. Indeed, the ruling of the Junta de Conciliación convinced the union that it had to call off the strike. Pasos agreed to reduce the number of firings from some 80 to 43, reaffirmed his commitment to withdraw the individual contracts, and promised no reprisals against the strikers. Although the CTN tried to put the best face on the solution, there was no doubt that the labor movement had suffered a serious setback.

Somoza's initial ambivalence and subsequent move against the strike reflected the complexity of its political ramifications. He surely enjoyed two immediate by-products of the strike: the image of PLI leader Pasos as an enemy of the people, and the increasing divisions within the opposition. The intransigence of General Pasos divided the anti-Somoza movement and undermined the possibilities for an alliance with the PSN. Although some progressives within the PLI, including their presidential candidate Aguado, unsuccessfully pressured Pasos to negotiate in good faith with the strikers, the Right overshadowed their efforts. The Conservative press, already on an anti-PSN campaign, claimed that "in the strike against PAYCO all the elements of a Communist Revolution are in gestation."[70] Likewise, General Pasos threatened, "I will tolerate no more Communist elements."[71] Pasos and the Conservatives charged on the one hand that Somoza supported the Communists, and on the other that Manuel Mora, the Costa Rican Communist leader, directed the strike. Similarly, ten Conservative and PLI deputies actively supported the strike-breakers' right to work.

Despite the political benefits that he derived from the strike, the rightist anti-Communist propaganda may well have pushed Somoza to act against the union. In October, while in the United States for medical attention, Somoza had enthusiastically signed up on the U.S. side of the Cold War by promising to keep communism out of Nicaragua. He repeated his vow against communism upon his return to Nicaragua. The charges by the Conservatives and Pasos were thus aimed at tarnishing the credibility of the dictator's new commitment to the Cold War effort in the eyes of the U.S. State Department. Somoza, however, parried the Conservative attacks by throwing them back at the opposition: "Just yesterday they [the union militants] were General Pasos's shock force that he used to attack the government. They aren't communists when they serve [his] political interests but they are when they demand rights for the workers."[72] The *somocista* press echoed the dictator's line, directly accusing the opposition of financing the PSN, and thus aiding the growth of the leftist labor movement. During the strike, Somoza himself deemphasized the domestic Communist threat.[73] Nevertheless, over the next few months, without engaging in mass jailings, the regime pursued a hostile policy toward the labor movement, exemplified by unfavorable labor court rulings, the banning of meetings and demonstrations, the denial of legal status to the CTN, and the support of the mining companies' and the San Antonio sugar mill's efforts to throw out the unions.

During the PAYCO strike, the Left reacted more vehemently against the opposition than against the regime. In their anger at Pasos and the Conservative press, they painted the rest of the opposition with the same reactionary colors. In denouncing PAYCO repression, the CTN stated:

---

70 *Diario Nicaragüense*, 22 November 1946.

71 *La Flecha*, 27 November 1946.

72 *La Nueva Prensa*, 23 November 1946.

73 Somoza's argument was quite nuanced. He sought to demonstrate not only the hypocrisy and elitism of the opposition, but the absurdity of their version of anticommunism. Thus he argued that the strikers were not Communists and that communism could not grow in Nicaragua because, "I will not tolerate it." In his effort to defuse the Communist issue, he came close to claiming that the workers involved in the PSN were not really Communists, or at least were not part of an international Red conspiracy (against which, of course, Somoza would struggle to the end).

"... and this is a clear indication of the disdain for workers ... [of the] near totality of those who aspire to direct the destiny of our country."[74] More significantly, on 24 November, less than a month after the PSN had pledged to support Aguado, the party urged the workers to boycott an opposition rally. The PSN boycott — in effect the withdrawal of some 5,000 demonstrators — caused the rally to fall far short of expectations. The boycott decision, taken during the strike, undoubtedly derived, in part, from the negative attitude of many opposition leaders toward the textile workers' union. The PSN communiqué, however, did not refer to the strike. Rather it charged that the national leaders of the opposition had blocked an alliance with the Left: "The opposition leaders in this capital ... reject the participation of the workers' party."[75]

The dramatic surge of anticommunism within the opposition, intensified by the strike, contributed heavily to the collapse of the popular–democratic alliance. The Left understood that the Red-baiting was meant for U.S. consumption: "... so that the United States decides to intervene in the internal problems of Nicaragua, naturally in favor of the opposition groups [because] the Somoza government is allied with the Soviet Union and the Creole Communists, ready to transform this piece of land into a Communist republic."[76] Although the embassy listened to the opposition, its reaction (if there was one) is undocumented. Dr. Mario Flores Ortiz, the PSN leader, however, does offer evidence of U.S. intervention. Delegated by the PSN to work out the details of the electoral alliance with the opposition in late 1946, Flores recalls that the PLI leader Enrique Espinoza Sotomayor called off the talks, informing the PSN leader: "We aren't going to ally with you because the American embassy does not look favorably on this alliance. If you want you can vote for us, but we aren't going to ally with you."[77] Espinoza's remarks probably precipitated the

---

74 *Voz Popular,* 9 November 1946.

75 *Ahora,* 24 November 1946. The communiqué distinguishes the attitude of the national leaders from those PLI militants in Chinandega, Masaya, León, and Matagalpa who collaborated with the labor movement. An embassy official attributed the small turnout for the pro-Aguado demonstration after the boycott to fear of the National Guard and to the "anti-labor bias" of the opposition during the strike. U.S. State Department, 817.00/12–146.

76 *Voz Popular,* 21 November 1946. It is, of course, possible that Somoza read this article and decided that he had to act to forestall this eventuality.

77 Interview with Dr. Mario Flores Ortiz, Managua, 1990. He states that when he approached Dr. Espinoza about the scheduled alliance talks, "Espinoza me dijo dejá de pensar en eso. Nosotros no vamos a aliarnos con uds. porque la embajada americana no ve con buenos ojos eso de alianza. Si uds. quieren, votan por nosotros pero nosotros no vamos a aliarnos con uds." Although Flores Ortiz is not certain of the exact date, he thought that the conversation took place around the time of the PAYCO strike (with which he was not involved directly). Octavio Caldera (Managua, 1990), at the time a student leader who worked directly with Espinoza during the electoral campaign, corroborated Flores Ortiz's assertion.

party's break with the opposition; they certainly stung the PSN's pride and moreover confirmed its suspicions about the opposition leaders' class bias. From that moment on, the Socialists were convinced that the anti-*somocistas* would attack the labor movement to curry the favor and active support of the United States.

The Socialists did not consider supporting Aguado without a formal electoral alliance. Rather, on 17 January 1947, the PSN issued a statement calling for abstention from the elections. The party argued that workers could not support the *somocista* party because it had "broken with democracy," and they should not vote for an opposition that had refused the collaboration of the PSN and had become "a nest of dangerous enemies of labor's modest conquests."[78]

The PSN's abstentionist policy coincided with a downward spiral in the Left's fortunes. The policy itself disillusioned many labor militants who supported Aguado (and voted for him). Meanwhile, as we have seen, the Somoza regime, anxious to earn some Cold War dividends, was thwarting labor organization throughout the country. In April 1947, the CTN recognized that "[its] movement [was] living through a period of crisis," admitting devastating union setbacks in the mines, the railway, the cigarette factory, and the San Antonio sugar mill.[79] The rapid decline of the labor movement following the PAYCO strike derived, at least in part, from its political isolation. Previously, the student movement and important sectors of the PLI had supported the unions, and to a degree blocked repression. Now even their closest friends in the opposition were convinced that the PSN had "sold out to Somoza," while the Socialists scoffed at the PLI's unrequited, servile attitude to the State Department.

The United States undoubtedly loomed large in the thinking of most opposition leaders. And there is little doubt that the opposition believed the U.S. State Department desired a break with the PSN. However, no documentary evidence exists to support the argument that the U.S. embassy forced a split between the Left and the opposition. And to have pushed for an opposition break with the PSN would have gone against the established U.S. policy of nonintervention in Latin American internal affairs. Nevertheless, it is quite possible that a nod or a wink was employed at that time in the fight against communism.[80]

---

78 *Ahora*, 17 January 1947.

79 See *Unidad*, 13 April 1947, and *Voz Popular*, 4 May 1947.

80 Part of the problem in analyzing the embassy's actions revolves around whether or not it viewed the PSN as part of the International Communist movement. Thomas Leonard (*The United States in Central America: Perceptions of Political Dynamics* [Montgomery, AL, 1984], p. 147) writes: "The Embassy was convinced [of] a Communist or quasi-Communist organization of local character only." On the other hand, in the fall of 1944, Ambassador Stewart reported that the PSN received its instructions from Mexico City. U.S. State Department, 817.504/11–1644. Similarly, Benson,

The dominant faction of the PLI was not anti-Communist in any mean-ingful sense. Rather than a commitment to the Cold War cause, the PLI leadership's recognition of the decisive importance of anticommunism in U.S. foreign policy framed their decision to jettison their allies on the Left. The PLI calculated that it could not expect U.S. intervention in the electoral process with the Socialists as allies – and they correctly assessed the probability of fraud without that intervention. In addition, the PLI feared that their alliance with the Conservatives would not survive a formal agreement with the electorally less significant PSN.

Although the opposition's break with the Socialists certainly demon-strated political pragmatism, it also revealed and reaffirmed the widely different conceptual spheres inhabited by the Center–Left opposition and the leftist workers. For the democrats, the goal of eliminating Somoza from power was primordial and all-encompassing. Although they sym-pathized with the labor movement, they could not understand (and thus did not trust) the PSN's insistence on guarantees for the post-Somoza era. The labor activists, on the other hand, could not understand the virtue of anti-Somoza unity when that involved ceding ground to the likes of Pasos and the rightist Conservatives who would surely trample the unions as soon as they took power. When the students accused them of selling out after their abstention declaration, the Socialists let their class resent-ment rise to the surface: "These children who aspire to congressional seats, have given their word to work together with us, but at the moment of truth they fall in behind the *caudillos politiqueros,* turning their back on us."[81]

The PSN, of course, could not foresee the consequences of losing their allies in the democratic opposition – a loss they might have mitigated had the party continued to support Aguado. The Left failed to recognize the degree to which the labor movement's growth from 1944–6 had depended on a uniquely favorable political conjuncture that included a general political enthusiasm (or at least acceptance) of the democratic ideals of the Allied cause. The rise of democratic ideology in Nicaraguan politics involved at least a tolerance for the Left and labor. Moreover, the political opening in 1945–6 provoked an intra-elite conflict that tended to protect the labor movement as long as one side or the other desired its political support. The local currents of the Cold War left the labor

---

in his 1946 Report on Labor, wrote of "the apparently well-founded belief that the Socialist Party is Communist inspired and directed through the Soviet Embassy in Mexico."

81 *Ahora,* 1 February 1947. It should be underscored, however, that the radical student leaders did much to overcome their cultural distance from the urban workers in Managua. Indeed, by 1947 they had a significant informal network of supporters in the working-class neighborhoods. Octavio Caldera recalls that because of their numerous publicized arrests and exiles, the student leaders had become "popular heroes" in the markets and popular barrios.

movement stranded, unprepared to survive alone and exposed on all sides to repression.

For its part, the democratic opposition made an even more serious miscalculation in November 1946. Their gamble on obtaining U.S. support failed miserably, and Somoza easily stole the election for his candidate Argüello. Similarly, the Conservatives proved to be problematic allies during the twenty-six days of the Argüello administration when the aged Liberal leader broke with Somoza. The PLI did not take into account the overall political effect wrought by the decline of the labor movement and the increased distance between the Socialists and the moderate Center–Left. In the departments of Chinandega, León, Masaya, and Matagalpa during 1946, the democratic forces and the labor movement had grown through a symbiotic process; the abrupt termination of that process thus also damaged the student movement and the PLI. Ironically, by the time the key condition that guided opposition politics was finally achieved after Somoza's overthrow of Argüello – the willingness of the United States to aid their cause – the democratic and labor movements were weak and divided.

Leonardo Argüello's fraudulent electoral victory, on 1 February 1947, pushed the opposition and the Left even farther apart.[82] The PLI and the students bitterly opposed the fraud; the Left criticized the elections in subdued tones, while negotiating with Argüello. With only tepid support from his Conservative backers, Aguado went to Washington to seek aid in nullifying the election. Although the State Department knew that Aguado would have won a fair election, it refused to intervene, judging, it seems, that Argüello would chart an independent course from Somoza.[83] Since January 1947, before the elections, the PSN had itself been acting on the assumption that Argüello would govern independently of Somoza and offer the labor movement at least a fair deal. His political program offered stronger commitments to the labor movement than that of the opposition. In private talks with the PSN, after it had broken with the anti-*somocistas*, Argüello apparently promised to make his program a reality. Following his fraudulent victory, the PSN continued to negotiate

---

82 Although Somoza certainly stole the election for Argüello, Knut Walter (The regime of Anastasio Somoza García, p. 262) is surely correct when he argues that the opposition estimate (107,591 for Aguado and 37,532 for Argüello) – repeated by embassy observers, and previously accepted by this author – were "as unlikely as that of the regime." Rather, Walter argues that Argüello's official tally of 104,958 may not have been inflated, but that "most likely it was the opposition that got short changed." (p.255) In addition, a three-to-one Aguado victory could not account for Somoza's strong rural support (I uncovered such evidence in the course of researching this essay).

83 See Leonard, *The United States and Central America*, p. 143.

with the president elect and offered him public support less than a month after the election. Some evidence suggests that in March the party signed a pact with Argüello in return for his commitment to ample union rights and democracy.[84]

The PSN's immediate acceptance of Argüello not only reinforced the anti-*somocistas*' belief that the party had sold out to Somoza, but moreover threw into doubt the Socialists' commitment to democracy. To a degree, the opposition assessment was correct, but less because of the PSN's Marxism than because of the Liberal *obrerista* roots of most of its leaders. The party's *obrerista* notion of democracy emphasized a commitment to worker citizenship in a polity previously reserved for the elite. Without guarantees and rights for workers and peasants, the PSN was not willing to fight for democracy. The PSN leaders addressed Argüello from within the Liberal–*obrerista* tradition.

In May 1947, the PLI and the students decided to support Argüello. As during the first days of his administration, he demilitarized state dependencies, began to reorganize the National Guard (including the removal of Somoza's son from the presidential guard), supported an initiative to legalize the Free University (set up during the student strike of July 1946), and began a dialogue with the unions. Not only did Argüello gain the support of the Left, the PLI, and the students, but he also won the loyalty of sectors of the National Guard, including the police chief of Managua. Perhaps as many as 150 officers in the National Guard pledged their support to Argüello. Moreover, the United States opposed any move by Somoza against Argüello. The Conservative *caudillo* Chamorro and the rightist PLI leader General Pasos were the only major political figures who did not back Argüello.

Perhaps Somoza's successful coup of 27 May was unavoidable. Nevertheless, it is worth emphasizing that during the weeks of the Argüello administration the Somoza dynasty was at its weakest point until 1978–9. Somoza's support (outside of passive peasant backing) was reduced to a divided National Guard, *somocista* congressional deputies, and the tentative backing of Chamorro and Pasos. Even the remnants of the *somocista* labor movement were divided over supporting Argüello or Somoza. Moreover, the coup was not a complete surprise. One week before the coup, Enrique Espinoza announced after the *somocista*-dominated Congress voted 28–18 against Argüello: "Now we await the *golpe de estado*."[85]

More significantly, there were groups ready to defend the Argüello government. One week before the coup, Colonel Alberto Baca, the police

---

84 Blandón (*Entre Sandino y Fonseca Amador*, p. 31) cites an accord between Argüello and the PSN published on 6 March 1947 in *La Estrella* in Panamá.
85 *La Flecha*, 21 May 1947.

chief of Managua, called in several student leaders to propose a plan for the armed defense of the Argüello administration. He offered the students several hundred rifles to be distributed when his group within the National Guard was ready to arrest Somoza. The students and their supporters would then join the struggle to put down the resistance of the pro-Somoza sectors of the National Guard. The students accepted the proposal and in a matter of days had organized a force willing to fight the *somocista* National Guard.

The students did not turn to the PLI and Conservative party leadership, but rather recruited their armed group from among supporters in the popular barrios. Although the students were moving to the Left (many defined themselves as socialists) and they had successfully created a network of supporters in the popular sectors, they did not reestablish contact with the PSN or the labor movement. The legacy of the failed strikes and the broken electoral alliance weighed heavily: in July 1947 the students and the labor movement once again found themselves fighting for the same cause, with very similar political agendas, and yet they were not talking to each other. Whether or not the students and their allies could have defeated Somoza with the labor movement's participation is, of course, debatable. On the one hand, the unions had declined in strength over the previous six months, but on the other, they were prepared to defend Argüello.

The students' strategy, devised on extremely short notice, lacked sufficient coordination with the National Guard's dissidents or with members of the Argüello government. As Octavio Caldera, one of the organizers, recalled:

A few days before the coup, we were organizing in the popular barrios. The police chief found out and he [Baca] called us in. He asks me, "What are you doing? Don't you see that it's all just about to happen. I just want the people to come when it blows up." So I answered, "How are the people going to come just like that? We have to organize them."[86]

In addition to the obvious lack of communication and the vastly different political styles between the Colonel and the students, the lack of coordination between the students, the National Guard dissidents, and the government posed an equally grave problem. Argüello acted as if he were not in touch with the conspiracy. On 25 May he ordered Somoza to leave the country, despite the fact that the preparations necessary militarily to enforce his order were not in place. Somoza struck the next night, arresting Baca and some 150 officers accused of supporting Ar-

86 Interview with Octavio Caldera, Managua, 1990.

güello. Caldera recalls the way he experienced the end of those days of hope:

> The day of the *golpe* an officer came to let me know. So at one in the morning my *compañeros* and I were waiting along the highway and we saw Guardia trucks pass by. And we waved to them in greeting, thinking [incorrectly] that they were the group in the Guardia who were going to oppose Somoza. So there we were at one in the morning waving at the Guardia.[87]

The Somoza coup in May 1947 signaled a dramatic political transition. Although Somoza directed his wrath against all of the pro-Argüello forces, he treated the students and the PSN – the two groups who most vigorously protested the coup – with a particular vengeance. For the first time, the regime directly made reference to a Communist problem in Nicaragua, in order to carry out its repression. The government (nominally headed by a puppet named Lacayo Sacasa) decreed the confinement of nine PSN leaders on the grounds that there existed in Nicaragua "elements affiliated with Communism."[88] On similar grounds, the regime imprisoned or drove into exile all student leaders. But communism was not the only crime in Nicaragua: to call for Argüello's return to power was also worthy of a prison term. The repression against the Left, although it had the most far-reaching consequences, was merely part of a general crackdown that drove over two hundred dissidents into exile and threw probably hundreds into jail, including many PLI and Conservative party members.

Following the coup, the United States adopted, for the first time, a belligerent attitude against the Somoza regime. One of the State Department's first moves was to withdraw its military mission to Nicaragua. Then, the United States voted, along with most Latin American governments, against allowing the Somoza regime to participate in the Rio conference of August–September 1947.[89] By refusing to recognize the de facto government, the U.S. government played a role in containing, to a degree, the regime's dictatorial excesses. The regime responded by releasing a number of prisoners, many of whom, however, would be rounded up again following a failed Conservative insurrection in mid-September.

The ideology and practice of anticommunism were key features of the regime's efforts to obtain diplomatic recognition from the United States.

87 Ibid.

88 *La Noticia*, 8 July 1947.

89 The local press, though tightly muzzled by that time, published the following declaration of an embassy official: "By voting against [the conference invitation to the regime] the United States maintained its policy of recognition of the Argüello government." *La Noticia*, 31 July 1947.

Thus, for example, a law was passed by the newly installed Constituent Assembly calling for military prosecution of acts of terrorism or communism. The Socialist party, with no protection from its battered labor movement and isolated from the rest of a defeated opposition, was easy prey for the regime. In January 1948, the National Guard rounded up between 50 and 100 Socialists as well as labor activists and PLI progressives. An astute State Department functionary commented that the antileftist repression responded to Somoza's need to accumulate "international capital in anti-Communism."[90]

The death of Leonardo Argüello in December 1947, removed a major obstacle to U.S. recognition for the regime and set the stage for negotiations with Carlos Cuadra Pasos and his rightist, *civilista* faction of the Conservatives. Cuadra Pasos saw negotiations as the only way to end the regime's reliance on repression of Conservatives and dissident Liberals, as he feared that it would provoke a civil war. He also approved of Somoza's decisive commitment to antileftist repression. After six weeks of negotiations, Somoza accepted most of the Conservative leader's demands. The pact, signed in February 1948, included an amnesty for political prisoners (although the leftists stayed in jail until August), immediate and increased representation for the Conservatives in the judicial and legislative branches of the government (in addition to governance over several departments), and the depoliticization of the National Guard as a precondition for free presidential elections to be held in 1951.[91]

The Conservative *caudillo* Emiliano Chamorro and the PLI denounced the Cuadra Pasos–Somoza pact.[92] But the Conservative Right, its opposition to Somoza softened by the prospects of representation and by the new Constitution – with concessions on land tenure and clerical issues – accepted the deal. The State Department looked positively on the Liberal–Conservative rapprochement (and on the anticommunism of the regime), and in late February proffered an invitation to the Pan-American Conference in Bogotá. This was if not tantamount to recognition, certainly indicative of a fundamental shift in U.S. policy since the Rio conference in September 1947. Before the conference began, at least three countries – Costa Rica, Colombia, and the Dominican Republic – had broken the hemispheric boycott by recognizing the government of Víctor Manuel Román y Reyes, Somoza's uncle. In May, immediately following the

90 U.S. State Department, National Archives, RG 59, 817.00/B 1–1048.

91 For a good account of the Cuadra Pasos pact, see Walter, The regime of Anastasio Somoza García, pp. 278–82.

92 Emiliano Chamorro surely belonged on the Right of the Conservative party since the 1890s. However, from 1946–50, his ideology veered toward the democratic Center. His long periods of exile in Mexico and especially in Guatemala (1947–9) had much to do with this shift. See his autobiography, *El último caudillo* (Managua, 1983), pp. 369–74.

conference, the United States followed suit, in part because of the necessity of hemispheric unity in the Cold War, and in part because the Cuadra Pasos pact – with its limited extension of the regime's political base – allowed Nicaragua to claim a place on the edge of the vastly expanded sphere of democratic nations.

U.S. recognition of the Somoza regime crowned the success of his postcoup strategy. With his own popular base diminished and his international legitimacy nonexistent, Somoza could only survive by making a hard turn to the Right. The regime's internal necessities – to clamp down on all "subversion" – meshed nicely with the international imperative to combat communism. At the same time, Somoza's visible commitment to anticommunism and political stability attracted the Conservative Right, who in turn allowed the regime to regain the semblance of legitimacy. In the new geopolitical world of the late 1940s, anticommunism counted for more than democracy.

In January 1950 the State Department engineered the start of negotiations between Somoza and a representative of Emiliano Chamorro. On 1 April, the negotiations bore fruit in the Pact of the Generals. The Somoza–Chamorro declaration began by justifying itself as a defense against the Communist threat. It then continued the course charted by Somoza–Cuadra Pasos in 1948: guaranteeing the minority party one-third of the seats in a Constituent Assembly, to be elected under bipartisan supervision in May, and minority party representation in the judiciary and in the state's autonomous institutions. Significantly, the PLI was left out of the deal. The pact barred it from participating in either the constituent or the presidential elections. Although bolstering the regime's local and international legitimacy, the Pact of the Generals divided an already weak and fragmented opposition. Somoza's overwhelming victory against the Conservative candidate was in large part due to the apathy of an opposition movement that three years earlier had come close to overwhelming the regime. The Left was too weak even to challenge Somoza's updated anti-Communist version of *obrerismo*, which he ably manipulated against the "reactionary" Conservatives.

Ironically, after failing to unite during their time of strength, in the depths of the Cold War, the ex-student Left and the remnants of the PSN came together in the Unión Nacional de Acción Popular (UNAP). Founded in 1948, over the next two years the UNAP made little progress in Somoza's semi–police state, although some leftists were able to work within the *somocista* unions. When the electoral campaign gave the Left some space to maneuver, they viewed a barren political landscape. Following the Pact of the Generals, UNAP activists wrote:

Nobody can miss the fact that we live in a time in which the indifference of the people is undermining the psychological structure of our citizens. We all know what this indifference means for the [popular] struggle. . . . We are passing through a period of moral crisis. UNAP, in truth, is trying to grow in a terrain more suited for that undesirable plant of servility than for our ideals. We must walk on the earth that our neanderthal politicians have fertilized and cultivated.[93]

Nicaragua's political evolution from 1944 until 1948 resembled that of many other Latin American republics. The country underwent a democratic opening, albeit uneven and limited, from 1944 until 1946, accompanied by major gains for the Left and for labor, followed by a period of repression against labor, the Left, and the democratic opposition from June 1947 until August 1948. Between 1948 and 1950 the Somoza regime consolidated an alliance with the Right that afforded it an important degree of domestic and international legitimacy.

The interaction of local and international forces that produced the conservative victory in Nicaragua parallels those of the rest of the continent. The beginning of the Cold War tilted a precariously balanced set of class relations decisively in favor of business and landed interests. Anticommunism had long been part of elite ideological baggage. But in 1946–7, under the stimulus of the growing U.S.–Soviet rivalry, elite groups transformed anticommunism from a largely polemical device into a key principle of their own political mobilization against both the labor movement and the Somoza regime.

Somoza's own conversion into an ardent anti-Communist in late 1946, although a response to opposition attacks, conformed to his belief that his regime's fate hinged on the goodwill of the State Department. The relative weakness and isolation of the labor movement in late 1946 facilitated Somoza's decision to suspend his populist project and move against the Left.

Economic factors, for example the need to create a secure climate for foreign investment, probably played a lesser role in the defeat of the Left in Nicaragua than elsewhere. In part this reflects the country's comparatively miniscule industrial base. Economic factors, however, did play a role in the move against labor. Somoza's own substantial economic interests not only distinguished his government from most others in Latin America (except the Dominican Republic), but also placed sharp limits on his populism. Moreover, it was no coincidence that the regime clamped down on labor first and hardest in the dynamic sectors of the economy – on the plains of Chinandega on the eve of an agro-export boom and in the foreign-owned gold mines. Nevertheless, the congruence of anti-Communist ideology and economic interests became more pronounced *after* the defeat of the labor movement, when rightist Conservatives moved to collaborate with the regime.

93 *Adentro,* 22 April 1950.

Although in broad outlines the rightist victory in Nicaragua paralleled that in the rest of the continent (except Guatemala), the outcome of the postwar conjuncture seems less inevitable in Nicaragua than elsewhere. The complexity and fluidity of labor's relations with the opposition movement created a unique political situation in Nicaragua in 1946 and in May of 1947. Somoza's attempted alliance with labor in 1944–45 resembled those of other Latin American authoritarian leaders like Vargas and Perón. But his early break (1945) with labor, during a period of relative civil and political liberty, created the conditions for a Center–Left advance. Those conditions matured in May 1947, when the new president Leonardo Argüello, with the support of sectors of the National Guard (and the tacit support of the State Department), decided to ally himself with the anti-Somoza opposition and the labor movement to eliminate the Somoza dictatorship.

The failure of the democratic opposition and the Left to take advantage of that opportune moment in May 1947 derived from their rupture the previous November and their subsequent decline. The local impact of the Cold War and perhaps the intervention of the U.S. embassy played an important role in the split in the democratic–popular alliance. Nevertheless, the break in the alliance need not have become a permanent one; the Left and the middle-class democrats did not compete for the same worker constituency (as for example in Venezuela). On the contrary, the competitors for labor were the Left and the *somocistas* (and to a minor extent the Catholic Church), and the Left had no appeal among the middle classes. Perhaps related to the lack of competition for a political base with the Left, the PLI in 1946–7 was not particularly anti-Communist. The PLI broke with the Left because its leaders believed that the State Department supported such a split and because they imagined that the United States was the direct and final arbiter of Nicaraguan politics (a belief that they shared with Somoza). Although the United States for decades had played a decisive political role in Nicaragua, during the period 1944 until mid-1947, the State Department, to the extent that it was concerned at all, probably would have preferred to see a democratic solution, even at the cost of an opening for a relatively small leftist labor movement.

The PLI leadership's belief in the necessity (and the possibility) of a U.S.-determined end to *somocismo* was symptomatic of the political and cultural gap between worker militants and the middle-class dissidents, who lacked an organic popular base. The labor Left emerged from *obrerismo*, a radical political tradition within the Liberal party and a language of worker pride and citizenship. Somoza's fluency in the language of *obrerismo* made cross-class communication even more difficult. For the opposition, Somoza's embrace of *obrerismo* cast doubts about the authenticity of the labor movement. Similarly, the Left had difficulty comprehending the centrality of anti-*somocismo* in the democrats' ideology and practice at the expense of concrete support for the labor movement. It was this political-cultural distance between labor and the democratic opposition that frustrated their alliance and thus decisively shaped the outcome of the postwar political and social struggle, permitting the Somoza regime to survive its worst crisis until 1978.

# 10

## Costa Rica

### *Rodolfo Cerdas Cruz*

The origins of the Civil War of March–April 1948 and the subsequent repression of the Communists and the more militant sections of the labor movement in Costa Rica can be traced to the 1930s.[1] The Depression accelerated the process of the formation of labor unions, notably those of the shoemakers, who were by then working in relatively large workshops of 200–300 workers, and the banana workers, who constituted a genuine agricultural proletariat. At the same time, it intensified class consciousness among labor leaders and strengthened the role played by organized labor in Costa Rican politics.[2] The decade of the 1930s witnessed the development of the Partido Comunista de Costa Rica (PCCR), which came to

Translated from the Spanish by Elizabeth Ladd.

1 An abundant bibliography exists on this period. Nevertheless, the events of 1948 await a complete in-depth study. There are partial contributions both by participants in the conflict and by academic researchers of undeniable importance. Particularly noteworthy in the first category are Partido Vanguardia Popular, *Los sucesos de Costa Rica: Un examen de la Guerra Civil* (San José, 1948); Rafael Obregón Loría, *Conflictos militares y políticos de Costa Rica* (San José, 1951); Alberto Cañas, *Los ocho años* (San José, 1952); Rosendo Arguello Chijo), *Quiénes y cómo nos traicionaron* (Mexico City, 1954); Manuel Mora, *Dos discursos en defensa de Vanguardia Popular* (San José, 1958); and José Figueres Ferrer, *El espíritu de 48* (San José, 1987). In the second category, see Oscar Aguilar Bulgarelli, *Costa Rica y sus hechos políticos de 1948* (San José, 1969); John Patrick Bell, *Crisis in Costa Rica* (Austin, TX, 1971); Bell, (*La Guerra Civil en Costa Rica* (San José, 1976); Miguel Acuña, *El 48* (San José, 1974); Jacobo Schifter, *La fase oculta de la Guerra Civil en Costa Rica* (San José, 1981); Schifter, *Costa Rica 1948: Análisis de documentos confidenciales del Departamento de Estado* (San José, 1982); Schifter, *Las alianzas conflictivas*, 2d ed. (San José, 1986); and Manuel Rojas Bolanos, *Lucha social y guerra civil en Costa Rica: 1940–1948* (San José, 1986).

2 On the early history of the labor movement in Costa Rica, see Alturo Fournier Facio, La United Fruit Company y las huelgas bananeras (Masters Thesis, Faculty of Law, University of Costa Rica, 1974); Raimundo Santos and Liliana Herrera, *Del artesano al obrero fabril* (San José, 1979); Vladimir La Cruz, *Las luchas sociales en Costa Rica (1878–1930)* (San José, 1980); Jorge Mario Salazar, *Política y reforma en Costa Rica: 1914–1958* (San José, 1981); Carlos Abarca et al., *Desarrollo del movimiento sindical en Costa Rica* (San José, 1981); and Carlos Luis Fallas Monge, *El movimiento obrero en Costa Rica (1830–1902)* (San José, 1983).

dominate the Confederación de Trabajadores Costarricenses (CTCR). It also saw the emergence of a middle-class business sector that had significant and growing conflicts with the economically and politically dominant agro-export coffee oligarchy, but which sought to promote a social and political program that was different and opposed to that of the Communist Party.

While the conservatives were trying to manage the new labor relations along the paternalistic lines that had existed between plantation owner and peon, the Communist Party and the CTCR attempted to introduce a legal framework, institutionalized in social security legislation and a labor code, to formalize workers' rights and, most importantly, collective bargaining, independent union organization, and the right to strike. The business sector also needed a clear, legal frame of reference for labor relations and the reproduction of the labor force that was stable, workable, and beyond the whims of traditional agrarian paternalism. Thus social reform united this middle sector with the program of the PCCR and its critique of the old oligarchical coffee society. Its own entrepreneurial capitalist ends, however, clothed by necessity in the progressive language of social democracy, placed it at odds with the Communists. The business sector also rejected the methods used by the Communists and, in particular, their alliance with the oligarchic governments of Calderón Guardia and Picado during the Second World War.

Between 1940 and 1944 Costa Rica was governed by Dr. Rafael Calderón Guardia, a traditional oligarch and reform-minded politician of the Partido Nacional Republicano (PNR). Calderón came to be distrusted by the coffee oligarchy for his actions during the Second World War in confiscating the property of pro-Axis sympathizers. It was the Second World War that also prompted Manuel Mora Valverde, the secretary general of the PCCR, known after the dissolution of the Comintern in 1943 as the Partido Vanguardia Popular (PVP), to offer his support to Calderón, and Calderón to accept it. The price of Communist support for Calderón was the Labor Code and other social legislation of 1942. When Teodoro Picado Michalski, a *calderonista,* was elected president in February 1944 with, it should be noted, 66 percent of the vote, the PVP and the Communist-led CTCR continued to provide the government with one of its main pillars of support.

For reasons that would be too lengthy to present in detail here, but that are discussed at length elsewhere,[3] the PCCR had acquired, almost from its very founding, a totally national character. Disconnected from

---

3 See Rodolfo Cerdas, *La hoz y el machete: La Internacional Comunista, América Latina y la revolución en Centro América* (San José, 1986).

the Communist International and its regional organization, the so-called
Caribbean Bureau, the PCCR had rapidly evolved into a political entity
directly associated with Costa Rican national problems, albeit from the
sectarian perspective of the labor movement. Several reports from the U.S.
legation in San José at this time indicate that this is how the PCCR was
seen by U.S. officials. For example, in the words of Minister Robert M.
Scotten, "it is not based on Marxist doctrine, but is rather a union
organization, and the best one can say about [it] is that it resembles our
own CIO."[4] Nevertheless, as early as 1942, there was a tendency to see
any legislative action that affected the interests of U.S. investors in the
country as "anti-American," particularly if it had to do with the United
Fruit Company, which, for example, began to take a harder line with
regard to social legislation.[5] There is thus evidence of a dual attitude: on
the one hand, U.S. officials recognized the predominantly national nature
of the Communist movement, and on the other, in putting U.S. commercial and business interests ahead of every other consideration, they
identified any action adversely affecting the economic interests of U.S.
investors in Costa Rica with Soviet communism. Nevertheless, it should
be stressed that throughout 1944, 1945, and 1946, indeed as late as
January 1947, the U.S. Embassy was still taking the view that the political
strength of the PVP arose from "a well defined programme to better Costa
Rican working conditions rather than from external (i.e., Soviet) support
which was considered non-existent."[6]

It has been argued that at the end of the Second World War the United
States intensified its policy against communism in Costa Rica; therefore
it supported both a series of opposition leaders and those anti-Communist
movements they wanted to see organized.[7] U.S. Ambassador Hawlett
Johnson, however, going against colleagues and departments in his own
embassy, tried to avoid a hostile stance toward Picado's government and
the PVP. Johnson had good personal relations with Picado: they frequently
went horseback riding together and he had an open invitation to the
presidential residence. He saw Picado as a convinced partisan and prac-
titioner of democracy. He felt that Picado was interested in improving

4 Schifter, *Alianzas conflictivas*, p. 168.

5 Minister Scotten, Chief of the U.S. Legation in Costa Rica, describes how Luis Anderson, United
  Fruit Company's lawyer in Costa Rica, "had read the Code with a glass of sal hepatica in his hand
  and expressed his opinion that if some Machiavellian type had wanted to harm the government
  and Costa Rica, he would have found no better weapon than the present Labor Code." Schifter,
  *Costa Rica 1948*, p. 107, citing Reed to Secretary of State, 21 April 1943. National Archives,
  Washington, D.C. (State Department, Costa Rica); hereafter NA, CR.

6 Schifter, *Costa Rica 1948*, p. 130, citing Johnson to Secretary of State, 9 Jan. 1947. NA, CR
  818.001/1–947.

7 Schifter, *Alianzas conflictivas*, p. 203.

the standard of living of the poor and that, unlike Calderón, Picado was not making himself rich off of public funds. Above all, he recognized that Picado "gave 100% cooperation to the United States and that his foreign policy was moulded on North American policy."[8]

Johnson also had a relatively positive view of Manuel Mora and the PVP. In his report to the State Department on a dinner he had with Mora on 6 December 1945, he indicated that he was impressed by the sincerity of Mora's words and the forcefulness with which he denied Soviet influence on the PVP. According to the ambassador, the government's program, supported by the PVP, "was no different from what the United States adopted in the form of social security, public works and other social reforms." He further considered that the PVP was "not really communist" and prohibited his staff from referring to the group as such.[9]

On the other hand, Johnson was very critical of the opposition to the regime, particularly the large capitalists who were opposed to the social reforms of the 1940s:

The large landowners of the country are totally opposed to any social change. They pay ridiculously low taxes and are accustomed to the old Spanish class system. They feel that a relatively moderate program like Popular Vanguard's will change the system in such a way that the peons, until now subjugated, will improve their financial and social position to a disproportionate extent.[10]

The positions adopted by the U.S. ambassador prompted the opposition to Picado's government to accuse him of communism, charges that he considered "lunatic": his policy was one of "absolute neutrality."[11]

The ambassador's attitude helped not only to preserve Picado's administration in power, but to prevent more open intervention by the United States in national politics. It was clear to Johnson that there was really no danger that the country would evolve toward communism, and that, "if Popular Vanguard was a communist party, it was so in a Latin American and Costa Rican way, owing its electoral attraction more to its program of social reform than to its international communist ideology."[12] A change of ambassadors in March 1947 in which Johnson was replaced by Walter J. Donnelly, until then an advisor at the U.S. embassy in Lima, maintained the broad lines of agreement between the embassy and the Costa

8 Schifter, *Alianzas conflictivas*, p. 208. The source cited is NA, CR, Johnson to Secretary of State, 3 January 1946, 818.00 Teodoro Picado 1–346.

9 Ibid., p. 209, based on NA, CR, Johnson to State Department, 6 December, 1945.818.008/ 12–645; ibid., 26 January 1945.818/002/1–2645 and 6 April, 1946.818.004/146.

10 Ibid. p. 209, citing NA, CR, Johnson to Secretary of State, 6 April 1946, 818.004/146.

11 Ibid., p. 209, citing NA, CR, Johnson to Secretary of State, 1 April 1946, 818.00/4–146.

12 Ibid., p. 211, citing NA, CR, Lester to Wise, 13 January 1947, 818.001/1–1547.

Rican government. There was thus no significant policy shift by the State Department at this stage toward Picado's government and its alliance with the *calderonistas* and the Communists.[13]

In the meantime, the young Archbishop of San José, Monsignor Víctor Manuel Sanabria Martínez, had boldly chosen to give the Catholic church a prominent role in the complex politics of the 1940s by supporting Calderón's progressive social legislation of the early years of the decade. In a private memorandum written fifteen years later (6 January 1956) from New York by Father Benjamín Núñez, director and founder of the Rerum Novarum confederation of labor, to the Apostolic Nuncio in Costa Rica, the church's position is explained as follows:

The resolution to organize a movement of this kind was not the result of improvisation on the part of His Excellency Sr. Víctor Sanabria, Archbishop of San José. On the very day he was promoted to this position in 1940, he indicated to Father Benjamín Núñez, the undersigned, his wish that the said priest leave immediately for some university to study in the area of social sciences, because, he said, "Until now we have not had one priest educated in these areas and we cannot involve ourselves in real social action without having at least one person, preferably a clergyman, to assume its initial leadership." Monsignor Sanabria had given a hint of his overall view of what he considered the social mission of the Church during the session of his First Pastoral, where it refers to the Social Question. In sum, the Prelate proposed to make a bold application, although gradual and progressive, of the great postulates of Catholic Social Doctrine, and its circumstantial derivations, to national realities, in such a way that the said doctrine would become the generating source and guiding principle of any systematic and organized action proposed to advance the overall well-being of the people of Costa Rica.[14]

This document reveals the Catholic church's intent, particularly that of its Archbishop, of participating in the social reform of the 1940s as an active protagonist and of competing, on the ideological, spiritual, and also the strictly organizational front, in the social field against the hitherto practically monopolistic influence of the Communist Party.

There was, however, a more immediate task: the defense of the recently enacted social guarantees, which were subject to the inevitable political tensions that surround such profound and significant changes. These tensions had three different sources: first, the opposition of capital, domestic and foreign; second, electoral manipulation on the part of the government, which saw the reform as merely an instrument to perpetuate itself in power; and third, the danger that the reform would be identified with,

13  Ibid. P. 212, note 151, citing NA, CR, United States, No. 1529, 24 March 1947.
14  Benjamín Núñez, "Informe sobre las relaciones entre el movimiento obrero católico costarricense y la Autoridad Eclesiástica," sent to the Apostolic Nunciature in San José from New York, January fifth 1956, typewritten, pp. 1–2.

and would serve to further broaden the influence of, the Communist Party. For Monsignor Sanabria, there was always a danger that the word "Communist" would be applied to this social legislation, possibly fatally wounding it or adulterating its fundamental propositions. "Fortunately," he concluded in a speech on 1 May 1945 specifically referring to the political and organizational manifestations of the Communist Party, and recognizing the basically national character of the party, "in Costa Rica there are no workers' groups which have not declared – and in good faith, while experience does not demonstrate the contrary, we have to take it as the truth – that their purposes are not exclusively and utterly Costa Rican." Sanabria was aware of the peculiarities both in the evolution of the Costa Rican Communist Party and in that of Costa Rican society and politics. As a result, he found joint participation by Communists and Catholics in the labor movement, and indeed direct action in the social struggle, acceptable. "In many countries the presence of a Bishop at a union meeting perhaps would make no sense, unless it were cause for . . . scandal," he declared. "In Costa Rica, given the specific circumstances, it is fully justified." [15]

In spite of Sanabria's progressive tone and his refusal to adopt a negative anti-Communist role, there should, however, be no confusion as to his position. The Archbishop knew that the church was, for labor, the only ideological alternative at the time to the Communists and to the opportunists who both supported social legislation. He supported workers' demands and situated them in a framework essentially opposed to Marxism–Leninism. The entente cordiale with communism was nothing other than peace in war. In his 1 May speech, Sanabria insisted on the need to create "independent union organisations that [were] pro-social justice, pro-worker, pro-social duty. He then continued, "Although it hurts to admit it, a good part of the social advances already achieved are due to [the Communists]. . . . Let us imitate them . . . learn from the enemy." [16] This is the origin of the rival organization to the CTCR, the Confederación Costarricense de Trabajadores Rerum Novarum, which was founded in 1943 by progressive leaders of the Catholic church and led by Father Benjamín Núñez.

Rerum Novarum was thus the product of the personal initiative of the Archbishop of San José and spiritual leader of Costa Rica's Catholic church, Monsignor Víctor Sanabria. It was he who selected Father Benjamín Núñez

15 "Discurso del Excelentísimo Señor Arzobispo de San José Mons. Dr. Don Víctor Sanabria Martínez" in "Memoria de la Primera Convención Solemne de la Confederación Costarricense del Trabajo Rerum Novarum," *Ediciones Rerum Novarum* 1 (1 May 1945): 17, 18.

16 Ibid., p. 23. For a more detailed study of Sanabria's thought, see Ricardo Blanco Segura, *Monseñor Sanabria* (San José, 1971) and *Obispos y Arzobispos de Costa Rica* (San José, 1966). See also James Backer, *La Iglesia y el sindicalismo en Costa Rica* (San José, 1978).

to be head of the organization and to study sociology and union organization in the United States. The Archbishop's protégé, however, was a strong personality and went his own way. In spite of his continued formal acceptance of ecclesiastical discipline and his affirmation of Catholic social doctrine, he was soon in conflict with the governments of Calderón Guardia and Picado because of their alliance with the Communist PVP and the Communist-led CTCR. For its part, the CTCR maintained a distrustful attitude toward Rerum Novarum from the beginning. They accused it of dividing the labor movement, over which the Communists had previously reigned practically alone. Later, they charged it with being linked to the national capitalist sector, the U.S. Embassy, and the labor movement in the United States, and with seeking to strengthen probusiness unionism.

Although these charges were denied by Rerum's leaders, Father Núñez did in fact request aid from the U.S. Embassy in San José:

On April 20, 1945, the Embassy agreed to lend moral support to Núñez, sending its attaché for civil affairs, Edward D. Cuffe, to attend a meeting at the house of Victor Manuel Yglesias, where methods for financing Rerum Novarum, Núñez' union, were discussed. Present were Father Núñez himself, Cuffe, and Howard Lindo, Alberto Dent, Carlos Rohrmoser, Fernando Alvarado, Manuel Jiménez, Rodolfo Montealegre and Victor Manuel Yglesias. They were all important coffee producers and opposed to the government of Teodoro Picado. Núñez explained at the meeting to these representatives and the American Embassy that the union was in a very difficult financial situation. The non-communist unions it had founded, which represented a democratic alternative for the country, could not make large economic contributions and therefore found themselves under-financed. According to the priest, he himself received only 300 *colones* a month in salary from Archbishop Sanabria, and the unions, in turn, contributed 1000 *colones* a month. This was not even enough to pay the lawyers and the debt Rerum had already run up . . . of nearly 7,000 *colones*.[17]

The result of the meeting was that the coffee owners decided to support Father Núñez with a contribution of 250 *colones* a month from each of them, and they would cancel the accumulated debt. Núñez tried to deny the political and social influence the agreement implied, earning the skepticism of the Embassy, which felt that Núñez would be receiving "financial support from a group opposed to Popular Vanguard."[18]

Later, in December 1946, Father Núñez appealed to Matthew Wall, President of the Central Committee of the American Federation of Labor (AFL), asking for economic aid to "support the democratic union movement in our country, Costa Rica, and other Central American countries."

17 Schifter, *Costa Rica 1948*, p. 123, citing Johnson to Secretary of State, 30 April 1945, NA, CR, 818.504/4–3045

18 Ibid., p. 124. According to Cuffe, Núñez himself confided to him that this financial group had supplied him with 10,000 colones so that Rerum could become independent on 1 May.

By way of introduction, the President of Rerum claimed that his Confederation had organized by then 90 unions and 10 confederations, and was opposed to the CTCR, an affiliate of the Confederación de Trabajadores de América Latina (CTAL), which he labeled a puppet of the Soviets. He said he needed $400 to strengthen Rerum and about $1,000 to organize other democratic unions in Central America. Serafino Romualdi answered Núñez that the letter had been read at the AFL convention and that they had voted to congratulate him on his democratic activity and to grant him a subsidy of $750 dollars a month to organize union confederations in Nicaragua and El Salvador, leaving open the request of aid for Rerum until they had received news of the work done in those two countries.[19] It was Romualdi's visit to Costa Rica at the beginning of 1947 as a representative of the AFL – looking for support for an anti-CTAL Latin American Labor Congress that was eventually held in Lima in January 1948 – that provoked the first public confrontation between Rerum and the CTCR.[20]

Sanabria himself was trying at this time to give his Catholic unionist conceptions a continental dimension, which necessarily came into conflict with both the Marxist unionism of the CTAL and Latin American conservatism. However, whereas in Sanabria's conception the predominant element seemed to be the specifically Catholic, or at least Christian and non-Marxist, perspective, for Núñez the most important dimension was by now anticommunism. Given his mentality, his education in the United States, his experience of social reform in Costa Rica, his opposition to the alliance of the government and the PVP, and his relations with the North American labor movement, it is not unreasonable to suspect Father Núñez's hand behind the memorandum sent by Monsignor Sanabria to the Holy See in August 1946.

19 Ibid, pp. 124–5. In both the first (partial) edition published by Editorial Universitaria in 1982, as well as in the complete edition, published by Libro Libre (*Alianzas conflictivas*, 1986), there is obviously an error in dates: in both, Schifter puts the date of the letter he found in the State Department as 16 December 1946, and the answer from Serafino Romualdi as 7 November of the same year. Checking the archival source for each, I found that for the Núñez letter Schifter cites NA, CR, Johnson to Secretary of State, 30 April 1945, 818.5043, and for Romualdi's, NA, CR, Johnson to Secretary of State, 16 December 1946, 818.5043. Without knowing the exact date, this leads us to assume that Núñez's letter is from 1945 or the beginning of 1946, and Romualdi's from the end of that year. In any case, the correspondence took place, and that is what is of interest.

20 See Backer, *La iglesia y el sindicalismo*. Schifter says: "Romualdi was, apparently, more interested in the creation of non-communist unions in Central America than in the strengthening of those belonging to Rerum Novarum. . . . Proof of this was the delivery of 'documents' which proved 'the existence in Latin America of Unions which are influenced by Moscow,' " which Romualdi sent to the State Department. *Diario de Costa Rica*, 25 September 1946, *Alianzas conflictivas*, p. 203. In *Costa Rica 1948*, p. 125, this paragraph was eliminated.

The majority of the labour organizations in Latin America (70%, 80%, 90%?) are affiliated directly with the CTAL. . . . Even for simple political reasons, above all at the present time, nearly all the governments of Latin America seem to distrust the CTAL and even fear it, and therefore a Confederation of Workers of non-Marxist inspiration and philosophy, that is, *not oriented towards Moscow,* ought to deserve their wholehearted sympathy.[21]

For tactical reasons, in the judgement of Sanabria (Núñez), who had initially left in the document the possibility of a strictly confessional union organization, the best thing was for the projected regional organization not to be solely Catholic, but to include neutral organizations.

In fact, in Latin America only two solutions to the social question present themselves, the sponsorship of CTAL, that is, the Marxist solution, and what is called the democratic solution, which at bottom is, with slight variations, the Catholic solution.[22]

Later, Núñez explained as follows:

I began to be interested in the existence of a continental union organization that, even if not inspired by social-Christian doctrine, would offer room for a worker's movement of this inspiration. *As early as 1944 I participated in talks which took place in Philadelphia between Latin American union leaders to explore the possibility of building a continental confederation that would be an alternative to and competition for the CTAL.* In April 1946 these plans, through talks held in Mexico, began to acquire major potential and finally they were crystallized at the meeting in Montevideo in October 1946. A Worker's Congress was convoked in Lima on January 1948. Rerum Novarum was represented by Luis Alberto Monge and Claudio González.[23]

By the beginning of 1948, the eve of the Civil War, the separation between Rerum and the Catholic church, or more precisely its spiritual and hierarchical leader Monsignor Sanabria, was irreversible.

The middle-class members of the business oriented Centro para el Estudio de los Problemas Nacionales, founded in 1940, moved in the opposite direction from the Catholic church – into a political alliance with the traditional oligarchy whose displacement was essential to opening up a field for their own historical project. While Sanabria's purpose was es-

---

21 Memorandum ("Acerca de la necesidad y posibilidad de establecer una Confederación de Trabajadores de la América Latina diversa a la CTAL") of 10 August 1946, sent to the Holy See by the Apostolic Nuncio Monsignor Luis Cantoz. Appendix to the typewritten document of Father Benjamín Núñez in his defense, "Informe sobre las relaciones entre el movimiento obrero católico costarricense y la Autoridad Eclesiástica," New York, 15 January 1956. Italics added.

22 Ibid.

23 Benjamín Núñez, "Un ensayo de aplicación de la Doctrina Social de la Iglesia," *Senderos* 4 (January– April 1981): 28. It was in Lima that the Confederación Interamericana de Trabajo (CIT), later affiliated with the International Confederation of Free Trade Unions (ICFTU), was formed.

sentially spiritual preservation in the face of Marxist atheism, a sort of ideological vaccine, the Centro had a genuine long-range strategy for the restructuring of the state, modernization, and the creation of a modern, democratic society and polity.[24]

In many ways this project brought the young intellectuals gathered in the Centro and their leader, José Figueres, then a member of Acción Demócrata (AD), close to the positions adopted by the PCCR. This was particularly true of their antiimperialist views, their nationalizing tendencies, and their critiques of traditional liberalism and the landowning oligarchy. In a word, they approached the first part of the *aprista* program of Víctor Raúl Haya de la Torre. However, the social origin of its leaders, their cultural background, their essential acceptance of the democratic, liberal heritage with respect to individual liberties, their ultimate vocation for a private business sphere and opposition to overnationalization, their style and temperament, their suspicions about the historical experience of the Soviet Union, their repugnance for Stalinist ritual and apologies, and their attraction to English and North American democracy, put the Centro on a different track from the Communists, which intersected here and there but parted on fundamental issues, methods, and procedures.

U.S. perceptions of the movement led by José Figueres were as much affected by its international as by its domestic commitments. Expelled by Calderón Guardias's government in 1942, Figueres went to Mexico where he cemented relations with other Latin American exiles. By 1943 he had begun to plan the formation of a multinational group of revolutionaries to overthrow the dictatorships in the region. (This was later formalized, under the auspices of the Guatemalan President Juan José Arévalo, in the so-called Caribbean Pact of December 1947.) The primary objective consisted of carrying out "redemptive missions" to topple the dictatorships of Anastasio Somoza in Nicaragua, Rafael Leonidas Trujillo in the Dominican Republic, and, less convincingly, Calderón and Picado in Costa Rica, and to achieve the immediate establishment of a united, democratic Central American Republic.[25] These commitments and the political implications of the revolutionary rise to power of a petty bourgeois intellectual of antiimperialist inclinations, along with the fact that the chain of conspiracy was directed against the Caribbean dictatorships that had come to power through U.S. intervention and were backed by the United States, placed Figueres and his plan directly at odds with the regional interests and objectives of the United States. To confront Somoza

---

24 See Susanne Bodenheimer, *The Social Democratic Ideology in Latin America: The Case of Costa Rica's Partido Liberación Nacional* (Rio Piedras, Puerto Rico, 1970).

25 Aguilar Bulgarelli, *Costa Rica y sus hechos políticos*, pp. 306–12. The whole text of the Caribbean Pact is reproduced here.

or to conspire against Trujillo would lead to a direct conflict with U.S. policy in the entire Caribbean Basin.

Another important reason to distrust the Caribbean Pact and its purposes was the economic nationalism that the conspirators shared. As Figueres said in a private letter to the Nicaraguan Edelberto Torres Rivas in May 1948:

It is necessary to destroy the capitalist in order to destroy the reactionary. Our first great battle must consist of the liquidation of the capitalist forces in Central America, since these are the enemies of the Central American Union and have been what props up all the dictatorships. . . . I have no objections to Marxist philosophy, not even those of a spiritual order which have made you reject it, but I do not commit the stupidities of Manuel Mora and face the Yankees and capitalism head-on. I will achieve more radical economic reforms than Mora and all his Party, and I will win more battles against Yankee imperialism in a shorter time than those people have achieved in twenty years, simply on the question of tactics. As Father Núñez puts it so well, "man fears words": I will make friends with the capitalists and the Yankee State Department and win the battle from inside, and I don't care what label I have to wear as I gain their confidence. Once they trust me, then I'll know what to do. . . . Another error you make, a reflection of your generally too frank attitude, is to let your countrymen know your program and general ideology. You ought to use any politician who is useful to you, without telling them your true purpose until after the victory. . . . I not only sympathize with the ideology you support but I am infinitely more radical than you, who consider yourselves so advanced.[26]

It is understandable, then, that the U.S. government viewed Figueres and his commitments with considerable distrust and perceived his intentions and orientation as clearly to the extreme Left. Accusations that Figueres was a Communist arose from, among other things, his antioligarchical and antiimperialist language. But in reality there is not, and never was, any room for confusion. Neither the influence of revolutionary *aprismo* nor the moderate socialist tenor of English laborism provided a basis for such mystifications. The essence was always populist, as the base of a discourse for gaining power, and the construction, from there, was of a capitalist model with a nationalist, distributive, modernizing, and development-oriented substructure. The ideological opposition between the Communist movement and the Centro para el Estudio de los Problemas Nacionales lay at the very roots of their propositions, and the hegemony of one or the other was the central issue, historically, in the violent confrontations of the forties.

Two different historical projects confronted each other electorally, through more powerful allies, at the start of the tragic year 1948. On

26 Argüello, *Quiénes y cómo nos traicionaron*, pp. 126–30; and Aguilar Bulgarelli, *Costa Rica y sus hechos políticos*, pp. 405–12, which reproduces the whole document.

one side was the governing National Republican Party whose candidate in the February elections was ex-President Calderón Guardia, the electoral caudillo seeking a return to office and the consolidation of the social gains of the 1940s. Its electoral strength came from the PVP and its workers' confederation, the CTCR, whose perspective leaned toward a profound transformation of the entire Costa Rican social and political system. On the other side, in opposition to the government and its Communist allies, stood the candidate of the coffee oligarchy, Otilio Ulate, raising the specter of the past by looking for the already impossible historical recovery of the traditional ruling class, whose decline had begun with the reforms promoted by Ricardo Jiménez as long ago as 1901.[27] In 1948 this group lacked the necessary global vision and modern perspective on development for Costa Rican society in the postwar period.

Costa Rica, however, was suffering from birth pangs. Within the opposition, waving the flag of democracy and capitalist modernization, opposed to the traditional coffee oligarchy out of historical necessity, and against *calderonismo* and communism for both ideological and opportunist reasons, was the group led by Figueres, the Centro para el Estudio de los Problemas Nacionales (now called the Partido Social Demócrata (PSD). This would have its baptism of fire in the Civil War of March–April 1948, and emerge victorious, subsequently giving birth to the Partido de Liberación Nacional (PLN). The old coffee oligarchy did not understand that behind what became the PLN there was more than just a group of youths with political and electoral aspirations; a historic project was in progress, the culmination of the long process of decline of their class. Lacking ideas in tune with the times, the traditional ruling class dedicated itself to the task of preservation, but they did so while leaving, in spite of themselves, room for the new arrivals. And the groups that eventually formed the PLN brought forward proposals that corresponded in significant measure with the aspirations of the great majority of the Costa Rican people.

In the run up to the February 1948 elections, the political climate in Costa Rica grew increasingly tense. Claiming government partiality in the electoral campaign, the opposition (which included Núñez and Rerum Novarum despite declarations of neutrality)[28] led a general strike between 23 July and 3 August 1947 with demands for electoral guarantees. When

---

27 See Samuel Stone, *La dinastía de los conquistadores: La crisis del poder en la Costa Rica contemporánea*, 3d ed. (San José, 1982).

28 Sanabria was opposed to this demonstration of strength (which replaced one not held on 1 May) because of the possibility of violence since the CTCR had called a counterdemonstration. Núñez insisted, however, threatening to leave the country if he was not allowed to participate. Núñez, "Informe sobre las relaciones," pp. 36–42. See also Aguilar Bulgarelli, *Costa Rica y sus hechos políticos*, pp. 201ff; Backer, *La iglesia y el sindicalismo*, p. 146.

the elections finally took place, it appeared that Ulate had won the presidency (and was declared the winner by a majority of the Electoral Tribune). But on 1 March, the Congress, voting strictly along party lines, annulled the results of the presidential election. Sporadic violence followed, and on 12 March, with the Proclamation of Santa María de Dota, José Figueres initiated a military revolt against the government. In the civil war that followed, the militias of the PVP provided the government's principal shock troops. Many of the leaders and members of Rerum Novarum joined the rebels; Father Núñez, in fact, became Chaplain of the Revolutionary Army.[29]

The complexity of domestic alignments in the Civil War of 1948 was exacerbated by the incursion of troops from Somoza's Nicaragua on the side of the *calderonistas* (although no Nicaraguan troops were ever engaged), and the threat that the conflict could spill over into other Central American countries. The fighting came to an end with a cease-fire at Ochomogo and a series of agreements (including safeguards for the PVP) under the so-called Pact of the Mexican Embassy (at the signing of which Núñez appeared alongside Figueres) on 18 April. The government of Teodoro Picado was overthrown. First a figurehead president, León Herrera, and then a Junta of the Second Republic, presided over by Figueres on behalf of the entrepreneur-politicians[30] of the newly formed PLN, took power with the support of Ulate and the Conservatives. On entering San José, Figueres had declared that he was not prepared to hand over power to "decadent and traditional politicians who oppose[d] social progress."[31] Following the drafting of a new constitution, elections were held in

---

29 Backer, *La iglesia y el sindicalismo*, p. 151–2; Aguilar Bulgarelli, *Costa Rica y sus hechos políticos*, pp. 360ff.

30 The label "entrepreneur-politicians" has been introduced here to refer to the first generation of the PLN, made up of middle business sectors who needed state support for the development of their private business interests. This was the source of their need to participate in politics, both to obtain and maintain state support and nationalized banking, and to modernize state structure in light of their new business needs, which were different from those of the traditional coffee oligarchy. This first generation is clearly distinguished from the second, the "politician-entrepreneurs," or bureaucratic bourgeoisie, which was composed of middle and lower middle sectors whose social advancement depended on their insertion into the public apparatus of government. Essentially bureaucrats and politicians, they involved the state in the field of business, broadening not only their own base of support and their own economic territory, but also deriving authentic privileges dependent on the jobs they carried out, without passing up ample opportunities for personal, private enrichment as a side effect of their influence and participation in public functioning. (See Rodolfo Cerdas, *La crisis de la democracia liberal en Costa Rica* (San José, 1972. (2nd edition, 1975); "Del estado intervencionista al estado empresario," *Anuario de Estudios Centroamericanos* 5 (1979): 81–97; "Costa Rica: Problemas actuales de una revolución democrática," *Democracia en Costa Rica* (1981); "La crisis política nacional: Origen y perspectivas," *La Crisis de la Democracia en Costa Rica* (1981): San José, 1991.

31 Schifter, *La fase oculta de la guerra civil* pp. 111–12; Acuña, *El 48*, p. 352.

December 1949. Ulate finally became president – but without real power. He was succeeded by Figueres in 1953.

The polarization of domestic politics in Costa Rica, manifested, in particular, by mounting anticommunism and culminating in civil war, had been reinforced by the international climate as the Cold War gathered momentum. By October 1947, a little before leaving for his next appointment, U.S. Ambassador Walter J. Donnelly had begun to modify his positive opinions about the Picado government and its Communist allies. He described the PVP as a party "not friendly to the United States," and declared that Manuel Mora, its president, "would not decidedly support the government in aligning itself with the United States" in the event of a war between the United States and Russia.[32] A new chapter then opened in the relations between the U.S. government and the Picado government in Costa Rica with the arrival of Ambassador Nathaniel Davis, who came to San José from the U.S. embassy in Moscow and was considered an expert on communism. Davis had a tendency to rushed and definite judgments and he was easily captivated by analogies between what was happening in Costa Rica and other international events. In addition to his authoritarian tendencies and contempt for Costa Rican politics, the new ambassador adopted an energetically anti-Communist posture, hostile to the Picado government and favorable to the opposition.

The U.S. attitude toward the conflict that erupted in civil war in March 1948 can be clearly defined by one central consideration: it was necessary to liquidate Communist influence in the government, communism being understood to mean all the political and social organizations directed by the PVP. Ambassador Davis was clearly sympathetic to Ulate, and against Calderón, primarily because this was the best way to keep out the Communists. Thus, in a note sent to the Secretary of State on 22 March 1948, ten days after Figueres's military revolt, Davis wrote:

The most favorable solution, obviously, from our point of view, would be a constitutional succession acceptable to the majority of the people that *would include the elimination of the communist influence in the government* and the suppression of all the private armies. The election of Ulate was a big step towards this goal, which [was] reversed by the annulment of the elections. To do it by force of arms would not serve our interests . . . recourse to such action could have negative effects inside and outside Costa Rica. On the other hand a military victory for the government, followed by the election of a first choice unacceptable to the opposition – Dr. Calderón in the extreme case – might possibly result in an increase in communist power, which is not to our advantage.[33]

32  Schifter, *Alianzas conflictivas*, pp. 225–6, citing NA, CR, Memorandum of conversation by Tapley Bennet, Jr., 30 September 1947, 818.00/10–947.
33  Ibid., p. 255. Italics added.

This same attitude was further promoted in a report by William Tapley Bennet, Jr., of the Division of Central American and Panamanian Affairs, sent to the State Department on 26 March 1948, in the middle of the Civil War. After commenting on the exaggerated influence of communism in the country, its infiltration into the administration, and its military strength, he concluded by making a comparison between the situation in Costa Rica and the situation prevailing in Eastern Europe.

The Embassy considers that the situation of uncertainty and insecurity currently existing in Costa Rica is similar in many ways to the situation that exists in Eastern Europe. Although this assessment may be exaggerated, perhaps it is worth remembering that Haya de la Torre of Peru, in a recent declaration to United Press, described Costa Rica as "the Czechoslovakia of the Western Hemisphere."[34]

The Ninth Conference of American States opened in Bogotá on 30 March. At that meeting, the U.S. government demonstrated its preoccupation with the rise of Marxism on the continent, and declared that it "could be forced into taking action the moment Communist activities endangered Latin American security or solidarity." Under U.S. pressure, a resolution was approved at the Conference that gave the following warning: "Due to its antidemocratic nature and its tendency towards interventionism, the political activity of International Communism is incompatible with the American concept of freedom." Consequently, the resolution resolved "to condemn the methods of any system which tends to suppress civil rights and liberties, and, in particular, those of international communism or any other authoritarian doctrine." The United States, then, officially inaugurated the Cold War in Latin America and put its new policy into practice in Costa Rica.[35]

At the same time, the U.S. Embassy was aware that the military action initiated by Figueres in Costa Rica was related to a major commitment resulting from the Caribbean Pact. This pitted Guatemala, which stood behind Figueres, against Nicaragua, which backed Picado and Calderón. Figueres, in turn, was allied with the conservative and antireformist capitalist sector of Costa Rica; Picado was a loyal ally of the Communists, who were, in turn, hated by Somoza. The Embassy feared that soon Honduras and Panama would take part, since it was obvious that Figueres's commitments would not stop in Nicaragua and would, at the first opportunity, extend to Honduras against the regime of Tiburcio Carías. The pursuit of Central American unity by Arévalo in Guatemala was, more-

34 *Foreign Relations of the United States: The Western Hemisphere, 1948*, vol. 9, (Washington, D.C., 1972), p. 503.

35 Schifter, *Alianzas conflictivas*, pp. 255–6, citing *Foreign Relations of the United States*, vol. 1 (Washington, D.C., 1948), p. 195. Quotation marks indicate quotes from the original.

over, a continuation of that country's quest for hegemony, independent of the ideological stamp of its government. It had functioned during the dictatorship of Jorge Ubico and now functioned under the progressive government of Arévalo. Somoza, suspicious of Guatemala, but above all of the Caribbean Pact, once again pitted himself against that country while supporting a government allied with the Communists that had embarked on a social reform inconceivable in Nicaragua. This made the alliances functioning at the time doubly contradictory, both within each alliance, for domestic reasons, and between each alliance, for reasons of regional politics.

First the North Americans tried, together with Somoza, to pursue a policy that would permit the liquidation of their two adversaries at a single blow: to strengthen Picado against Figueres by supplying the government of Costa Rica with arms, but making this aid contingent on the elimination of the Communist influence in the country. On 22 March, Picado was received in Nicaragua by Somoza and the U.S. chargé d'affaires, who offered their aid to the government of Costa Rica. The formula for obtaining it was as follows:

Vicente Urcuyo, Costa Rica's ambassador to Nicaragua, would sign a document in which our government asked for aid from Nicaragua *to get rid of communism and Figueres in Costa Rica*. When this petition was received, arms and men (possibly the National Guard) would be sent immediately to exterminate these two groups. . . . Picado rejected the proposition. . . . [It] meant the preservation of his and Calderón's government, but the price was too high: foreign intervention, the even more fearsome unleashing of passions, and a much more costly struggle in terms of the lives of his citizens. But beyond that it was also the betrayal of the Communist group which had given him their support in the electoral struggle, in the government and in times of trouble. Teodoro preferred to lose the presidency rather than lose the country and blemish his name with a betrayal.[36]

The United States then systematically blocked every possibility that the government of Costa Rica might acquire arms, although the Guatemalan government was supplying arms to Figueres. The aid obtained by Picado's government in Mexico, through relations with Vicente Lombardo Toledano, was delayed until the eleventh hour, and neither the government nor the forces supporting it could count on it or on any other war material to defeat the insurrection. After a conversation with the President on 6 April, Ambassador Davis reported: "I consider, after analyzing Picado's words, that the government's situation is desperate unless they can manage to get supplies from outside. The government has no other recourse but to fight to the finish with armaments inferior to those

---

36 Aguilar Bulgarelli, *Costa Rica y sus hechos políticos*, pp. 337–8. Italics added.

Figueres has obtained from abroad."[37] The objective sought was clear enough: to force the government into a negotiation with the opposition and isolate both the PVP and Figueres. These latter two, although for different reasons, constituted a threat to the interests of the United States in Central America and the political stability of established governments in the region.

At the same time, the State Department put pressure on Somoza over Nicaraguan policy toward Costa Rica. The United States had to rely on him in order to fulfill their political objectives there. Somoza, therefore, capitalized on this to further his own ends vis-á-vis both the Communist threat and the threat of Figueres and the Caribbean Pact. The United States had been putting pressure on Somoza to step down from power and permit the establishment of a democratic political system. Somoza had been resisting this and had only agreed to step down in favor of his uncle, who the United States refused to recognize. The change of U.S. policy toward Nicaragua and the recognition of Víctor Román y Reyes, Somoza's uncle, as puppet president signified a triumph for the dictator and a clear warning to Figueres to restrain his impulse to keep his promises to the Caribbean Pact.

Both the intervention by Somoza at the end of the Civil War and the events that culminated in the Pact of the Mexican Embassy, which put an end to the conflict, evidenced a policy of growing coordination between the State Department and the dictatorial regime in Nicaragua. Thanks to U.S. pressure, Somoza's troops had to retreat from Costa Rican territory, but this was also a catalyst for the ultimate political compromise, which was marked by eloquent threats of direct U.S. intervention. By then, however, the Picado government was practically overthrown, and the search for a political solution had given rise to a negotiation in which the government surrendered. This provided Figueres with political space, something the U.S. government had not counted on, and it complicated, from the regional angle, the consequences of the insurrectionary victory against the Costa Rican government.

Under these conditions, Figueres was forced to break the promises and accords he had made with his adversaries, especially the Communists. The subsequent persecution of the latter was not only a manifestation of the political passions of the moment, but the expression of policies that sought to convey assurances and expressions of loyalty to the United States, which suspected the true intentions of Figueres once he was in power. Nevertheless, the main concern of the United States was not Figueres's

---

37 Schifter, *Alianzas conflictivas,* p. 262, quoting NA, CR, Davis to Secretary of State, 6 April 1948, 818.00/4–648.

triumph, which was now seen as a convenient way out of the situation, but rather the possibility that the Communists, who controlled airports, railroad stations, and the capital city, could even now seize the government. Both Davis and other Americans linked to U.S. business in Costa Rica feared a denouement of this kind. This undoubtedly accelerated Picado's fall and the rise of Figueres's power.

On the 17 July 1948, in flagrant violation of the promises made at the Mexican Embassy only three months earlier,[38] the government's Junta issued Decree 105, which declared communism illegal and its organizations dissolved, regardless of the name they adopted. Later, the measure acquired constitutional sanction, introduced by a majority vote in the Constitutional Assembly (Article 98, paragraph 2), which prohibited "the organization and functioning of parties which, through their methods of action, ideological programs and international links, threaten the sovereignty of Costa Rica." This was followed by decrees that empowered employers to dismiss workers affiliated with the PVP without the compensation legally stipulated by the Labor Code, which was consequently repealed.

On 8 June 1949, Father Núñez, who had been appointed Labor Minister, began a procedure in the labor court to dissolve the CTCR.[39] The confederation's legal defense managed to delay the process, overturning the court's verdict before the Court of Appeals. The latter, in spite of government pressure, continued its efforts to retain due process of law in the country. The procedures followed by Núñez clearly responded to a question of form, with which he hoped to cover up the singular phenomenon of a union leader persecuting and dismantling a

---

38 The publication in 1987 of Figueres's memoirs, *El espíritu del 48,* edited with the help of Núñez, rekindled the debate about the Mexican Embassy pact of 18 April 1948. Figueres entitles the relevant chapter (p. 275ff) "A Letter That Did Not Exist" and reproduces in full a letter by Núñez himself explaining what occurred. According to this version, the list of promises he gave to Manuel Mora, the Communist leader, was drawn up by Mora himself, not Núñez; he (Núñez) never had any intention of fulfilling any part of the pact and Mora expressly knew it, but he (Mora) needed the document to convince the party members to surrender their arms. For this reason, Núñez limited himself to printing his name, but not writing his signature, on the document. Mora, of course, alleged exactly the opposite. But with the party divided, he found that among the leaders of other Communist factions there were some, like Arnaldo Ferreto, who accepted Núñez's claims. Mora and Ferreto debated the theme in the newspapers of their respective parties, *Libertad* and *Libertad Revolucionaria. Libertad,* 5–11 December and 12–18 December 1986, 30 January–5 February and 27 February–6 March 1987; *Libertad Revolucionaria,* 28 November–4 December; 5–11 December, 1986, 23–29 January, 30 January–5 February, 13–19 February, 20–6 February, 27 February–5 March, 1987; see also *La Nación,* 22 January 1987.

39 Backer, *La iglesia y el sindicalismo,* pp. 156–7.

union confederation for political reasons from his post in the Ministry
of Labor. The final agreement dissolving the CTCR was delayed only
until 9 September 1951.

The Junta actively pursued not only the dissolution of the CTCR but
of all the unions affiliated with it. When the workers tried to rebuild
their organizations, they were harassed, their meetings broken up, their
leaders arrested, their propaganda destroyed, and so forth; this was particularly true of the bakers', printers', and shoemakers' unions, which had
strong Communist traditions. In the Pacific banana zone, Núñez personally threatened the banana union members with violence when they held
the general strike of 1949. The most serious event, although not personally
attributable to Father Núñez, was the assassination of the principal peasant
and union leaders of the Workers' Federation of Limón.[40]

The repressive climate on the political and union scenes seriously ham-
pered the process of the recovery of the labor movement. Although it
might be supposed that the participation of Rerum's leaders in the Civil
War and the presence of Núñez in the Ministry of Labor would contribute
to the strengthening and development of at least the anti-Communist
unions, what happened was the reverse. In spite of having no competition
and being linked to high-ranking government officials, Rerum Novarum
practically disappeared in the years following the armed conflict of 1948.
Most of its leadership, above all, Father Núñez, came to form part of
what would be the National Liberation Party, leaving secondary leaders
in the union field who were incapable of stemming the decline in discipline
and cohesion that characterized the confederation, whose activities were
now subordinated to the electoral interests of the new party.[41]

The internal crisis suffered by Rerum Novarum was accompanied by
an ideological division motivated by the influence that the labor attachés
of the Argentine Embassy had gained over some of its leaders. An important group wanted to follow a Peronist line and affiliate themselves
with the Agrupación de Trabajadores Latinoamericanos Sindicalistas (AT-
LAS) and not the Confederación Interamericana de Trabajo (CIT). The
Peronist group was expelled at Rerum's 1950 Congress, taking with it
more than 1,500 union members who then established the Confederación
Nacional de Trabajadores (CNT). This new confederation, however, did
not survive the fall of Perón in 1955 and the subsequent loss of financial
and political support. Núñez, for his part, maintained at all times an
active militant stance against the Peronists and their organization.

Relations between Rerum and the church during this period did not

---

40 Backer, *La iglesia y el sindicalismo,* p. 157. See also Bell, *Guerra civil en Costa Rica,* and Rojas,
   *Lucha social y guerra civil.*
41 Backer, *La iglesia y el sindicalismo,* pp. 158, 160.

improve. In June and July 1948, with Father Núñez already Labor Minister, friction actually increased over a suspension of construction works by the Metropolitan Curia, which gave rise to a conflict between the union, affiliated with Rerum, and Archbishop Sanabria, who was directly affected as a representative of the organization. The situation worsened for political reasons, given Sanabria's resistence to going along with the policy of labor repression. Monsignor Alfredo Hidalgo, Vicar General of San José, delivered a speech on 16 January 1949, in which he clearly denounced the persecution loosed against the losers of the Civil War. He announced that there would not be peace and tranquility in the country until "the pact signed by the combatants before the Diplomatic Corps on Ochomogo Hill" was honored.[42] Relations became progressively cooler and the separation wider, if that was possible, between Rerum Novarum and the church hierarchy. Rerum Novarum finally terminated its relationship with Sanabria, who had functioned equally as a source of ideological and Catholic doctrinal inspiration and as a brake on anticommunism, which, in the end, got out of control not least because of the confederation's links with the United States and the onset of the Cold War.

The defeat in the Civil War of 1948 was a devastating blow to the PVP and left Costa Rica practically without an organized labor movement. Rerum Novarum could not capitalize on the rise of Father Núñez to the Ministry of Labor, nor even on the dissolution and persecution of its rival, the CTCR. An atmosphere of visceral anticommunism immobilized the workers, and the international climate of the Cold War strengthened this tendency day by day. The process of recovery was very slow, not only because of the imprisonment and physical elimination of labor leaders, but also because of the death of Archbishop Sanabria and his replacement by the anti-Marxist Monsignor Rubén Odio. The entire Costa Rican labor movement lay prostrate for several decades. Between 1948 and 1951, the Communist Party, the PVP, its workers' movement, the CTCR, and the independent union confederation, the Rerum Novarum, had all been virtually eliminated in Costa Rica. This represented the first victory of the Cold War in Central America.

42 Ibid., p. 161.

# 11

## Guatemala

*James Dunkerley*

The experience of Guatemala during the decade following the Second World War was exceptional within Latin America. As in most of Central America, an antidictatorial movement strongly influenced by the war took root in 1944. However, in contrast to all of the countries of the isthmus (except Costa Rica), this movement succeeded not only in overthrowing a dictatorship established in the wake of the Depression – that of General Jorge Ubico (1931–44) – but also in resisting the ensuing right-wing backlash. Then, in contrast to the general trends in Latin America as a whole (except Argentina), the regimes of Juan José Arévalo (1945–51) and Jacobo Arbenz (1951–4) for almost a decade pursued policies of progressive socioeconomic reform, accepted and sometimes encouraged the spread of unionization, and fostered a nationalist sentiment that increased pressure on foreign enterprise and tension with the United States. In contrast to the Peronist experience in Argentina, the Guatemalan governments desisted from taking a resolutely anti-Communist line and came to rely on the support of independent radical forces in the labor movement. As a result, the Arbenz regime was eventually overthrown, in perhaps the most open and emphatic example of U.S. Cold War interventionism to be seen in Latin America, when the CIA organized a counterrevolutionary invasion from Honduras in June 1954.

The counterrevolution, or "liberation," of 1954 may be seen as marking Guatemala's overdue reversion to the pattern of regional politics, although it was precisely by virtue of the long delay that the reactionary backlash was so singular in its degree of public and covert U.S. backing, and in its consolidation of an anti-Communist political culture that subsequently impeded even the most modest reforms for over three decades. Indeed, the differences in both local and international conditions between 1954 and 1945–8 – the context for the "Cold War resolution" almost everywhere else – greatly reduce the usefulness of direct comparison between the experience of Guatemala and that of much of the rest of Latin America.

At the same time, a detailed study of Guatemala that restricted itself to the immediate postwar years would yield a distinctly partial history and exclude many developments – the right-wing coup attempt of 1949, the agrarian reform, and the formal establishment of a national Communist Party in the shape of the Partido Guatemalteco del Trabajo (PGT) in 1952 – integral to the character of the reformist regime and to Washington's decision to eradicate it. The question to be addressed is, therefore, why it was that Guatemala took the better part of a decade to conform to regional type.[1]

The political liberalization opened by the revolution of October 1944 and the project of socioeconomic reform that emerged with increasing strength from 1947 can only be understood in the light of the national experience over preceding decades, in particular the 1930s. With the exception of Costa Rica, autocratic government based on the military prevailed throughout Central America during the years of the Depression. However, this was an essentially new form of regime for the region. Only in Guatemala had it been the established type of government since the early republic. Partly as a result of this, Ubico possessed greater autonomy from the landlord class than did most of his peers, even Somoza, whose fortune and power were consolidated in the 1940s. Equally, the presence of large U.S. companies controlling a strategically vital banana enclave was unexceptional in regional terms. Yet nowhere else was the enclave both controlled by a single enterprise, the United Fruit Company (UFCO), and inserted into a buoyant coffee economy over which it could exercise considerable influence by virtue of an effective monopoly of rail transport.[2] Hence, although in 1929 coffee accounted for 77 percent of the export

---

1 This approach, of course, reverses that normally taken with respect to postwar Guatemala, namely, how and why did Washington overthrow the Arbenz regime? Studies of the 1954 intervention and its immediate background are now sufficiently detailed to render a further account unnecessary. The standard contemporary account, written from an unbending anti-Communist position, is Ronald M. Schneider, *Communism in Guatemala* (New York, 1958). For a more moderate and critical appraisal, see Richard H. Immerman, "Guatemala as Cold War History," *Political Science Quarterly* 95 (1980–1981): 629–53, and *The CIA in Guatemala: The Foreign Policy of Intervention* (Austin, TX, 1982). A less scholarly if equally detailed study that attributes a much greater role to the United Fruit Company is provided in Stephen Schlesinger and Stephen Kinzer, *Bitter Fruit: The Untold Story of the American Coup in Guatemala* (London, 1982). José M. Aybar de Soto, *Dependency and Intervention: The Case of Guatemala in 1954* (Boulder, CO, 1978), adopts a rather more schematic perspective.

2 There was no banana enclave in El Salvador, where the coffee oligarchy was, if anything, stronger than that in Guatemala. The UFCO faced subordinate competition from Standard Fruit in Honduras, but that country continued to lack a significant dominant class based on export agriculture and only adopted coffee in the 1940s. Banana production was never established on a stable basis in Nicaragua, whereas in Costa Rica the UFCO possessed a monopoly of neither cultivation and export nor the railway network.

revenue and bananas only 13 percent, the profile of UFCO within the economy was particularly high and the object of discontent amongst an appreciable local bourgeoisie that was frequently prejudiced by the company's differential freight rates.[3]

These two long-term conditions — the strength of an autocratic government and the singularly contentious character of a foreign enterprise — were to have considerable resonance in the late 1940s. They provided exceptional potential for the expression of political democracy and nationalist sentiment across class lines, thereby delaying for a short but critical period the appearance of social conflict and ideological polarization. On the one hand, liberal constitutionalism enjoyed unusual resilience due to the strength of antidictatorial feeling and the weakness of independent political traditions and organization on both the Right and the Left. On the other, core economic reforms were slow to generate major confrontation because they affected UFCO's interests more sharply than those of local capital. In a sense, then, it could be said of the postwar reformist experience in Guatemala that it initially derived strength from the very weakness of domestic political forces, and that it ultimately proved vulnerable precisely by virtue of the strength with which foreign interests were confronted. The fact that the project of democratic reform was defeated primarily by external forces undoubtedly corresponds to Washington's local and international requirements in the early 1950s, but should also be seen in the context of long-term domestic developments.

Ubico was the heir to a formidable local tradition of personalist and autocratic government that began during the conservative epoch under Rafael Carrera (1838–65) and continued into the liberal, free-trade era with the regimes of Justo Rufino Barrios (1871–85) and Manuel Estrada Cabrera (1898–1920). To some degree this proclivity for dictatorship derived from the fact that under the Spanish, Guatemala City had been the center of colonial administration of the isthmus, the local elite being accustomed to dominating the rest of the Captaincy General and possessing an armed force sufficient for this objective, which continued well into the republic. However, coercive government corresponded in more direct terms to the fact that the country had a very large indigenous population — at least 65 percent of the population of 1.8 million in 1930, and an equal proportion of that of 2.4 million in 1945. This Indian population was split into some two dozen ethnic groups, but it possessed powerful communitarian traditions that always coexisted uneasily with — and sometimes openly challenged — the minority *ladino* population of all classes that upheld the Hispanic state. Following the expansion of coffee from

---

3 Victor Bulmer-Thomas, *The Political Economy of Central America since 1920* (Cambridge, 1987), pp. 37, 77.

the mid–1870s, both class and ethnic tension was abetted by the expropriation of communal lands in the foothills, and the need to supply the *fincas* with a seasonal labor force from the densely populated highlands. The provision of harvest labor was initially attempted through the application of the colonial mechanism of *mandamiento,* or direct obligation. Yet within a decade, the liberal state shifted to reliance on debt peonage, which operated through market forces, and it continued to depend on a powerful military force that monitored seasonal migration and pursued evaders under the direction of departmental *jefes políticos.*

In 1934, Ubico replaced debt peonage with a labor system based on a vagrancy law that made all landless and most subsistence peasants liable for plantation labor as well as unpaid work on roadbuilding, which was greatly accelerated during the 1930s.[4] This important organizational alteration was presented by Ubico as a major democratic advance, but it appears to have been onerous in economic terms for the rural poor. However, it did provide appreciable support for the *finqueros,* who were hit by the Depression and to whom Ubico refused to concede a devaluation, making only a modest overture in reducing export taxes. The authority of both the central state and Ubico himself may be seen in these measures, which were complemented by the abolition of traditional Indian municipal government (replaced by centrally appointed intendants) and all independent entrepreneurial associations, including the Chamber of Commerce.

Such suppression of the established vehicles for expression of two very different, but highly important, corporate interests was facilitated by the fact that the partial relaxation of political control and the economic buoyancy during the 1920s had failed to produce either a coherent system of oligarchic political parties, or a strong popular challenge. This is somewhat surprising since the overthrow of Estrada Cabrera in 1920 had been achieved with the subordinate, but significant, participation of the urban middle class and the poor, and the regimes of Generals Mariano Orellana and Lázaro Chacón had also permitted at least some competition and expression of opposition to the particularly leonine contract secured by the UFCO in 1927. It should, however, be noted that the racial question divided the popular movement not only between town and country, but also within the countryside; the newly organized banana labor force was small and isolated from the highland communities that comprised the majority of the rural population. Significantly, Guatemala alone in Central America lacked a Communist organization at the end of the 1920s, and its urban trade unions were exceptionally weak. Social mobilization in

4 Between 1932 and 1943 the country's roads were extended from 1,375 to 6,375 miles (Bulmer-Thomas, *Political Economy,* p. 71).

the wake of the 1929 Crash was more easily contained in Guatemala than in the rest of the isthmus.[5] Equally, the landlord-dominated bourgeois forces failed to remedy their longstanding lack of political organization, in part simply because the requirements of coercive control of both Indian and peasant had not diminished; in part because their economic vanguard lay in the very small community of German planters who accounted for over a third of coffee exports, but resisted real engagement in political life; and in part because the anti-Estrada Cabrera campaign had rapidly collapsed into conflict over the idea of Central American union, which had once been integral to the psyche of the dominant class, but was now rendered anachronistic by U.S. hegemony. Moreover, the antagonism caused by the UFCO was qualified by the absence of any real alternative to it, Washington's support for the company, and the fact that it had not yet secured complete control of, nor fully exploited the sole means of, bulk transport to the Atlantic on the line owned by International Railroads of Central America (IRCA). Finally, the Guatemalan elite remained traumatized by the experience of popular revolution in neighboring Mexico. Its fears of mass mobilization, political radicalization, and anticlericalism greatly diminished the desire to curb military authority or seek a political control based on a modicum of popular participation, like that visible for a while in the rest of Central America.

As a consequence, when Ubico was elected unopposed early in 1931, he was readily able to revive a longstanding dictatorial tradition rooted in a social system divided by race and an economy based largely on coerced labor. In the process, he curtailed the particularly insecure democratic and reformist tendencies that had emerged in the 1920s. Although his election to all intents and purposes constituted a coup, its formality facilitated full and comparatively easy relations with Washington from the start. Similarly, Ubico's support for the UFCO in the disputes of the late 1920s provided him with important company patronage and underpinned an unusually generous contract in 1936. Under this contract, the enterprise was relieved of its previous obligation to build a Pacific port

5 It is frequently asserted that a Communist Party was established in 1922 on the basis of the Unión Obrera Socialista [1921], but this organization never took root despite receiving informal Comintern recognition. In 1928 two militants of the Federación Regional Obrera de Guatemala (FROG) participated in the sixth Congress of the International, and in 1929 the FROG was recognized by the Red Trade Union International. Claims for the establishment of a Communist Party in 1929 are also made, but there is no evidence that this took organizational shape beyond informal meetings of FROG militants. The PGT recognizes its origins to go back no further than 1949. See Víctor Manuel Gutiérrez, *Breve historia del movimiento sindical de Guatemala* (Mexico, 1964); Huberto Alvarado Arellano, *Apuntes para la historia del Partido Guatemalteco del Trabajo* (Guatemala City, 1975). For the weakness of the labor movement at the end of the 1920s and in the early 1930s, see José Luis Balcarcel, "El movimiento obrero en Guatemala," vol. 2 of *Historia del movimiento obrero en América Latina,* ed. Pablo González Casanova (Mexico, 1985).

and was thus enabled to consolidate its control over IRCA and the influence it could weild through it.

Guatemala remained in political stasis throughout the thirteen years of *ubiquismo*. Opposition was rapidly eradicated; the Left through a spate of executions, expulsions, and imprisonments in the wake of the Salvadorean revolt of January 1932, and middle class dissidents by similar means, and on a rather larger scale, some two years later. Ubico subsequently experienced no difficulty in enforcing the prohibition of all independent political parties, trade unions, and civic bodies, and he suffered virtually no challenge from within the army even after the officer corps was expanded and a more modern institutional ethic engendered within it by the establishment of the Escuela Politécnica under a U.S. officer. True to the literary depiction of the Caribbean despots of this era, Ubico presided over all aspects of government with extraordinary zeal, employed a very small bureaucracy, a highly active secret police force, and enough eccentric behavior to instill unusual awe in both the oligarchy and the lower orders.[6] Like his peers in the neighboring states to the south, he never dispensed with the formal trappings of democratic procedure since his personal power ensured absolute compliance and rendered unnecessary any direct organizational emulation of the European fascist regimes that he greatly admired.

Such comprehensive domination by a single man (who, together with a clique of minions, inevitably drew maximum pecuniary advantage from his power) was not as extraordinary as it might appear; it took place in a very small country where the Depression had had a sharp impact on a backward economy, and in a society still regimented along nineteenth-century – and sometimes sixteenth-century – lines. In 1930 Guatemala's GDP was a mere $449 million and its GDP per capita $245; agriculture prevailed as the overwhelming source of export and tax revenue, the value added by a manufacturing sector dominated by artisanal workshops amounting to a mere $70 million.[7] Urban culture was limited to the capital, which had a population of only 150,000; the second town, Quezaltenango, had no more than 20,000 inhabitants. Moreover, once the immediate discontent caused by the economic crisis in 1930–2 had been suppressed, Ubico's rule was fortified by a slow but constant economic recovery – GDP per capita rose from $197 in 1932 to $392 by 1940 – in which nonexport agriculture proved to be especially buoyant. By the end of the decade, the staples of coffee and bananas were returning a

---

6 Ubico, a lover of motorcycles, was constantly on the move and would frequently make unannounced visits to the provinces. Although an amateur drummer and admirer of Napoleon, he was less eccentric than General Maximiliano Hernández Martínez in El Salvador.

7 Bulmer-Thomas, *Political Economy,* pp. 308, 312, 322.

reasonable profit and upholding a domestic budget only slightly lower
than that of the 1920s.[8] For the central forces in Guatemalan society –
the coffee *finqueros* and the peasantry (both Indian and *ladino*) – the Depression did not produce rupture so much as contraction, stasis, and then
measured recuperation. Manufacturing grew much more slowly from a
very low base, and the urban middle class was sharply affected by budget
reductions (some 50 percent between 1928 and 1932), reduced employment, and inflation. Of all the social sectors seeking political expression
in the 1920s, the *ladino* artisan class and the middle strata were most
directly prejudiced by Ubico's rise to power since they expected more
than the historically subordinate *campesinado,* and lost more than the
bourgeoisie.

In most respects, the impact of the Second World War in Guatemala
conformed to regional type. Neither in 1939 nor in 1942 did Ubico relax
or alter the internal regime, but he was obliged to adjust foreign policy
according to the needs of realpolitik rather than ideological enthusiasm
(he had recognized Franco at the earliest opportunity). War was declared
on the Axis in the wake of Pearl Harbor, bases were provided for U.S.
troops, and full collaboration was offered to Washington over the Inter-
American Highway (which bolstered Ubico's roadbuilding plans) and to
the UFCO over the cultivation of strategically important *abacá* (hemp).
The closely regulated and extraordinarily sycophantic press provided coverage of the conflict, but it clearly sought to reduce discussion of the
underlying ideological issues, with respect to which the oligarchy and the
Right had – for once – to embrace geographic fatalism. All the same,
the political cost of the war to the regime did not appear substantial until
the spring of 1944, before which there was no sign of reorganization
within the labor movement or middle class.

Equally, the broad economic impact of the war proved to be less
disastrous than at first feared once the Central American states were
allocated generous quotas under the Inter-American Coffee Agreement of
November 1940. In 1932, Guatemala had sold over 28 percent of its
coffee to Germany and had received 11 percent of its imports from Germany. However, the Nazi regime's shift to paying for such commodities
in Aski marks (which could only be exchanged at face value for German
goods) meant that from 1935 Guatemala sought alternative markets with
the result that although in 1939 27 percent of imports were derived from
Germany (largely by virtue of accumulated Aski mark credit), only 12
percent of coffee exports went to that country. Equally, since trade with
the UK in 1939 amounted to only 1.8 percent of exports and 2 percent
of imports, Guatemala was less severely hit than some other countries,

---

8 Ibid., pp. 81–2, 312.

such as Costa Rica, by the loss of this market. Unsurprisingly, the banana trade was most sharply affected by the outbreak of war, the volume of exports falling by some 40 percent in 1939–40, although UFCO continued to make profits and issue a dividend throughout the war. Against this, a strictly modest fall in the volume of coffee sales following the quota agreement (to an average of 99.6 million lbs. per annum in 1939–43, from 104.2 million lbs. in 1934–8) kept the overall level of export revenue somewhat above that of the second half of the 1930s (an average of $87.5 million a year in 1939–43 against $82.6 million in 1934–8). On the other hand, a sharp fall in imports fueled inflation because prices had been falling since 1937 (1937 = 100; 1939 = 93; 1941 = 81; 1943 = 122; 1945 = 174) and contributed to a significant diminution of GDP per capita, from $392 in 1940 to $249 in 1944. Import substitution industrialization was barely perceptible, the value added by manufacturing rising from $60 million in 1939 to only $70 million in 1944.[9] Under these conditions, the urban artisan class continued to experience a very gradual recovery from its poor position of a decade earlier, but mercantile interests and the salaried work force remained under acute pressure, the latter especially so.

Perhaps the single most critical effect of the war was on the important German community. By the end of the nineteenth century, immigrant planters had invested 200 million deutsche marks in the purchase of 300,000 hectares of prime coffee land, predominantly in the department of Alta Verapaz; at the outbreak of the First World War, their 170 estates accounted for 35.8 million lbs. of total coffee exports of 52.5 million.[10] During that conflict, Estrada Cabrera had placed restrictions on the Germans and their property, but strenuously resisted imposing the outright controls eventually demanded by Washington, rapidly devolving property that had been "intervened" after the armistice. Subjected at an earlier stage to greater pressure for the expropriation of all Axis-owned property on the "Proclaimed List" during the Second World War, Ubico had little choice but to acquiesce in the deportation of German nationals to the United States. Moreover, in 1941 the general did not resist the "intervention" (temporary state management) of what became known as *fincas nacionales* since these still amounted to over 300,000 hectares, accounted for at least a third of the national coffee crop, and defrayed between 10 and 15 percent of the national budget.[11] However, Ubico was intent at

9 Ibid., pp. 91–2, 350, 79, 93, 330, 95, 332, 322.

10 Ralph Lee Woodward, *Central America: A Nation Divided* (New York, 1976), p. 165; Julio Castellanos Cambranes, *Coffee and Peasants in Guatemala: The Origins of the Modern Plantation Economy in Guatemala, 1858–1897* (Stockholm, 1985), p. 145.

11 Mario Monteforte Toledo, *Guatemala: Monografía sociológica* (Mexico City, 1959), p. 429; Leo A. Suslow, *Aspects of Social Reform in Guatemala* (New York, 1950), p. 66.

all costs to avoid the outright nationalization of German property, a move that he viewed as "communistic." By early 1944, Cordell Hull was insisting that U.S. Ambassador Boaz Long push the dictator to take this step, threatening to reduce the country's coffee quota if it was further delayed. In the subsequent exchange, Long effectively defended Ubico's position, noting the importance of the properties to fiscal revenue (although this was not the major issue at stake) and the constitutional difficulties involved. Hull, however, remained insistent, and although in the wake of the Salvadorean revolt of April 1944 Long diligently reported Ubico's fears of the political dangers of full expropriation, the dictator was finally obliged to announce the nationalization just a few days before he was ousted from power at the end of June 1944.[12]

In itself the issue of the nationalization of German properties cannot be considered a central feature of the overthrow of the dictatorship, but it does appear to have stiffened the resolve of the State Department – and even of the ambassador – to maintain a strictly neutral stance in the final mobilization against Ubico.[13] The exchanges between Guatemala City and Washington did not receive great publicity, and for the bulk of the population the precise status of German property already managed by the state could not have excited the degree of interest already directed toward the achievement of civil liberties. On the other hand, it is distinctly worthy of note that because Ubico's short-lived heir, General Federico Ponce, ratified the expropriation, the Arévalo and Arbenz regimes inherited a large amount of land (with a labor force in excess of 20,000), which first provided important revenue and then – in addition to Ubico's own expropriated estates – enabled an agrarian reform to be realized without a major assault on locally owned private properties. Under Arbenz's reform law of June 1952, some 365,000 acres of the 920,000 acres expropriated over the next two years belonged to the *fincas nacionales*,

---

12 Hull to Long, United States National Archives (henceforth USNA), 740.00112A European War, 1939/36499a, 28 February 1944; Long to Washington, USNA, 740.00112A European War, 1939/36572, 18 April 1944; Long to Washington, USNA, 740.00112A European War, 1939/36610, 16 May 1944; Long to Washington, USNA, 740.14112A/89, 13 June 1944.

13 "A confidential American informant was sent to the Embassy this morning by a Cabinet Minister to report that a group of doctors and nurses are planning a sitdown strike along Salvadoran lines and to inquire whether American doctors and nurses could be counted on to handle emergency cases. I replied that this would constitute intervention in internal politics in violation of our well known policy" (Long to Washington, USNA, 814.00/1464, 21 June 1944). "The Department assumes that the 'good offices' referred to in your telegram . . . relate exclusively to the transmission of messages between the contending factions and do not involve the preparation and submission of formulas of settlement, etc." (Washington to Long, USNA, 814.00/1470, 21 June 1944. See also, Washington to Long, USNA, 814.00/7-744, 7 July 1944; Long to Washington, USNA, 814.00/7-1444, 14 July 1944).

whereas most of the remaining land belonged to UFCO, and only 3.9 percent of locally owned private land was affected.[14]

The transition from reactionary dictatorship to liberal constitutionalism took place over the last half of 1944. Continuous demonstrations in the capital in the final week of June forced Ubico to surrender office on 1 July. In October, a relatively bloodless coup led by junior officers overthrew the tyrant's chosen successor, General Ponce, and established a short-lived junta, which in December called the elections that were easily won by Arévalo. Given the complete absense of popular organization, political activity, and open military discontent over the previous ten years, this was an extraordinary turn of events. It was not, however, a period of constant mass mobilization or great ideological turmoil. The drumming of Ubico from office was almost exclusively a middle-class affair, lacking trade union support for the simple reason that there were no unions in existence until 3 July, when the teachers established a national association (to be rapidly followed by the railway workers, laborers on UFCO's Tiquisate plantation, and a welter of small artisanal bodies). Equally, it was the captains and majors who dispatched Ponce in October, and although the rebel officers did distribute arms to the students, there was minimal participation in the revolt by members of the new Confederación de Trabajadores de Guatemala (CTG), formed less than three weeks earlier. On neither occasion was there any organized left-wing presence, although a number of individuals later prominent in the Communist PGT – José Manuel Fortuny, Alfredo Guerra Borges, Carlos Pellecer – were to the fore in the antidictatorial campaign centered on the Universidad de San Carlos (USAC). The very smallness of USAC (less than 700 students) meant that these individuals were subsequently able to establish a personal as well as political identification with the constitutionalist movement – a matter repeatedly stressed (and often exaggerated) by State Department reports in the early 1950s: "Communist political success derives in general from the ability of individual Communists and fellow travellers to identify themselves with the nationalist and social aspirations of the Revolution of October 1944."[15]

Neither in June nor in October 1944 did the U.S. embassy take undue fright at events or note the presence of any dangerous radical elements beyond suggesting that Arévalo might be supported by leftists.[16] Indeed,

14 Long to Washington, USNA, 814.00/7–1444, 14 July 1944; Mario Monteforte Toledo, "La Reforma Agraria en Guatemala," *El Trimestre Económico* 19 (1952); Neale J. Pearson, "Guatemala: The Peasant Union Movement, 1944–1954" in *Latin American Peasant Movements*, ed. Henry A. Landsberger (Ithaca, NY, 1969), p. 343; Nathan L. Whetten, *Guatemala: The Land and the People* (New York, 1961), p. 163.

15 National Intelligence Estimate, USNA, 11 March 1952, UNA, NIE–62.

16 Long to Washington, USNA, 814.00/10–1344, 13 October 1944.

if in July Boaz Long proved to be somewhat misguided in his optimistic assessment of General Ponce's popularity ("the first ten days of the new Government augur well for the future"), the October coup's emphatic demonstration of his error did not dissuade Chargé William Affeld from cabling Washington within a week of the revolt to indicate that the junta represented "the establishment of democratic ideals and procedure."[17] Such a response is not surprising in view of the fact that three weeks earlier Long had received a letter from the acting director of the Office of American Republics, Norman Armour, in reply to his concerns about the burgeoning autocratic tendencies of Ponce's regime:

A number of us in the Department are deeply concerned at political developments in Guatemala and elsewhere in Latin America. The problem of support for democratic processes is not an easy one and was discussed at some length this morning. The idea was advanced that we might have President Roosevelt or the Secretary include in an early address a statement more or less along the following lines: "we wish to cultivate friendly relations with every government in the world and do not feel ourselves entitled to dictate to any country what form of government best suits its national aspirations. We nevertheless must feel a greater affinity, a deeper sympathy and a warmer friendship for governments which effectively represent the practical application of democratic processes."[18]

The effective adoption by the embassy in mid-October of this policy toward Ponce amounted to a distinct cold shoulder. However, there is no evidence to suggest that what was still a small and unimportant legation offered any encouragement to Majors Francisco Arana and Jacobo Arbenz to stage the coup of the 20th when the sensitivity of U.S. policy to such an event would be particularly high, especially in the wake of the confusing and bloody events in neighboring El Salvador.[19] It can be said with some confidence that during 1944 Washington stuck closely to protocol, which in practical terms meant leaving both Ubico and Ponce unprotected against the forces of democratic reform by more than formal recognition. At no subsequent point – even in the weeks prior to the June 1954 intervention – did the State Department stray from its view that the events of 1944

17 Long to Washington, USNA, 814.00/7–1444, 7 July 1944; Affeld to Washington, USNA, 814.01/10–2644, 26 October 1944.
18 Armour to Long, USNA, 814.00/9–2644, 3 Oct. 1944.
19 In April 1944, junior officers staged an abortive coup against General Hernández Martínez, the Salvadorean dictator, who subsequently shot the rebel ringleaders, causing such a popular outcry and loss of control that he was obliged to flee the country in early May. There then followed five months of popular mobilization in an election campaign, which was halted in a reactionary coup headed by Colonel Osmín Aguirre y Salinas on 21 October – one day after the Guatemalan revolt, the celebration of which in San Salvador was savagely repressed by Colonel Aguirre's troops.

were positive, progressive, and popular. In an interdepartmental memorandum of May 1950 it was noted that:

In 1944 one of the most ruthless of all Guatemalan dictatorships was overthrown by what amounted to a truly popular uprising supported by all segments of the population. Popular elections followed, and Juan José Arévalo, a liberal and progressive-minded ex-teacher, was elected President by an overwhelming popular vote. Shortly thereafter Guatemala embarked on a social, economic and political program which in general terms aimed at improving the standard of living of the masses, protecting them from the abuses of the old feudal system, and achieving freedom and democracy for the Guatemalan people. This program was at its outset commendable.[20]

At the end of 1944 it would not have required undue prescience to predict the "pro-labor attitude," "nationalist tendency," and "deep-seated mistrust" of UFCO that the document goes on to attack, but the events of that year offered few signals of future difficulties for Washington. The June campaign against Ubico had begun on a simple platform of autonomy for the USAC, and owed much to the example of the mobilization against General Maximiliano Martínez in El Salvador in April. Even when Ubico's police repressed the demonstrations and killed a teacher, the offensive remained within purely constitutionalist parameters and was conducted in an eminently civic manner. The UN charter was proclaimed to the masses and Ubico was subjected to a petition signed by 311 professionals who requested the application of the Four Freedoms on the grounds that, "Guatemala cannot remove itself from the democratic imperatives of the era. It is impossible to frustrate with coercive means the uncontainable impulses of that generous ideology which is being reaffirmed in the world's conscience by means of the bloodiest of struggles between oppression and liberty."[21]

Once Ubico was out and General Ponce installed, there was a discernable lull in political momentum, as if the urban populace was shocked by the relative ease of the operation. Ponce was sufficiently astute to convene elections for October and cancel the most draconian of the dictator's edicts. However, as soon as it became apparent that the general's intended *continuismo* stood in danger from the candidacy of Arévalo, a military leadership that had undergone few changes since Ubico's departure simply staged a fraud whereby Ponce won, in Affeld's words, "by a handsome, not to say fantastic margin, garnering 48,530 votes out of a total of

20 Memo by the Director of the Executive Secretariat, Under Secretary's Meetings, 29 May 1950, USNA, Under Secretary's Meetings, Lot 52 D 250.
21 Quoted in Manuel Galich, *Por qué lucha Guatemala: Arévalo y Arbenz: Dos hombres contra un imperio* (Buenos Aires, 1956), pp. 334–6.

44,571."[22] As has been seen, such a maneuver could no longer be guaranteed North American indulgence, and although popular opposition was temporarily cowed by the truckloads of Indians brought into the capital by Ponce, it was evident that *ubiquismo* without Ubico lacked any future. The constitutionalist agenda remained open, at a higher level of popular expectation, and beyond the point of repudiation of a specific individual. Moreover, between June and October the high command had failed to subborn the junior officers, who by dint of their position, pay, training, and family ties had been influenced by the democratic movement as well as fortified by the replacement of their longstanding *caudillo* by nondescript figures deprived of political skills because of his concentration of power. As a result, whereas elsewhere in Central America the army halted the constitutionalist tide, in Guatemala it acted to guarantee its success.

This close association of the officer corps with the establishment of democratic government was central to the capacity of the reformist regime to secure the general neutrality of the military over the following years. The army acquired uncommon popularity from its leadership of the October revolt, and despite receiving a reduced share of the (increased) budget under both Arévalo and Arbenz, it lost little influence in policy making compared to that held under the dictatorship, while it retained the bulk of its prior administrative powers, particularly in the provinces. No less importantly, it encountered very little antimilitarism from the Left.[23] Of course, the momentum provided by this unusual convergence in the antidictatorial movement was subsequently placed under considerable stress. From 1948 new arms supplies were withheld by Washington – a policy that, as military envoys continually pointed out, reduced both logistical capacity and institutional esteem.[24] Equally, the existence of

---

22 Affeld to Washington, USNA, 814.00/10–1744, 17 October 1944.

23 In August 1949, a month after the assassination of Colonel Francisco Arana and the abortive coup attempt by rightists, the Partido de Acción Revolucionaria (PAR) issued a manifesto calling on the masses to support the army and praising the military as a professional institution at the service of the people (*Nuevo Diario,* 19 August 1949). At the time, the PAR's leadership was still under the strong influence of the Marxists of Vanguardia Democrática Guatemalteca (VDG), which operated inside the party as a clandestine "entryist" group. After the counterrevolution, the PGT recognized that it had been "far too soft" with the military leadership (PGT, *La intervención norteamericana en Guatemala y el derrocamiento del régimen democrático* [n.p., 1955], pp. 3–4, 30–6).

24 In a typical case, Colonel Oscar Morales López insisted, when visiting the State Department in December 1950, that the renewal of arms sales was necessary for the containment of communism (USNA, 714.562/12–2950). Morales was politely rebuffed although the United States was no longer able to defend its policy on the grounds that Guatemala had not ratified the Rio treaty, duly undertaken in September 1950 but complicated by the country's claim on Belize. In an internal policy statement of May 1951, the State Department identified the army as weak and indicated that the United States unofficially provided support to the Guatemalan military, although no details were given (USNA, 611.14/5–251).

even the modest and informal groups of armed civilians, first in the shape of the Caribbean Legion patronized by Arévalo, and then in the popular militias organized by the Left early in 1954, challenged the army's formal monopoly – if not its real exercise – of military power. Furthermore, as vividly illustrated by the abortive coup of July 1949, consensus over the desirability of constitutionalism by no means extended to the social reforms – still less the popular mobilization – that followed in its wake. Nonetheless, the failure of the army to lead a counterrevolutionary movement when it had the coercive means so to do owed a great deal to the fact that the bulk of the officer corps had accepted the violent displacement of the *ubiquista* old guard, which both removed the leading conservatives from the scene and constituted sufficient institutional trauma to make support for the ethos of democracy a necessity as well as a virtue. As in the case of the State Department, the celebration of 1944 by the military was never subsequently foresworn, even by the Right after 1954. Until that date, the palpable absence of a coherent political alternative to progressive reform, outside of regression to a dictatorship led by one of Ubico's acolytes – the *caudillo* died in New Orleans in 1946 – made the regime tolerable to most, as well as desirable to some.[25] The purely generational aspects of the 1944 revolution may have been exaggerated, but it is significant that what may be dubbed "right- and left-wing" interpretations of it were contested within the ranks of those who had staged the revolt – Arana championing the former and Arbenz the latter – while the postinterventionist regime was led by officers associated with the dictatorship. Nor should one ignore the fact that although Arbenz was on the Left of the political spectrum, he was also a highly respected officer who safeguarded institutional interests from the presidential palace, receiving in return a high degree of loyalty. In sum, although UFCO and those elements in Washington considering the overthrow of reform – the State Department itself apparently resisted serious investigation of this course until late 1953 – could identify sympathetic officers, they could not find enough support to make a major move.[26]

25 In one of his first speeches after the intervention, Carlos Castillo Armas went out of his way to distinguish the social gains made in the wake of October 1944 from the practice of communism (*El Imparcial*, 6 July 1954).

26 A detailed assessment of U.S. policy is beyond the scope of this essay, but it should be mentioned that in May 1950 the State Department warned UFCO executive Thomas Corcoran not to pursue his idea of influencing the November 1950 election (USNA, 714.00/5–1550). Equally, in October 1952 it acted to impede a planned overthrow of Arbenz by Somoza, who, it was recognized, would not have entertained taking on the Guatemalan military had he not been encouraged (supposedly in error) by Truman's assistant military aide, General Neil Mara, to believe that Washington would offer support (USNA, 714.00/10–352). A CIA memo of December 1952 to the State Department scrupulously noted that the Agency had given "no overt or covert" assistance to the anti-Arbenz plot (USNA, 714.00/12–1252). In May 1953, the Department recognized

Washington's inability to depend on the military as a counterrevolutionary force was not made fully clear until July 1949, when army commander Colonel Francisco Arana was assassinated. For the first four years of the Arévalo regime, Arana seemed the obvious candidate to lead any Thermidor, and in all probability his control over the military misled the United States as to the ideological reliability of the officer corps as a whole. Arana's ambition to succeed Arévalo in the presidency lay behind his defense of the civilian administration against a plethora of ill-organized rightist plots, this distinctly interested loyalty obscuring substantial political differences with Arbenz and the reformist current in the army. It was only from late 1948, when it was clear that Arana's candidacy would not be supported by any political party, that he himself was perceived – from all the evidence, correctly – to be preparing a coup.[27] His assassination can, therefore, be viewed as a preemptive strike to defend the regime – whether Arbenz was directly involved is less evident – and a decisive act inasmuch as a successful coup by Arana would almost certainly have followed the Salvadorean path in eliminating all but the rhetoric of reform. Nevertheless, the failure of the military uprising in response to Arana's death strongly suggests that by that stage matters depended on far more than the initiatives of individuals. Arana's own fatal delay in staging a challenge, and the subsequent collapse of his supporters' effort, owed much to the fact that Arévalo had hitherto acceded to military invigilation and tabled a set of strictly modest reforms that were applied with notable caution.

By this stage, the State Department had begun to modify its assessment of Arévalo as a weak and vacillating character who survived largely by shifting with the tide.[28] It was, in fact, moving to the view that the president had deliberately lulled both his army commander and Wash-

---

that Arbenz's hold over the junior officer corps was not so strong as that he had over the high command, yet reiterated that in the event of an invasion, Guatemala would have a clear case for complaint in the OAS (National Intelligence Estimate, 19 May 1953, reprinted in *Foreign Relations of the United States: American Republics, 1952–54*, vol. 4, p. 1071).

27 See, for example, USNA, 814.00/7–846; 814.00/11–1248, on Arana's discontent with Arévalo and possible links with a coup.

28 Early in 1945, the State Department, suspicious of Arévalo's "radical tendencies," cabled the embassy in Buenos Aires to check up on his politics. It was informed that it was their "considered opinion that anyone reasonably well informed about his teachings, writings and general activities would be inclined to pass over such suspicions as being so utterly without foundation as to call for no response" (USNA, 814.00/1–1345). At the beginning of 1947, the embassy in Guatemala said the president was "far more of a student than a politician" (USNA, 814.00/1–247). Even after the controversy of the labor code, the embassy stated, "He appears to have a realistic approach to the problem [although] inherent sympathy for the laboring classes may swing him at the crucial moments" (USNA, 814.504/12–1947). At the end of his term, Arévalo was described to Truman as "an extreme leftist rather than a Communist" (USNA, 611.14/9–950).

ington into a false sense of confidence. After all, the "hidden agenda" approach to reform in this period was avidly pursued by the Costa Rican Partido Liberación Nacional (as Figueres's group was to become) and Acción Democrática in Venezuela, both of which organizations were closely allied to Arévalo. There is, however, no evidence that the "spiritual socialism" espoused by the president was not as anti-Communist and social democratic in substance as he repeatedly declared it to be.[29] Furthermore, unlike his regional peers, Arévalo was a member of no party, and he owed a great many of the 255,000 votes cast for him in December 1944 (out of a total of 295,000) precisely to his independence, the political "purity" gained by years of exile in Argentina, and his personification of the liberal democratic values thrown up by the antidictatorial movement. Although his support for the Caribbean Legion – the source of appreciable concern in Washington – was somewhat anomolous within his generally cautious and legalistic approach, this was realized independently of the parties, depended on military acquiescence, and in no sense amounted to patronage of radicalism per se. Arévalo was undoubtedly a more adept politician than has been generally recognized, but he remained throughout his office a solitary and highly vulnerable figure whose moderate program survived primarily because it cohered with the objective limits and possibilities of the time.

In the political sphere, Arévalo's program was effectively condensed in the Constitution of 1945, which replaced the charter of 1879 in a manner fully consonant with other constitutions of this period. Property was identified as possessing a "social character," thereby providing a legal resource for state intervention, and the franchise was extended to all adults except illiterate women, still a substantial proportion of the population. The university was granted both autonomy and an increased budget, but parties with international affiliations were proscribed in line with the standard continental form for outlawing Communist organizations (although none yet existed in Guatemala). In the same vein, vagrancy was abolished – without major effect on either rural order or agricultural production – and the restoration of municipal government in 1946 re-

---

29 Arévalo described himself as an admirer of the New Deal, and in advocating "spiritual socialism" he fused motifs of that secular mysticism common among the Central American middle class with a less familiar developmentalist vision: "We are socialists because we live in the twentieth century. But we are not materialist socialists. We do not believe that man is primarily stomach. We believe that man is above all else a will for dignity. . . . Our socialism does not aim at an ingenious distribution of material goods or the stupid economic equalisation of men who are economically different. Our socialism aims to liberate man psychologically and spiritually . . . the materialist concept has become a tool in the hands of totalitarian forces. Communism, Fascism and Nazism have also been socialist. But theirs is a socialism that gives food with the left hand while the right mutilates the moral and civic values of man" (Juan José Arévalo, *Escritos políticos* [Guatemala City, 1945], p. 199).

turned autonomous administration to the Indian communities. None of these measures upset the United States or any but the most ultramontane domestic forces; they met the central demands of the broad antidictatorial movement and yet altered the balance of social forces to a strictly limited degree. Moreover, their introduction greatly mollified the newly formed parties, three of which – the Frente Popular Libertador (FPL), Renovación Nacional (RN), and the Partido de Acción Revolucionaria (PAR) – came to dominate formal politics. All publicly backed Arévalo and served in his cabinets. Yet none ever managed to establish a clear monopoly on either the legacy of 1944 or government patronage, still less popular support.[30]

This weakness, which encouraged sectariansim and impeded all attempts to establish a single revolutionary party, may be ascribed in good measure to the lack of middle-class political tradition and the rapid, bipartisan manner in which the central political reforms were introduced. It was also encouraged by the fact that the virtues of Arévalo's independence were followed by the necessities of Arbenz's similar status, derived from his position in the army. Its effects were to dilute the identification of government policy with the pronouncements of any single organization, particularly the PAR, diffuse the clientelist links of the nascent labor movement, and provide cover for Communist activities, allowing the Marxists to remedy some of their own weaknesses by exploiting those of the PAR, entering it, and eventually dominating its leadership. The corresponding debility of oligarchic political organization meant that while in practice the FPL pursued a quite conservative line, there was no constant and clearly defined polarization of ideological positions. Instead, Arévalo presided over and Arbenz arbitrated between a stream of claims to patronage, parliamentary competition failing to produce a viable challenge for the presidency, as was evident from the absence of significant opposition in the November 1950 poll.[31] As a result, party politics became a secondary activity, buoyant in expression but feeble in organization. At one level, the stridency of competing claims to revolutionary bona fides alarmed Washington simply because it was conducive to a radicalization of the general nationalist sentiment from which no

30 The activities of the parties are too labyrinthine to discuss here. There was an almost constant series of ruptures and alliances between 1945 and 1948, general unity during the crisis of 1949, and renewed conflict from 1951 to 1954, qualified only by resistence to Arbenz's attempt to foster an officialist party, which never got off the ground. In the 1949 congressional elections, the FPL won 30 seats, the right-wing alliance 15, the PAR 11, the RN 5, and independents 3.

31 Miguel García Granados, formerly of the FPL, won 29,000 votes in the election. The FPL was the only party to campaign against Arbenz and Ydígoras but ran two candidates and eventually withdrew.

party could afford to stray. Yet until the formation of the PGT in late 1952, no single organization incarnated this line; the fluidity and ambiguity of both policies and personnel shifted the locus of "real" politics to the much less tangible sphere of influence. This lack of organizational resolution eventually permitted the attribution of positions and sympathies to Arévalo and Arbenz on the basis of the guilt by association and "duck test" methodology of the McCarthy era.

If the absence of a finite representation of the radicalism immanent in the 1944 revolution was in itself a key factor in delaying a reactionary response, it possessed more than symbolic importance and accurately reflected the slow and erratic manner in which the 1944 agenda of political democracy elided into that of economic nationalism and social reform. Perhaps the most critical factor in this process was the overbearing presence of the UFCO, which provided the reformists with a target of exactly that definition, which the conservative forces lacked. Yet even in this case, Arévalo advanced slowly and with moderation. The nationalist issues at stake were incorporated in the democratic and legal agenda through his insistence that the labor question be resolved by enactment of a new code and UFCO's position dealt with by negotiation. Although a series of strikes and invectives in Congress during 1946 convinced the UFCO that the IRCA might be expropriated, Arévalo permitted Arana to contain the railway workers, whose union leadership, the SAMF, had already signaled its independence from the radical tendencies emerging within the CTG by splitting with it early in 1945. Moreover, in August 1945 Arévalo prohibited any unionization of rural workers until the promulgation of the labor code, and in January 1946 he ordered the closure of the Marxist-dominated Escuela Claridad, a workers' night school. Indeed, when the code was finally introduced early in 1947, it appeared to ratify this conservative approach; although it provided the expected clauses as to union rights (eight-hour day, etc.), it also restricted the existence of rural unions to those enterprises with a labor force of at least 500 workers where a minimum of 50 wished to form a union, 60 percent of whose members would have to be literate in order to receive registration. However, the UFCO claimed that this was deeply discriminatory and aimed directly at the corporation, which had refused to renegotiate its 1936 contract and now threatened to withdraw from the country. Although the State Department sought to modify some of the company's claims – most notably that it was the only enterprise affected – Washington applied considerable pressure on Arévalo.[32] The final result of this was that the

---

32 At the end of July, the Guatemalan foreign minister was visited by the State Department's chief of Central American affairs (Robert Newbegin) who requested a precise response to the claims of discrimination. In August and September, the U.S. ambassador visited Arévalo to press the

code was amended to permit unions on all rural estates so that whereas early in 1948 there were only 11 organizations, by 1953 at least 345 were in existence.[33] In effect, by challenging the supposedly nationalist element of a markedly conservative law, the UFCO and the State Department had contrived to make the legislation much more extensive, while failing to relieve the company of its unprecedented vulnerability to labor organization, which began to flex its muscles in a series of strikes in 1948–9. There is a certain irony in the fact that the final code was more democratic than the original version, and that the whole affair deepened the conviction of the State Department as well as the UFCO that Arévalo was decidedly, if not dangerously, pro-labor.

This belief was further hardened when, in December 1949, the president introduced the Law of Forced Rental, which realized the social property clauses of the 1945 Constitution in obliging the leasing of uncultivated estate lands at a rent of no more than 5 percent of harvest value. This act was not, however, used to a significant degree against the UFCO, and indeed was never extensively applied. As was the case with the proposed (and eventually thwarted) income tax law, the measure stood to prejudice local capital more directly than foreign interests, and perhaps for this reason it was never zealously employed. In fact, U.S. investment in Guatemala rose during this period, albeit modestly, from $86.9 million in 1943 to $105.9 million in 1950, the climate for entrepreneurs being supported by the establishment of the Instituto Nacional de Fomento de Producción (INFOP) that provided state credit to the private sector, the investment of which accounted for 8 percent of the GDP in 1950 compared to 3.8 percent in 1944.[34] Wages also rose appreciably, in the urban sector by as much as 80 percent and in the countryside to around double the level of the late 1930s, although rates varied and were seldom paid fully in cash.[35] In the five years after the war, the economy was buoyant rather than booming – although banana exports rose 34 percent between 1944 and 1949 – and much of the increase in pay was determined by the establishment of formal minimum rates, together with a significant expansion of government expenditure on services and the freeing of the labor market in the coffee sector. Consequently, one should neither discount the pressure on capital nor overemphasize the role of organized labor in obtaining economic gains.

point home (USNA, 814.504/8–447; 814.504/8–847; 814.504/9–2247). By the end of the year, Arévalo had agreed to present most of the required revisions to Congress (USNA, 814.504/12–1947).

33  Pearson, "Peasant Union Movement," p. 350.
34  Bulmer-Thomas, *Political Economy,* p. 120.
35  Handy, *Gift of the Devil: A History of Guatemala* (Toronto, 1980), p. 108; Pearson, "Peasant Union Movement," p. 336.

The development of an organizationally coherent and politically pugnacious labor movement was markedly uneven, even after the introduction of the labor code. The early establishment of unions on UFCO plantations placed the company under pressure that was unprecedented, yet qualified by three years of state restrictions on labor activity. There was effectively no organization elsewhere in the countryside until after 1947, and the urban unions were constrained by the small size and artisanal character of industry – in 1953, 1,070 enterprises with a total labor force of 20,500 at an average of 19 workers per plant – the absence of virtually any syndicalist tradition, and ideological differences that combined the essence of disputes witnessed elsewhere in the 1920s with those determined more directly by contemporary developments. As a result, no rural confederation was established until May 1950; the urban movement remained divided until October 1951; and the two coexisted uneasily even after the introduction of the agrarian reform in June 1952. Both the recent formation of plantation and sectoral unions and the delay in national unification and political activism served to shield the labor movement from precipitate repression and to provide the small Communist group with the opportunity to deepen its organizational influence in a manner similar to that of the PAR. Hence, although there was no open Marxist organization in Guatemala until the end of 1952, by 1947 Communists were acting as the general secretaries of the PAR (José Manuel Fortuny) and the CTG (Víctor Manuel Gutiérrez).

The division between the CTG and the SAMF-dominated Federación Sindical de Guatemala (FSG) began over the question of affiliation with Vicente Lombardo Toledano's Confederación de Trabajadores de América Latina (CTAL), which the CTG joined at the earliest opportunity. This link proved to be of enduring importance, in a sense compensating for the previous decades of isolation. After 1948, when the conditions for union politics underwent a sharp change in Mexico, relations did not diminish despite the fact that Lombardo now lacked the authority of earlier years. This was partly because the Mexican Left could support a popular antiimperialist cause in Guatemala without major risk on either side of the border, and partly because many Central American and Spanish exiles found the country's provincial but politically uplifting climate preferable to the uncommon chill of post-*charrazo* Mexico. Arévalo was periodically prevailed on to expel clutches of foreign radicals whose political credentials were more manifest than those of local activists. But his own experience of exile, sympathy for the Spanish Republic and Central American union, together with the fact that the foreigners bolstered the state's administrative skills as well as those of the Left, ensured that the "alien question," which had, of course, been at the heart of J. Edgar Hoover's original U.S. anti-Communist drive in 1919–20, never developed into the campaign sought by Washington and the indigenous Right. It is unclear to what extent the experience and advice of Mexican radicals prompted the Guatemalan Communists to embrace the entryist strategy. Until 1950 there existed few feasible alternatives and when, in November 1949, Gutiérrez's radical union militants broke with Fortuny's predominantly middle-class group and left both the clandestine Partido Comunista Guatemalteco (PCG; formed in September 1949) and the PAR within which it was operating, Lombardo's efforts at mediation came to nought.[36] At the same time, it is possible to overestimate the importance of the CTAL in determining the division between the CTG and the FSG that impeded labor unification for five years. Under the control of Manuel Pinto Usaga, the SAMF, which effectively controlled the FSG, was not so much apolitical as opposed to the adventurism of the Communists with whom its leaders battled for influence within the PAR.[37] Pinto Usaga was a persistent thorn in the side of the IRCA, and because he facilitated the 1949–50 truce with Gutiérrez and the eventual unification of the urban unions in the Confederación General de Trabajadores de Guatemala (CGTG), he was particularly odious in U.S. eyes (a "veiled Communist" – one step up from a "pro-Communist" and in some senses more reprehensible than the full-blooded, open variety). However, the railway workers' prolonged resistance to Communist influence clearly implied that unification was a key factor in restraining union radicalism.[38]

At the time of the counterrevolution, the CGTG claimed to have more than 100,000 members in 500 affiliated unions. Because this was a very considerable proportion of the urban working population, and because the general secretaryship of the confederation was held by Víctor Manuel Gutiérrez, it could be said that the Guatemalan working class was under Communist control. That this was not the case was not simply due to the fact that numbers on paper bore only an approximate relation to the practice on the ground, but also to the intrinsic limits of national union leadership – abetted by the overwhelmingly rural and unintegrated character of the economy – together with the deeply uneasy relations between the "workerist" Marxists headed by Gutiérrez and the "politicians" led by Fortuny. This division took place almost immediately after the clandestine PCG was formed inside the PAR in the autumn of 1949 – that is, once the Communists were moving toward a more than purely cellular form of existence – and lasted until March 1952. It therefore covered a particularly critical period of labor activism during which both the urban CGTG and the rural Confederación Nacional Campesina de Guatemala

---

36 Schneider, *Communism in Guatemala*, pp. 66–7.
37 Ibid., p. 63.
38 Ibid., pp. 171–2.

(CNCG) were established, and when Arbenz was elected president with union backing. At this time, the State Department estimated the number of Communist activists to be between 500 and 1,000 – in all probability it was closer to the lower figure, which would also have included many *simpatizantes* – a relatively small group that had only four deputies in Congress, no representatives in the cabinet, and less than two dozen militants in senior administrative posts.[39] However, U.S. perceptions of a much greater Marxist influence were not mere flights of fancy, and the fact that this political community was divided precisely over the question of union work (the entryist issue was an extension of this dispute) since one leader headed the country's largest confederation, gave the debate a more than purely sectarian character. The tension between Gutiérrez and Fortuny certainly enabled the SAMF – FSG bloc to move toward the CTG, and once Gutiérrez established the Partido Revolucionario Obrero de Guatemala (PROG) independently of both the PCG and the PAR, he created a third pole in left-wing politics in a manner that signaled distance from the Communist core, and yet did not lead to significant competition with it. The effect of this was to enhance Gutiérrez's own reputation with the broad union membership and to thwart the threat of an anti-Communist current within the new CGTG. Gutiérrez returned to the fold shortly before the establishment of the PGT – pressure from Moscow seems to have been instrumental – but for three years his autonomous line kept union politics simultaneously fluid and radical.[40] In the eyes of the Right and Washington, these comings and goings made little difference – Gutiérrez remained a committed Marxist and the CGTG an avowedly radical organization – yet they demonstrate both the organizational weakness of Guatemalan communism and how that weakness proved to be an advantage by averting a major rupture within the radical labor bloc at a time when politics as a whole was rapidly polarizing.

The key point in this polarization was the assassination of Arana on 18 July 1949, and the subsequent abortive coup of his followers that left some 150 dead and 300 wounded – a toll far higher than that of October 1944. Arbenz's distribution of weapons to the students and workers, together with the call for a general strike, thwarted the uprising, converted Arbenz into the undisputed protector of the reformist regime, and provided the labor movement with both increased confidence and a clear

---

39 In March 1952, the State Department figure was 500; two years later it was put at between 2,000 and 3,000 (National Intelligence Estimate, 11 March 1952, *Foreign Relations 1952–4*, vol. 4, p. 1033; USNA, 714.00/4–1954). According to Mario Monteforte Toledo, the party had 1,300 activists at its peak (*Guatemala*, p. 316).

40 Schneider notes that Gutiérrez visited Moscow in December 1951 and that upon his return in February 1952 the PROG voted to dissolve itself in the name of unity (*Communism in Guatemala*, p. 67).

alliance. It may be stretching matters to suggest a parallel with the events of October 1945 in Argentina, but some underlying similarities are certainly evident. Following debate within the unions over tactics, Arbenz's candidacy in the November 1950 elections was fully supported. Sealed four years into the regime, within the parameters of liberal democracy, and at a point where the unions were acquiring organizational resources and demands for economic reform were on the rise, the military–labor alliance was forged in peculiarly advantageous circumstances at a local level, while the international context was equally unpropitious. Internally, the fact that Arévalo was able to serve out the last eighteen months of his term unassailed from either the Right or the Left provided an aura of continuity and, despite the fact that he did not endorse Arbenz (or any other candidate), effectively bestowed the democratic mandate of October 1944 on the decidedly more Bonapartist regime that succeeded it.

This sense of legitimacy was heightened by the fact that Arbenz's principal opponent at the polls was General Miguel Ydígoras Fuentes, who was closely associated with the Ubico dictatorship and was seen to repudiate the revolution *tout court* rather than simply dispute its terms from within. Arbenz's decisive victory – by 267,000 to 74,000 votes – was not challenged by Washington, which had pursued a policy of extreme caution during the campaign so as not to excite nationalist fervor. Moreover, at this stage the State Department still perceived Arbenz as an opportunist with whom it could negotiate.[41] Such a policy of watchful waiting may have been encouraged by the fact that the State Department's labor officers and the embassy staff remained embroiled in a dispute over the legal and political acceptability of the 1947 labor code and its ramifications for the UFCO.[42] Equally, although North American sensibilities continued to be aggravated by such matters as the playing of nationalist tunes instead of the "Stars and Stripes" to greet the Puerto Rican team to the Central American Olympics in Guatemala City, it remained a fact that, in the wake of the Chinese Revolution and at the onset of the Korean War, Guatemala voted with the United States on most issues in the UN. However, its new government – as distinct from certain political elements within the country – showed and admitted to no disposition to alter existing external policy, meddled in the affairs of its neighbors less than any prior regime, and desisted from promoting communism to the same degree as it asserted its right to exist as a national force.

The argument as to whether it was a general Cold War logic or the more direct interests of the UFCO that prompted the shift from watchful

---

41 *Foreign Relations 1950*, vol. 2, p. 877; USNA, 714.001/11–1560.
42 USNA, 611.14/5–1750, Memo, Fishburn to Miller, 19 April 1950; USNA, 611.14/5–1750, Wells to Washington, 17 May 1950.

waiting and discrete pressure in 1951 to indirect armed intervention in 1954 is somewhat artificial in that these factors are only partially distinguishable. As has been indicated, the professional diplomats continued to be cautious and upheld the strategy of diplomatic pressure and economic isolation (although this never came to include a boycott of coffee and bananas) until late 1953. By then the general panorama was quite distinct from that prevailing when Arbenz assumed office. The replacement of Truman by Eisenhower (and Dean Acheson by Foster Dulles) must be considered a factor of significant – if not decisive – importance, both in general terms and because senior officials of the new administration possessed especially close ties with the UFCO.[43] The degree to which Eisenhower's election condemned the Guatemalan revolution is open to discussion, at least insofar as the new administration continued Truman's policy of negotiation with the revolutionary regime that came to power in Bolivia in April 1952. But Eisenhower was prepared to tolerate nationalization of the tin mines and an agrarian reform in Bolivia because they did not greatly affect U.S. capital, whereas in Guatemala less radical measures did so directly. There is no indication that the Guatemalan authorities considered that the introduction of an agrarian reform law in June 1952 – when the U.S. presidential campaign was underway – and the legalization of the PGT in December – when Eisenhower had already defeated Stevenson – constituted a decisive provocation to the United States, which had been exerting growing pressure over both the "persecution" of the UFCO and the alleged indulgence of communism since 1947. Of course, they had relatively few precedents on which to draw in assessing the likely consequences of their acts, which fell clearly within the parameters of the Constitution and far short of, say, Lázaro Cárdenas's nationalization of the oil industry in Mexico. They may well, therefore, have adjudged such moves as unlikely to prejudice in a critical fashion the already poor relations with Washington, while greatly improving domestic support. The agrarian reform indubitably enhanced the local popularity of the government. Both measures, however, and particularly the registration of the PGT, gave the advocates of counterrevolution exactly those substantive targets for condemnation and the mobilizing issues that had previously been lacking. They served to give the initiative to those both inside Guatemala and abroad who believed that, in the words of U.S. Ambassador John Peurifoy, "if [Arbenz] is not a Communist, he will certainly do until one comes along . . . normal approaches will not work in Guatemala."[44]

The agrarian reform, Decree 90, of 27 June 1952, was a purposefully

43 For details of the links, see Schlesinger and Kinzer, *Bitter Fruit.*
44 USNA, 611.14/12–1753.

modest measure defended by Arbenz as the best means by which to promote capitalism in the countryside. All farms under 90 hectares (219 acres) and those of up to 300 hectares (488 acres), two-thirds of which were under cultivation, were exempted, as were all forests, communal lands, and completely cultivated properties.[45] Equally, redistribution of the *fincas nacionales* absorbed much of the shock anticipated by the landlord class, which was not severely hit but responded with vehemence to Central America's first modern agrarian reform. Such repudiation was entirely predictable for a deeply reactionary sector sustained by forced labor until seven years earlier and determined to avoid the "Bolshevik path" of Mexico. It may, indeed, have been more concerned by the level of peasant mobilization than distribution. By 1952 the rural labor movement was organized at a national level, that in the towns was finally unified, and the two were acting in erratic but unprecedented concert. Thus, although mobilization in the countryside did not approach the levels witnessed in Bolivia at the time (still less those in Mexico of earlier decades), the issue was profoundly worrying for landed capital, which was quick to denounce the existence of openly declared Communists in the CGTG and the Departamento Agrario Nacional (DAN), which administered the reform. In fact, the PGT possessed an exceptionally weak apparatus in the countryside, and although both the church and the landlords railed against the "Bolsheviks" in the CNCG, the domestic anti-Communist scare campaign never took firm root or seriously challenged the regime. However, the reform was hotly denounced by the UFCO, which, with some 15 percent of its 650,000 acres of plantation under threat, was by far the most prejudiced party and particularly vulnerable to the device of assessing compensation on the basis of tax returns since these had always been exceptionally modest.[46] The threat was, therefore, far greater than that proffered by the labor code of 1947, and the State Department now rallied to the corporation's defense without qualification. Although Arbenz's complementary economic policies of building a road to the Caribbean coast to break the monopoly of the IRCA railway and developing a state-owned electricity plant to compete with U.S.-controlled supply had been recommended by the 1950 World Bank mission, these measures were now perceived as constitutive of a coherent and dangerous nationalist project. In sum, by the end of 1952 the United States had come to oppose Arbenz's economic program in itself, the interpretation that it was conducive to radicalization now being of secondary importance.

45 For details of the agrarian reform, see Guillermo Paz, *Guatemala: Reforma agraria* (San José, 1987); Handy, *Gift of the Devil*, pp. 126ff.; Pearson, "Peasant Union Movement"; and Mario Monteforte Toledo, "La Reforma Agraria."
46 Handy, *Gift of the Devil*, p. 142.

The problem of communism projected to the U.S. public in terms of an uncomplicated "Red Conspiracy" was, in fact, always discerned in Washington less in terms of a Bolshevik takeover – the evidence for which was negligible – than in terms of Moscow and the PGT edging Guatemala into a neutralist stance.[47] Although it might be argued that Mexico had been able to approximate this position over the previous three decades, the terms of that country's relative autonomy were quite distinct and required persistent policing, which had always included restricting Mexican influence in the isthmus. The general political conditions of 1953– 4 made any reduction of U.S. hegemony implied by neutralism particularly dangerous, and the Mexican government was in any case entirely unwilling to defend Guatemala's shift toward such status beyond reaffirmation of the principles of nonintervention and sovereignty in the diplomatic sphere. Lacking the support of a nonaligned bloc in the UN, let alone in the Organization of American States (OAS) where the United States concentrated its campaign, the Arbenz regime was far too weak to resist Washington's offensive for any length of time. The Guatemalan defense necessarily had to focus on the rule of law. This created a number of difficulties for Washington in that it was confronted with a case where a properly constituted government in control of national territory was supported, rather than subverted, by a Communist organization. Nonetheless, neither the terms of the Rio treaty nor the modus operandi of the OAS depended on strict observance of constitutionality. Furthermore, the U.S. conviction that the difference between the real and "hidden" agendas in Guatemala was now a matter of mere formality determined that realpolitik would prevail, even if Foster Dulles took care to employ surrogate forces as the public actors in Arbenz's downfall. Arbenz's second line of defense – that his domestic policies were intrinsically desirable and fortified capitalism while Guatemala's foreign relations provided no basis for concern whatsoever – was of little avail. It is noteworthy that Arbenz did not, in fact, embrace the notion of a developmentalist "third way" to the degree evidenced by, for example, Juan Perón or the Bolivian Movimiento Nacionalista Revolucionario (MNR).

These two elements – constitutionalism and the modesty of economic reform – may be deemed purely marginal in the context of U.S. management of the hemisphere. More important was Washington's inability to separate the military from the regime. Even after Colonel Elfego Monzón, Arbenz's minister of the interior, was impeached and removed from office for suppressing the Communist paper *Octubre* in 1952, the army resisted staging a coup that would have greatly eased the U.S. position

---

47 National Intelligence Estimate, "Probable Developments in Guatemala," 19 May 1953, *Foreign Relations 1952–4,* vol. 4, p. 1061.

by rendering the extensive domestic and diplomatic campaign of the first six months of 1954 unnecessary. Certainly Washington was able to make a virtue of a necessity and undertake an operation that had a considerable "demonstration effect" well beyond the Caribbean Basin. But it should be remembered that even after the formidable effort at destabilization and the use of CIA bombers, the invasion from Honduras led by Colonel Carlos Castillo Armas very nearly failed to achieve its objective and was in palpable danger of collapsing in ignominious defeat. In the event, the army's refusal to repeat its actions of October 1944 and July 1949 in withholding weaponry from the civilian population extinguished the possibility of further deviance from Washington's mandate. The inability of the unions and *campesinado* to stage independent resistence demonstrated that, even after the accelerated mobilization of 1950–4, the popular forces still lacked the power to enforce a domestic stalemate at the moment of external intervention.

For a number of days after Arbenz's departure, the officer corps continued to operate on the assumption that there was further room for maneuver; senior officers disputed Ambassador Peurifoy's designation of Castillo Armas as the new president. However, the Guatemalan masses were rapidly and violently disabused of any such notion. Within a matter of months, most unions had been dismantled, almost all redistributed land returned to its former owners, left-wing organizations had been effectively proscribed, and their leaders either exiled, jailed or, less often, executed. The UFCO's contracts were restored at only slightly less than their earlier levels of generosity, and the apparatus of liberal democracy was evacuated of any substance. All this did not exactly amount to a return to the status quo ante – neither debt peonage nor the vagrancy laws were restored. However, the counter revolution was enforced with such determination that the Guatemalan Left subsequently remained deeply suspicious of legal and electoralist strategies (and was amongst the first to adopt the "Cuban road," which its own experience played no small part in encouraging), while the traumatised and profoundly relieved Right henceforth viewed reformist policies as inherently conducive to Bolshevism, resisting for three decades all but the most superficial amendments to the free market and dictatorial rule. Cold War politics persisted far longer in Guatemala than almost anywhere else in Latin America. Its polarities were long delayed, but they were finally established with such a vengeance that the subsequent influence of Cuba's revolution, which engendered significantly new terms in hemispheric politics, was always overshadowed by that of Guatemala in 1954. The price of one period of exceptionalism was another, of much greater length and incomparably greater human suffering.

# CONCLUSION

## The postwar conjuncture in Latin America and its consequences

*Leslie Bethell and Ian Roxborough*

The period between the final stages of the Second World War and the beginnings of the Cold War, that is to say, the years 1944–5 to 1947–8, constitute an important, but neglected, conjuncture in the history of Latin America in the twentieth century. Notwithstanding the region's great political, social, and economic diversity, ruling groups in the majority of the twenty Latin American republics experienced, confronted, and contained during this period significant and strikingly similar challenges from below. The nature and, more important, the outcome of the 1944–8 conjuncture established the institutional and ideological framework for the political, social, and economic development of Latin America during the following three decades (until, that is, the breakdown of the postwar "model" in the 1980s).

The final year of the war and the year immediately following the end of the war witnessed, more particularly in those countries living under a dictatorship or a narrowly oligarchic regime, a process of liberalization and democratization prompted mainly by middle-class and student groups, but with a degree of popular mobilization. There was almost everywhere a rapid growth of parties of the reformist Center–Left and the orthodox Marxist Left, especially Communist parties. In addition, most noticeably in those countries that already had a sizeable working class, there occurred an upsurge of labor militancy together with the political incorporation of organized labor, often for the first time.

At the end of the Second World War, and to a large extent because of the Second World War, not only was there in Latin America a forward march by democracy, the Left, and labor, but there was also a shift in the nature of political-discourse and ideology. There were expectations in Latin America, as elsewhere in the world, that a new era of democratic government was about to commence. And democracy was seen by many to imply a commitment to popular, more particularly working-class participation in politics, and social and economic improvements for the poorer sections of the population. Democracy increasingly became identified with development and welfare. This was the vision of the Latin American Left, both Communist and non-Communist. It was complimented by the aspirations of a new generation of Latin American "structuralist" economists and technocratic modernizers, many of whom in 1948 joined the United Nations Economic Commission for Latin America (ECLA/CEPAL) in Santiago. Central to their strategy for postwar economic development in Latin America was a planned acceleration of the import substitution industrialization (ISI) of the 1930s and the war years. This would be sustained by an alliance of domestic industrialists (the "national bourgeoisie"), who would be guaranteed adequate profit levels behind protective barriers, and organized labor, which would be offered expanding employment, rising wages, and improved welfare provision, and led by an interventionist state, which would create the appropriate market conditions, provide infrastructure, and invest in industry itself where private initiative was not forthcoming. They explicitly rejected the view that Latin America could or should return to a model of capital accumulation, growth, and development based on primary exports.

The United States had emerged from the Second World War with unrivaled supremacy, both economic and political, in Latin America. The new economic ideas emerging from Latin America generated considerable unease among U.S. policy makers. During the final years of the war, the United States had formulated an increasingly clear and articulate vision of a liberal international economic order based on free trade and free flows of capital. Protectionism, government intervention in the economy, and forced industrialization were, like commodity agreements and trade blocs, anathema, but these were issues for the medium and long term. In the short term, the United States supported postwar political liberalization and democratization in the region. And at this time the United States was not opposed to the advance of labor and of the Left (including the Communist Left).

There existed in Latin America at the end of the Second World War, therefore, a unique conjuncture of domestic and international circumstances favorable to significant political and social change. Is it too fanciful to see a window of opportunity, at least in the industrializing countries, for the beginnings of a Latin American version of social democracy? Democracy, whatever its shortcomings, would be advanced and consolidated. Organized labor and the Left would be permanently incorporated into democratic politics (an incorporation institutionalized through electoral contests in which parties with a solid basis in the working class would compete). And despite inevitable problems in maintaining the balance between consumption and investment, and between profits, wages, and employment, class conflict (urban, if not rural) would be replaced by a measure of class compromise around the ISI project; there would be more or less permanent bargaining between relatively autonomous labor unions, industrialists' associations, and the state over economic policy and macroeconomic management.

The odds were always heavily weighted against it, and it was in many ways premature. Despite the significant changes that had begun to take place during the 1930s and during the Second World War, the urban working class was, outside of Argentina, Chile, and Uruguay, still a relatively small segment of society. And precisely because of the rapidity and scope of the changes that were occurring, the growing working classes of countries like Mexico, Colombia, Peru, Venezuela, and Brazil still had relatively little sense of class cohesion and solidarity and were relatively poorly organized. Nor was the emergence of a national bourgeoisie entirely unproblematical. Even in the larger and most industrialized countries of Latin America at the end of the Second World War, industry was not yet the dominant sector of the economy, even if it was seen by some at least as the motor of future development. Industrialists also often felt themselves to be a new and relatively weak actor on the national stage. In some cases they were immigrants, uneasily jockeying for admission to the ranks of the elites. In other cases, the industrialists were too firmly embedded in the social and political, as well as economic, networks of established agrarian elites to develop any clear sense of themselves as a separate class with a distinct economic and political vocation. And in all cases, dependence on state support and on international capital and technology further militated against the development of a national bourgeoisie with a clear sense of mission. Only at a regional level in some countries did anything like a self-conscious bourgeoisie emerge.

Moreover, the emerging alliance of industrialists, sections of the middle class, and organized labor was also weak. The political movements and parties that sustained it were relatively new, untested instruments, and were often riven by strategic and ideological division. Even the more progressive elements in their leaderships had to concern themselves with the need to control and institutionalize their mass following, to restrict and channel its demands, and to juggle the interests of their supporters against the demands of political survival and the constraints of economic necessity.

At the end of the Second World War, the Latin American elites, both economic and political, were still largely based on landownership. In Latin America, unlike large areas of Asia, for example, their position had not been eroded, much less destroyed, by the shattering impact of the war. With the exception of Mexico (which alone in Latin America had experienced social revolution), landed elites who controlled the great mass of peasants and rural workers through a variety of clientelistic systems continued to exercise disproportionate political power, at both local and national levels. In the state apparatus itself, conservative forces retained a considerable foothold. At the same time, despite the Young Turk movements of the twenties and thirties (*tenentismo* in Brazil, for example), and despite the modernizing drive of the military in some of the larger countries, the higher echelons of the military continued to be dominated on the whole by profoundly conservative men. Other social, political, and cultural forces of the ancien régime were still powerful. The Catholic church, in particular, continued to exercise a conservative influence in many countries, most notably in Colombia, but also in Brazil, Argentina, and Chile. Progressive tendencies within Catholicism, such as Christian Democracy and liberation theology, would not appear until much later in the postwar period.

Thus in the years immediately after the Second World War, the dominant socioeconomic and political groups in Latin America were willing and determined to confront and defeat, or at least contain, popular forces, especially once the meaning of the postwar democratic advance emerged, and the threat to their political and social control posed by popular mobilization, labor militancy, and the growth of the Left was fully recognized. And this willingness and determination was reinforced by the changes taking place at the international level. These were, above all, political: that is to say, the imperatives of the Cold War and, above all, the determination of the United States to contain communism internationally. There already existed pressing domestic reasons for an attack on the Left (as well as on labor and even on democracy itself). But whatever the reality or otherwise of the threat of Communist subversion, the Latin American elites willingly embraced the anti-Communist crusade that the United States desired to impose on the region as further ideological justification for the shift to the Right.

The international imperatives reinforcing domestic resistance to sweeping political and social change in the postwar period were also economic. There was always a tension, as we have seen, between the emerging reformist, inward-looking Latin American model of economic development based on ISI, and the liberal international economic order established by the United States at the end of the war. Moreover, the new ISI model, like the old export-led model, required substantial imports of foreign capital and technology – now more for manufacturing industry than for mining, agriculture, public utilities, and transportation. With Europe devastated by the war, the United States was the only source of external finance and technological know-how. And, since the United States rejected Latin American demands for development aid (there would be no Marshall Plan for Latin America), there was no alternative to U.S. direct investment. To attract private U.S. capital into the manufacturing sector, Latin

America had to offer not only favorable legislation and a protected domestic market, but also political stability and an environment free of
labor strife and Communist agitation. Although not planned as such, a
degree of conservative institutional reorganization was a necessary precondition for Latin America's unprecedented economic growth from the
1950s to the 1970s.

If, broadly speaking, the first phase of the postwar conjuncture was
characterized by popular mobilization and reformist aspirations, the second phase – and the precise timing of each phase varied somewhat from
country to country, and often there was considerable overlap between the
two – was essentially one of containment of the popular forces, even roll
back, and the realities of reaction. The resolution of the immediate postwar
crisis took the form of a decisive defeat for labor, the Left, and democracy.
Throughout the region, governments launched an offensive against labor.
In some countries, this took the form of antistrike legislation, and almost
everywhere independent militant labor organizations were divided, weakened, and brought under state control. Communist parties were for the
most part outlawed and subjected to systematic and sustained repression
– out of all proportion to the threat they posed. Parties of the non-
Communist Left were put on the defensive, and in some cases also subjected to repression. At the same time – and often linked to the offensive
against both organized labor and the Left in general, and the Communist
Parties in particular – in some countries (e.g., Brazil and Chile) restrictive
legislation reduced the scope of democracy. In others (e.g., Peru and
Venezuela in 1948) military coups brought to an end the postwar democratic openings.

Insofar as a window of opportunity for political and social change in
Latin America had opened at the end of the Second World War, it had
been firmly slammed shut by the end of 1948. The only exceptions were
Guatemala and Argentina. In Guatemala, a democratic, reforming regime
survived until its brutal overthrow in 1954. In Argentina, Juan Domingo
Perón presided over a government that, although it did not always behave
democratically, had been democratically elected and was, at least rhetor-
ically, pro-working class. However, in the late forties, Perón moved
rapidly to eliminate rivals in the labor movement and to suffocate dissent
from within the ranks of Peronism. And as the immediate postwar boom
in Argentina petered out, the real wage gains of organized labor began
to be eroded. Eventually, the Peronist regime itself was overthrown by
the military in 1955.

The contrast with Western Europe at the end of the Second World
War is revealing. Conditions there were much more favorable for the
construction of an enduring social democracy. There was already a considerable experience of democracy. The Right had been discredited during

the war. The Communist Left had emerged from the war with its prestige enormously enhanced, especially within the labor movement; and there were social-democratic (and Christian-democratic) alternatives to the Communists. Organized labor had already been (at least partially) incorporated into the political system, and labor movements were both mature and predisposed toward class compromise. Finally, the United States, for strategic reasons, offered the Marshall Plan for economic reconstruction, which more than anything else would underpin postwar social democracy in Western Europe.

In the United States itself, as in Latin America, the postwar conjuncture led to the reinforcement of conservatism. Both the experience of the Depression years and the war itself had produced a considerable strengthening of leftist, progressive forces in the United States. At the end of the war, the United States experienced increased labor mobilization, a rapid growth in leftist political influence, and an attempt to break the Republican–Democratic duopoly of power. There was, however, no sharp break with the past. On the contrary, the United States after the war turned away from the New Deal and the progressive coalitions of the 1930s and moved to the Right. The war had eliminated mass unemployment and doubled the GNP. The age of mass consumption had arrived. Along with high and rising living standards went unprecedented political conservatism. Left-wing leaderships in the labor unions were defeated and forced out of office, a new Red scare led to an onslaught on real and supposed Communist influence in many spheres of American life, and an "end of ideology" was proclaimed. A conservative, and at times reactionary, consensus dominated domestic politics at least until the 1960s when a variety of challenges (the Civil Rights movement, student movements, Vietnam, urban rioting, etc.) began to erode it. As Michael Harrington has said, "1948 was the last year of the 1930s."

Conservative consolidation in Latin America was more fragile and problematic than in the United States, but equally long lasting. Many of the parties of the democratic Left/Center-Left had been permanently weakened or forced by the struggle to survive to move to the Center/Center-Right. And with the exception of Chile, the orthodox Marxist Left had been virtually eliminated as a viable political force in Latin America. In the 1960s, in the wake of the Cuban revolution, the Left turned to the elitism and utopianism of revolutionary guerrilla strategy, but this only led to further heavy defeats. Gradually, at different times, with different rhythms, and in response to different stimuli (political, ideological, and, above all, economic – not least because of the problems of highly inequitable growth, perennial balance of payments crises, and endemic inflation associated with the ISI model) labor reemerged as an important political actor throughout the region, challenging the economic bases of the postwar order, but producing heightened anxiety among conservative elites and provoking an inevitable backlash. As for Latin American democracy, it remained fragile and precarious throughout the postwar period. In 1954, a decade after the beginning of the postwar wave of democratization, only four countries could reasonably be described as democratic. There was a further brief period of democratization in the late fifties and early sixties, but from the mid-sixties to the mid-seventies country after country resorted to authoritarian solutions to economic, social, and political problems, mostly in the form of military dictatorships. Where democracy survived, with few exceptions it did so fitfully and invariably under the tutelage of the armed forces.

Not until the 1980s did Latin America once again turn toward democracy. By 1990, apart from Cuba, which still retained its Communist regime despite the winds blowing from Eastern Europe, most countries in the region could plausibly claim to be democracies, or at least on their way to becoming such. (Mexico's Partido Revolucionario Institucional continued to win elections that many observers regarded as fraudulent, but even there a considerable space had been opened up for genuine political contestation by opposition parties.) Latin American democracies, both old and new, however, faced massive challenges as they sought to strengthen fragile democratic institutions in a context of continuing indebtedness, the collapse of the postwar ISI development model, declining economic growth rates, high and hyperinflation, the fiscal crisis of the state, severely reduced living standards for the majority of the population, worsening income inequalities and thus a deepening social crisis.

In the late eighties and early nineties, economic and ideological imperatives led one Latin American government after another, backed by the United States and a wide range of international financial agencies, to implement sweeping structural reforms of a neoliberal kind. The frontiers of the state were rolled back and state-owned enterprises privatized; economies were deregulated and opened to international competition, inducing industrial restructuring and, in some cases, deindustrialization. Public sector employees were dismissed and industrial workers laid off; real wages that were already low dramatically declined.

The Latin American labor movements confronting these tremendous problems were bigger, better organized, and more sophisticated than in earlier decades. However, torn between intransigent opposition to neoliberal reforms and passive acquiescence (in the hope of maintaining at least a fragile and subordinate alliance with the state), organized labor was divided, weakened, and once again put on the defensive almost everywhere. The political parties of the Left in Latin America were also more formidable (and more genuinely and explicitly committed to democracy) than in earlier decades. And (in most cases) they were no longer constrained by authoritarian governments or U.S. pressure for the containment of Communism. But a coherent, well-articulated and credible alternative to neoliberalism had yet to emerge from the Latin American Left. This was in part a consequence of the crisis of Marxism as an intellectual force and the retreat of the Left (Marxist and non-Marxist) internationally. But it also reflected the weakness of social democracy in Latin America, which, we have argued in this volume, was in part a consequence of the defeat of a nascent social democratic project in the immediate aftermath of the Second World War.

Although the 1980s and early 1990s offered new opportunities for progressive "openings" for broadly social democratic projects of economic, social, and political transformation in Latin America, they also brought new, potentially greater, dangers of conservative "closures." It is too early to tell what the outcome of the present conjuncture will be. On the whole we are pessimistic. The new order emerging in the early 1990s, as in the late 1940s, seems likely to take the form of a conservative consolidation of some kind (not excluding the possibility of another defeat for democracy and a return to authoritarian rule). Here is a further justification – if any is needed – for studying the origins of the previous order in Latin America that emerged as the outcome of the conjuncture formed by the end of the Second World War and the beginning of the Cold War.

# Index

335